FAIRY TAIL

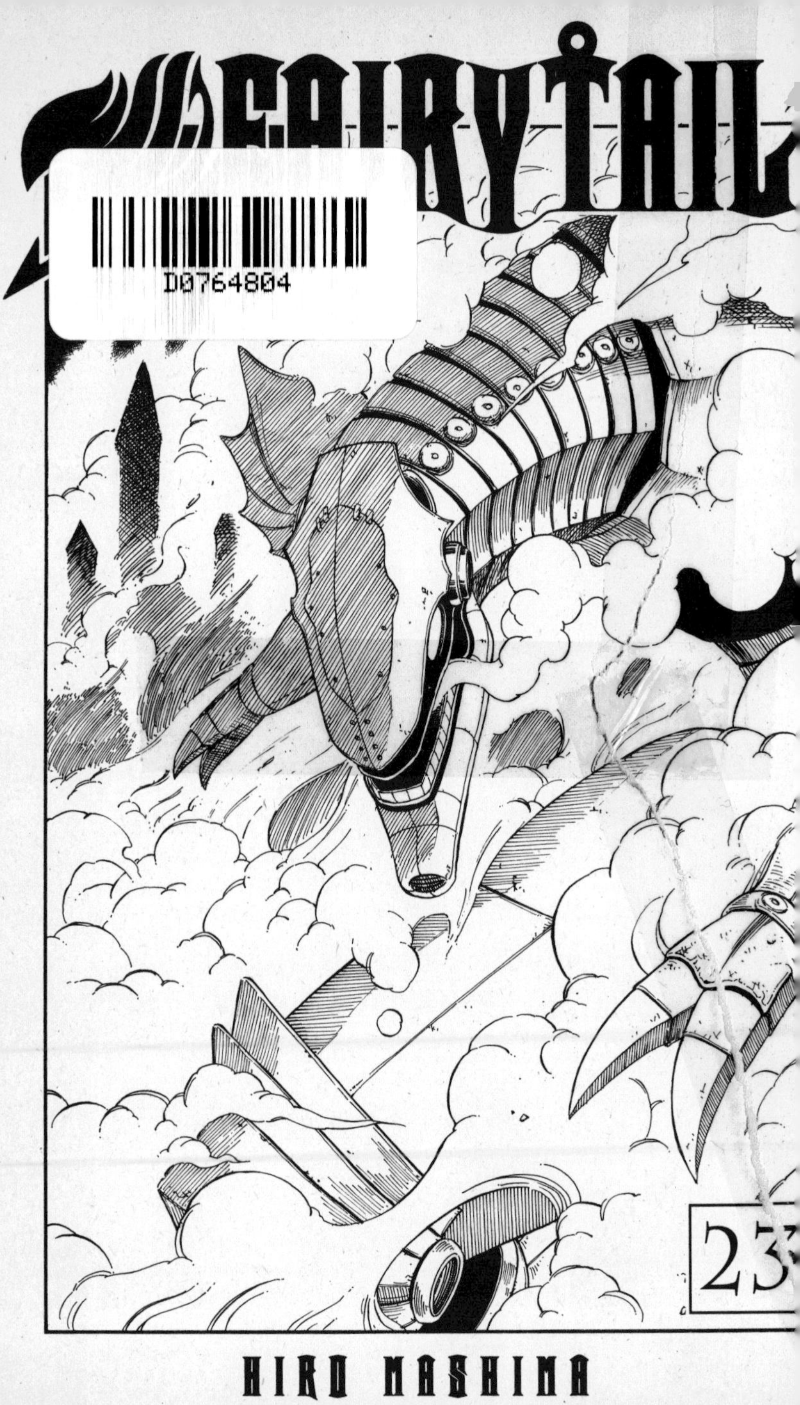

23

HIRO MASHIMA

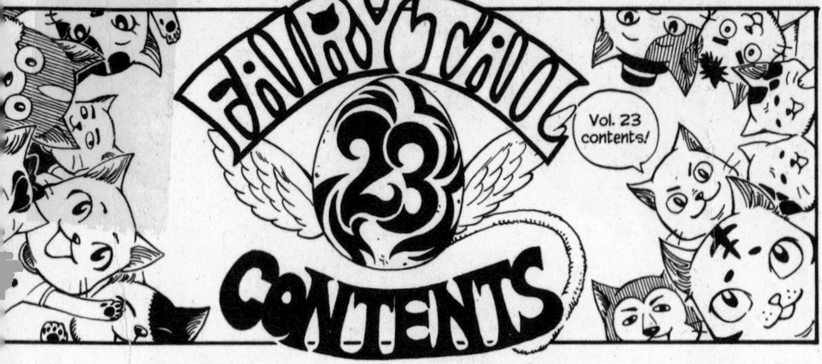
Fairy Tail
23
CONTENTS
Vol. 23 contents!

Published in serial form by Weekly Shônen Magazine 2009 Volumes 44 - 51

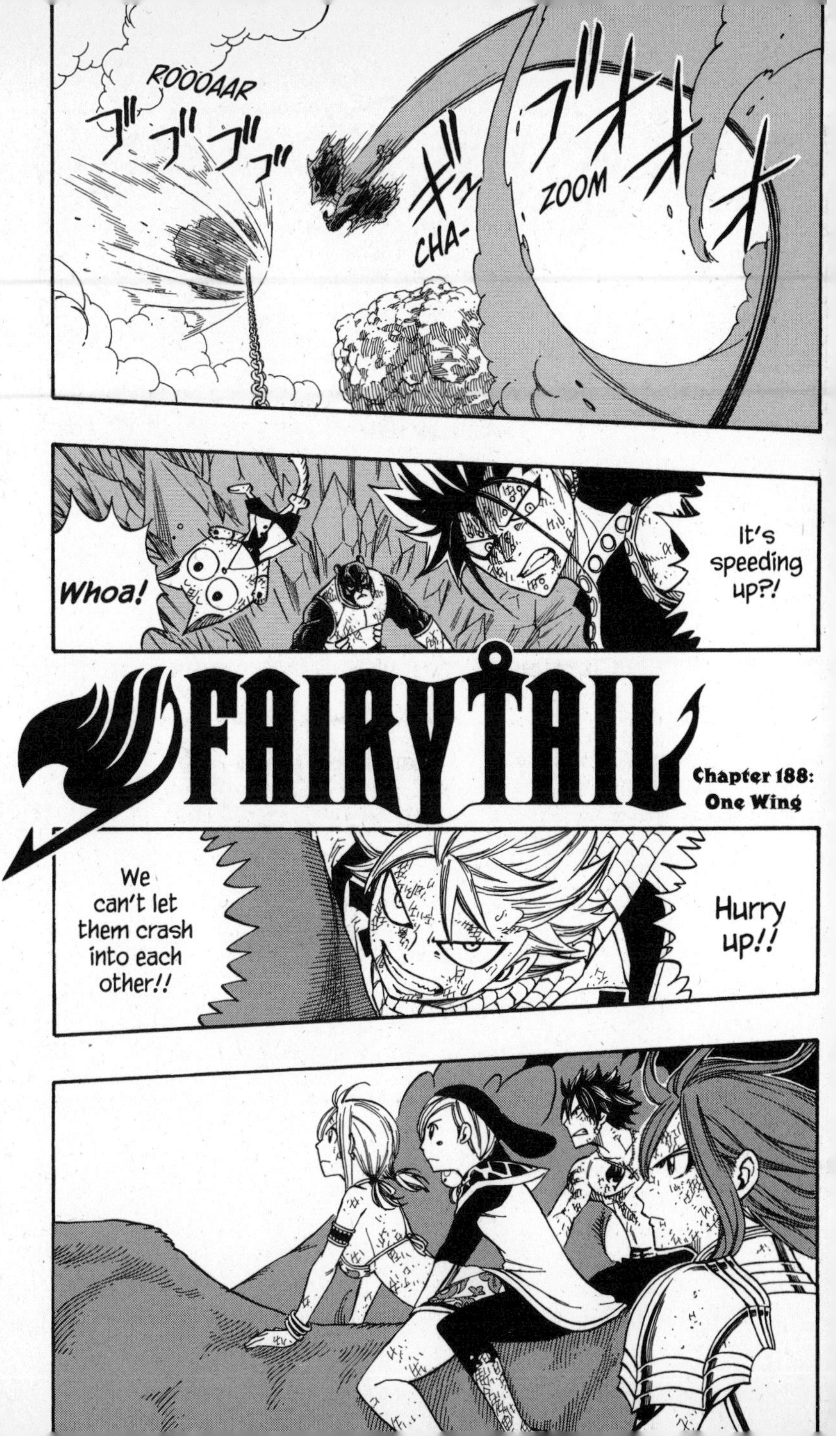
ZOOM
CHA-
ROOOAAR
It's speeding up?!
Whoa!
FAIRY TAIL
Chapter 188: One Wing
Hurry up!!
We can't let them crash into each other!!

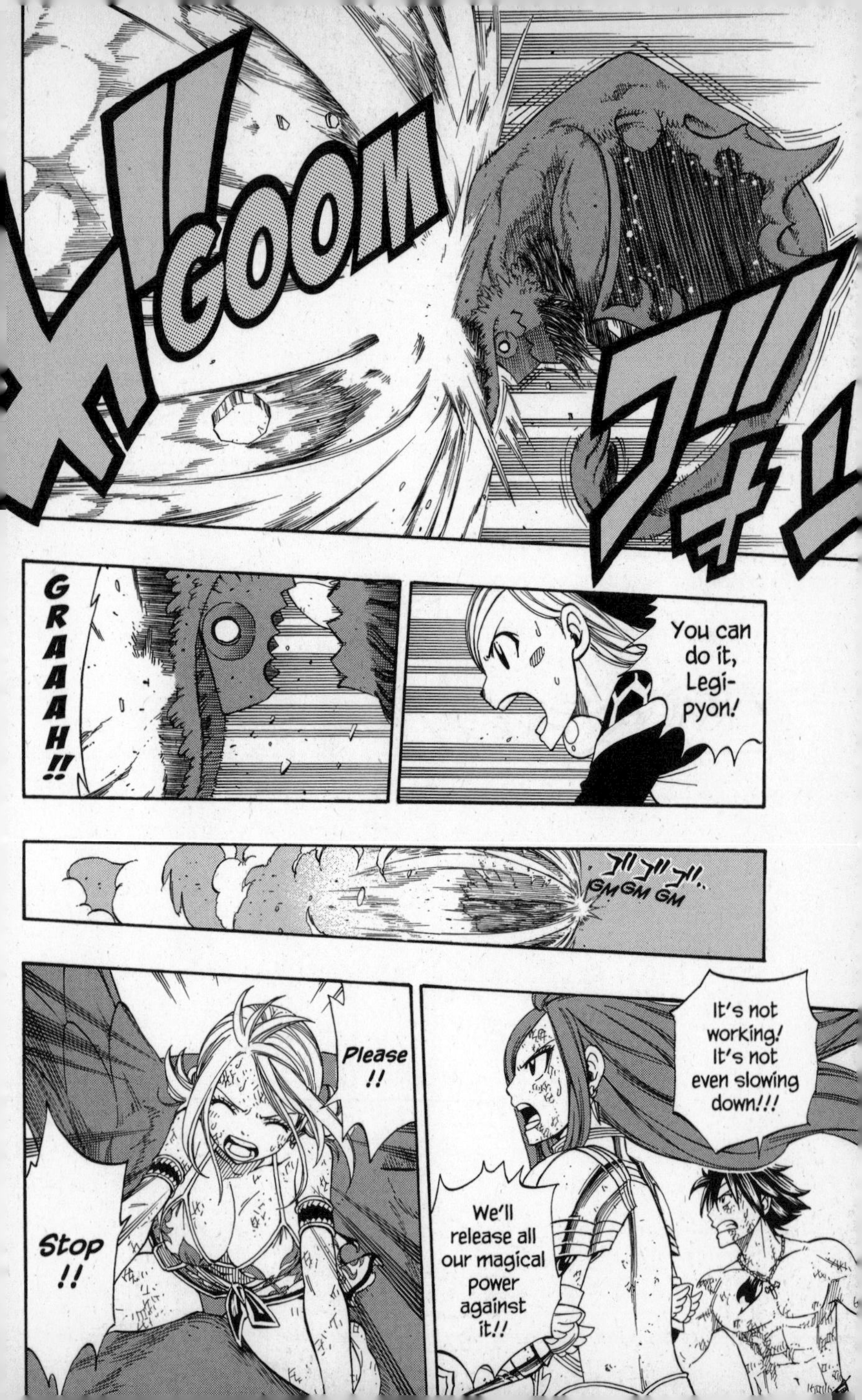
GOOM
You can do it, Legi-pyon!
GRAAAAH!!
GM GM GM
It's not working! It's not even slowing down!!!
We'll release all our magical power against it!!
Please !!
Stop !!

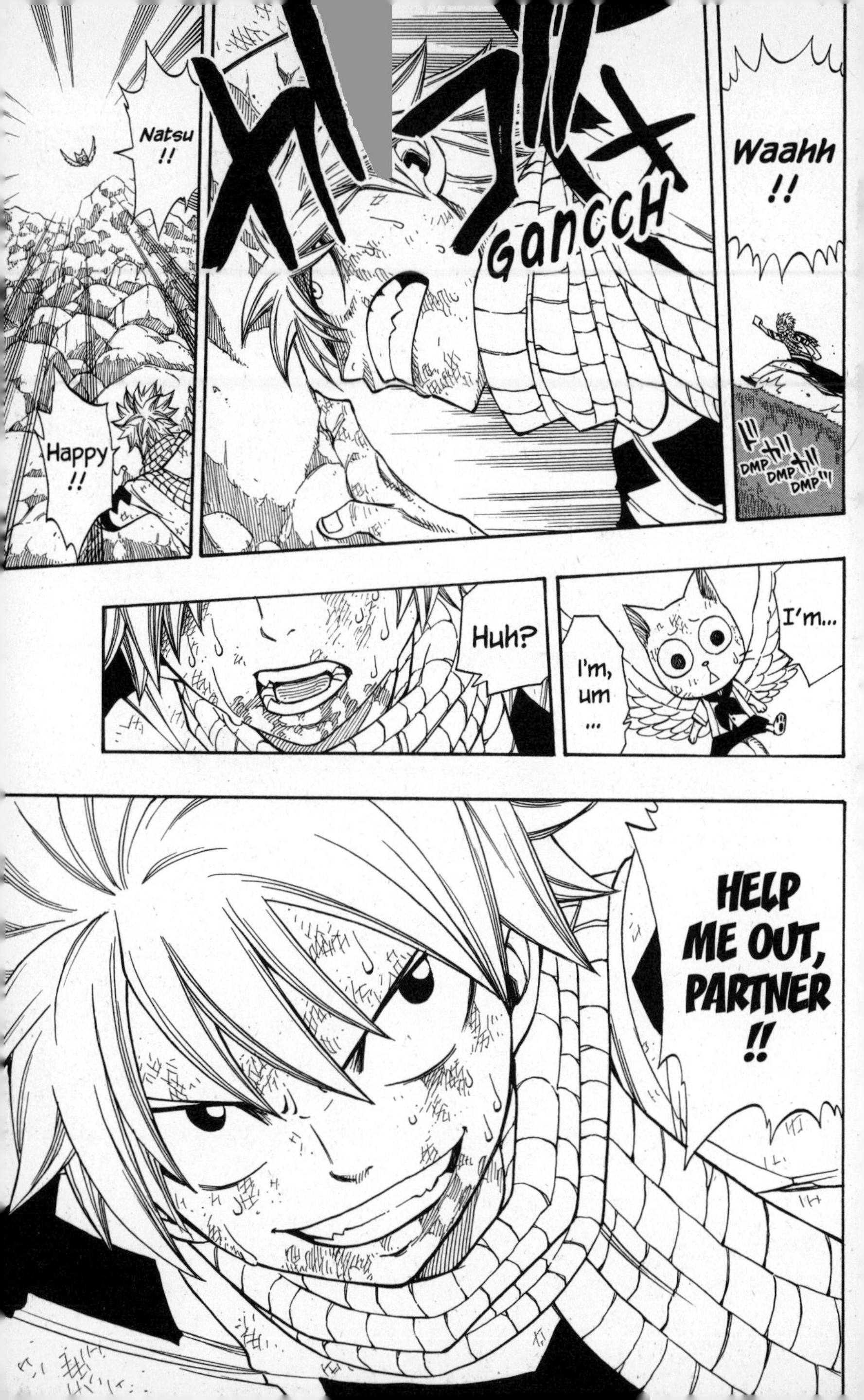
Waahh !!
DMP DMP DMP
GANCCH
Natsu !!
Happy !!
I'm...
I'm, um ...
Huh?
HELP ME OUT, PARTNER !!

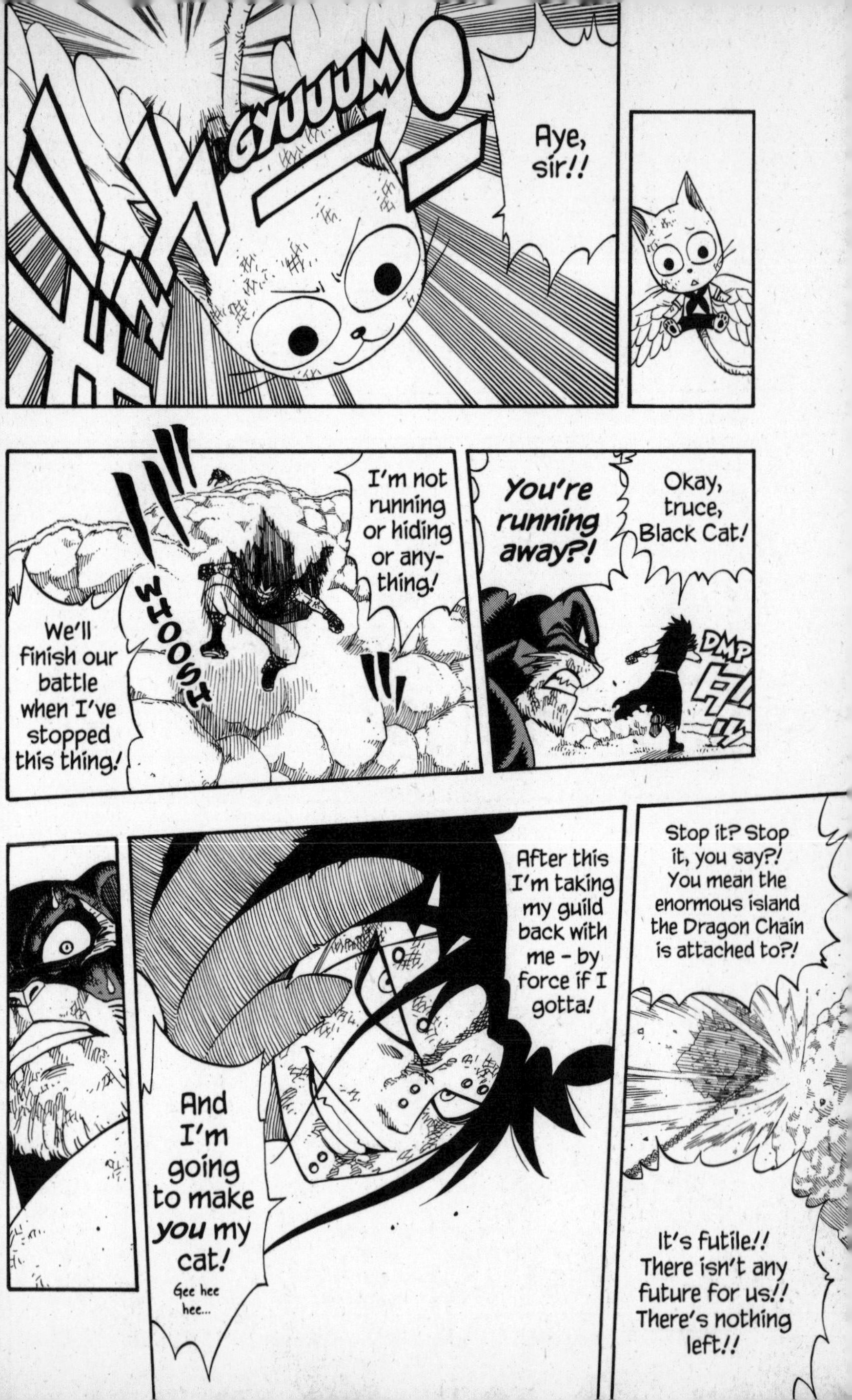
Aye, sir!!
GYUUUM
Okay, truce, Black Cat!
You're running away?!
DMP
I'm not running or hiding or anything!
We'll finish our battle when I've stopped this thing!
WHOOSH
Stop it? Stop it, you say?! You mean the enormous island the Dragon Chain is attached to?!
It's futile!! There isn't any future for us!! There's nothing left!!
After this I'm taking my guild back with me - by force if I gotta!
And I'm going to make *you* my cat!
Gee hee hee...

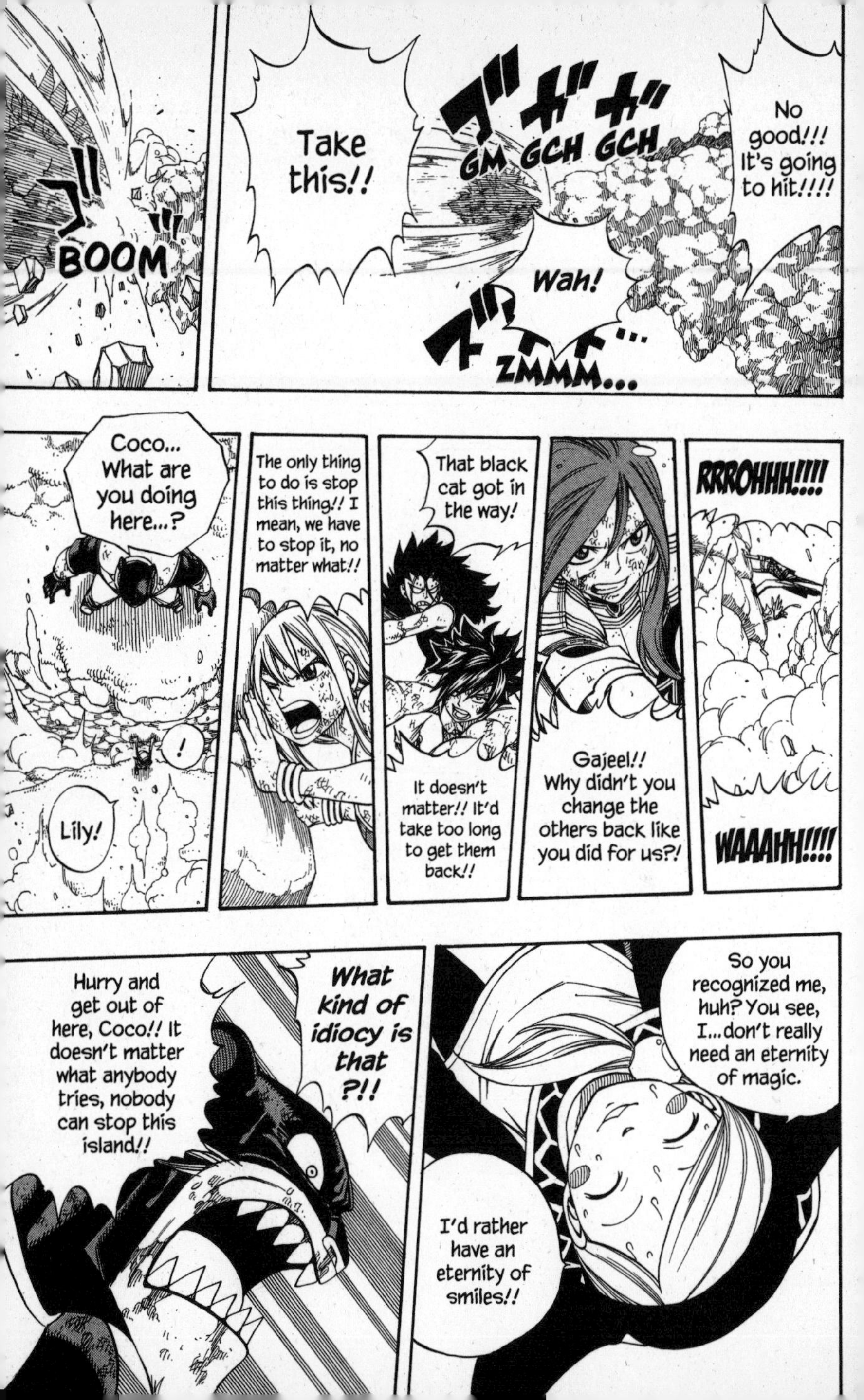
No good!!! It's going to hit!!!!
GM GCH GCH
Take this!!
Wah!
ZMMM...
BOOM
RRROHHH!!!!
WAAAHH!!!!
Gajeel!! Why didn't you change the others back like you did for us?!
That black cat got in the way!
It doesn't matter!! It'd take too long to get them back!!
The only thing to do is stop this thing!! I mean, we have to stop it, no matter what!!
Coco... What are you doing here...?
!
Lily!
So you recognized me, huh? You see, I...don't really need an eternity of magic.
I'd rather have an eternity of smiles!!
What kind of idiocy is that?!!
Hurry and get out of here, Coco!! It doesn't matter what anybody tries, nobody can stop this island!!

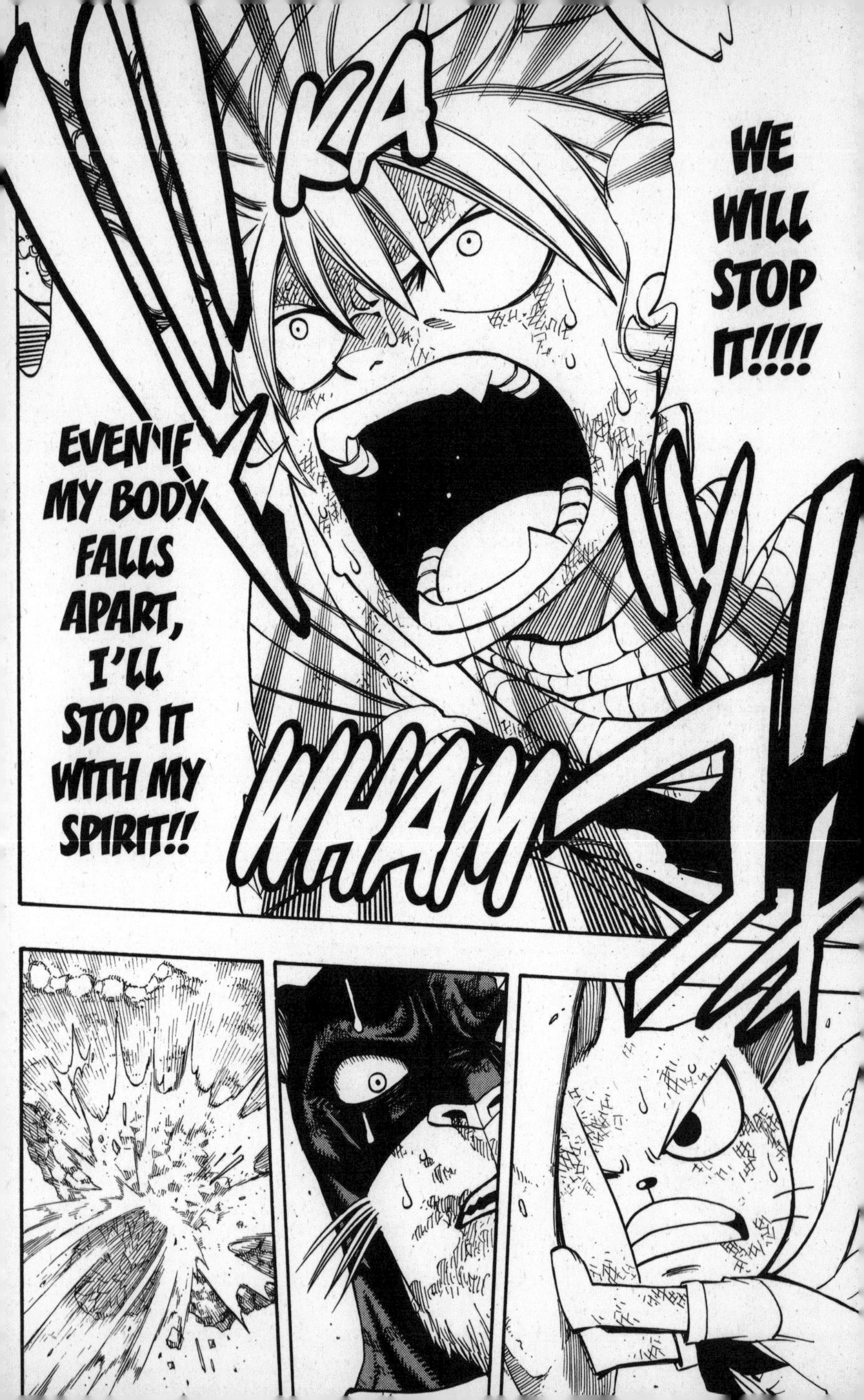
WE WILL STOP IT!!!!
KA
EVEN IF MY BODY FALLS APART, I'LL STOP IT WITH MY SPIRIT!!
WHAM

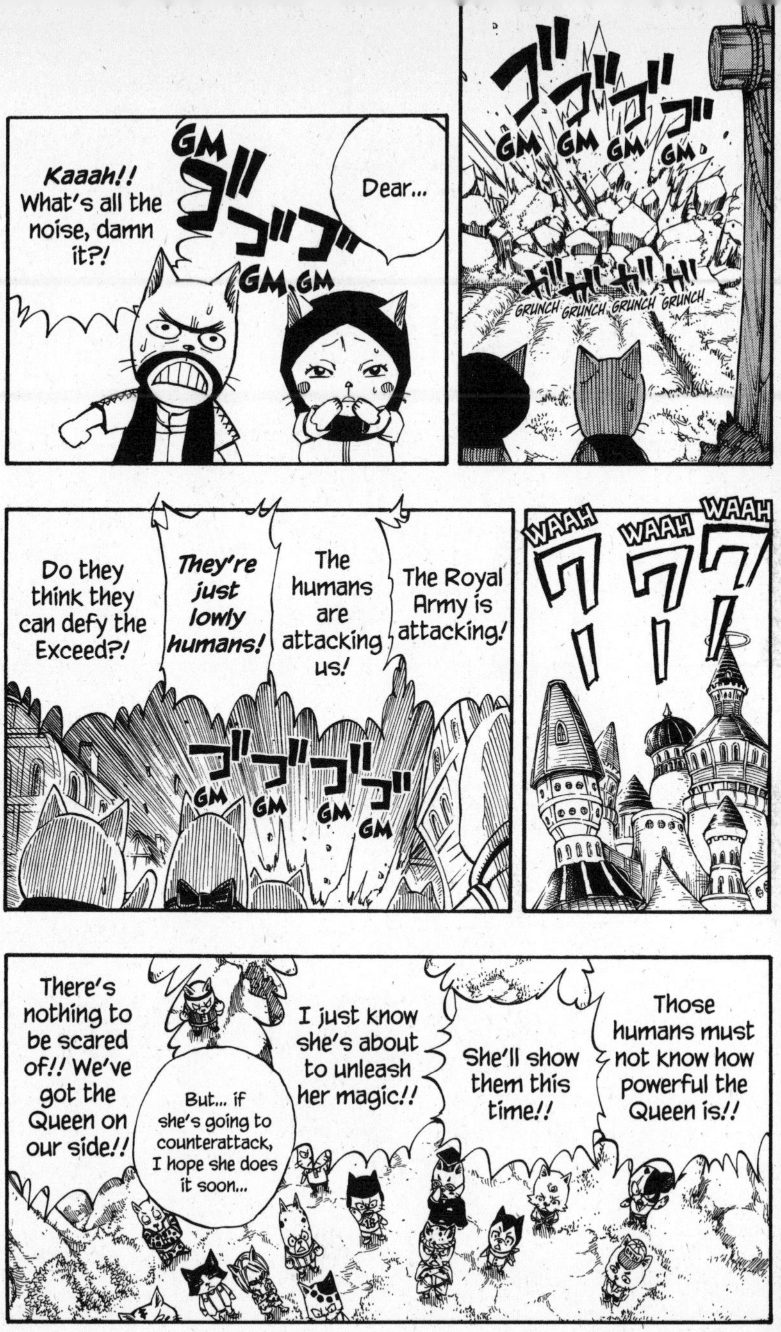
GM GM GM GM
GRUNCH GRUNCH GRUNCH GRUNCH
Dear...
GM
Kaaah!! What's all the noise, damn it?!
GM GM
WAAH WAAH WAAH
The Royal Army is attacking!
The humans are attacking us!
They're just lowly humans!
Do they think they can defy the Exceed?!
GM GM GM GM
Those humans must not know how powerful the Queen is!!
She'll show them this time!!
I just know she's about to unleash her magic!!
There's nothing to be scared of!! We've got the Queen on our side!!
But... if she's going to counterattack, I hope she does it soon...

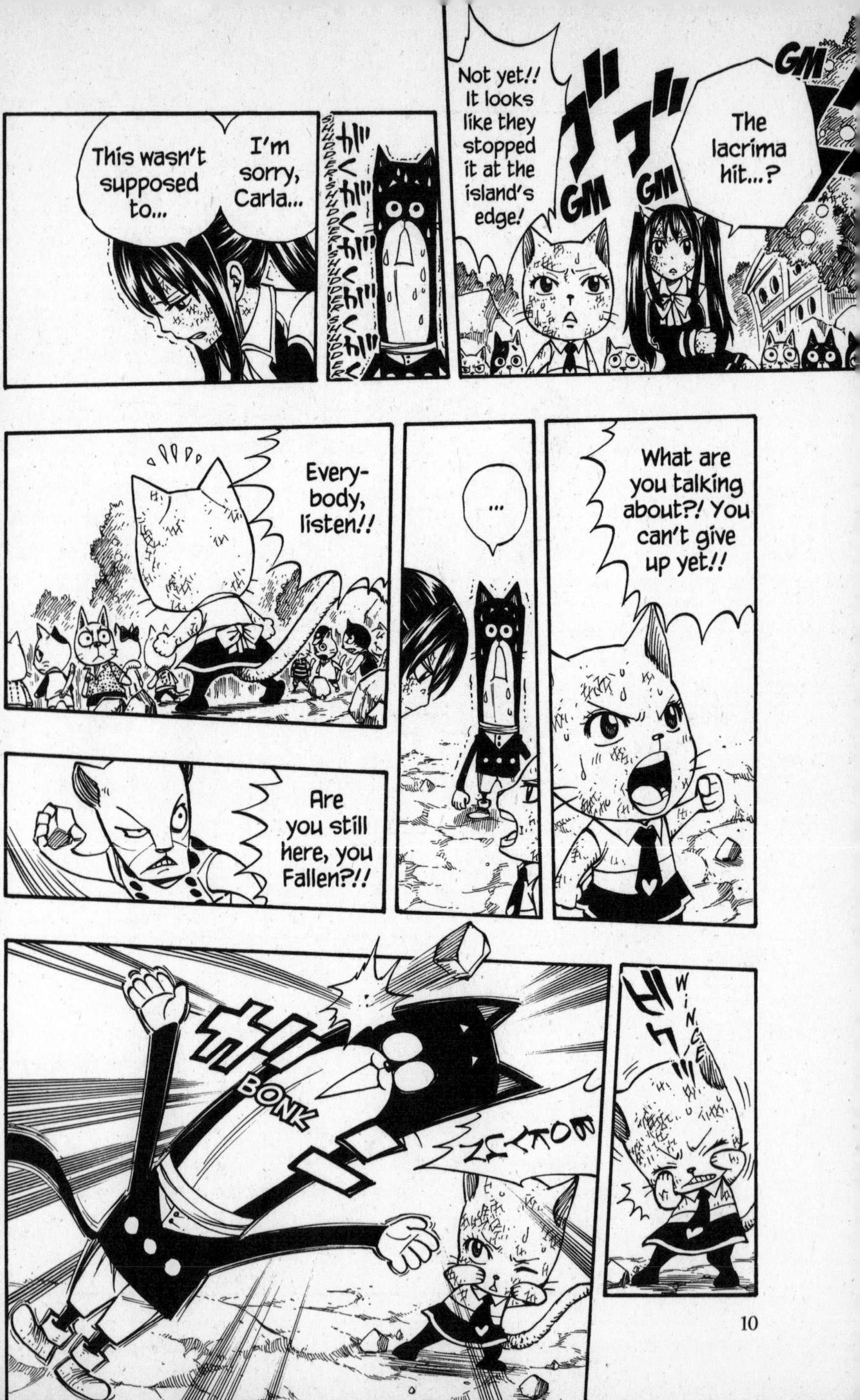
GM
GM
GM
The lacrima hit...?
Not yet!! It looks like they stopped it at the island's edge!
SHUDDER SHUDDER SHUDDER SHUDDER
I'm sorry, Carla...
This wasn't supposed to...
What are you talking about?! You can't give up yet!!
...
Every-body, listen!!
Are you still here, you Fallen?!!
WINCE
BONK

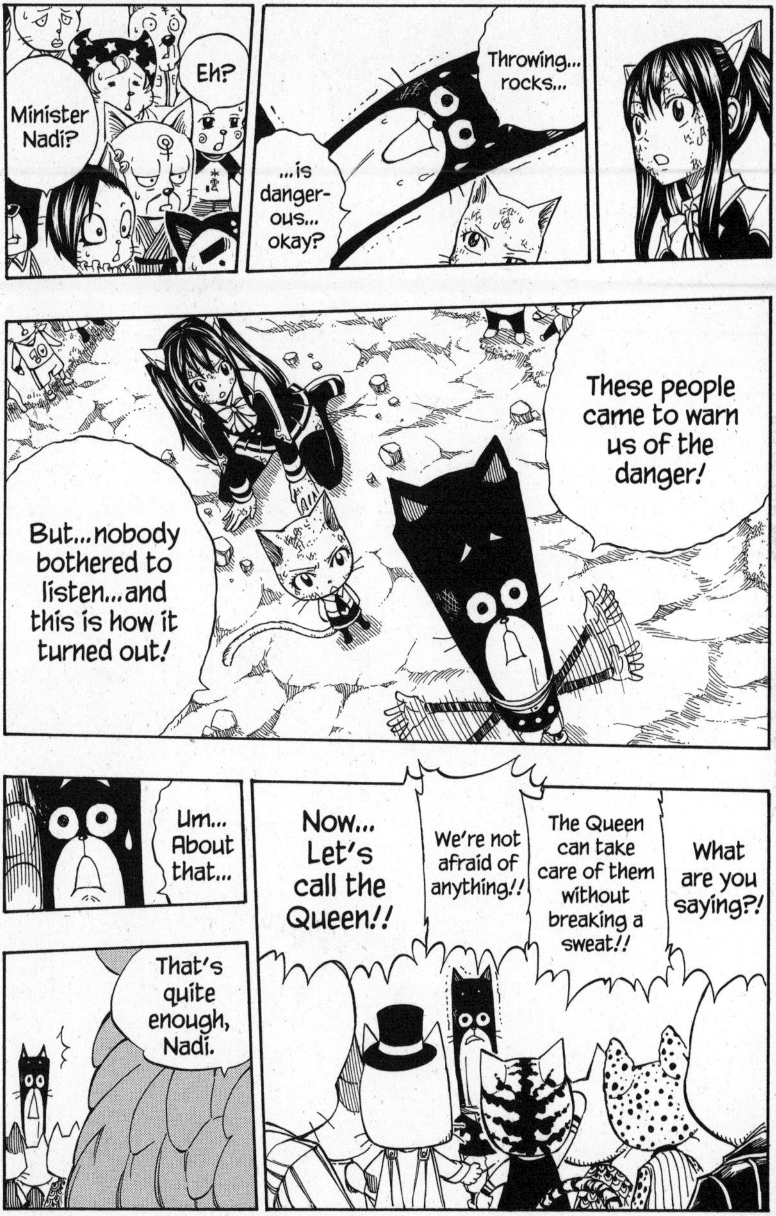
Throwing... rocks...
...is danger-ous... okay?
Eh?
Minister Nadi?
These people came to warn us of the danger!
But...nobody bothered to listen...and this is how it turned out!
What are you saying?!
The Queen can take care of them without breaking a sweat!!
We're not afraid of anything!!
Now... Let's call the Queen!!
Um... About that...
That's quite enough, Nadi.

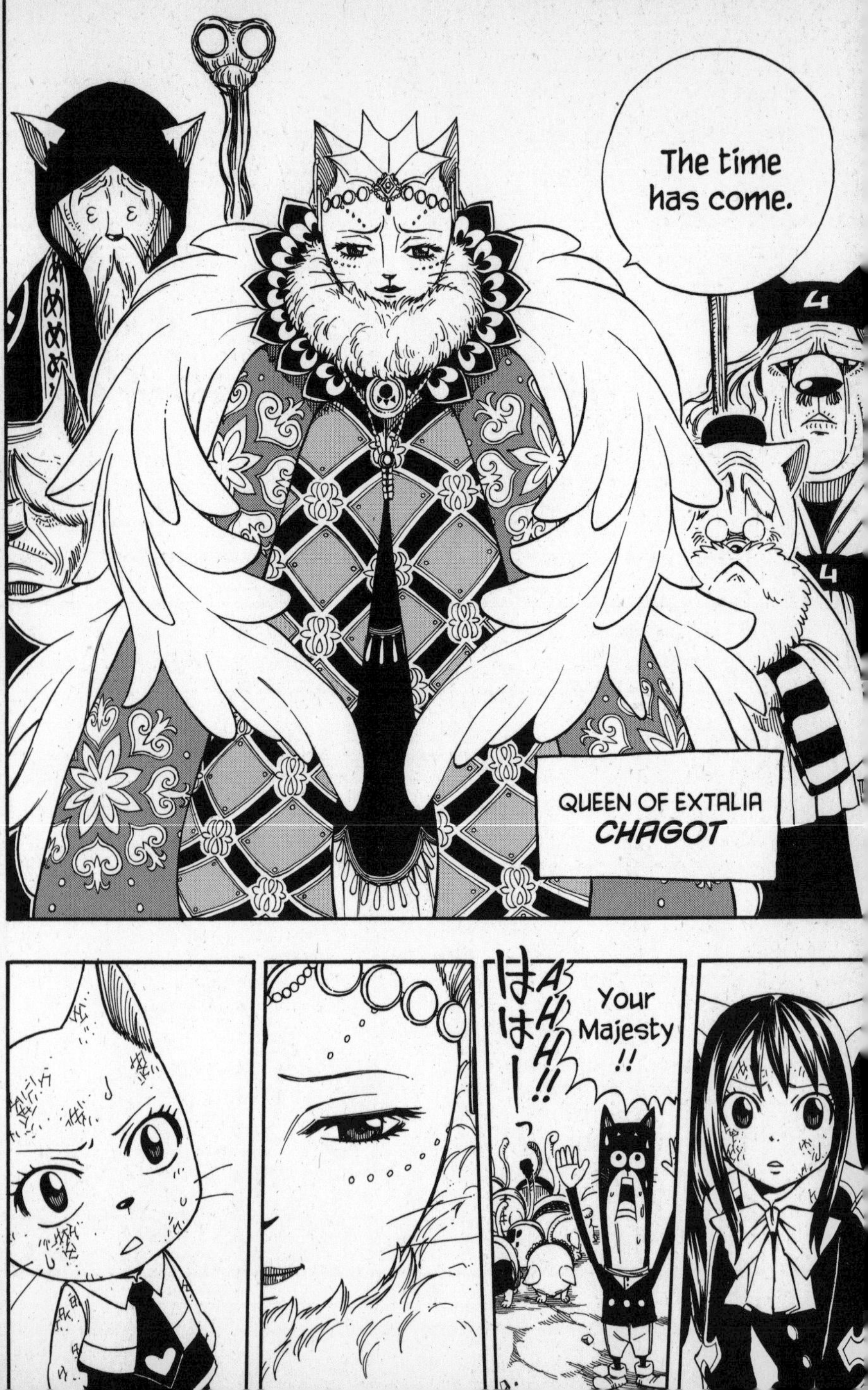

The time has come.
QUEEN OF EXTALIA
CHAGOT
Your Majesty !!
ははーっ
AHH!!

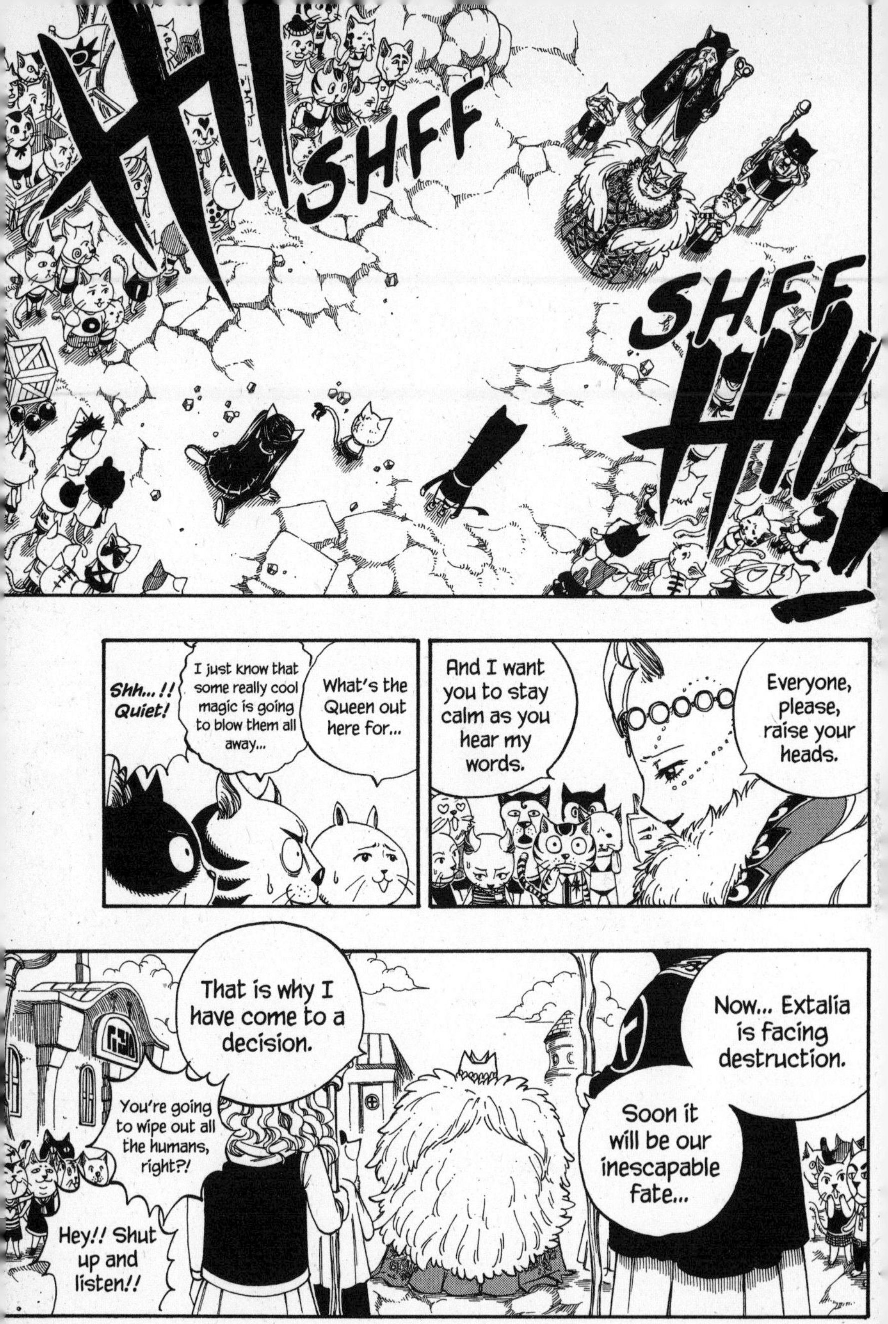
SHFF
SHFF
Everyone, please, raise your heads.
And I want you to stay calm as you hear my words.
What's the Queen out here for...
I just know that some really cool magic is going to blow them all away...
Shh...!! Quiet!
Now... Extalia is facing destruction.
Soon it will be our inescapable fate...
That is why I have come to a decision.
You're going to wipe out all the humans, right?!
Hey!! Shut up and listen!!

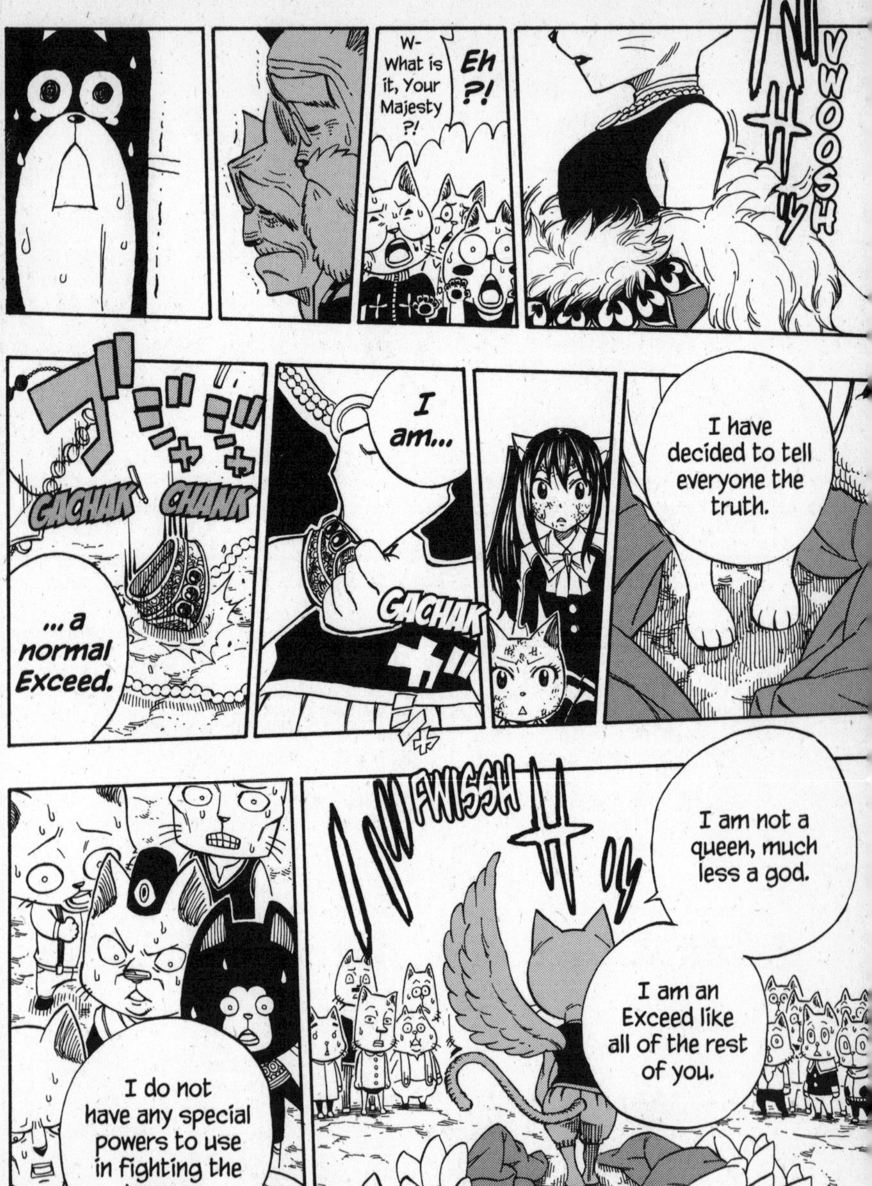
VWOOSH
Eh?!
W-What is it, Your Majesty?!
I have decided to tell everyone the truth.
I am...
GACHAK
GACHAK
CHANK
... a normal Exceed.
FWISSH
I am not a queen, much less a god.
I am an Exceed like all of the rest of you.
I do not have any special powers to use in fighting the humans.

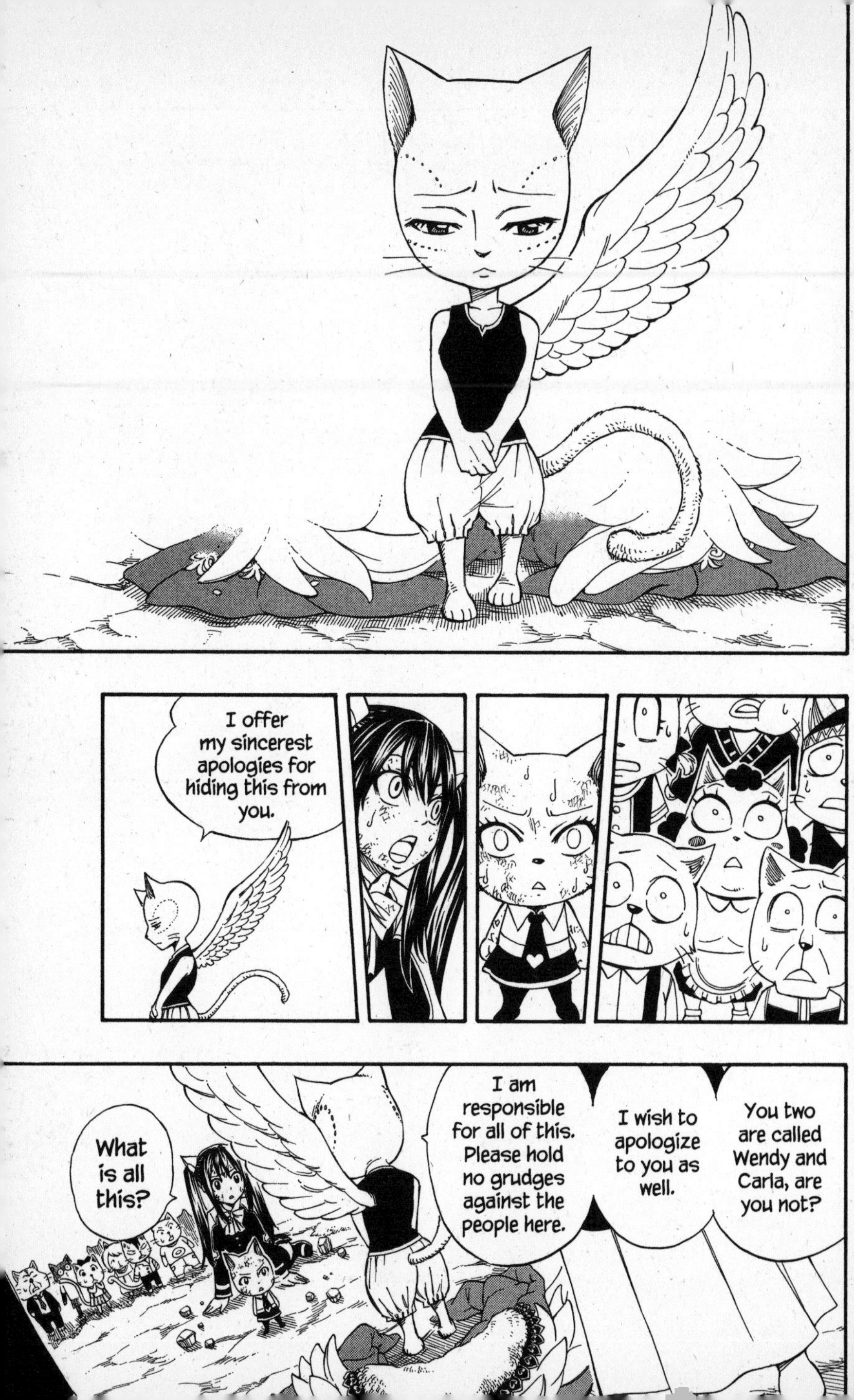
I offer my sincerest apologies for hiding this from you.
You two are called Wendy and Carla, are you not?
I wish to apologize to you as well.
I am responsible for all of this. Please hold no grudges against the people here.
What is all this?

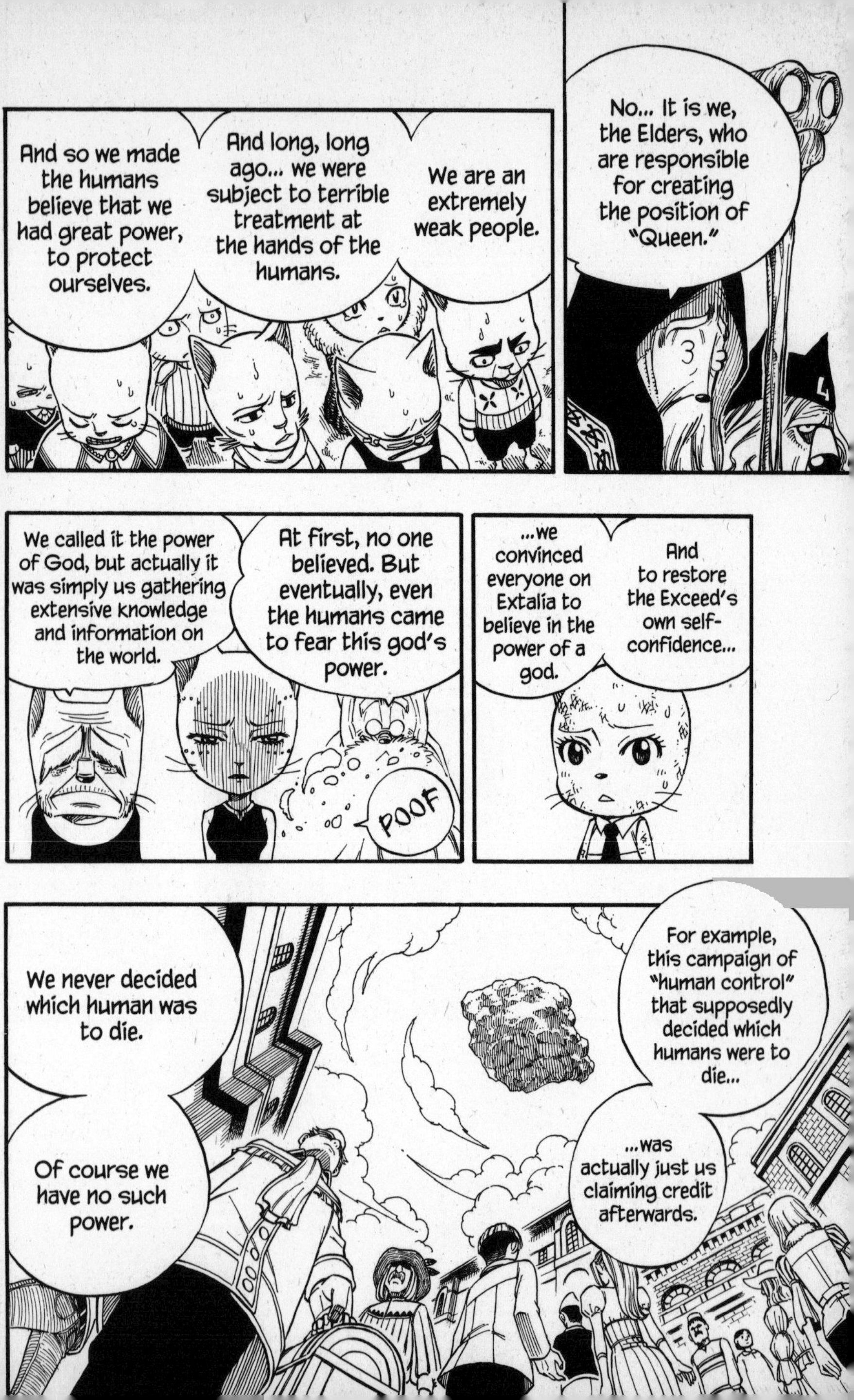
No... It is we, the Elders, who are responsible for creating the position of "Queen."
We are an extremely weak people.
And long, long ago... we were subject to terrible treatment at the hands of the humans.
And so we made the humans believe that we had great power, to protect ourselves.
And to restore the Exceed's own self-confidence...
...we convinced everyone on Extalia to believe in the power of a god.
At first, no one believed. But eventually, even the humans came to fear this god's power.
We called it the power of God, but actually it was simply us gathering extensive knowledge and information on the world.
POOF
For example, this campaign of "human control" that supposedly decided which humans were to die...
...was actually just us claiming credit afterwards.
We never decided which human was to die.
Of course we have no such power.

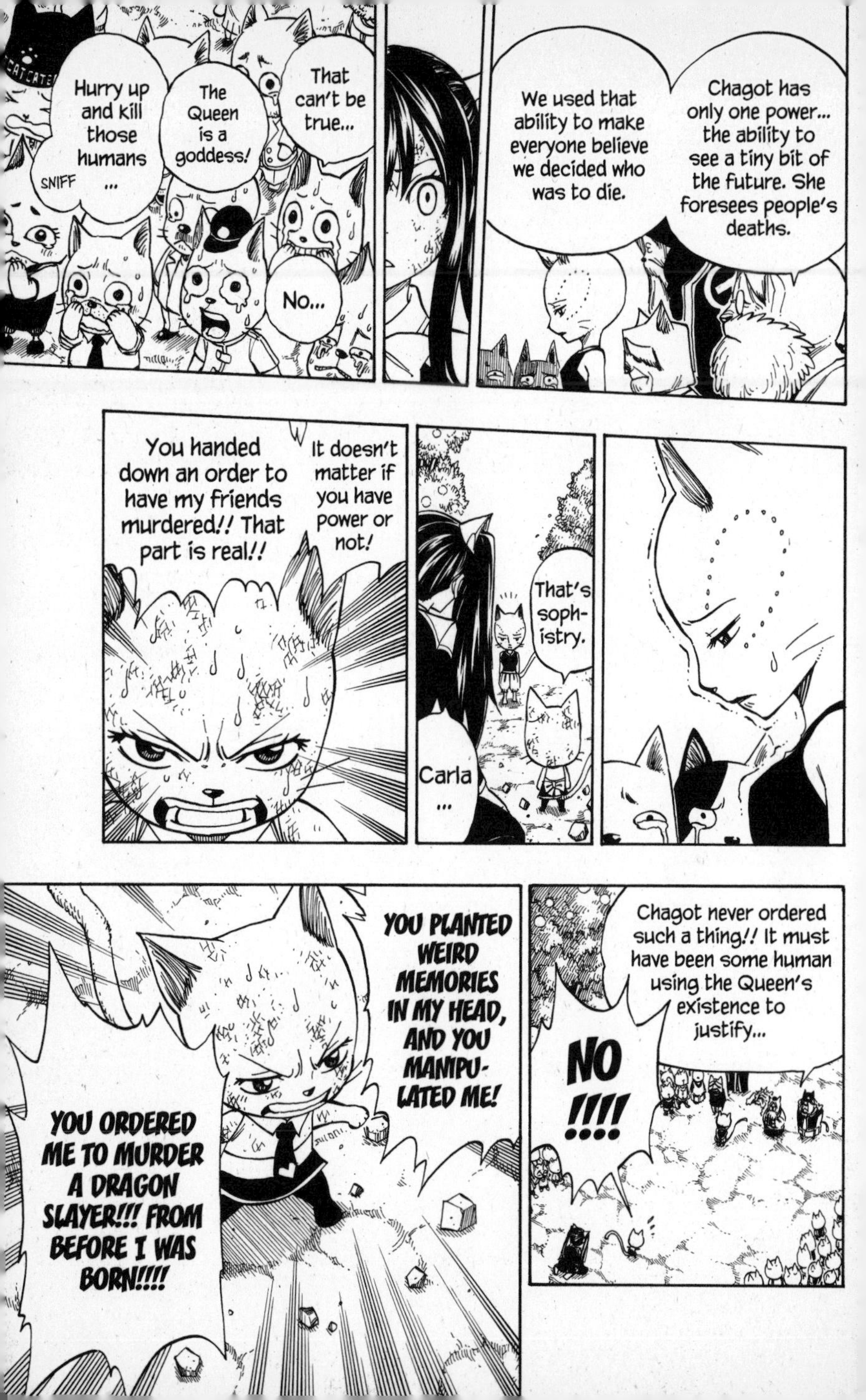
Chagot has only one power... the ability to see a tiny bit of the future. She foresees people's deaths.
We used that ability to make everyone believe we decided who was to die.
That can't be true...
The Queen is a goddess!
Hurry up and kill those humans ...
SNIFF
No...
That's soph-istry.
Carla ...
It doesn't matter if you have power or not!
You handed down an order to have my friends murdered!! That part is real!!
Chagot never ordered such a thing!! It must have been some human using the Queen's existence to justify...
NO !!!!
YOU PLANTED WEIRD MEMORIES IN MY HEAD, AND YOU MANIPU-LATED ME!
YOU ORDERED ME TO MURDER A DRAGON SLAYER!!! FROM BEFORE I WAS BORN!!!!

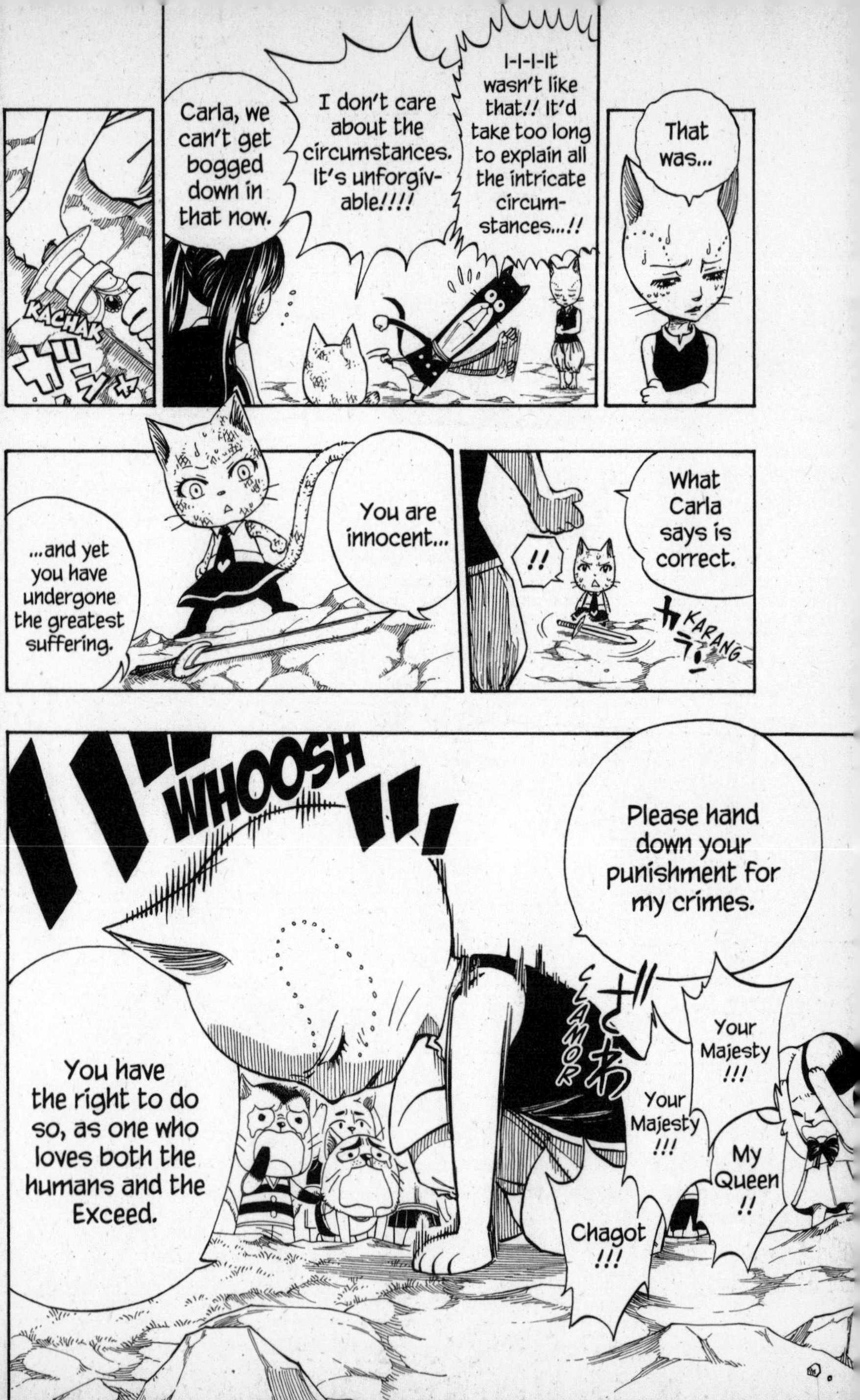
That was...
I-I-I-It wasn't like that!! It'd take too long to explain all the intricate circumstances...!!
I don't care about the circumstances. It's unforgivable!!!!
Carla, we can't get bogged down in that now.
KACHAK
What Carla says is correct.
!!
KARANG
You are innocent...
...and yet you have undergone the greatest suffering.
Please hand down your punishment for my crimes.
CLAMOR
Your Majesty!!!
Your Majesty!!!
My Queen!!
Chagot!!!
WHOOSH
You have the right to do so, as one who loves both the humans and the Exceed.

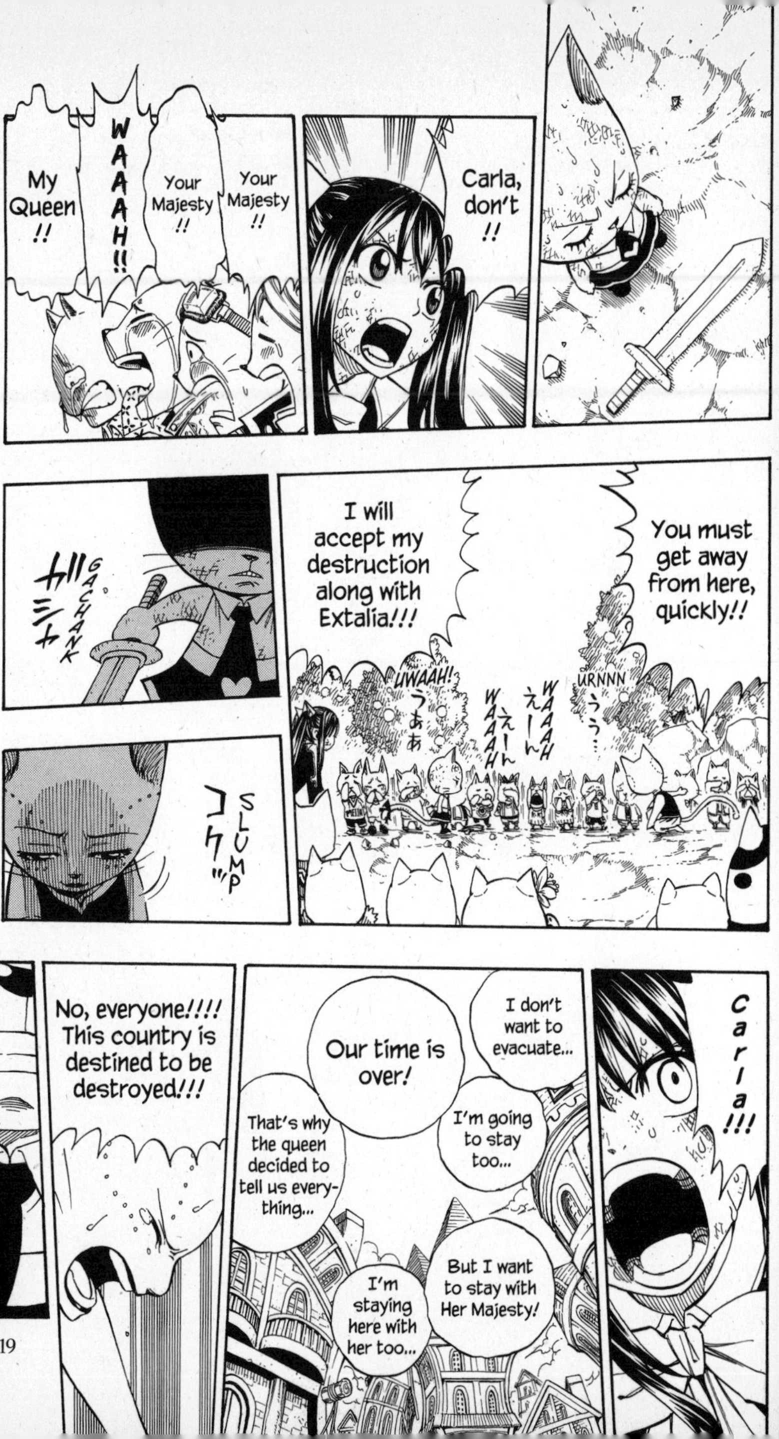
Carla, don't!!
Your Majesty!!
Your Majesty!!
WAAAAH!!
My Queen!!
You must get away from here, quickly!!
I will accept my destruction along with Extalia!!!
URNNN
うう…
WAAAH
えーん
WAAAH
えーん
UWAAH!
うああ
GACHANK
ガシャ
SLUMP
コク"
Carla!!!
I don't want to evacuate...
Our time is over!
I'm going to stay too...
That's why the queen decided to tell us everything...
But I want to stay with Her Majesty!
I'm staying here with her too...
No, everyone!!!! This country is destined to be destroyed!!!

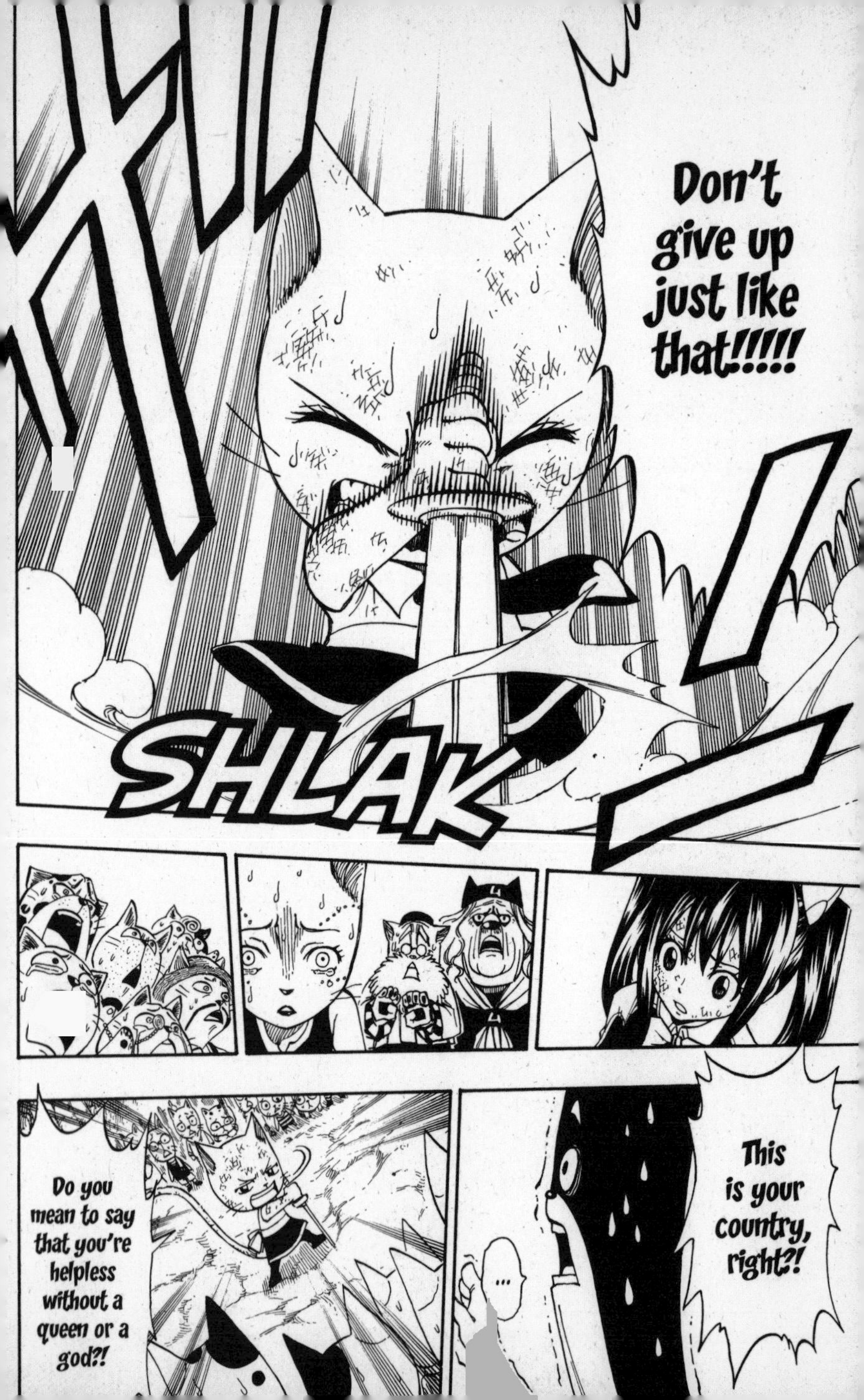
Don't give up just like that!!!!!
SHLAK
This is your country, right?!
...
Do you mean to say that you're helpless without a queen or a god?!

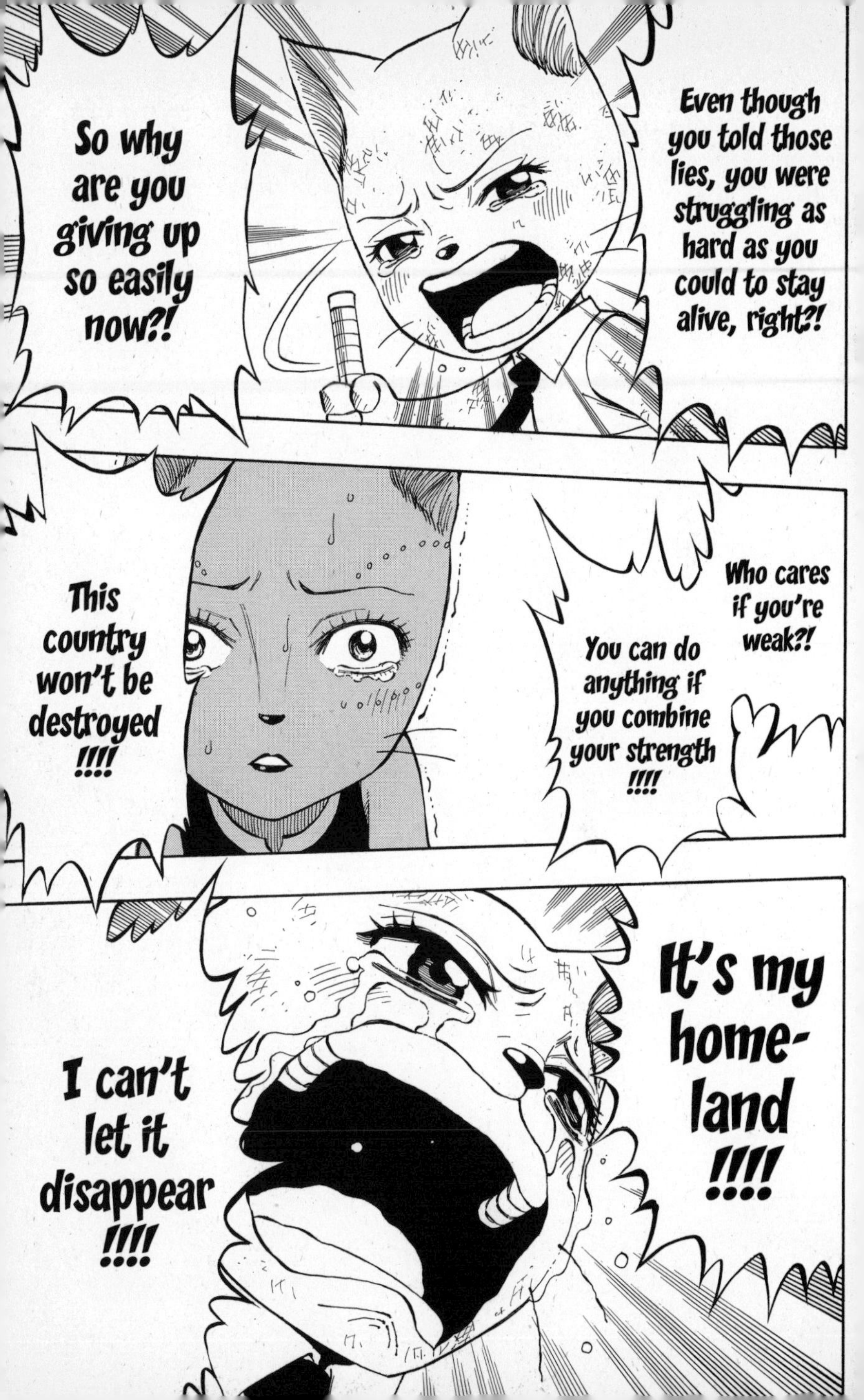
Even though you told those lies, you were struggling as hard as you could to stay alive, right?!
So why are you giving up so easily now?!
Who cares if you're weak?!
You can do anything if you combine your strength!!!!
This country won't be destroyed!!!!
It's my home-land!!!!
I can't let it disappear!!!!

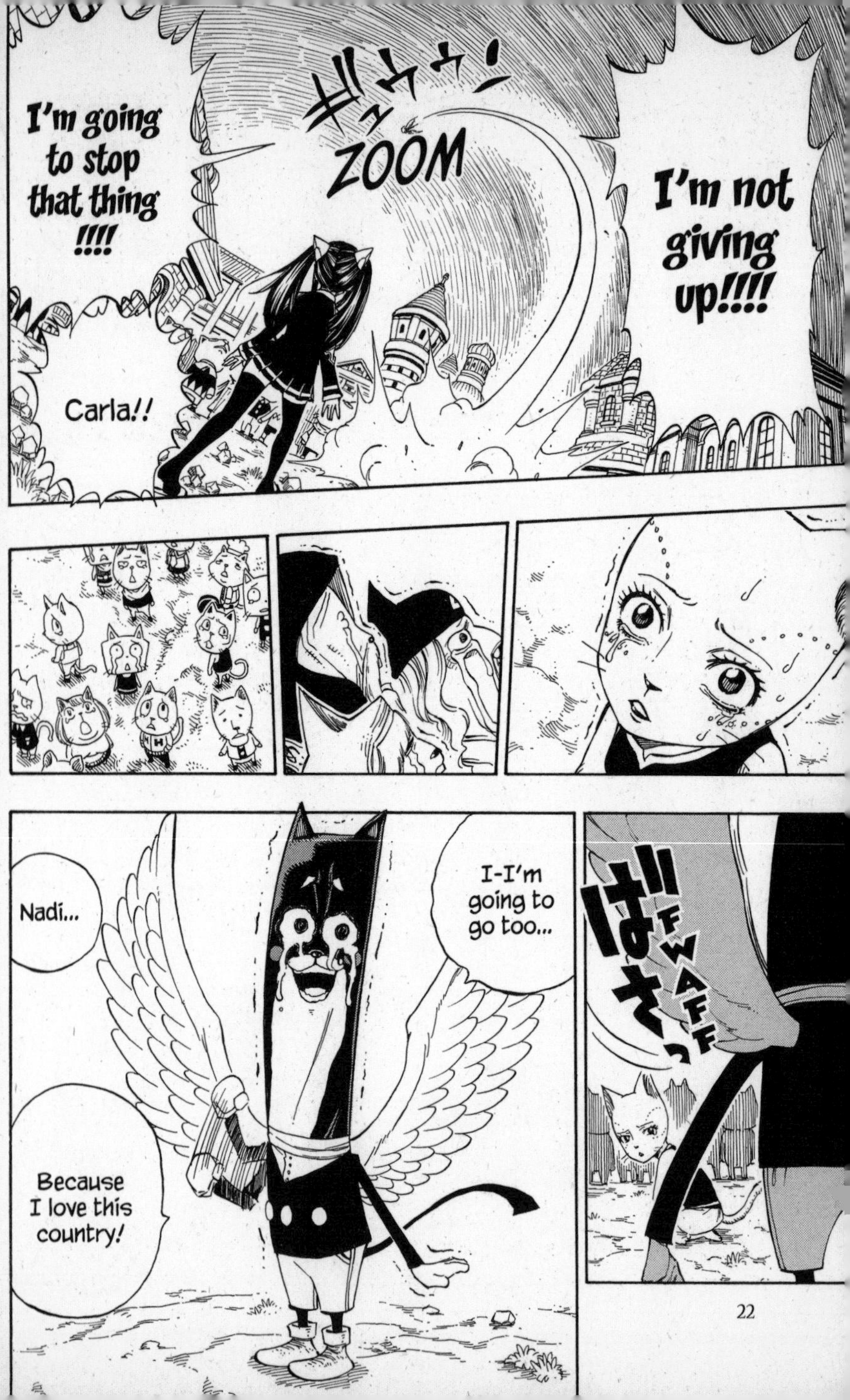
I'm not giving up!!!!
ZOOM
I'm going to stop that thing!!!!
Carla!!
ばさっ
FWAFF
I-I'm going to go too...
Nadi...
Because I love this country!

FAIRY TAIL

フェアリーテイル

Chapter 189: The Boy From Back Then

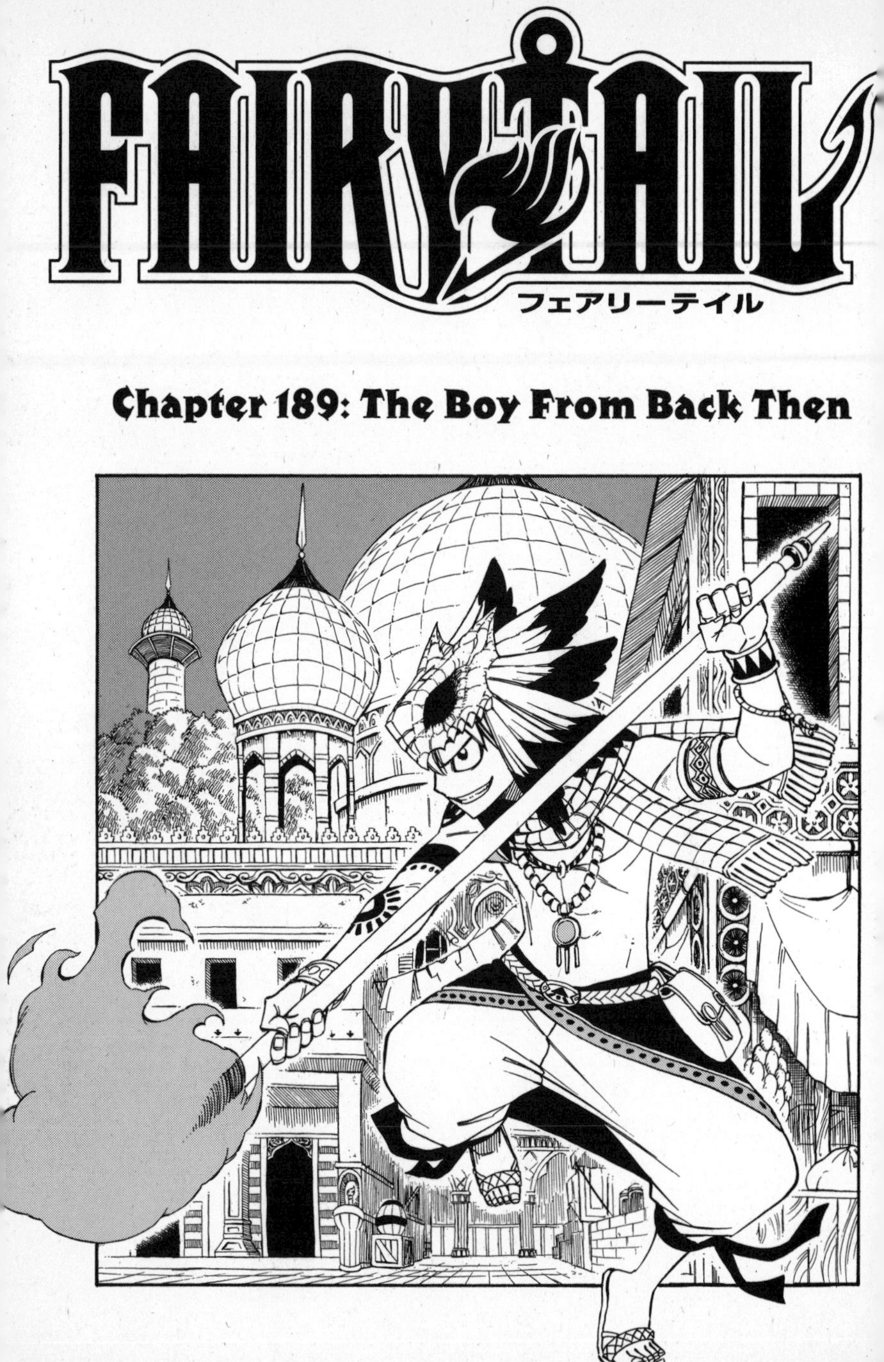

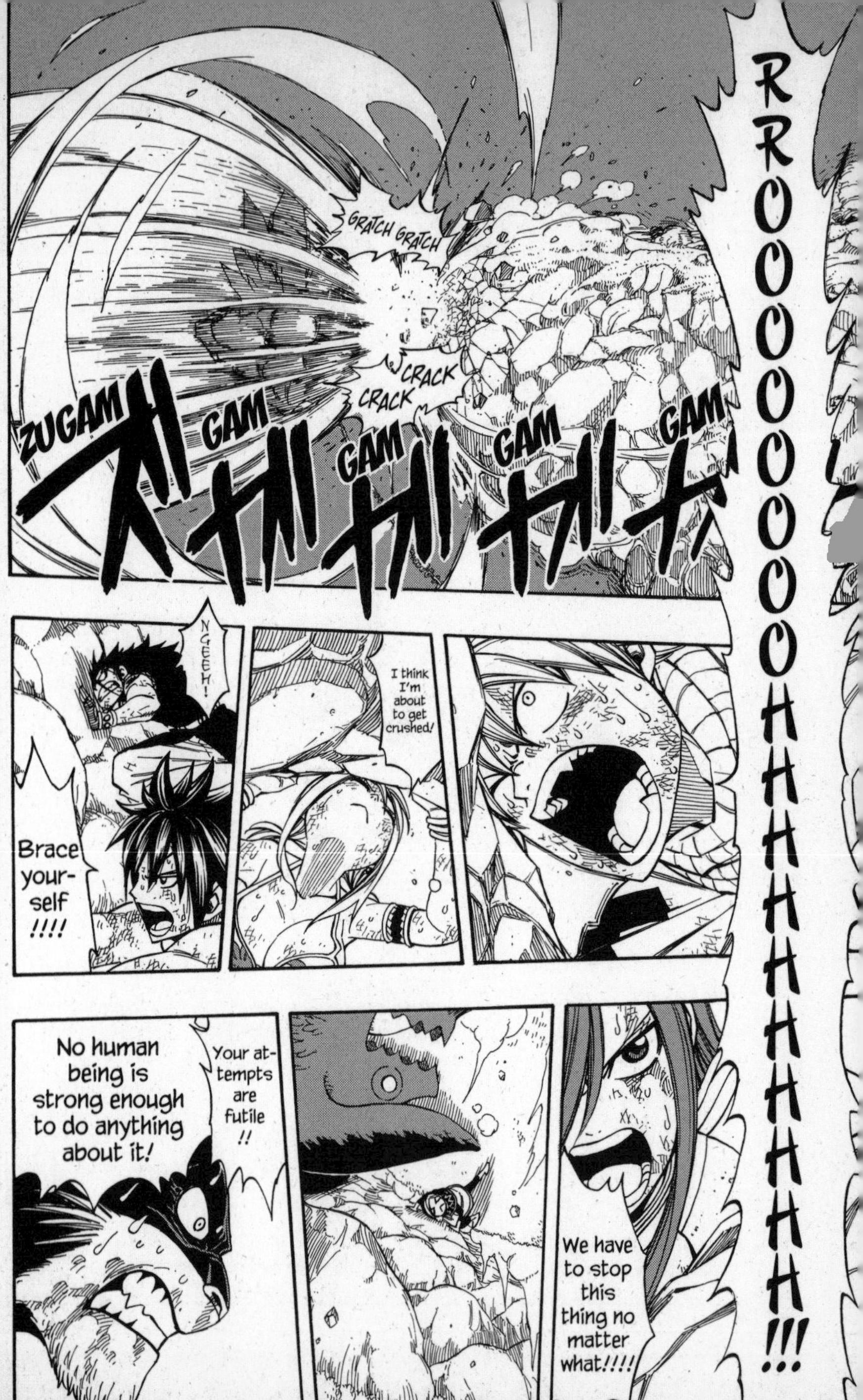
RROOOOOOOOOOOOHHHHHHHHHHHH!!!
GRATCH GRATCH
CRACK CRACK
ZUGAM GAM GAM GAM GAM
I think I'm about to get crushed!
NGEEEH!
Brace your-self!!!!
We have to stop this thing no matter what!!!!
Your at-tempts are futile!!
No human being is strong enough to do anything about it!

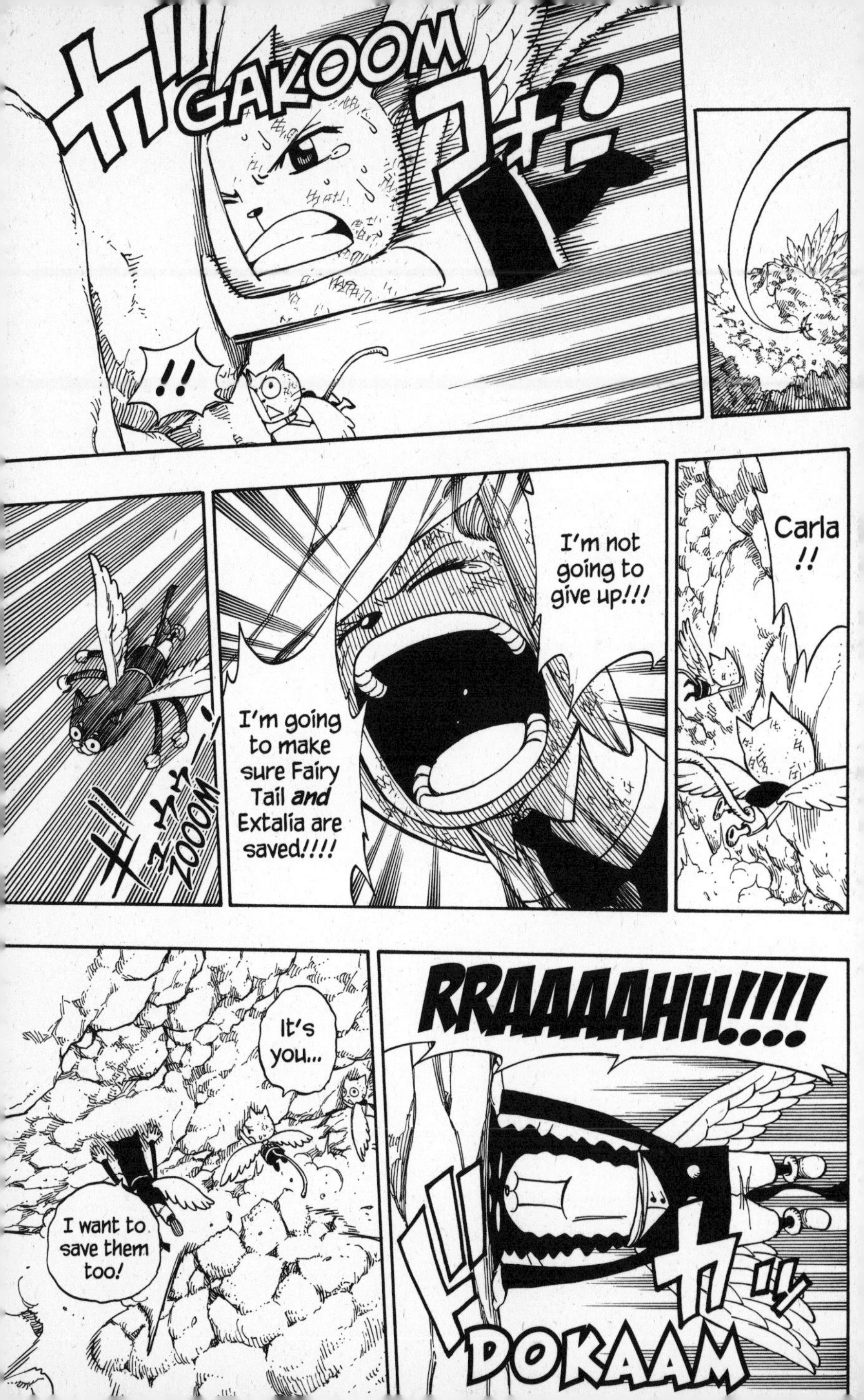
GAKOOM
!!
Carla !!
I'm not going to give up!!!
I'm going to make sure Fairy Tail *and* Extalia are saved!!!!
ZOOOM
RRAAAAHH!!!!
DOKAAM
It's you...
I want to save them too!

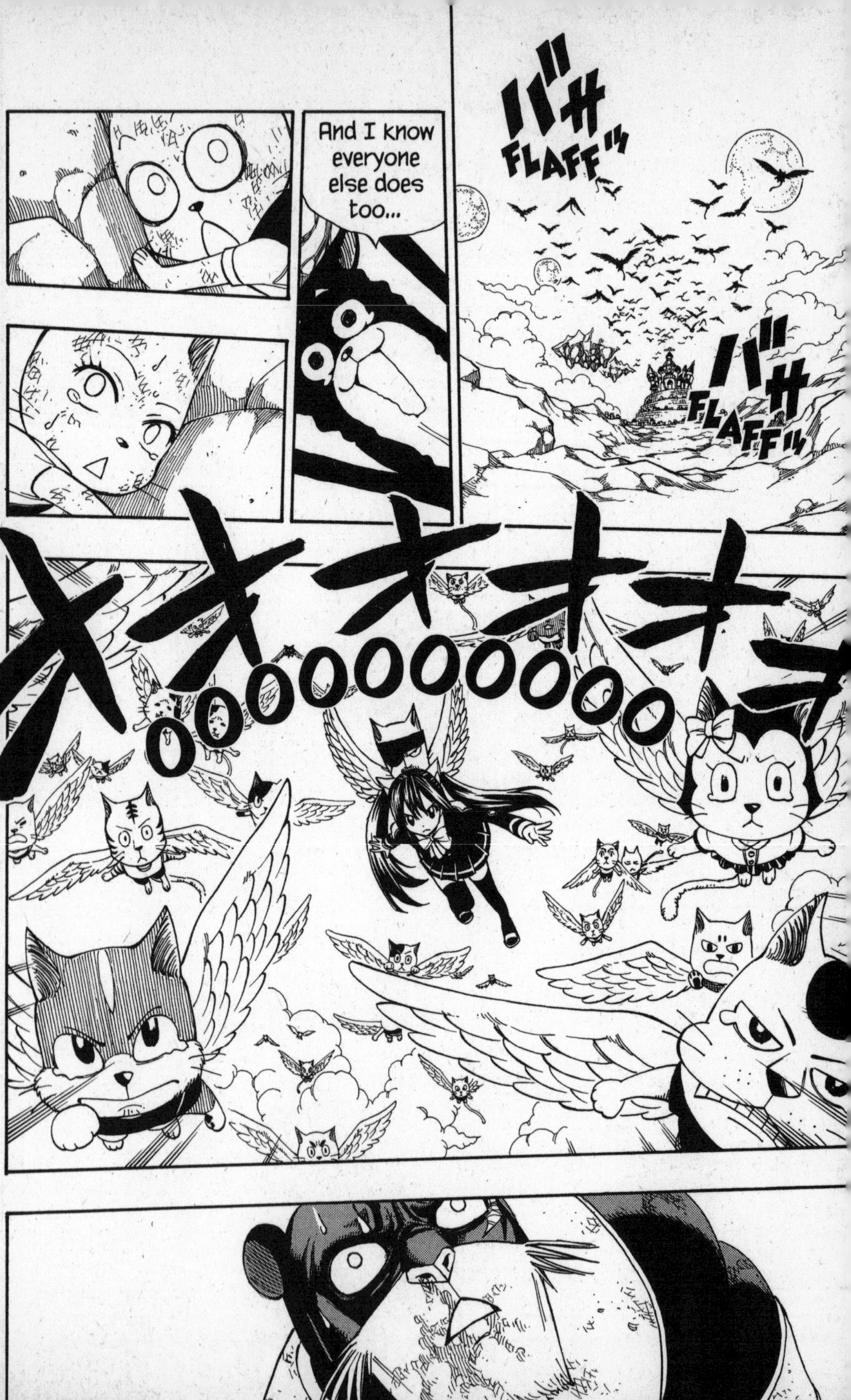
バサ
FLAFF
バサ
FLAFF
And I know everyone else does too...
オオオオオ
OOOOOOOOOO

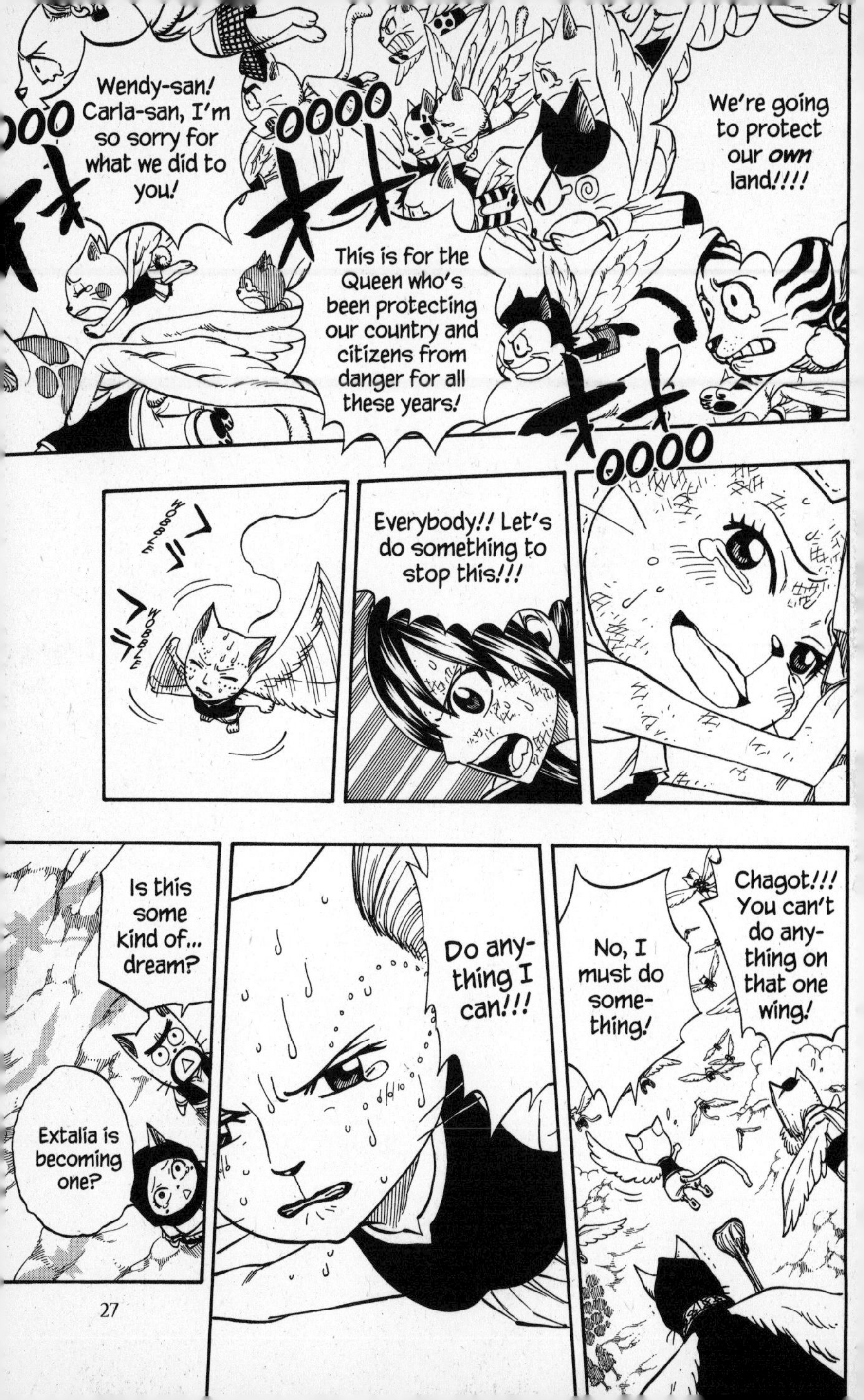
We're going to protect our *own* land!!!!
OOOO
This is for the Queen who's been protecting our country and citizens from danger for all these years!
OOOO
Wendy-san! Carla-san, I'm so sorry for what we did to you!
OOO
OOOO
Everybody!! Let's do something to stop this!!!
WOBBLE
WOBBLE
Chagot!!! You can't do anything on that one wing!
No, I must do something!
Do anything I can!!!
Is this some kind of... dream?
Extalia is becoming one?

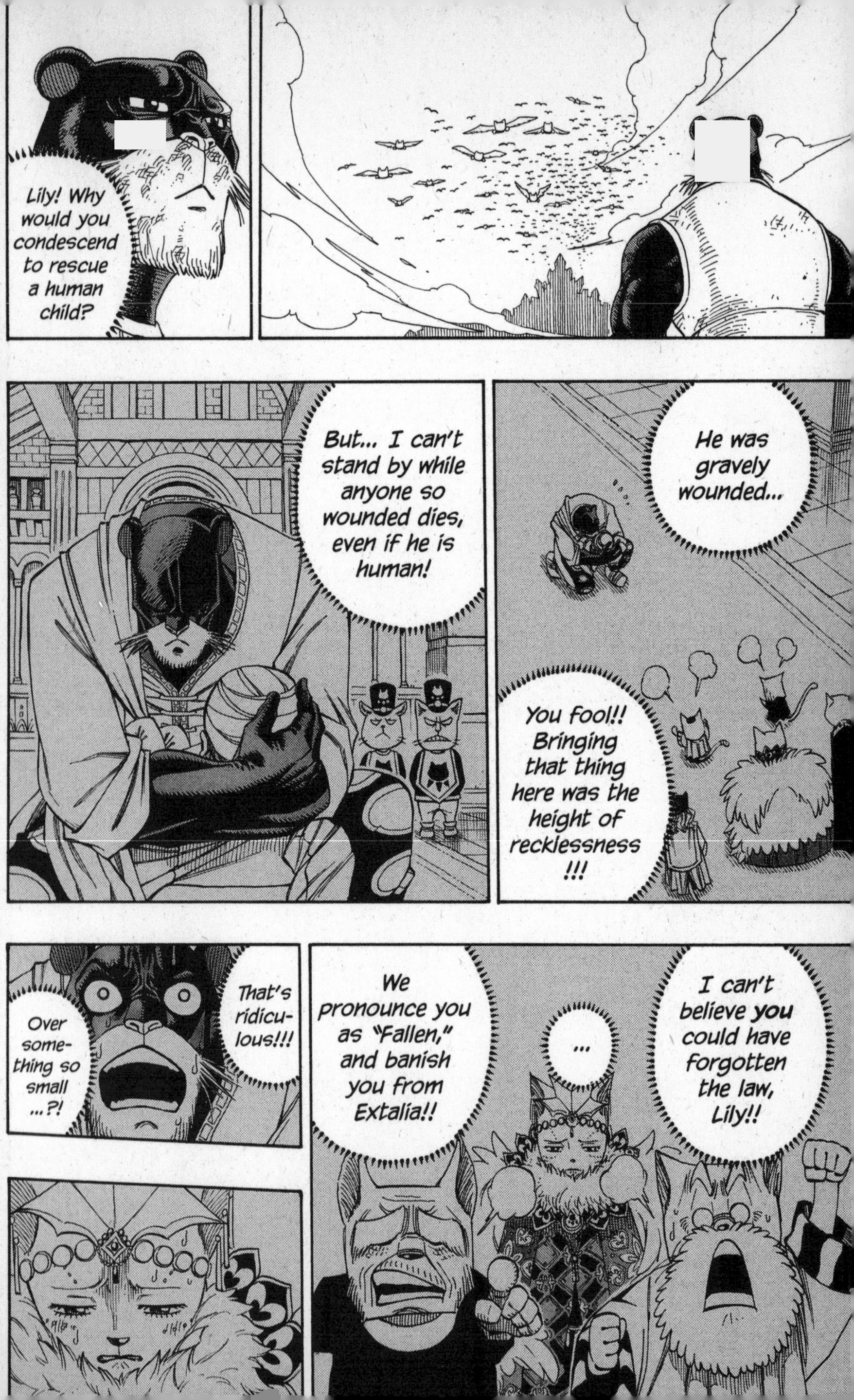
Lily! Why would you condescend to rescue a human child?
He was gravely wounded...
You fool!! Bringing that thing here was the height of recklessness!!!
But... I can't stand by while anyone so wounded dies, even if he is human!
I can't believe **you** could have forgotten the law, Lily!!
...
We pronounce you as "Fallen," and banish you from Extalia!!
That's ridicu-lous!!!
Over some-thing so small ...?!

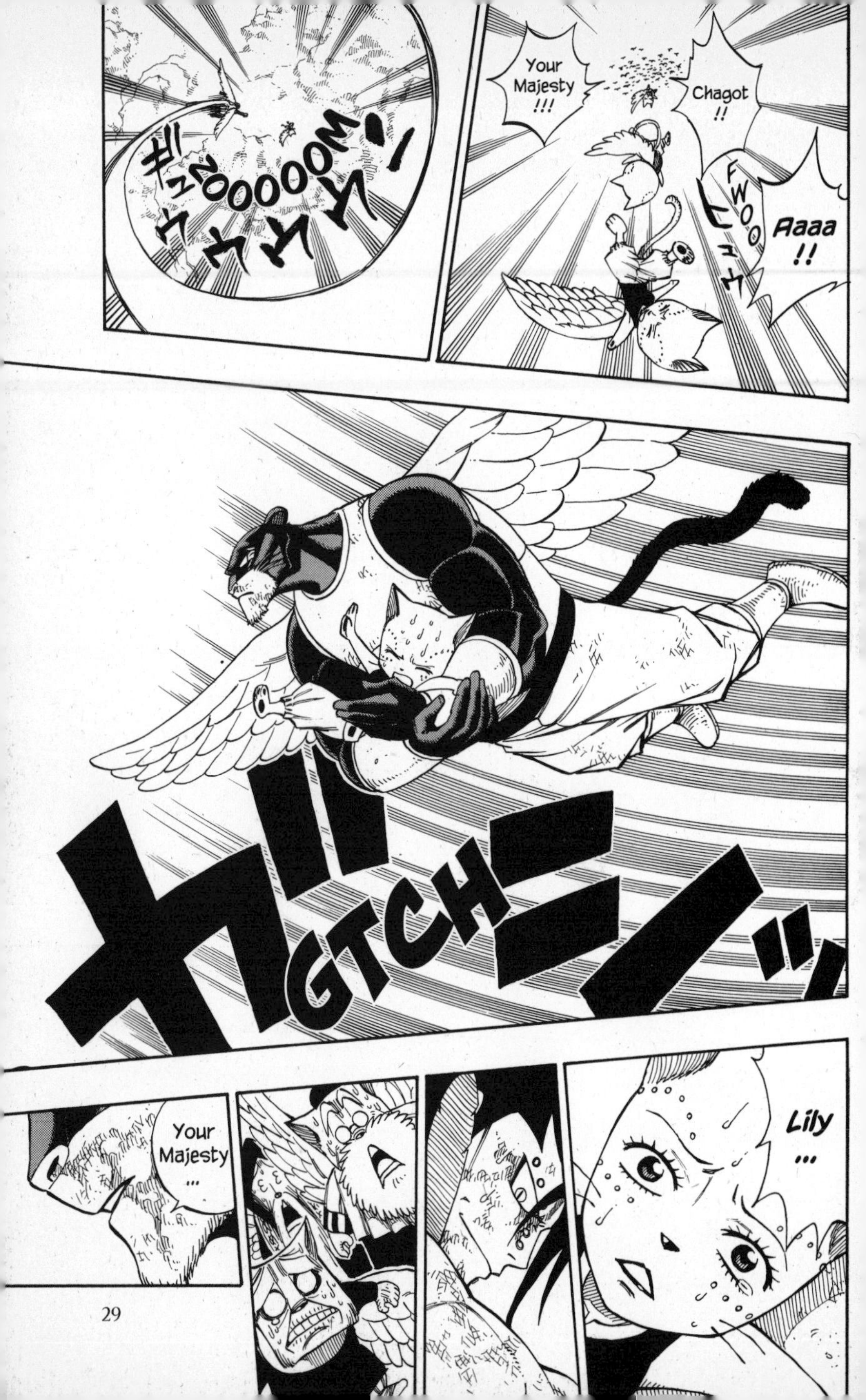
Your Majesty !!!
Chagot !!
FWOOM
Aaaa !!
ZOOOOOM
GTCH
Lily ...
Your Majesty ...

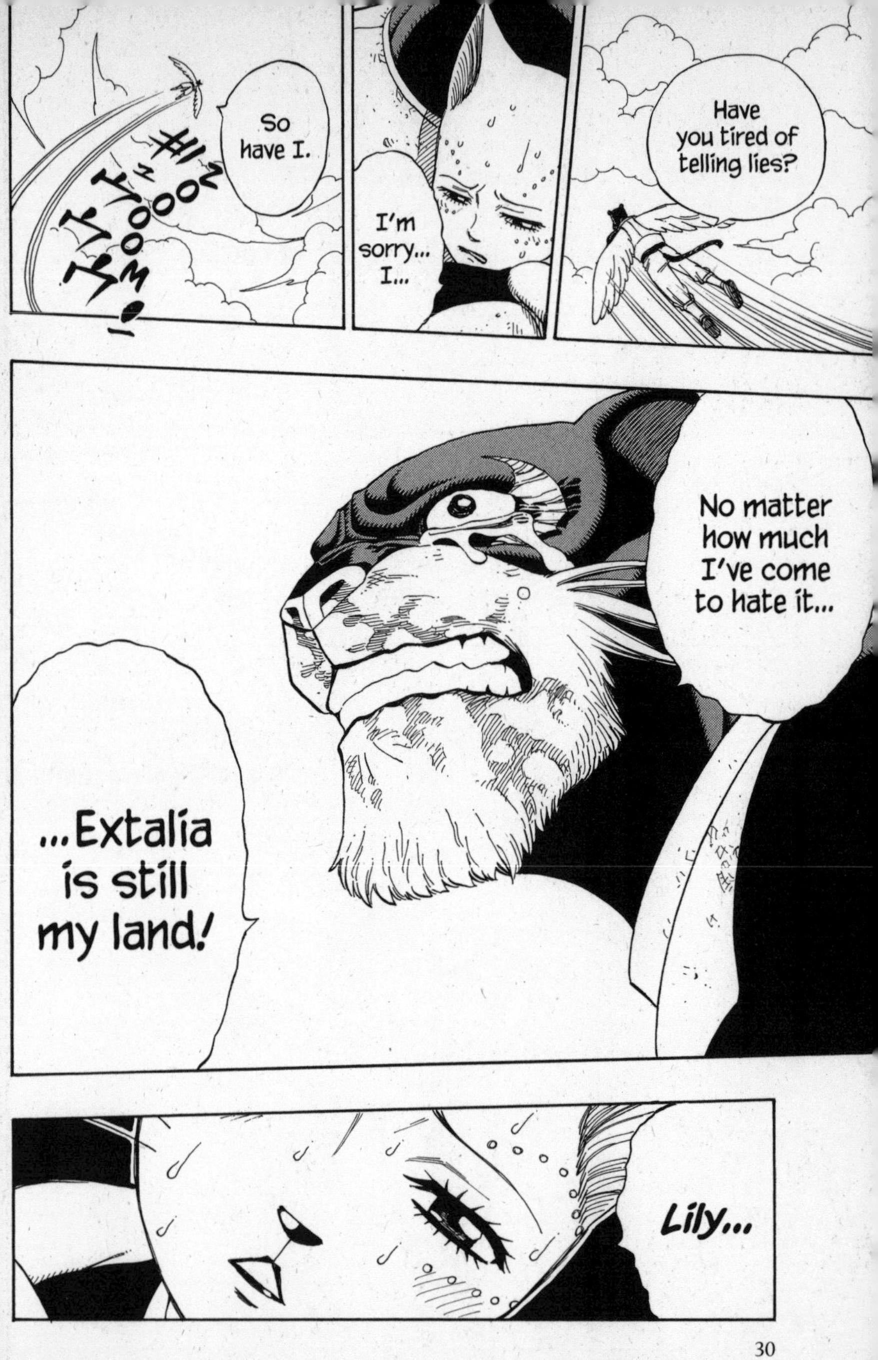
Have you tired of telling lies?
I'm sorry... I...
So have I.
ZOOOOM!!
No matter how much I've come to hate it...
...Extalia is still my land!
Lily...

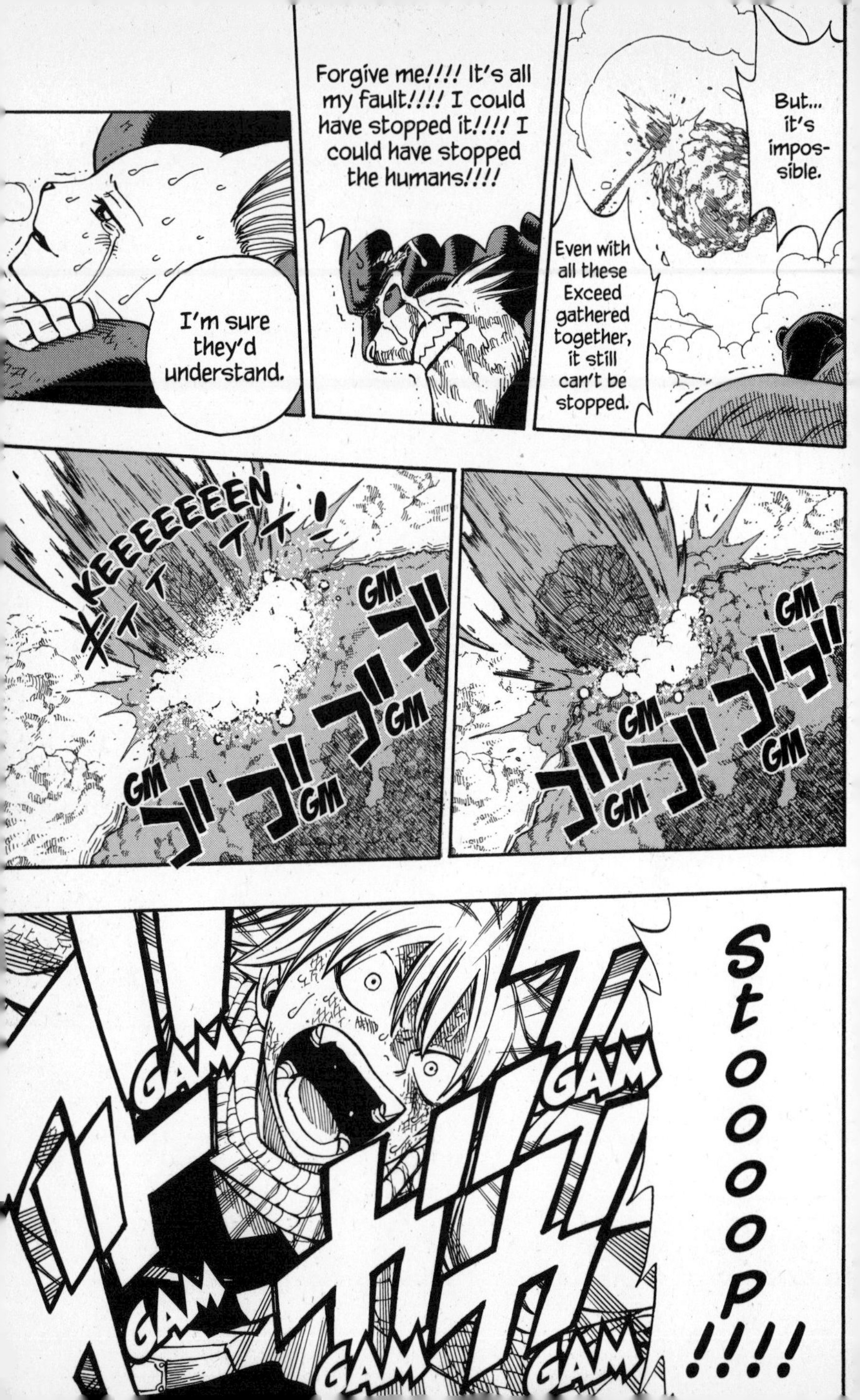
But... it's impossible.
Even with all these Exceed gathered together, it still can't be stopped.
Forgive me!!!! It's all my fault!!!! I could have stopped it!!!! I could have stopped the humans!!!!
I'm sure they'd understand.
GM GM GM GM
ゴゴゴゴ
KEEEEEEEN
キイイイイ
GM GM GM GM
ゴゴゴゴ
Stooooop!!!!
GAM GAM GAM GAM GAM

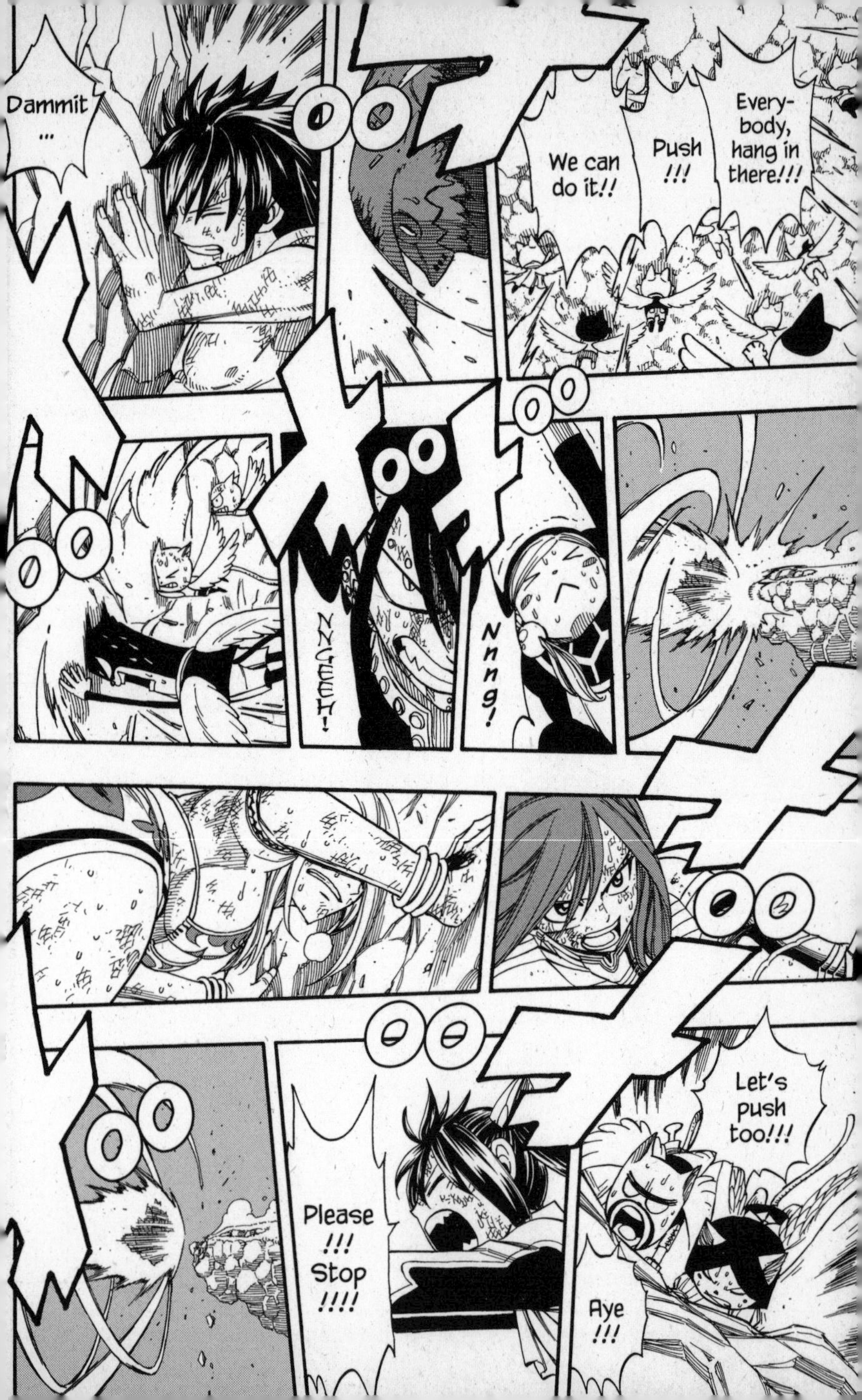
Every-body, hang in there!!!
Push!!!
We can do it!!
Dammit...
Nnng!
NNGEEH!
Let's push too!!!
Aye!!!
Please!!! Stop!!!!

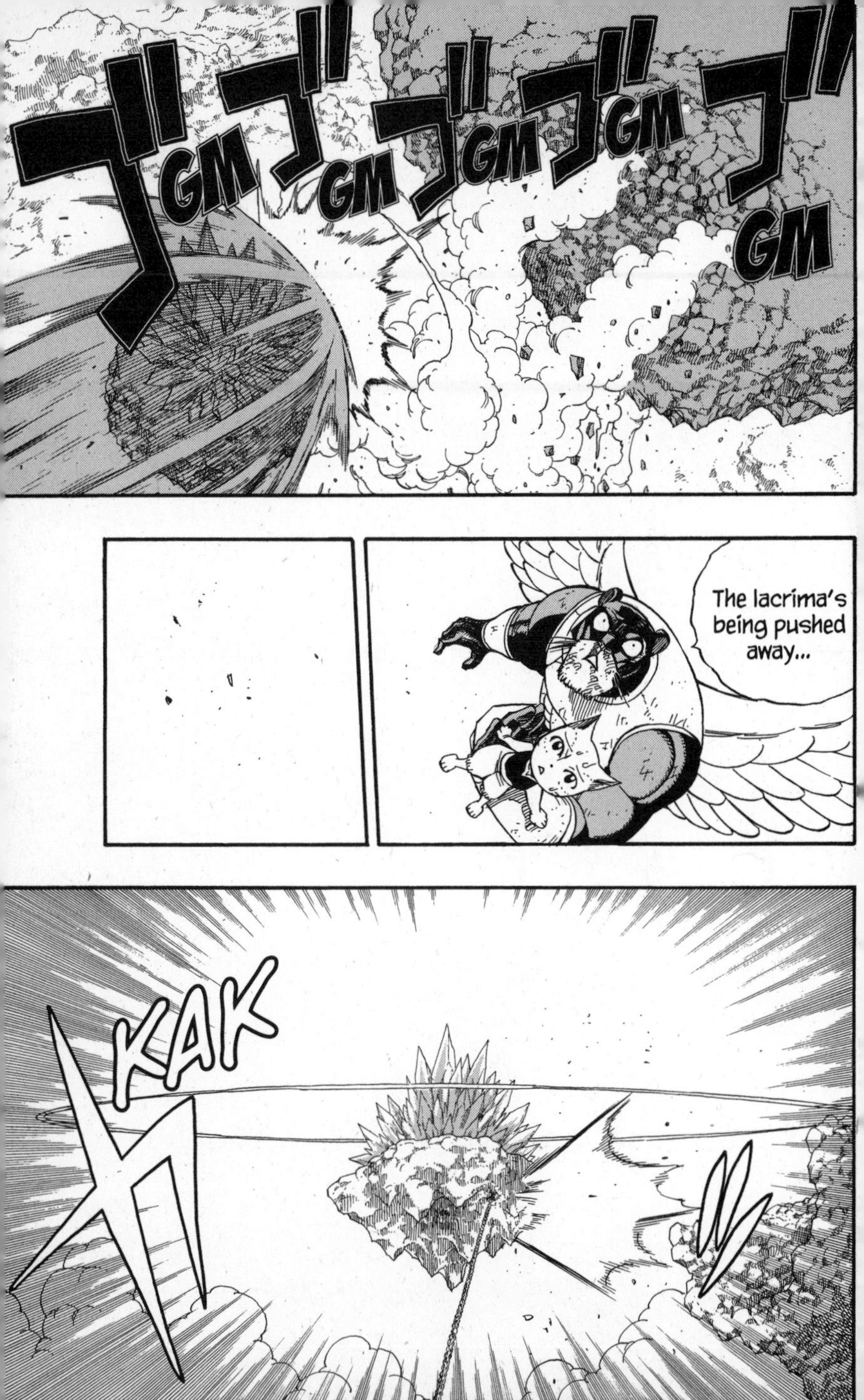
ゴGM ゴGM ゴGM ゴGM ゴGM
The lacrima's being pushed away...
KAK

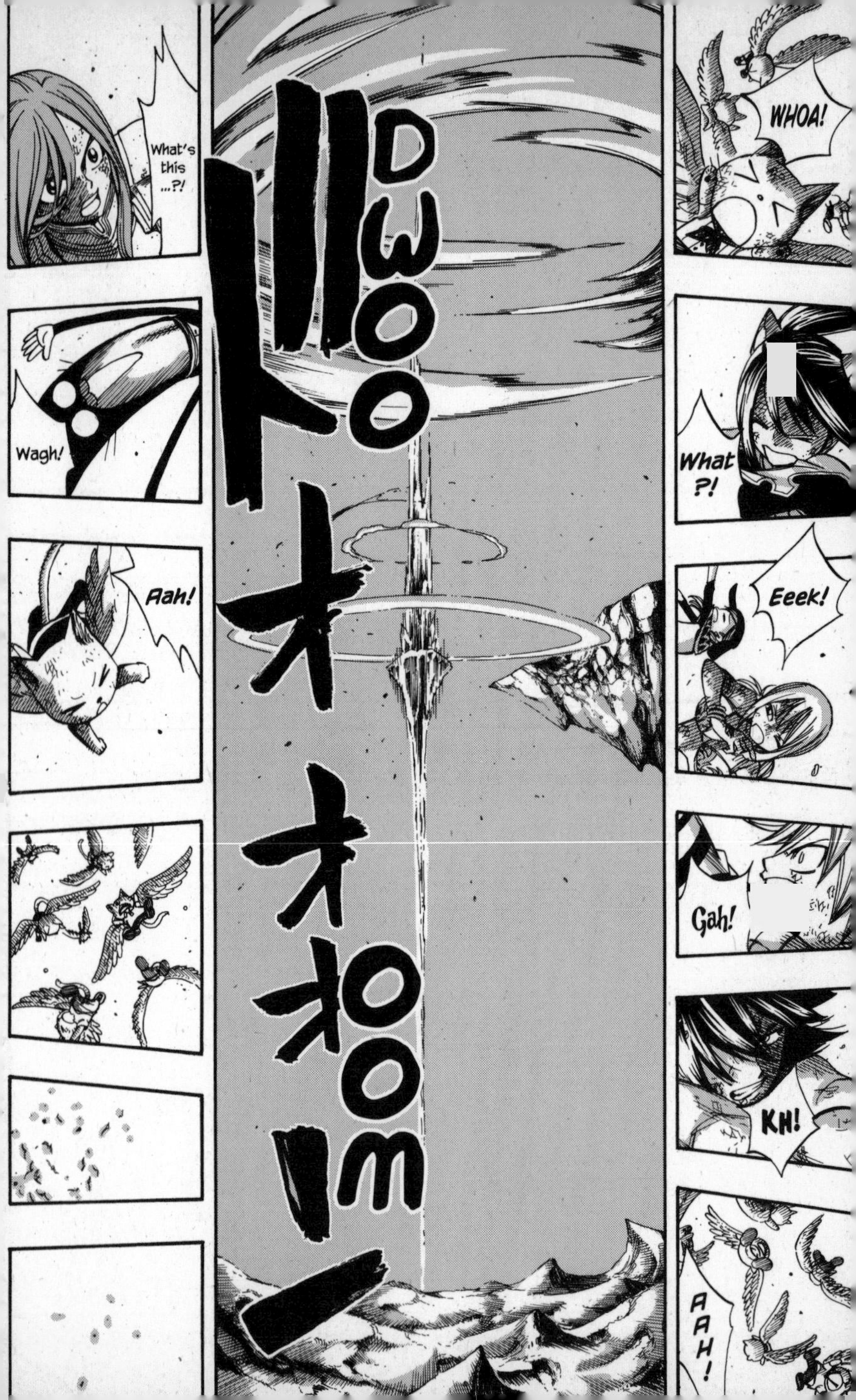
WHOA!
What ?!
Eeek!
Gah!
KH!
AAH!
DWOOOOOM
What's this ...?!
Wagh!
Aah!

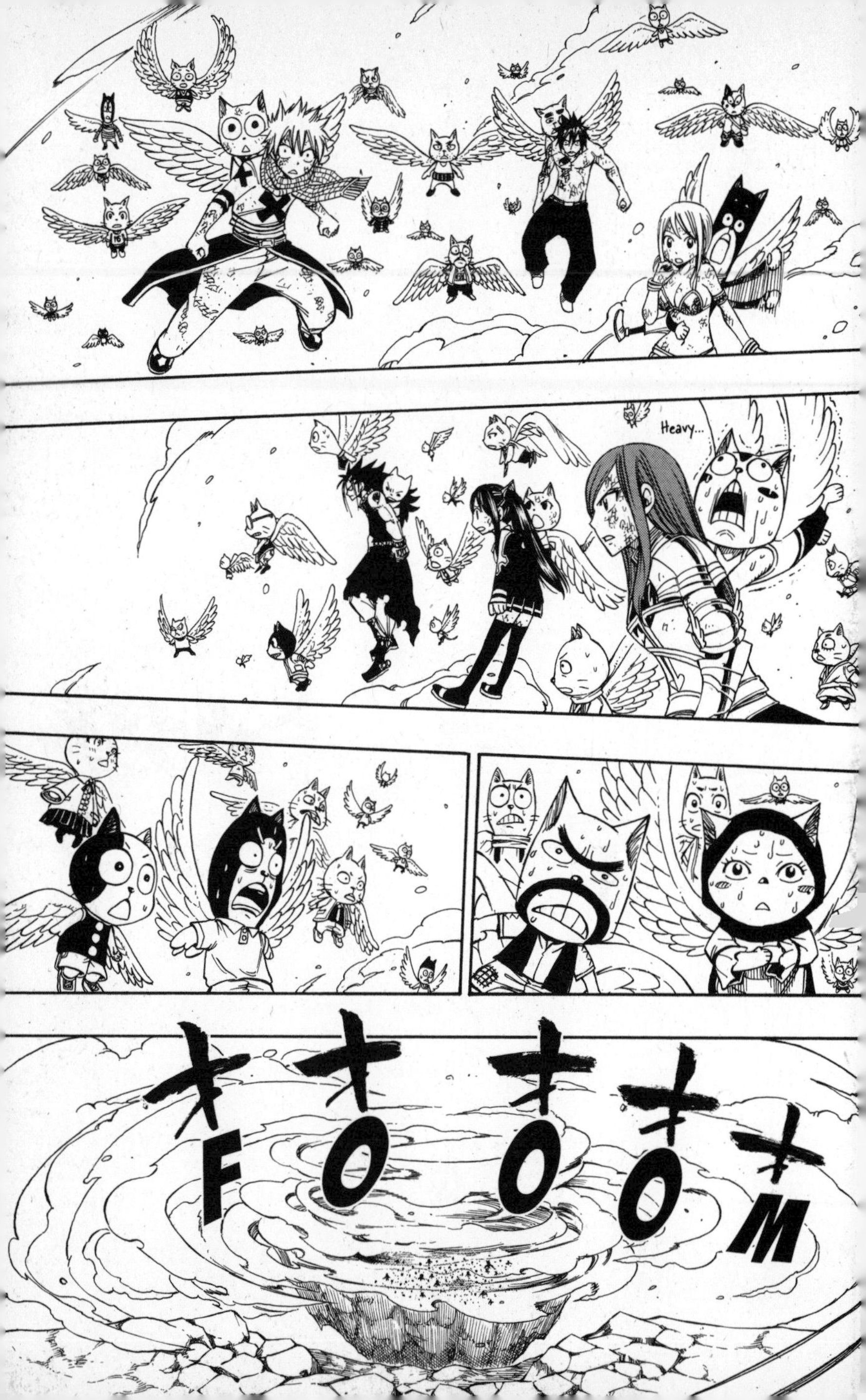
Heavy...
FOOOM

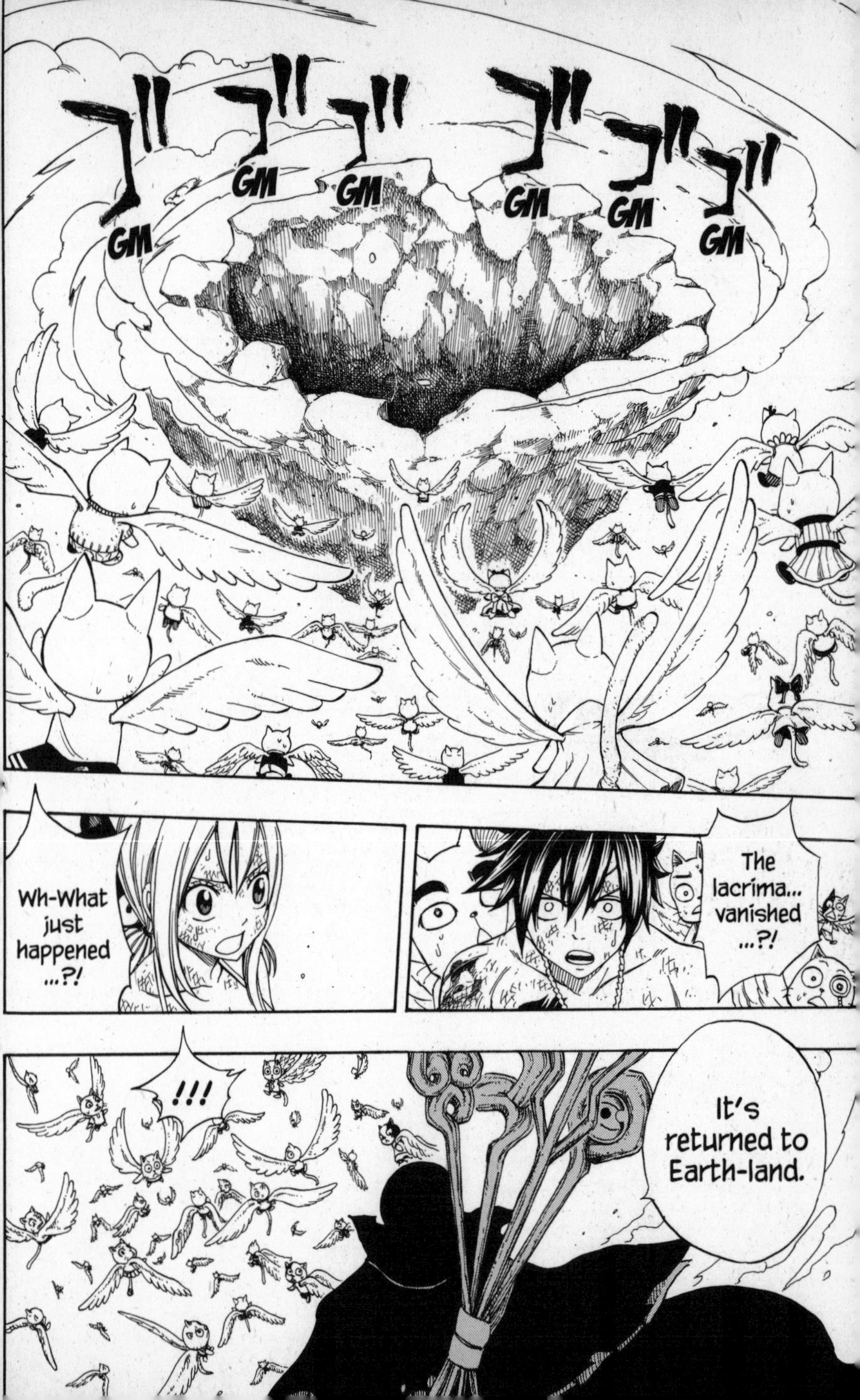
GM GM GM GM GM GM
The lacrima... vanished ...?!
Wh-What just happened ...?!
It's returned to Earth-land.
!!!

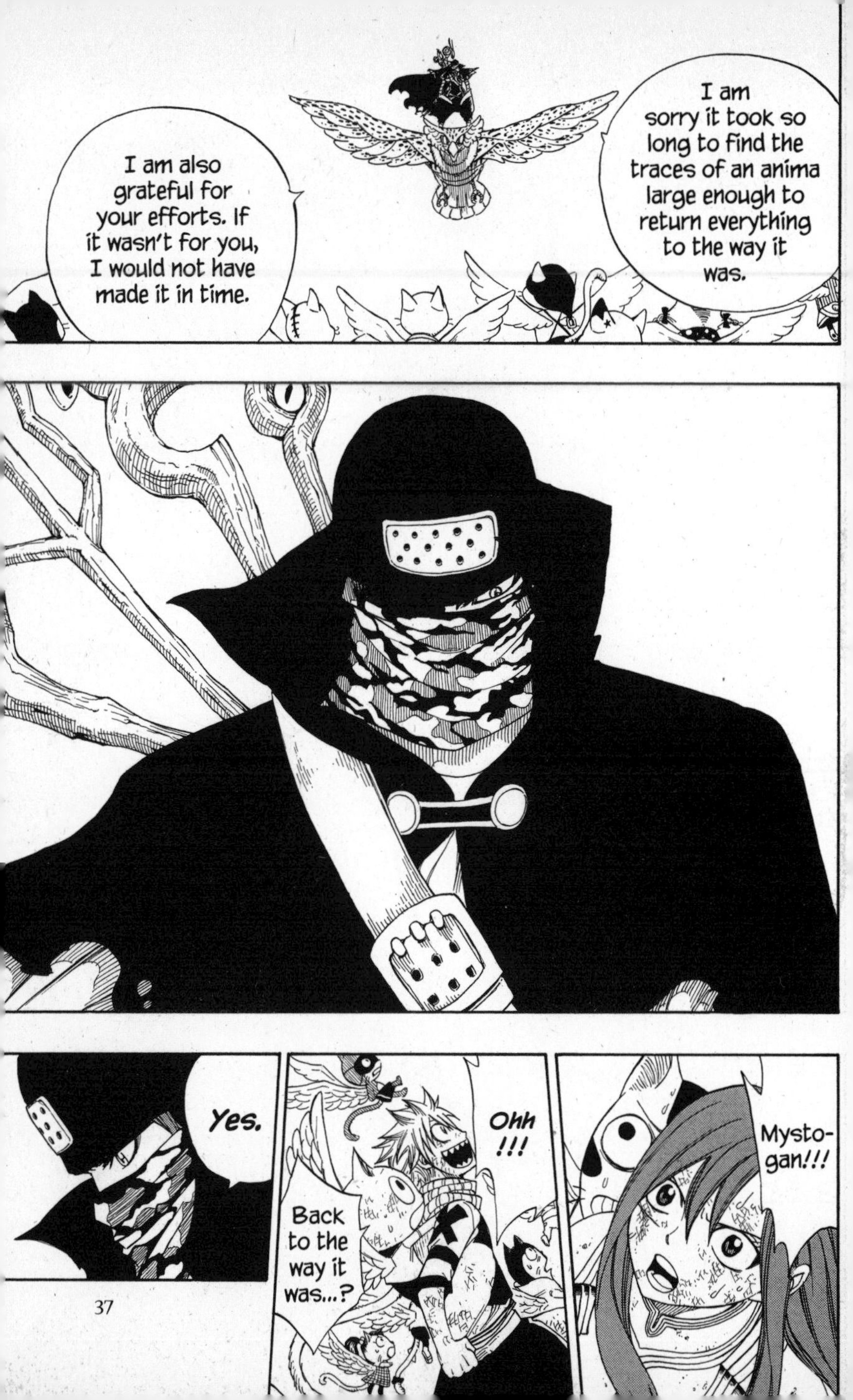
I am sorry it took so long to find the traces of an anima large enough to return everything to the way it was.
I am also grateful for your efforts. If it wasn't for you, I would not have made it in time.
Mysto-gan!!!
Ohh!!!
Back to the way it was...?
Yes.

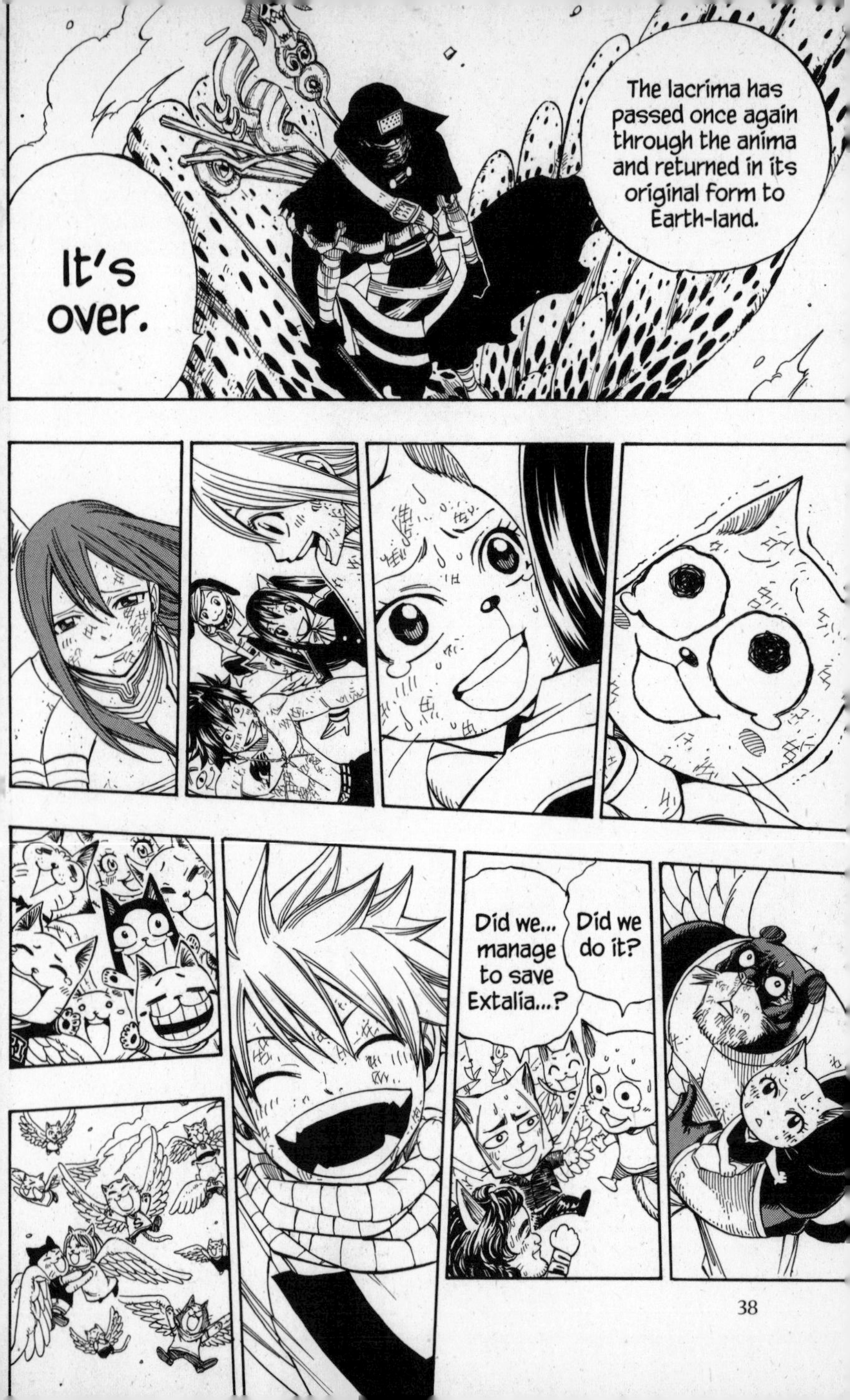
The lacrima has passed once again through the anima and returned in its original form to Earth-land.
It's over.
Did we do it?
Did we... manage to save Extalia...?

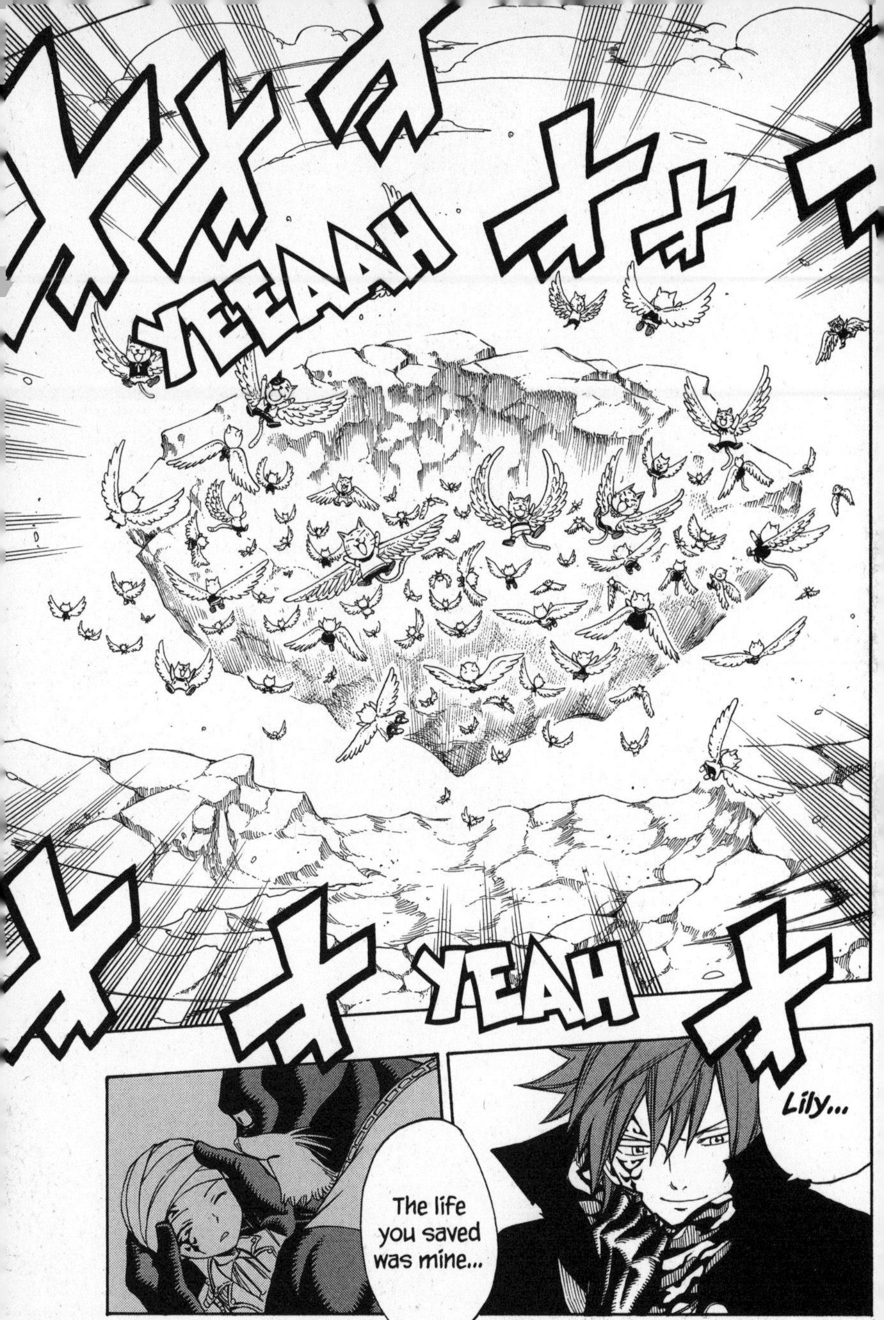
YEEAAH
YEAH
Lily...
The life you saved was mine...

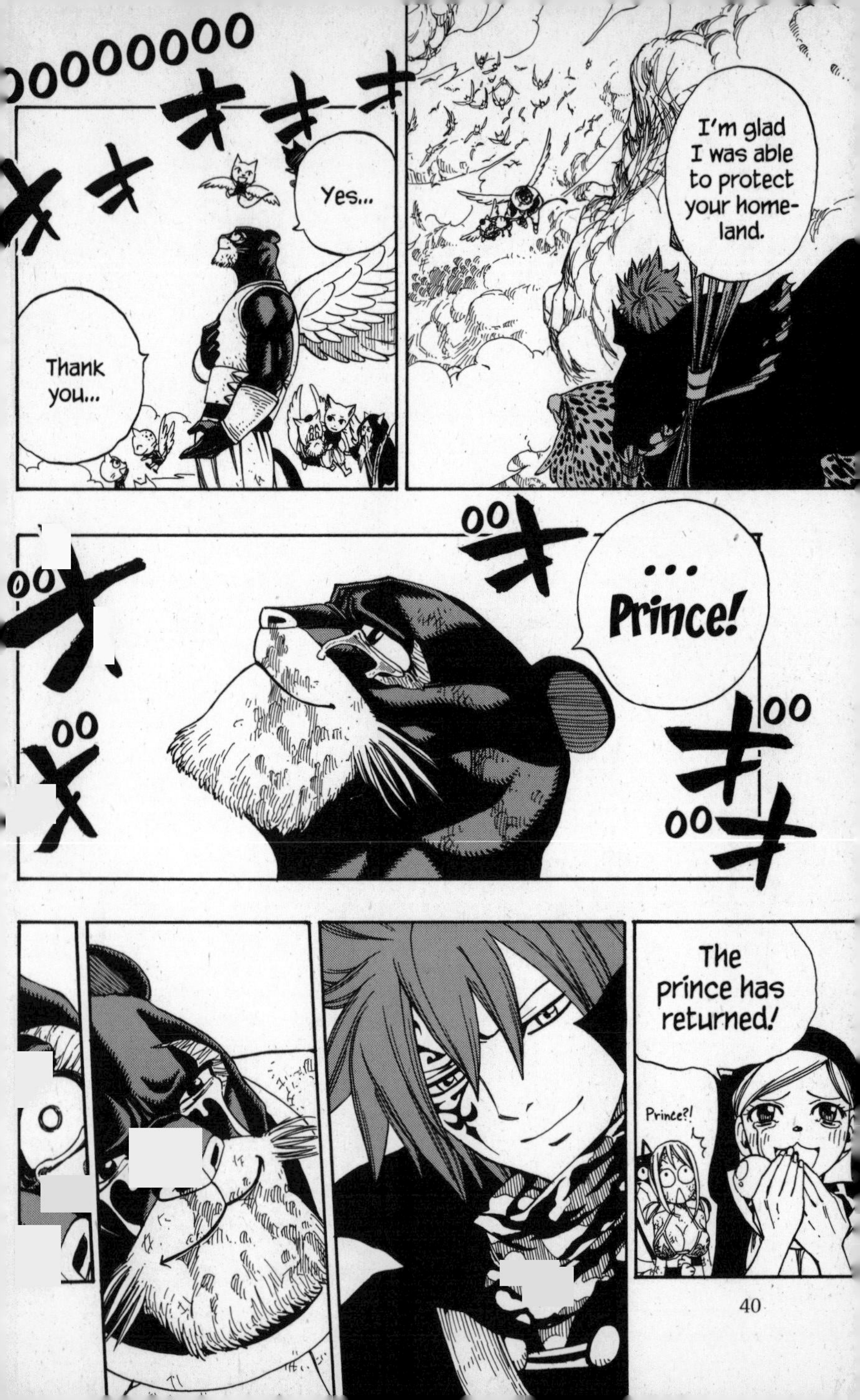
I'm glad I was able to protect your homeland.
Yes...
Thank you...
...Prince!
The prince has returned!
Prince?!

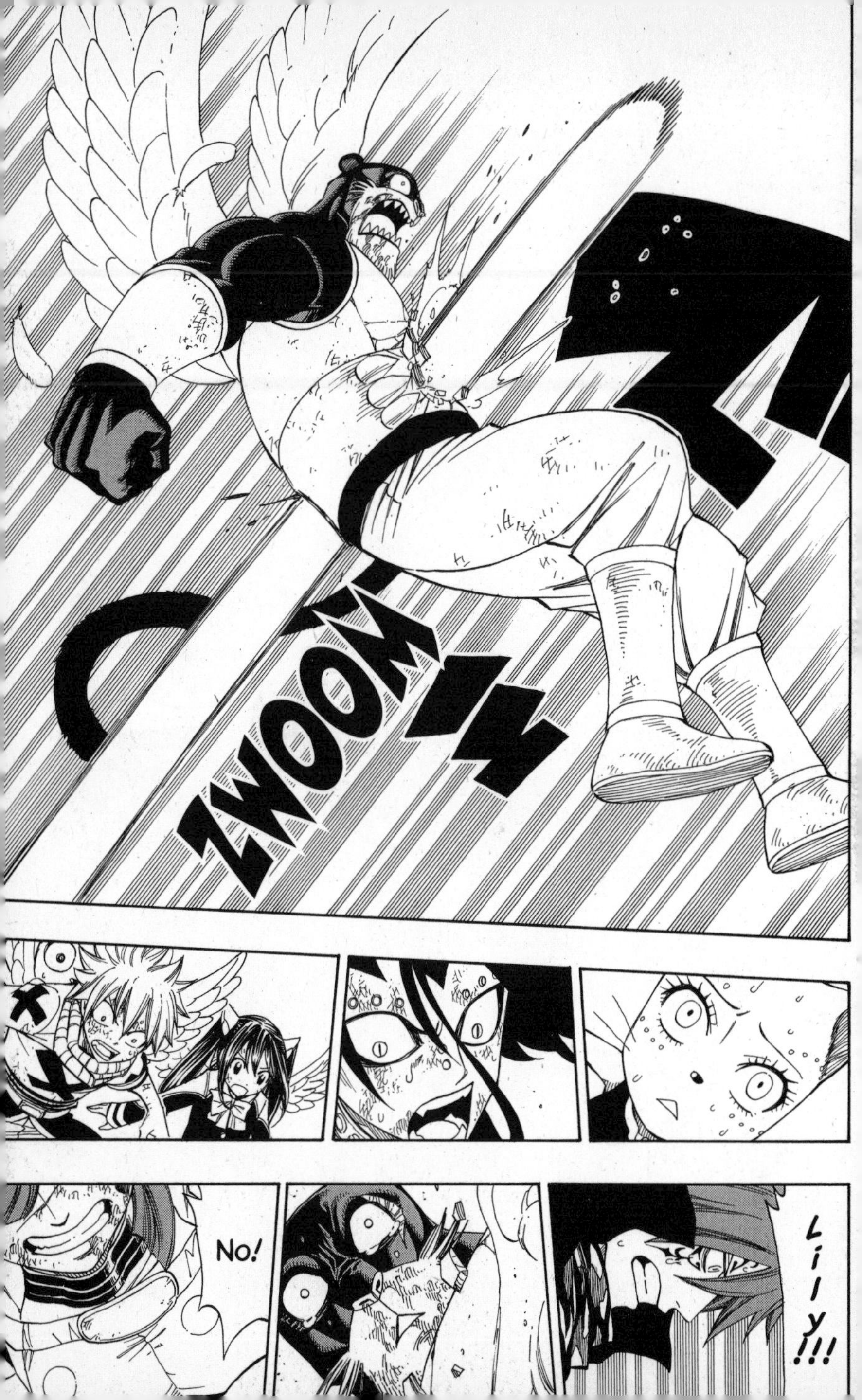
ZWOOM
Lily!!!
No!

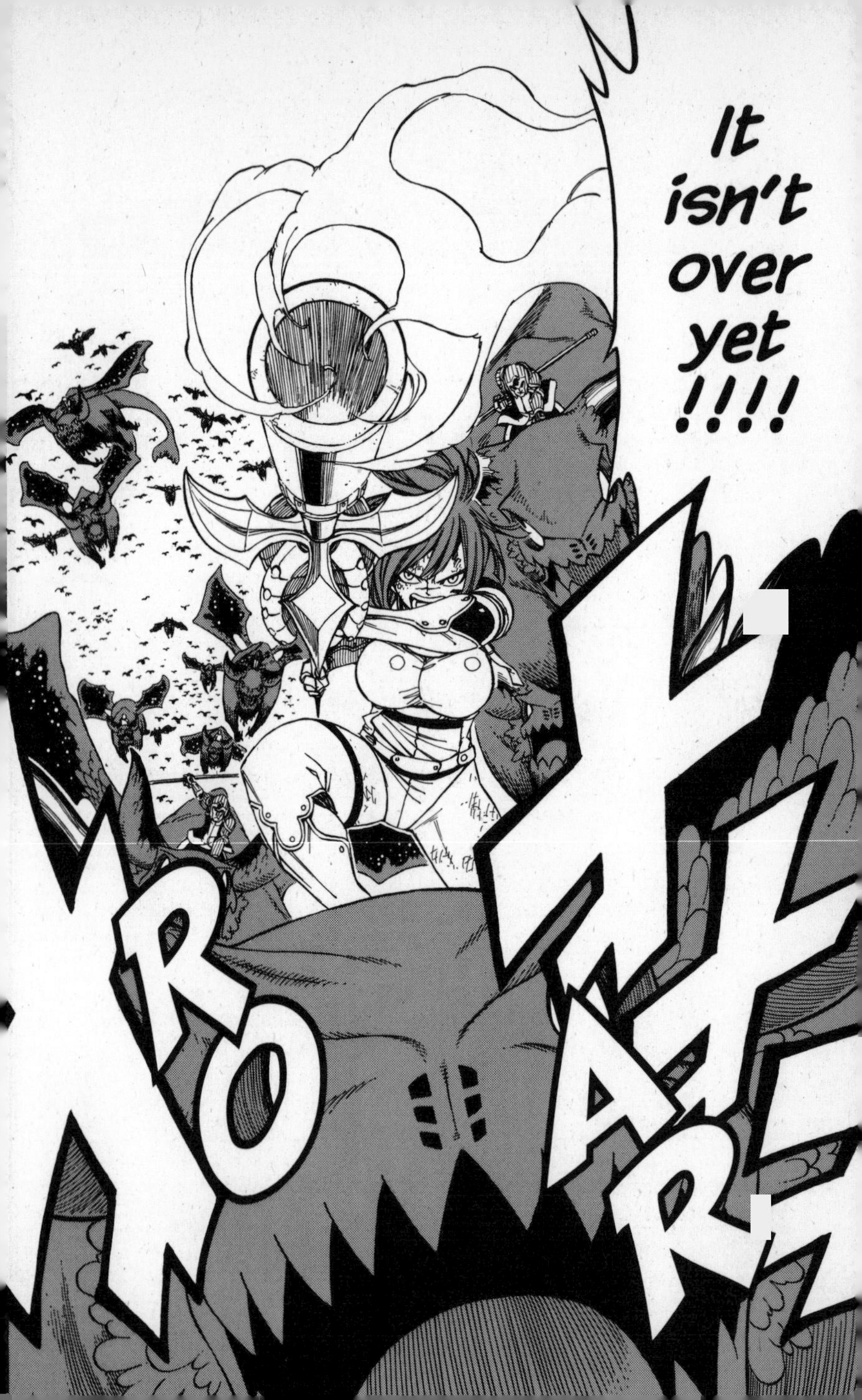
It isn't over yet!!!!
ROAR

FAIRY TAIL

フェアリーテイル

Chapter 190: Dragon Sense

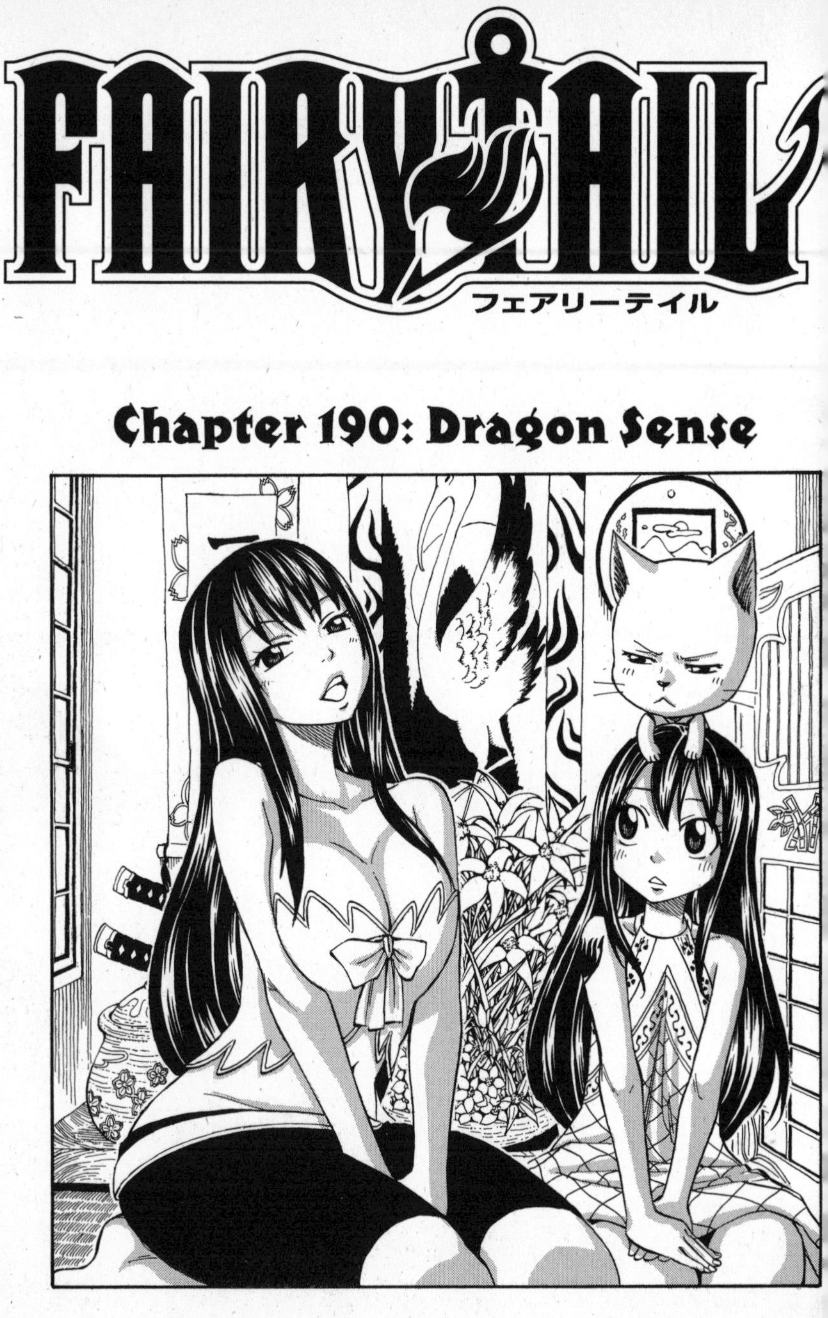

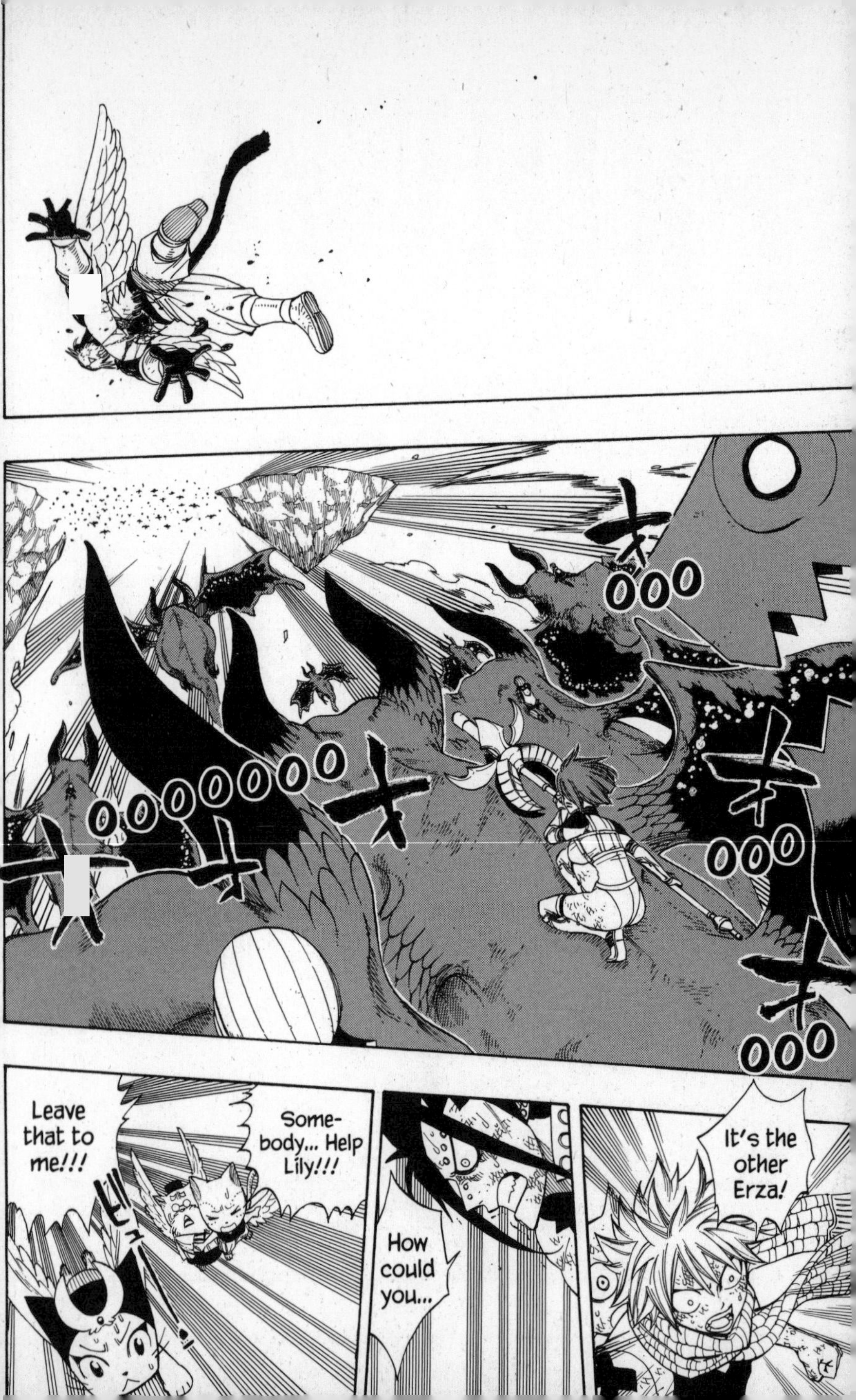
It's the other Erza!
How could you...
Some-body... Help Lily!!!
Leave that to me!!!

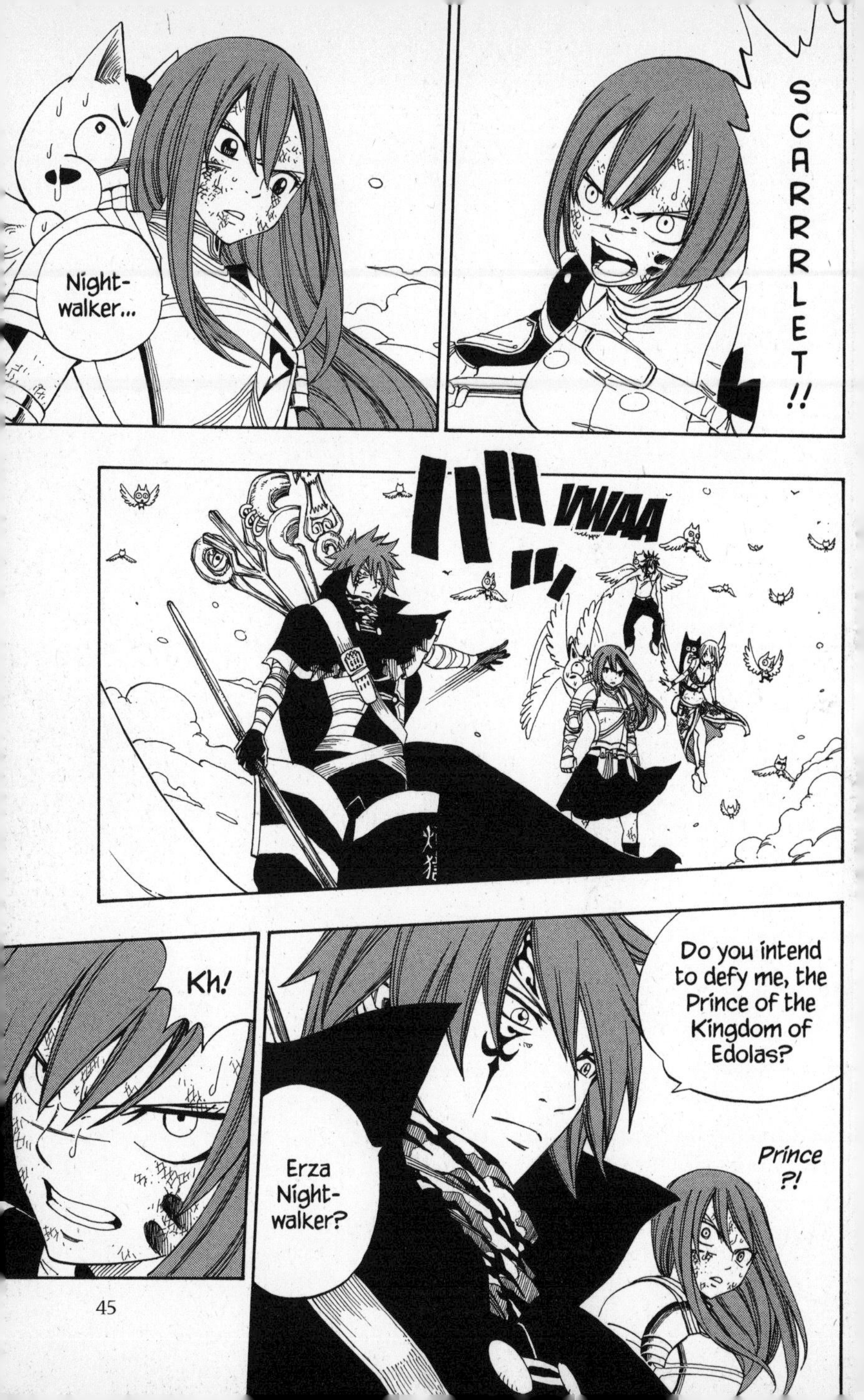
SCARRRLET!!
Night-walker...
VWAA
Do you intend to defy me, the Prince of the Kingdom of Edolas?
Erza Night-walker?
Prince ?!
Kh!

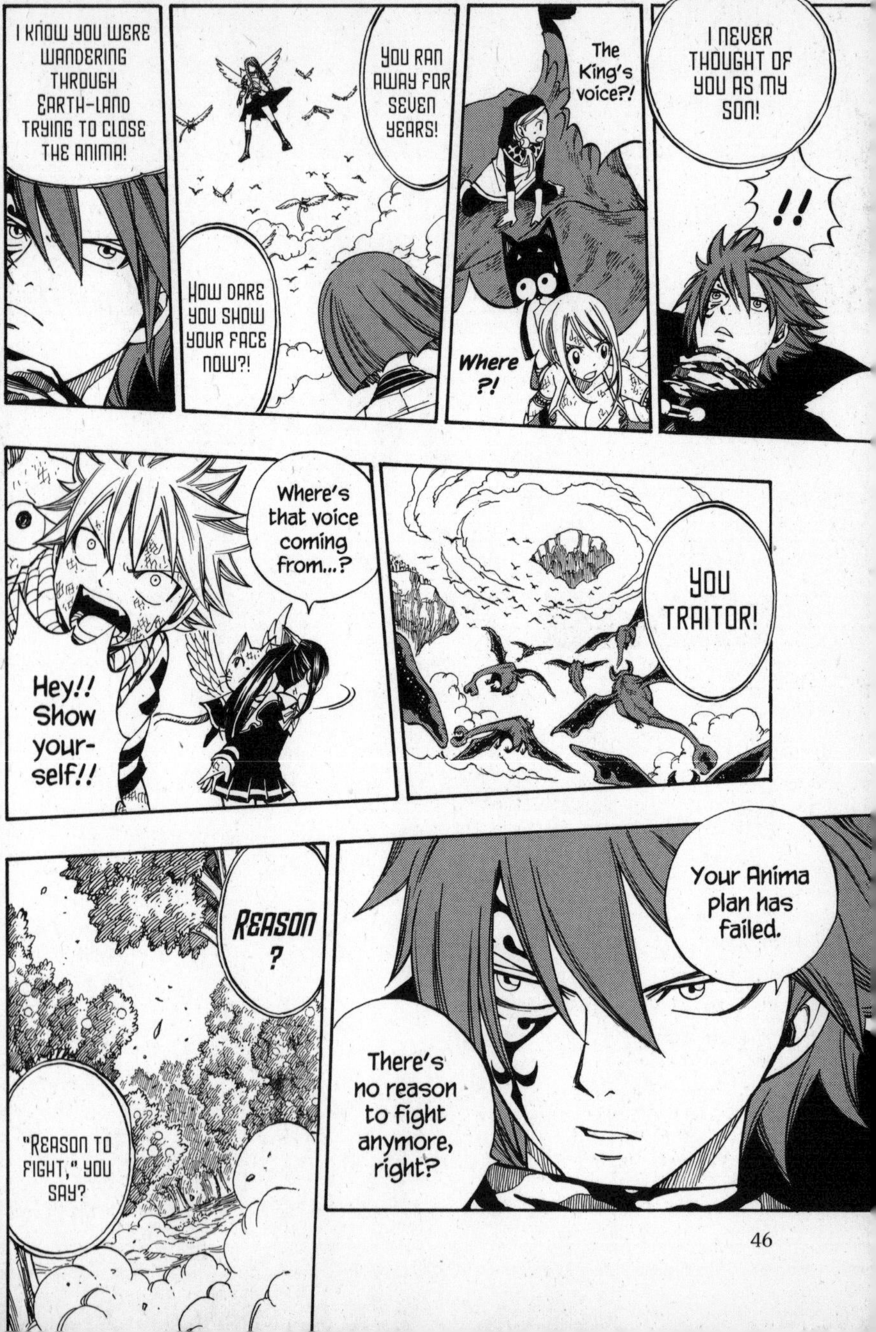
I NEVER THOUGHT OF YOU AS MY SON!
!!
The King's voice?!
Where?!
YOU RAN AWAY FOR SEVEN YEARS!
HOW DARE YOU SHOW YOUR FACE NOW?!
I KNOW YOU WERE WANDERING THROUGH EARTH-LAND TRYING TO CLOSE THE ANIMA!
YOU TRAITOR!
Where's that voice coming from...?
Hey!! Show your-self!!
Your Anima plan has failed.
There's no reason to fight anymore, right?
REASON?
"REASON TO FIGHT," YOU SAY?

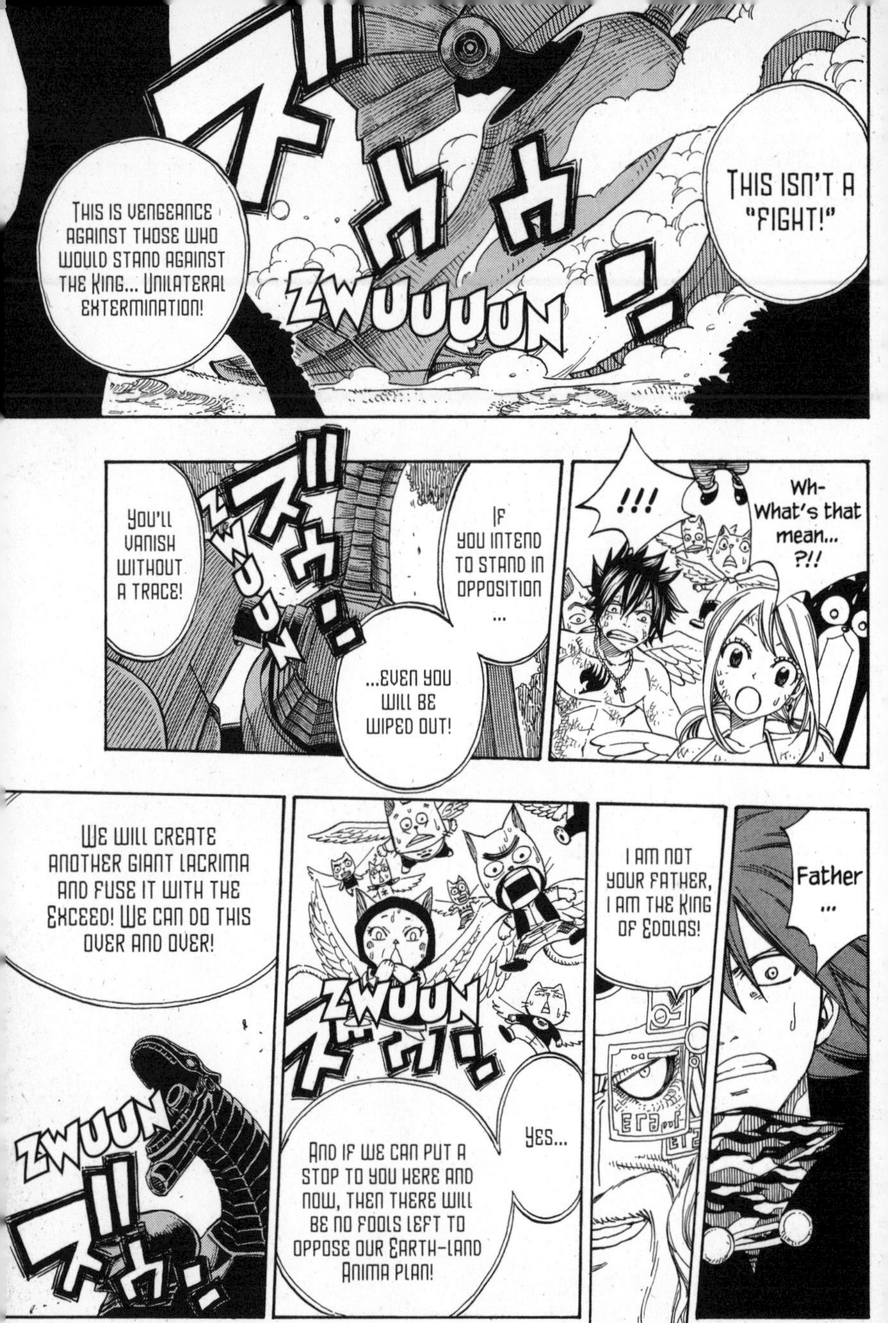
This isn't a "FIGHT!"
This is vengeance against those who would stand against the King... Unilateral extermination!
ZWUUUUN
Wh- What's that mean...?!!
!!!
If you intend to stand in opposition...
...even you will be wiped out!
You'll vanish without a trace!
ZWUUUN
Father...
I am not your father, I am the King of Edolas!
Yes...
And if we can put a stop to you here and now, then there will be no fools left to oppose our Earth-land Anima plan!
ZWUUN
We will create another giant lacrima and fuse it with the Exceed! We can do this over and over!
ZWUUN

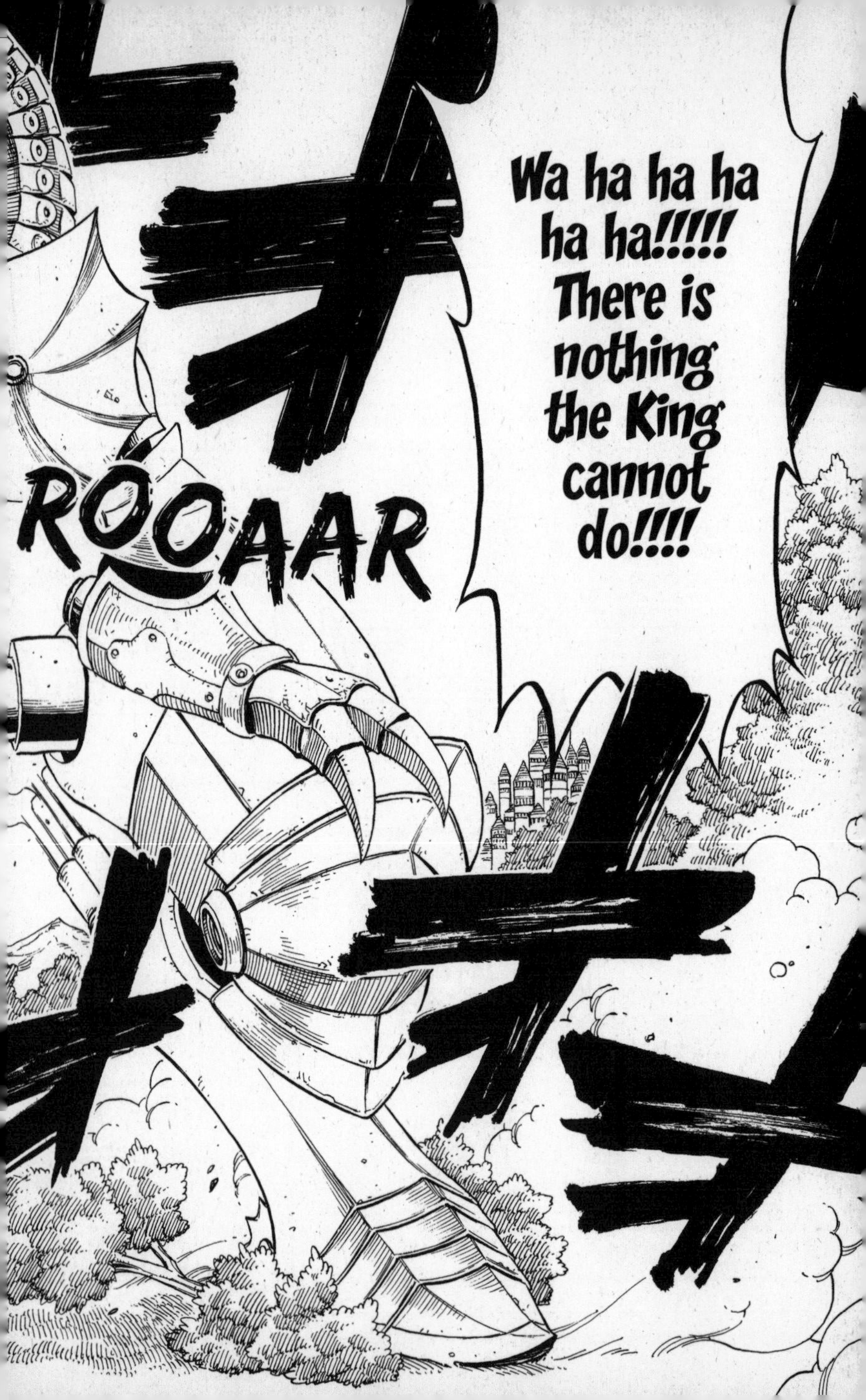
Wa ha ha ha ha ha!!!!! There is nothing the King cannot do!!!!
ROOAAR

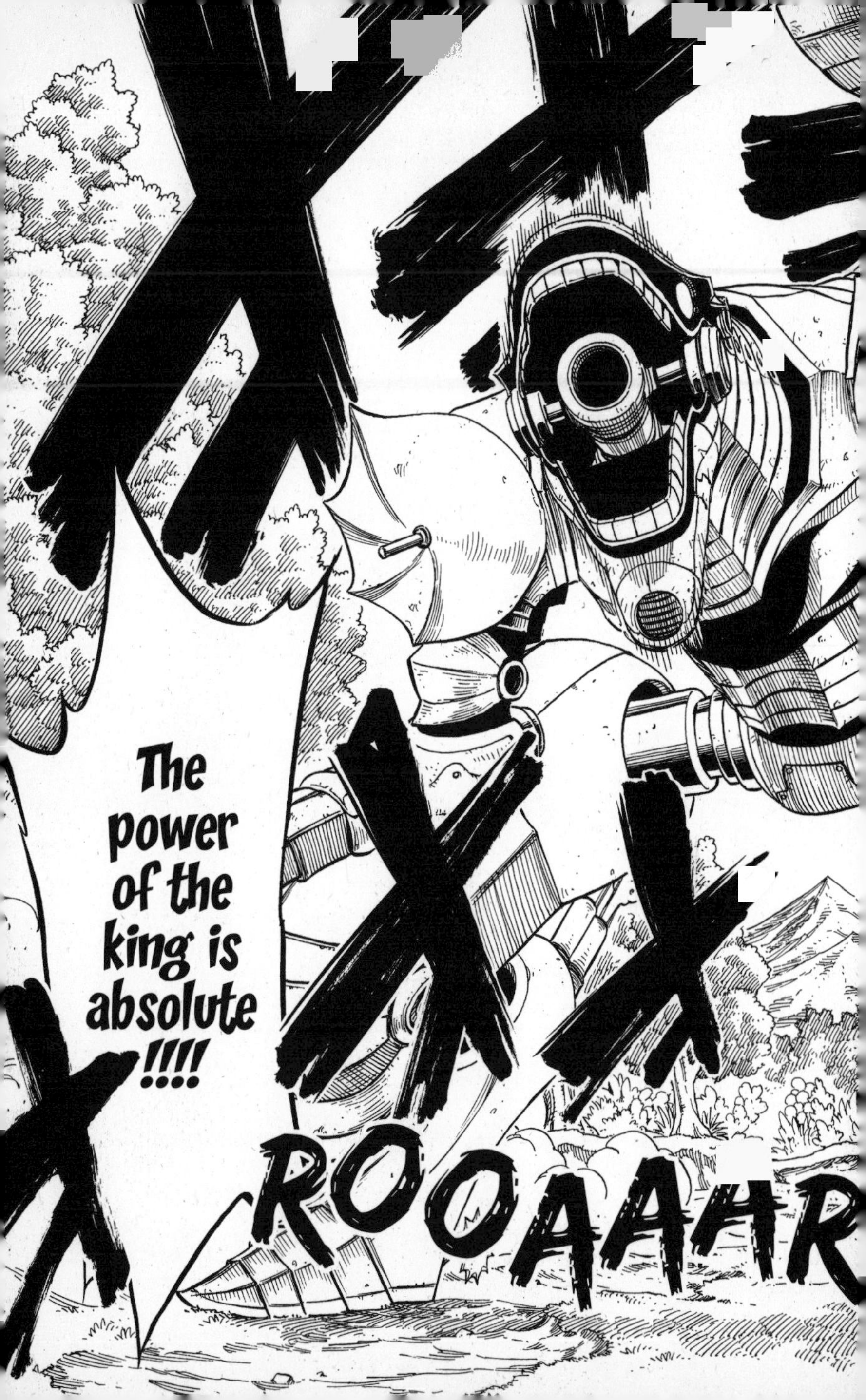
The power of the king is absolute!!!!
ROOAAHR

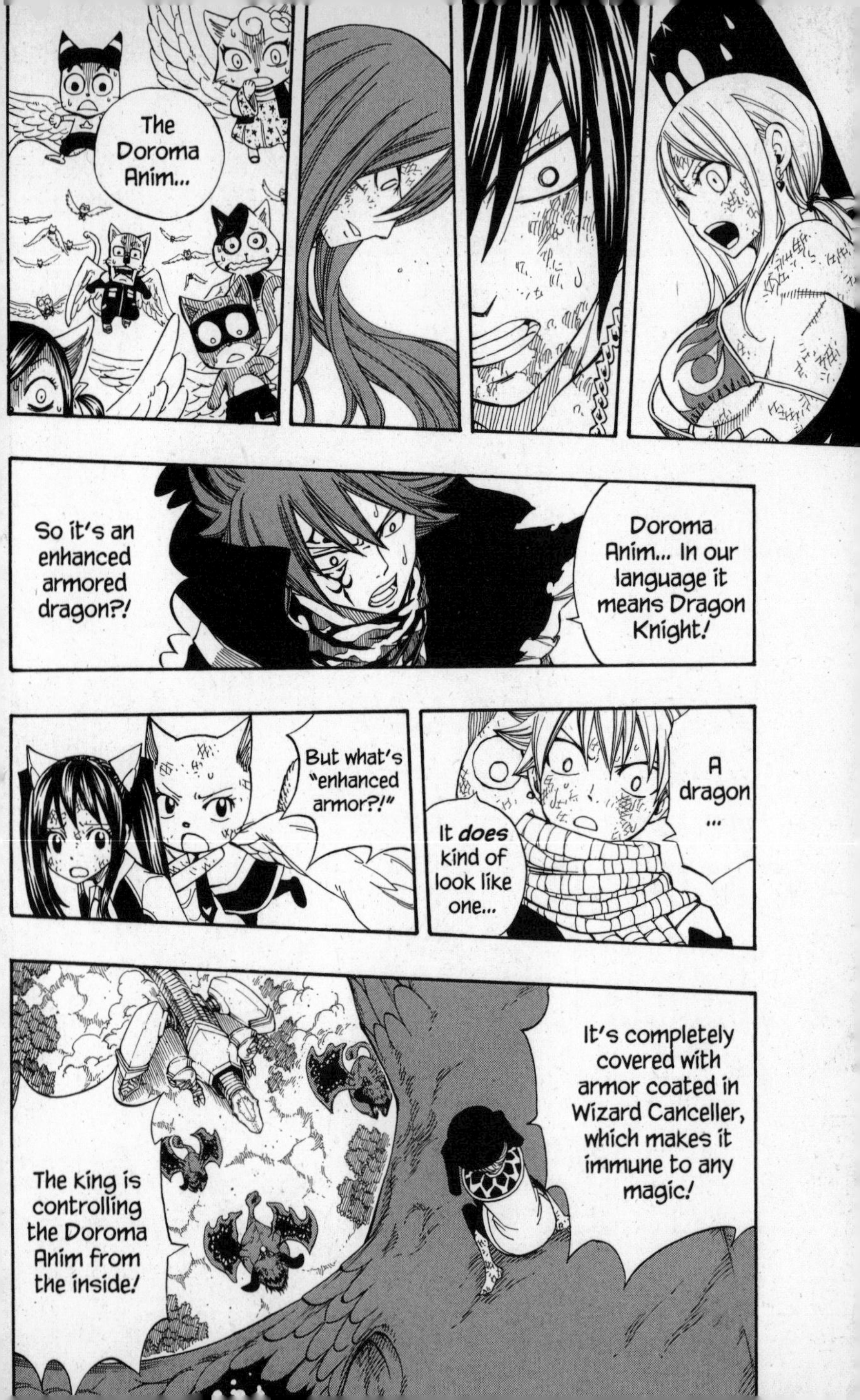
The Doroma Anim...
Doroma Anim... In our language it means Dragon Knight!
So it's an enhanced armored dragon?!
A dragon...
It *does* kind of look like one...
But what's "enhanced armor?!"
It's completely covered with armor coated in Wizard Canceller, which makes it immune to any magic!
The king is controlling the Doroma Anim from the inside!

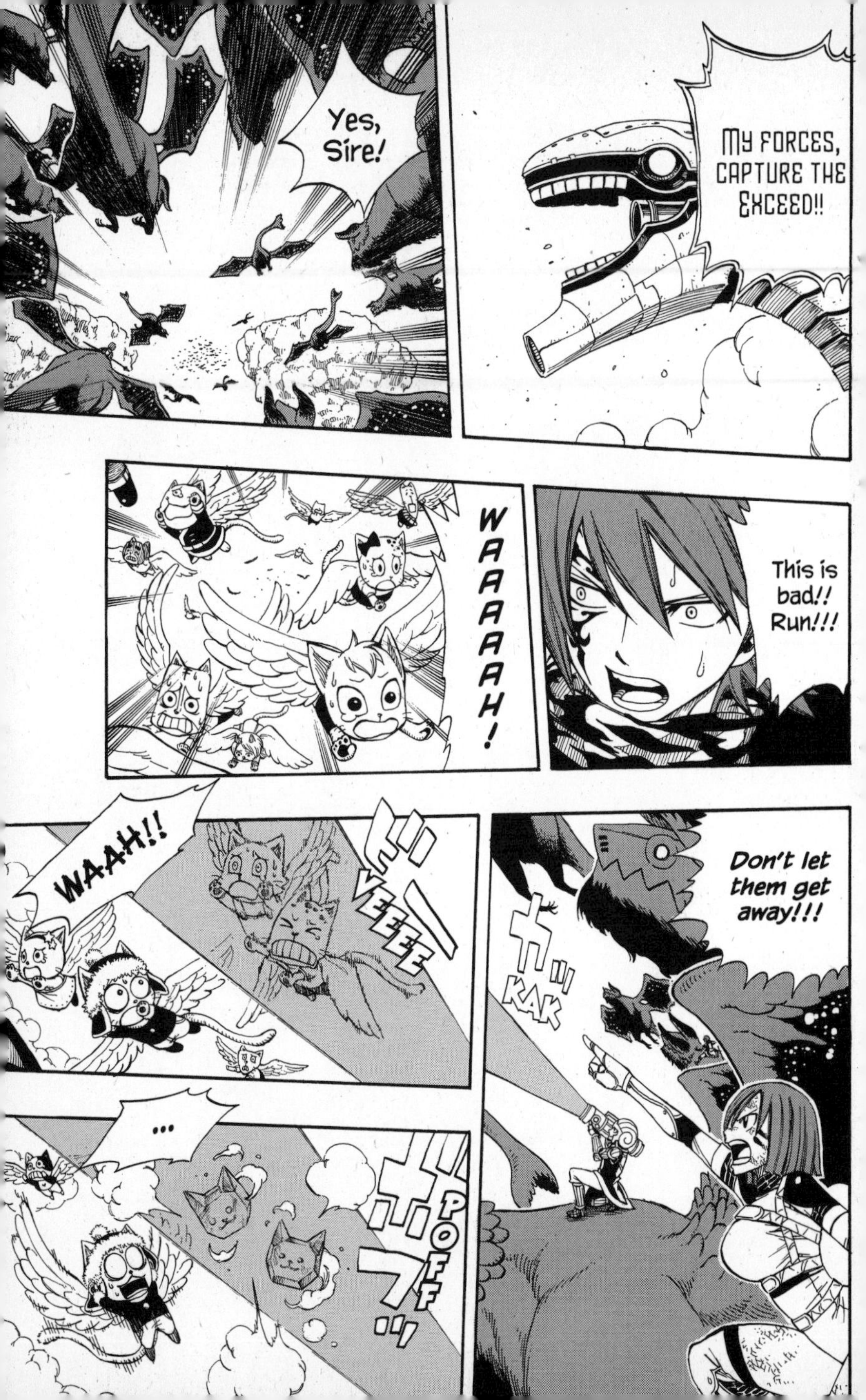
My forces, capture the Exceed!!
Yes, Sire!
This is bad!! Run!!!
WAAAAAAH!
Don't let them get away!!!
KAK
WAAH!!
VEEEE
...
POFF

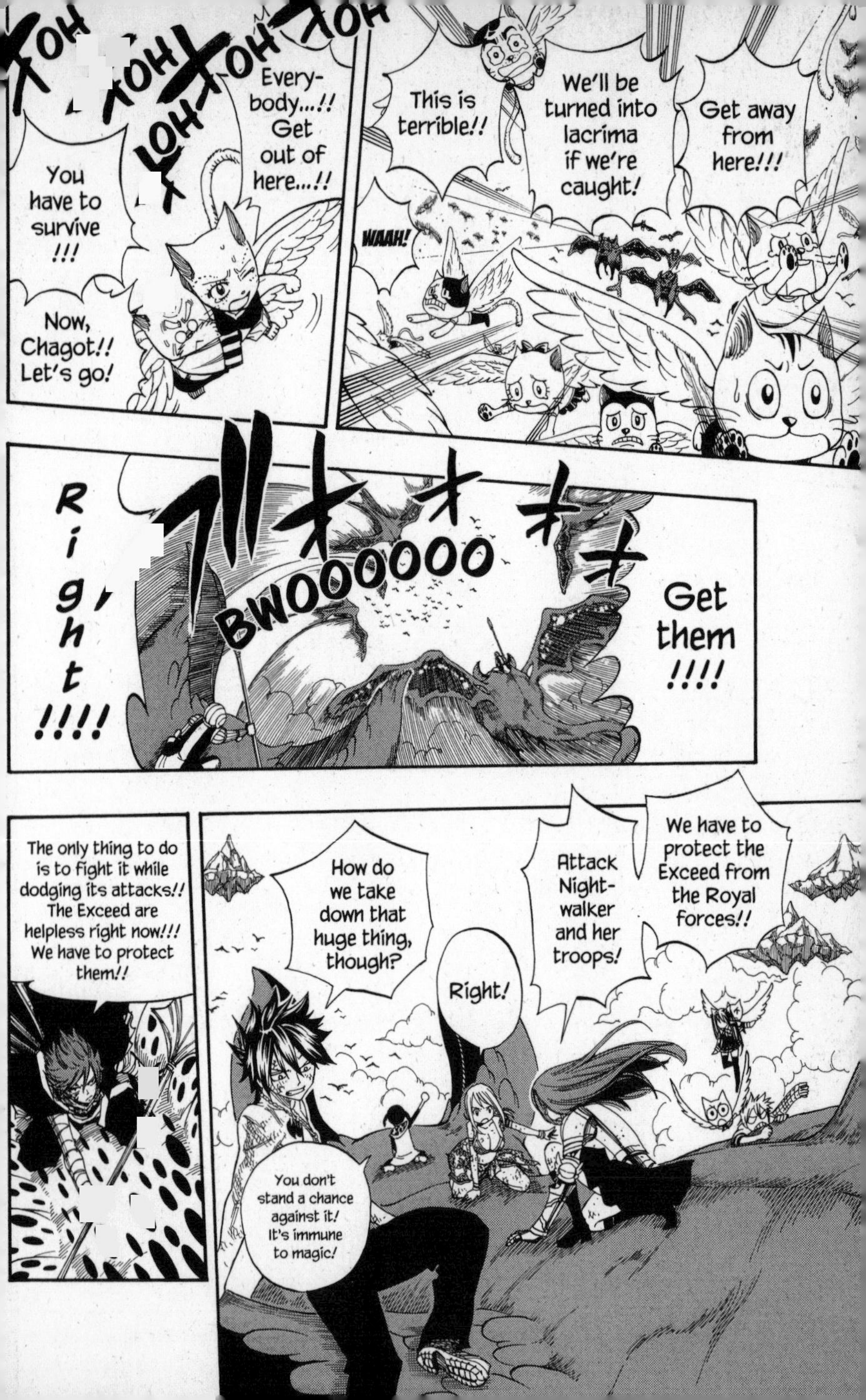
Get away from here!!!
We'll be turned into lacrima if we're caught!
This is terrible!!
WAAH!
Every-body...!! Get out of here...!!
TOH TOH TOH TOH TOH TOH
You have to survive!!!
Now, Chagot!! Let's go!
Get them!!!!
BWOOOOOO
Right!!!!
We have to protect the Exceed from the Royal forces!!
Attack Night-walker and her troops!
Right!
How do we take down that huge thing, though?
You don't stand a chance against it! It's immune to magic!
The only thing to do is to fight it while dodging its attacks!! The Exceed are helpless right now!!! We have to protect them!!

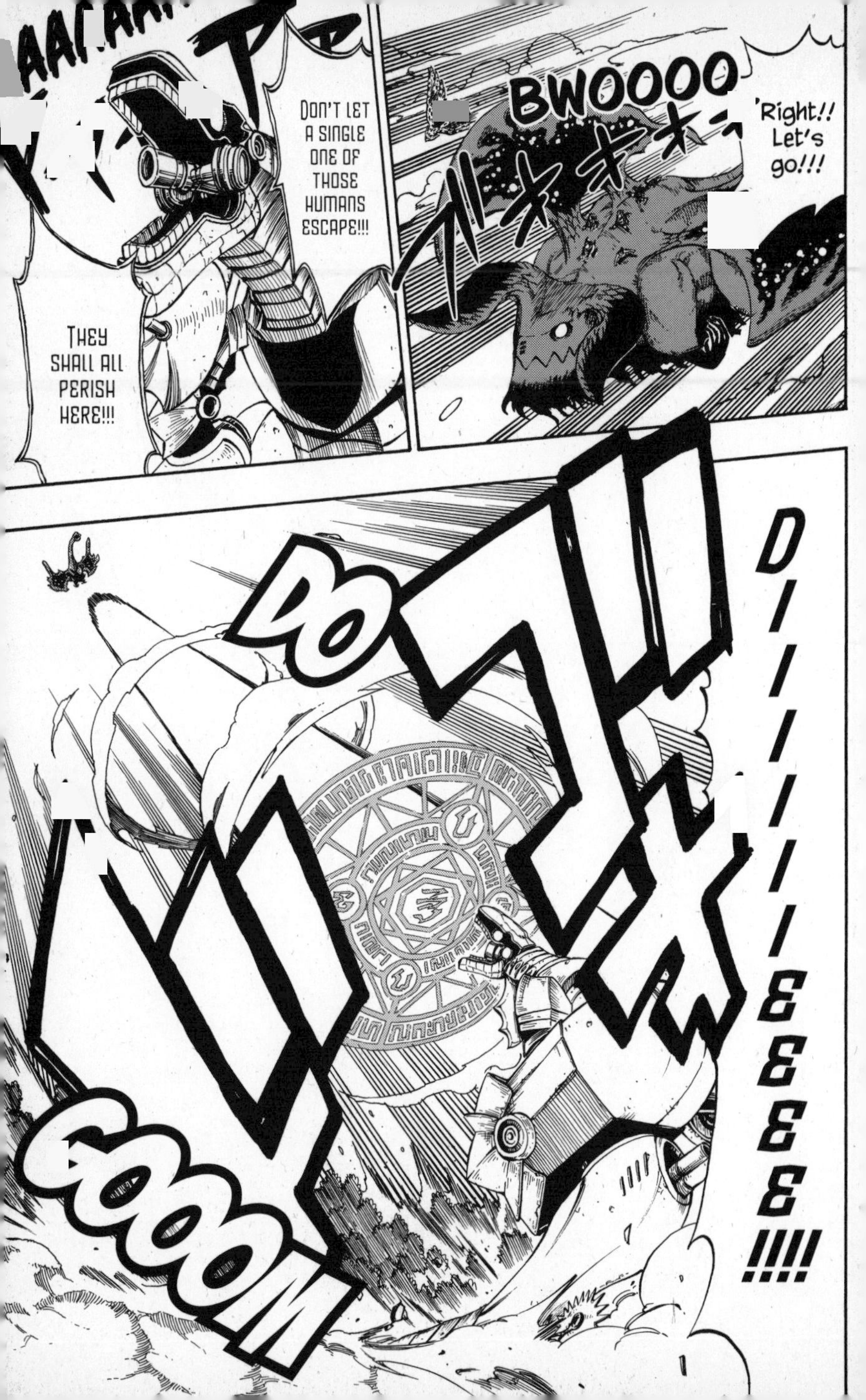

Right!! Let's go!!!
BWOOOO
Don't let a single one of those humans escape!!!
They shall all perish here!!!
DO
GOOOM
DIIIIIIIEEEEE!!!!

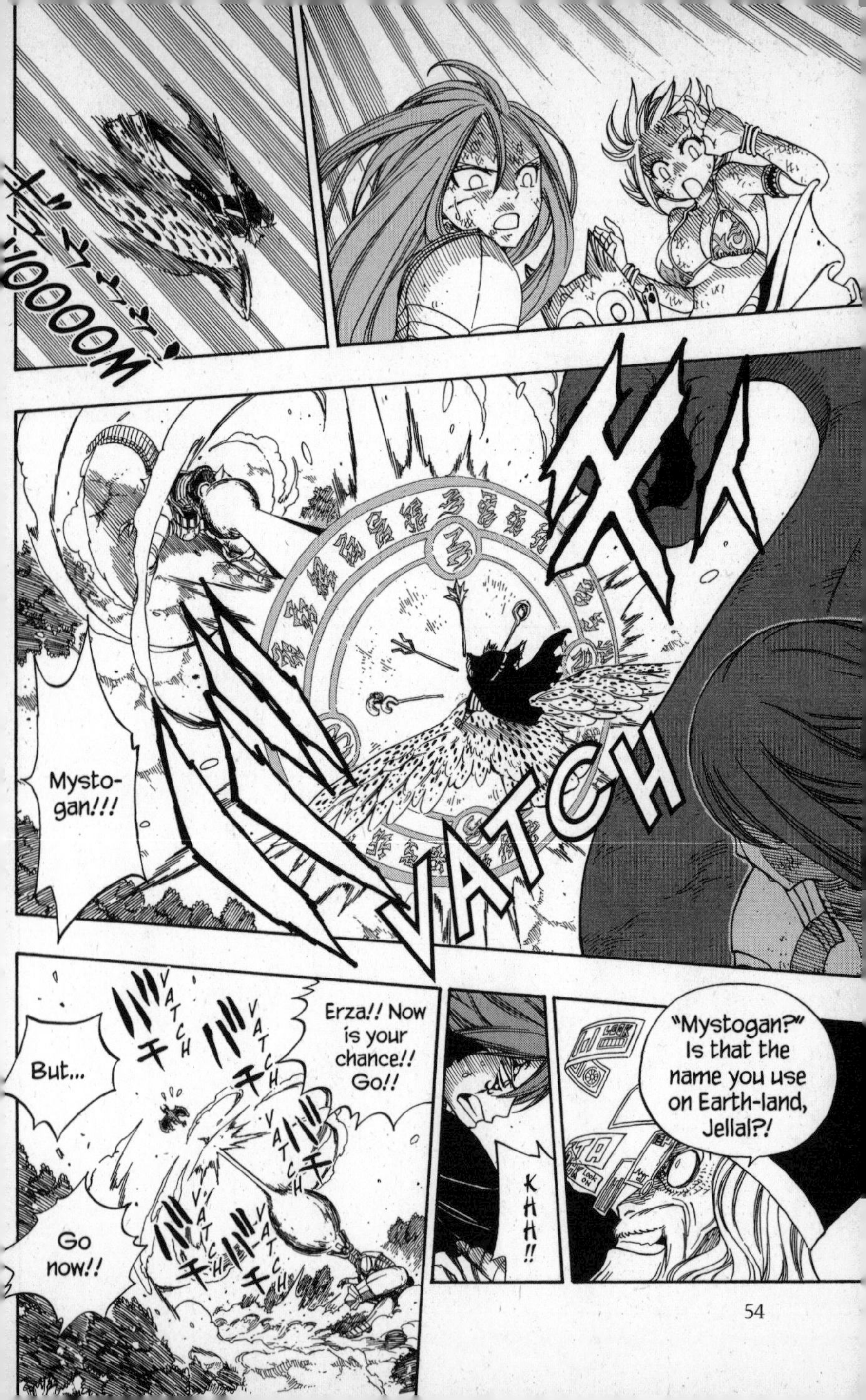
WOOOOOM
VATCH
Mystogan!!!
"Mystogan?" Is that the name you use on Earth-land, Jellal?!
KHHH!!
Erza!! Now is your chance!! Go!!
But...
Go now!!
VATCH

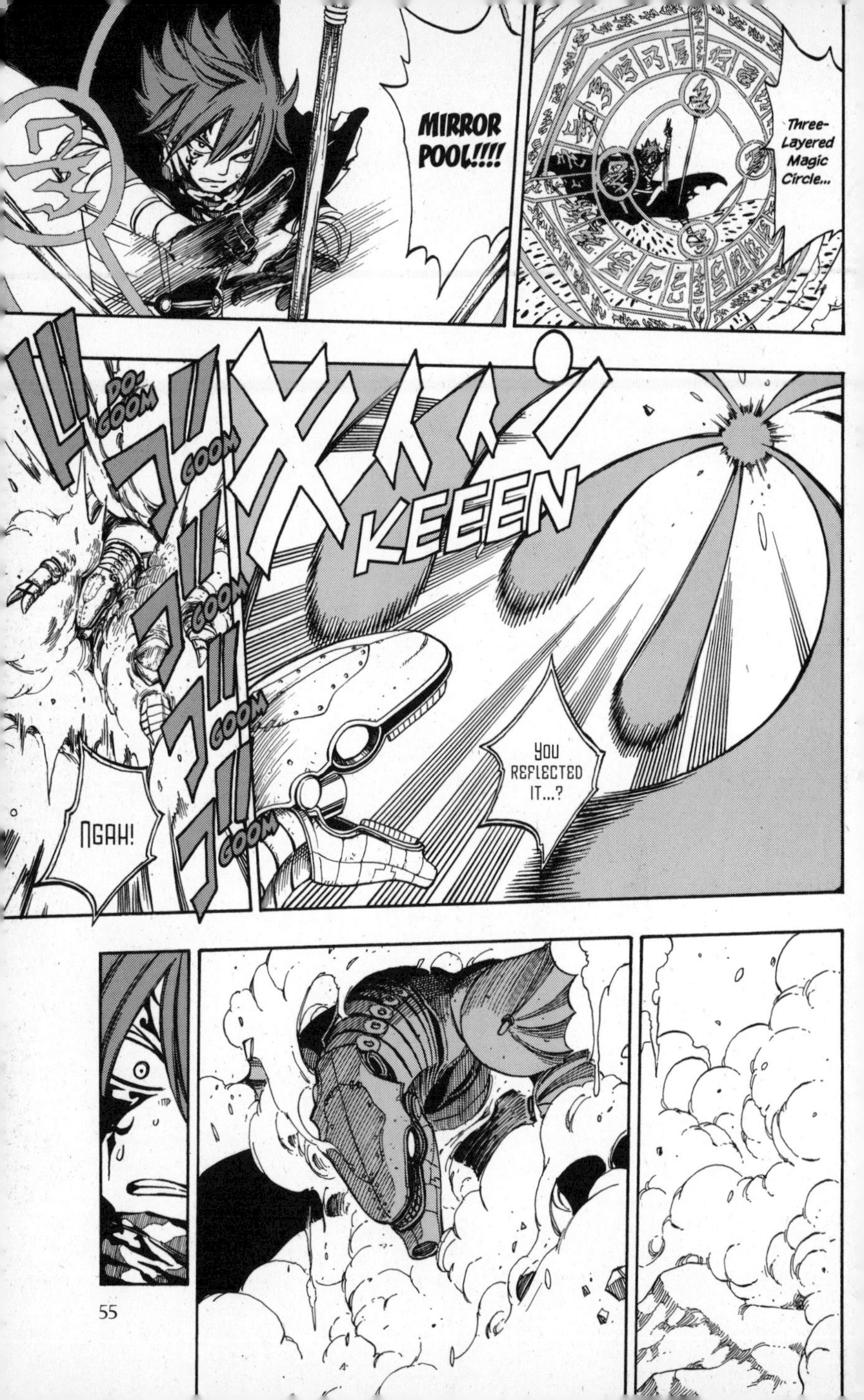
Three-Layered Magic Circle...
MIRROR POOL!!!!
KEEEN
YOU REFLECTED IT...?
DO-GOOM
GOOM
GOOM
GOOM
GOOM
NGAH!

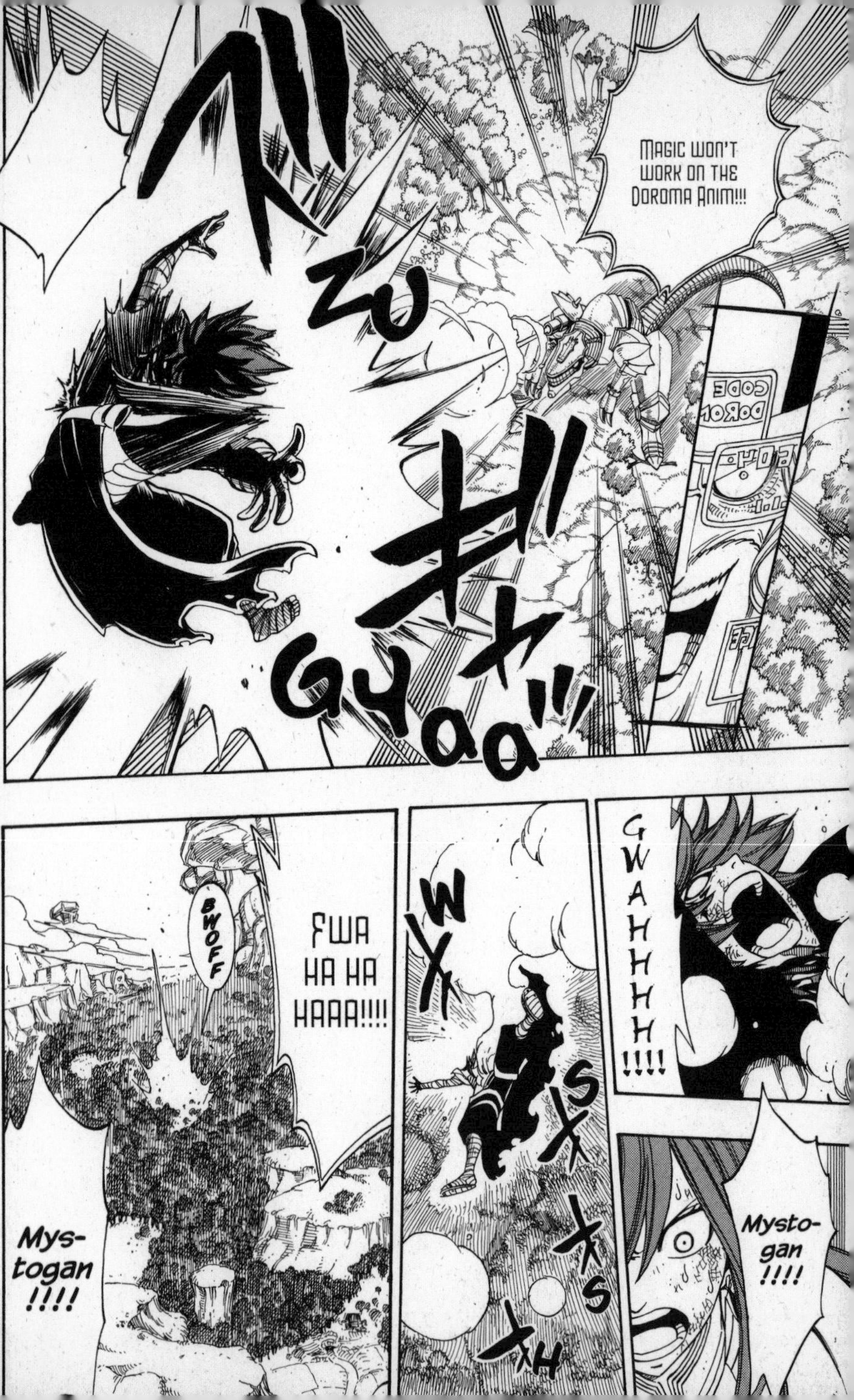

Magic won't work on the Doroma Anim!!!
ZU
GYAA!!
GWAHHHH!!!!
Mysto-gan!!!!
FWA HA HA HAAA!!!!
BWOFF
Mys-togan!!!!

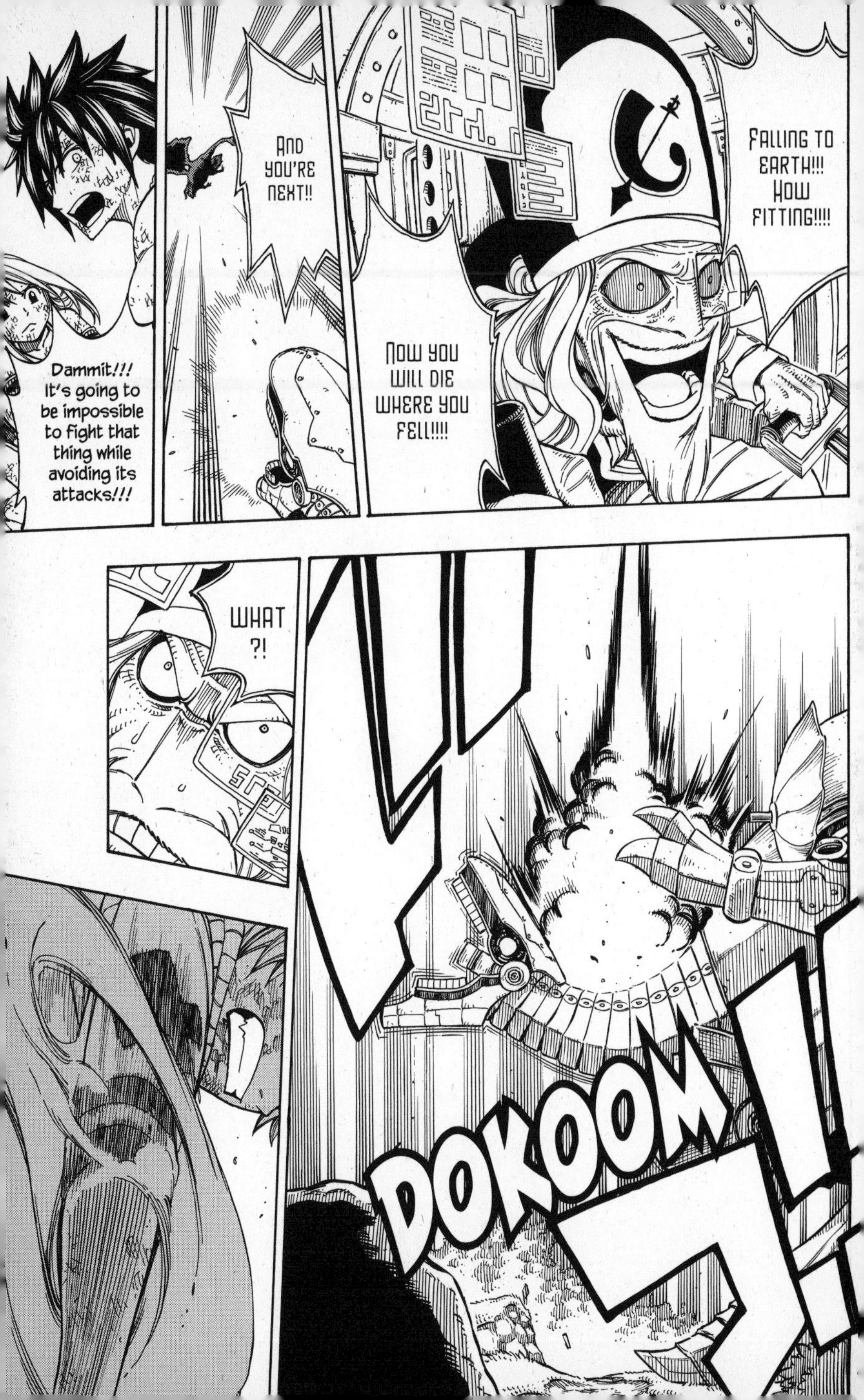
FALLING TO EARTH!!! HOW FITTING!!!!
NOW YOU WILL DIE WHERE YOU FELL!!!!
AND YOU'RE NEXT!!
Dammit!!! It's going to be impossible to fight that thing while avoiding its attacks!!!
DOKOOM!!
WHAT ?!

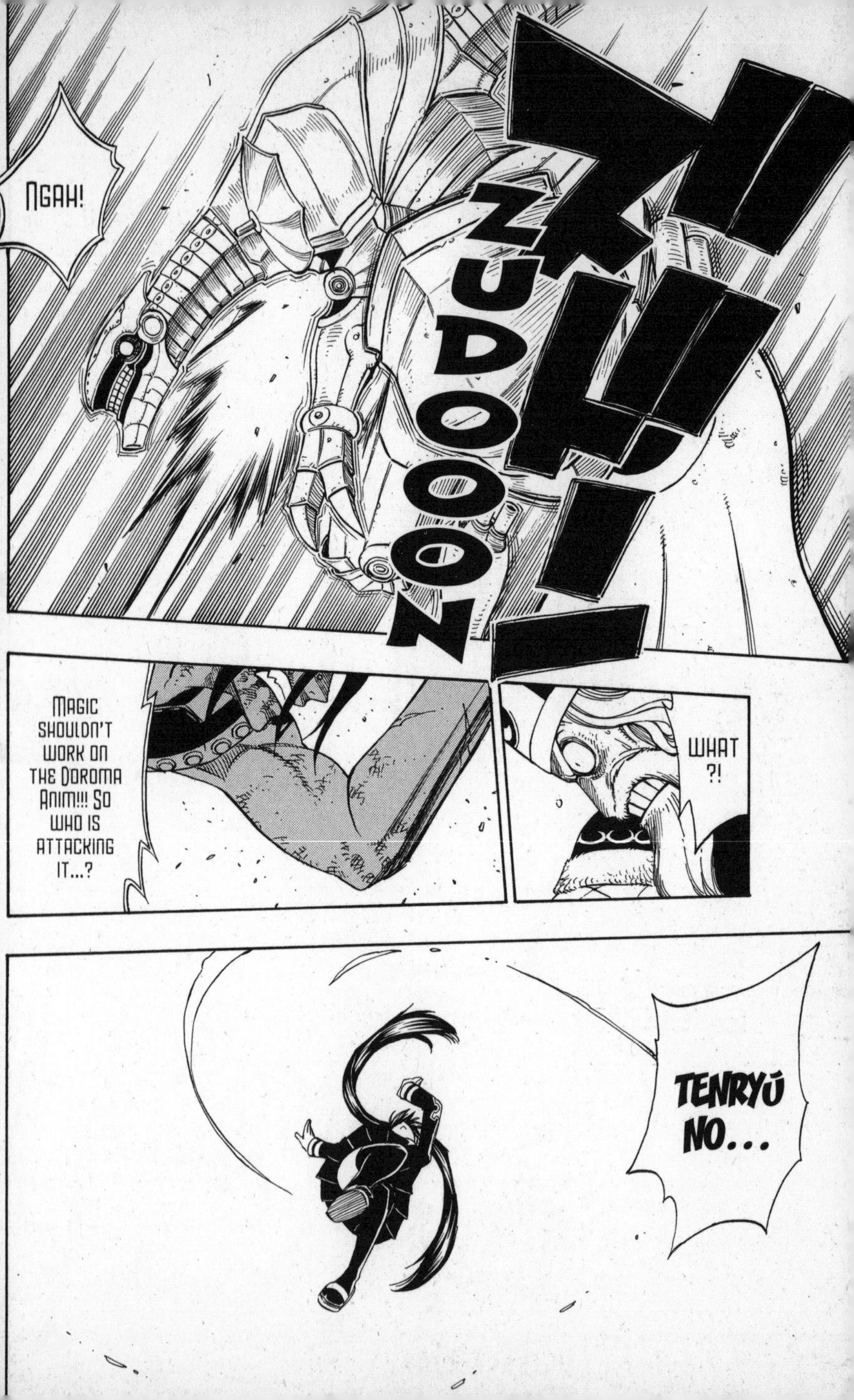
ZUDOOON
NGAH!
WHAT?!
MAGIC SHOULDN'T WORK ON THE DOROMA ANIM!!! SO WHO IS ATTACKING IT...?
TENRYŪ NO...

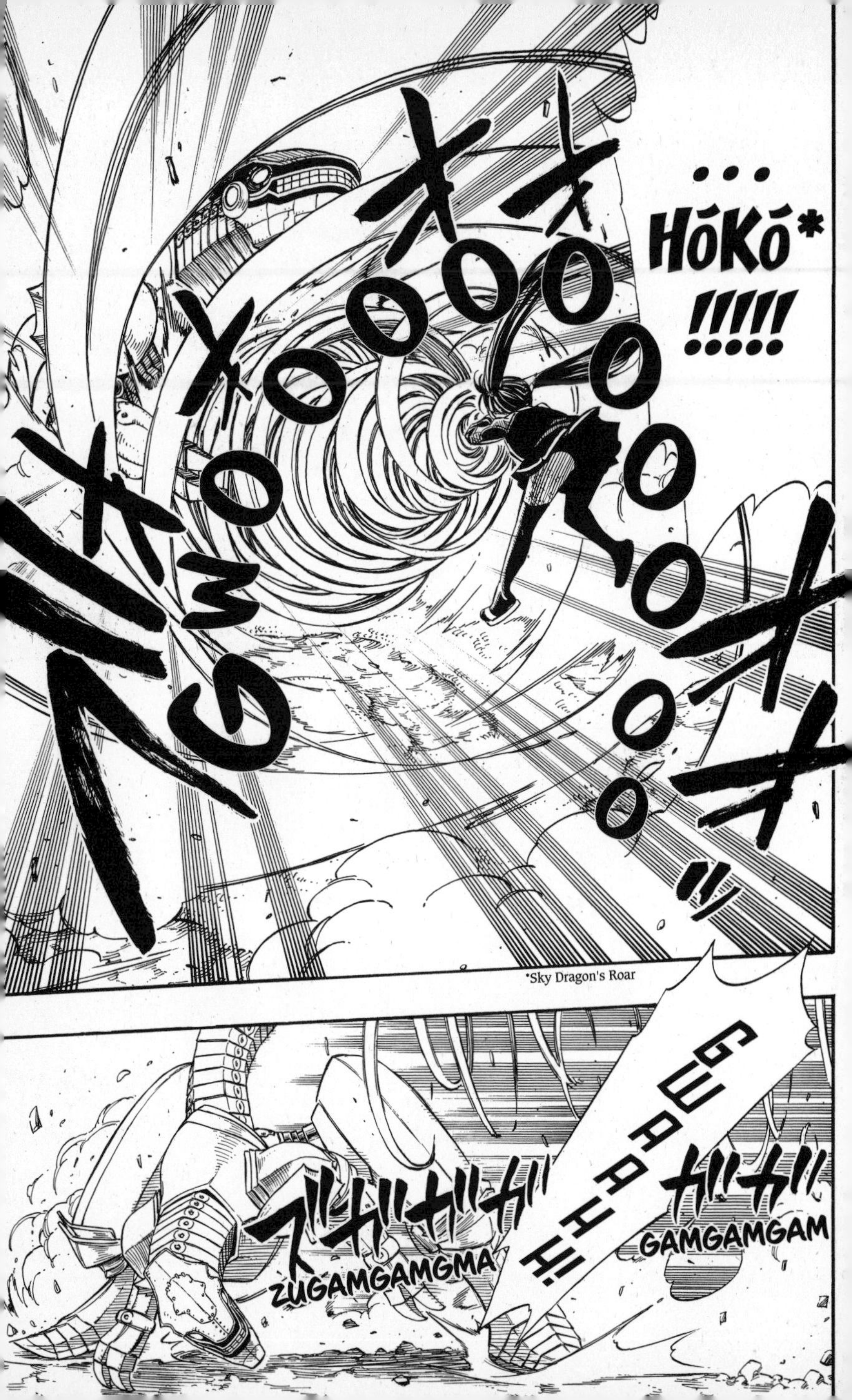
...HŌKŌ* !!!!!
*Sky Dragon's Roar
GUAAAH!!
GAMGAMGAM
ZUGAMGAMGMA

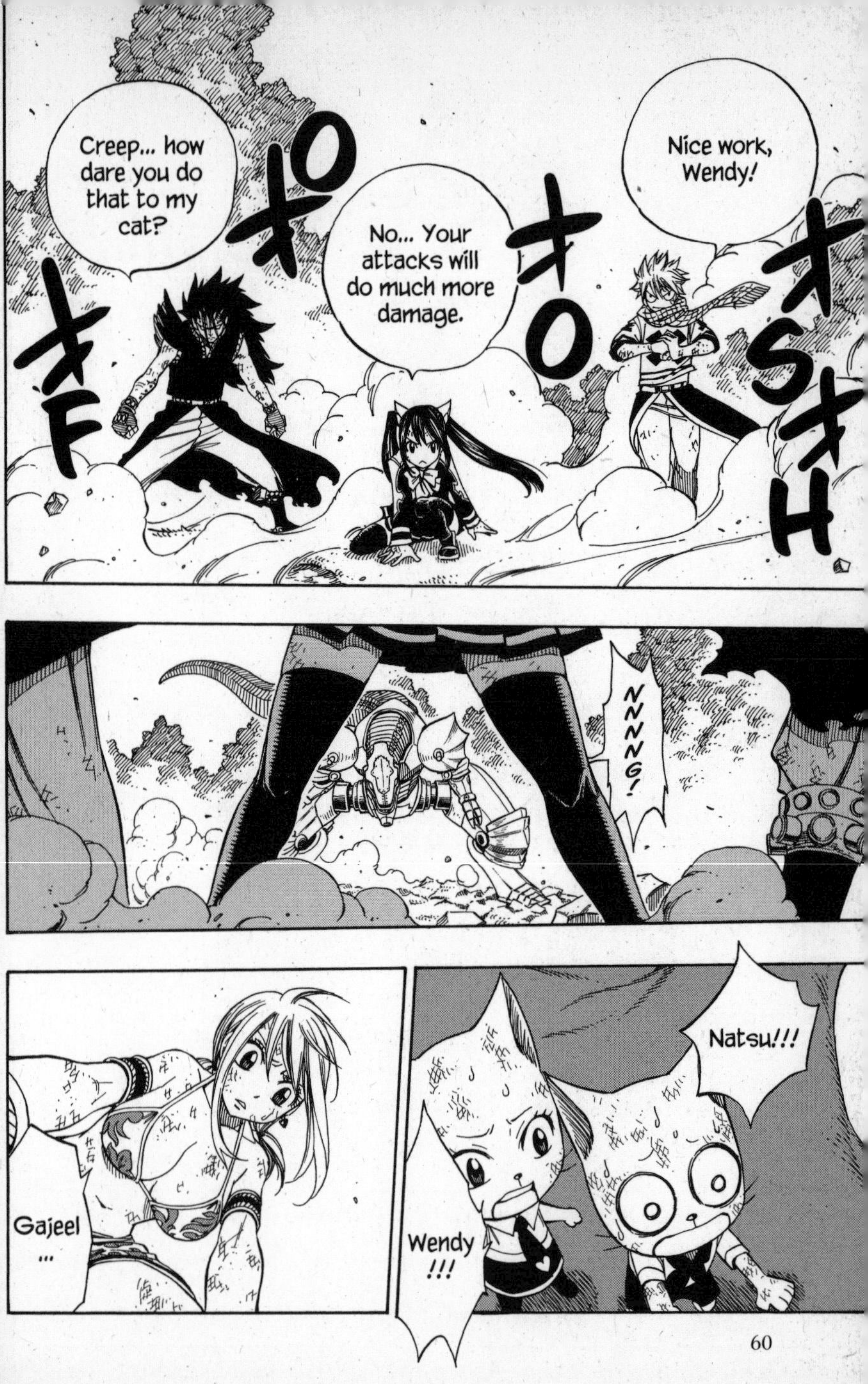
Nice work, Wendy!
No... Your attacks will do much more damage.
Creep... how dare you do that to my cat?
FOOSH
NNNNG!
Natsu!!!
Wendy !!!
Gajeel ...

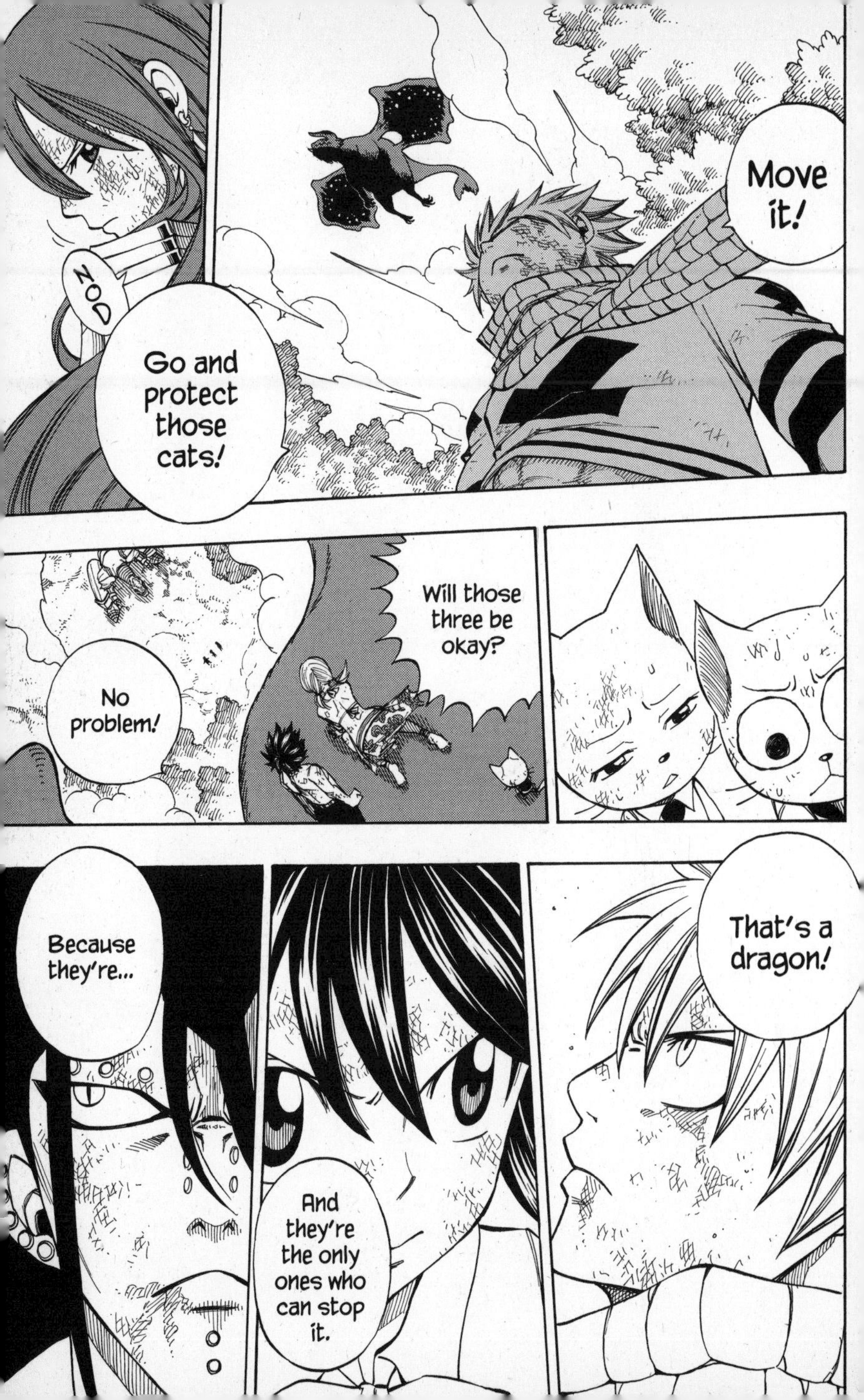
Move it!
Go and protect those cats!
ZOD
Will those three be okay?
No problem!
That's a dragon!
And they're the only ones who can stop it.
Because they're...

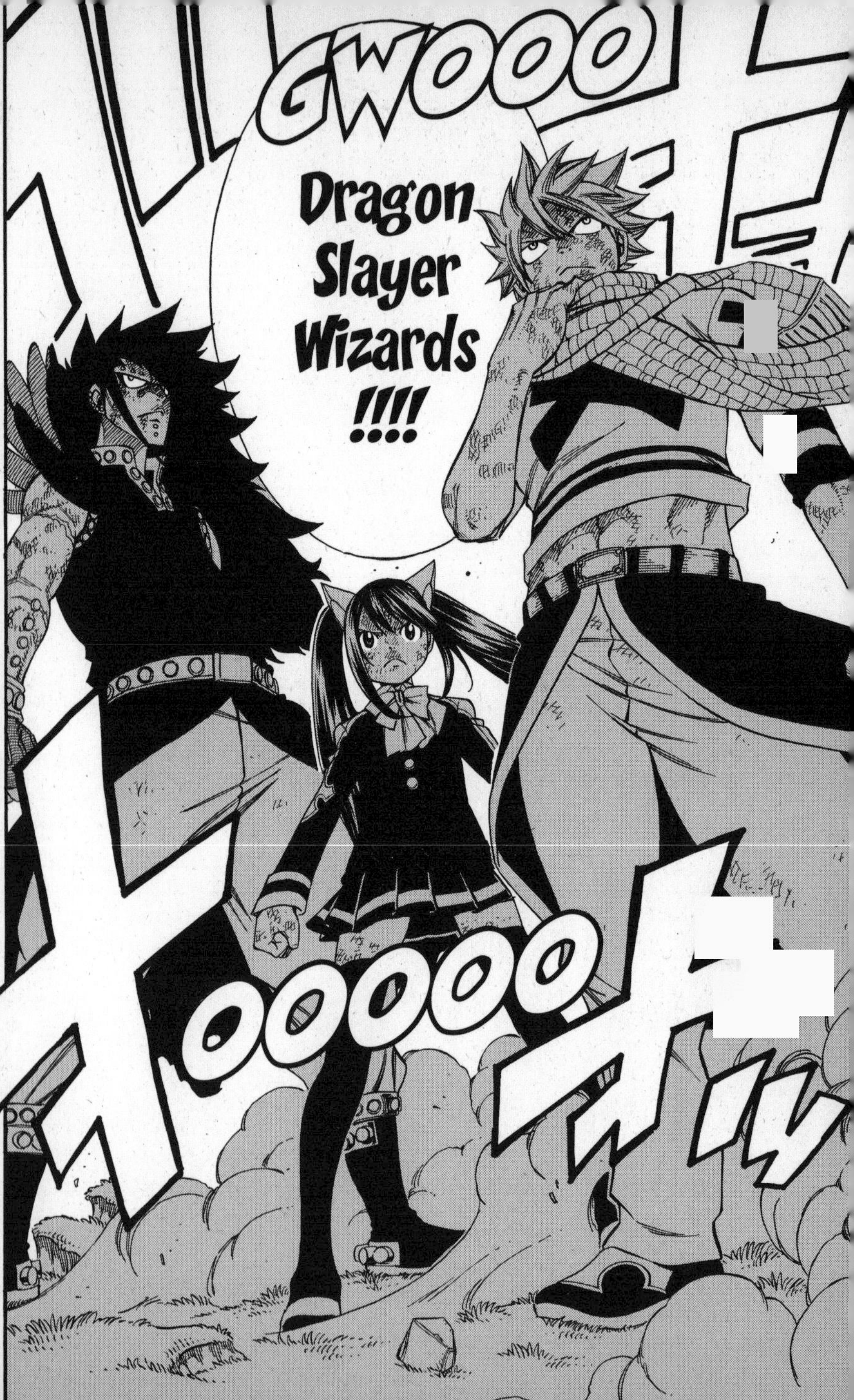
GWOOO
Dragon Slayer Wizards!!!!
OOOOOO

FAIRY TAIL

フェアリーテイル

Chapter 191: Three-Man Cell

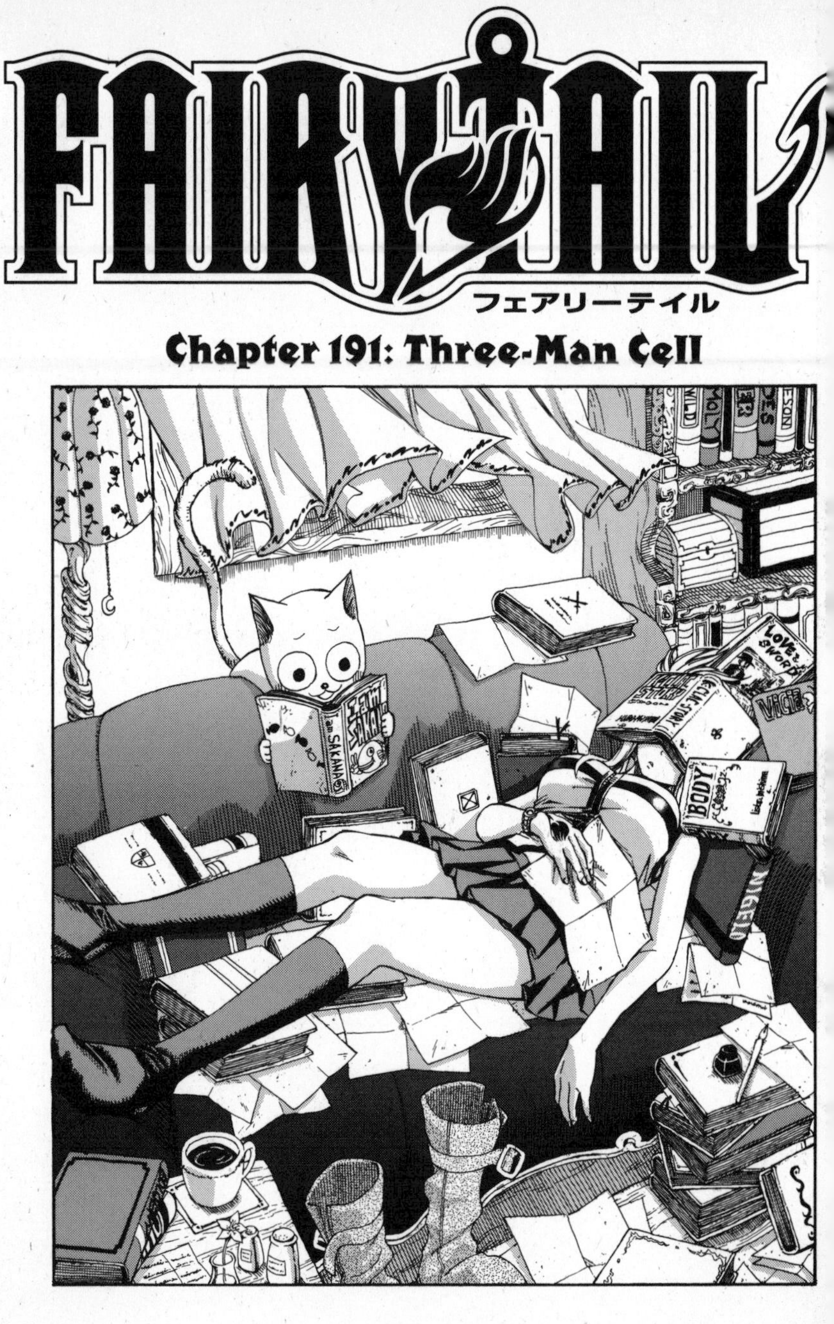
I am SAKANA
BODY

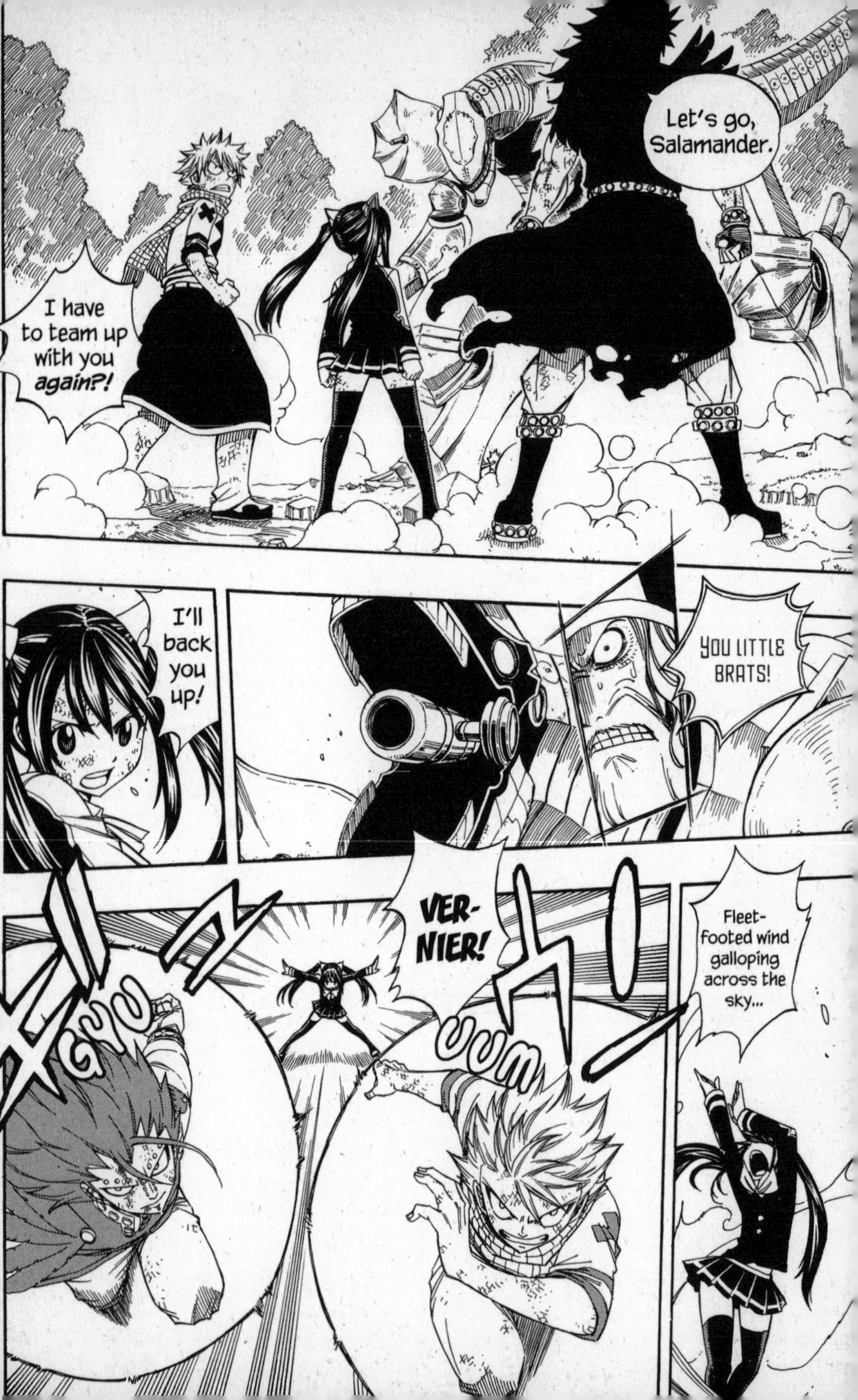

Let's go, Salamander.
I have to team up with you *again?!*
YOU LITTLE BRATS!
I'll back you up!
Fleet-footed wind galloping across the sky...
VER-NIER!

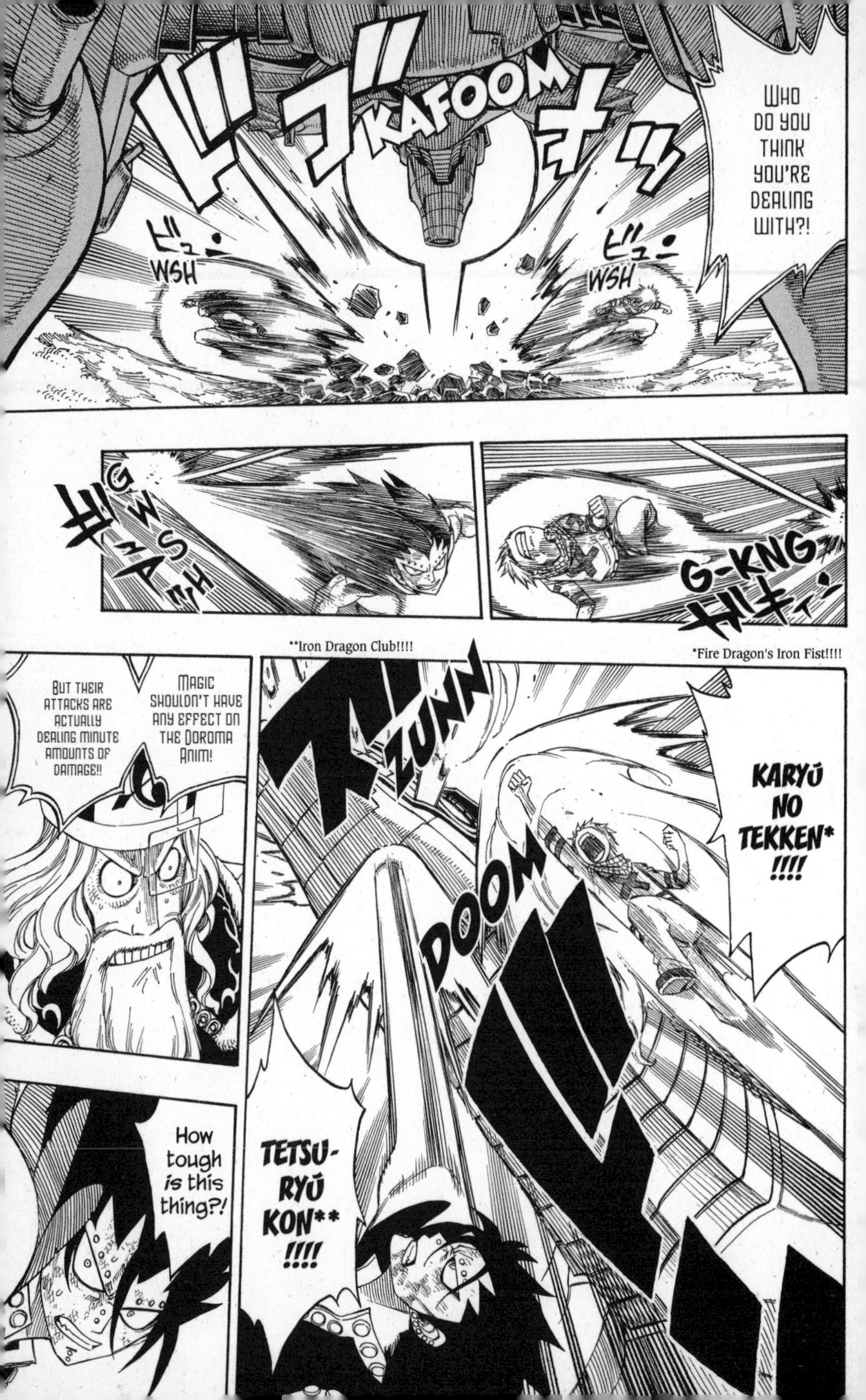
KAFOOM
Who do you think you're dealing with?!
WSH
WSH
G-KNG
GWSSH
KARYŪ NO TEKKEN* !!!!
ZUNN
DOOM
TETSU-RYŪ KON** !!!!
Magic shouldn't have any effect on the Doroma Anim!
But their attacks are actually dealing minute amounts of damage!!
How tough is this thing?!

*Fire Dragon's Iron Fist!!!!

**Iron Dragon Club!!!!

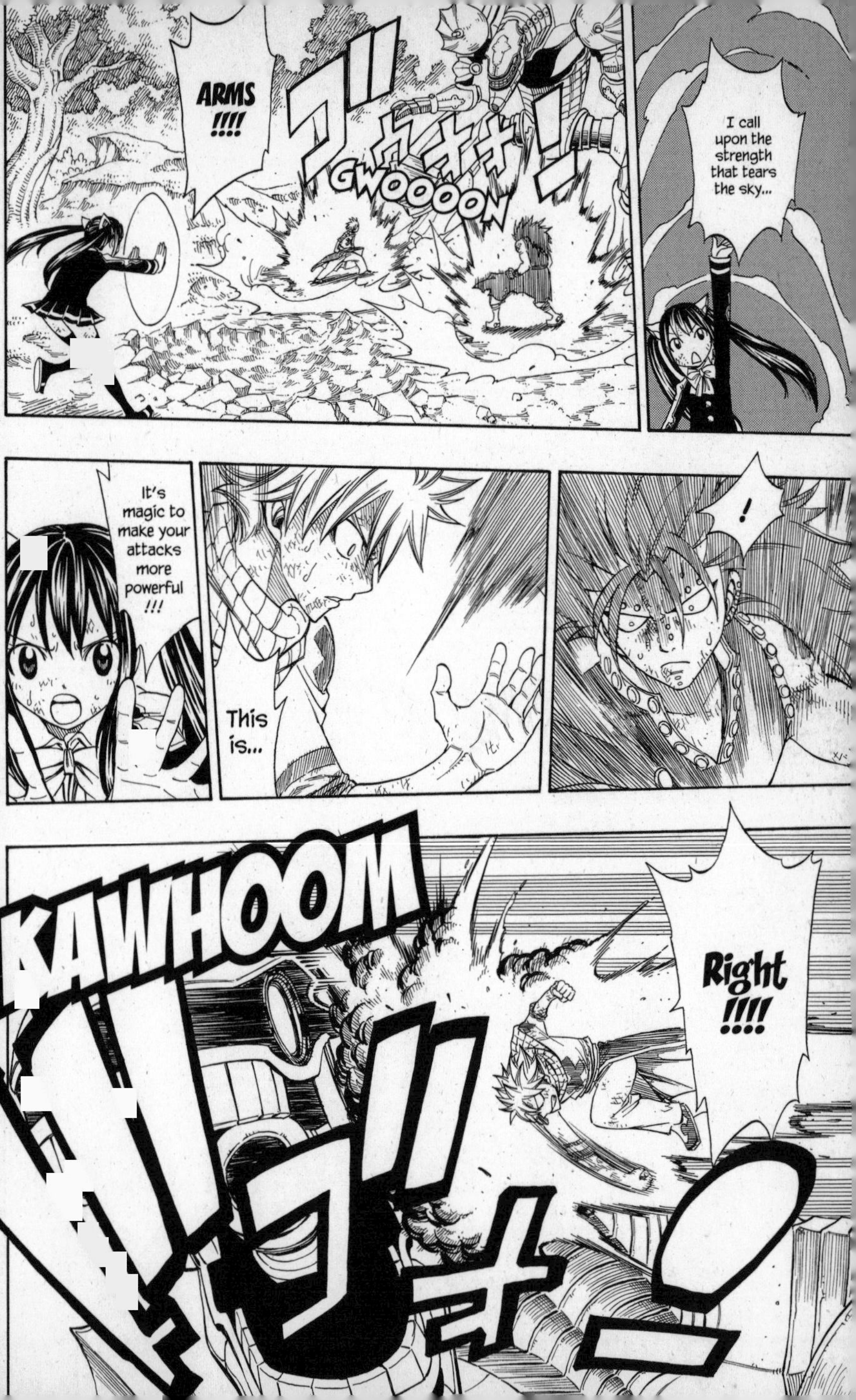
I call upon the strength that tears the sky...
ARMS !!!!
GWOOOOON
!
This is...
It's magic to make your attacks more powerful !!!
Right !!!!
KAWHOOM

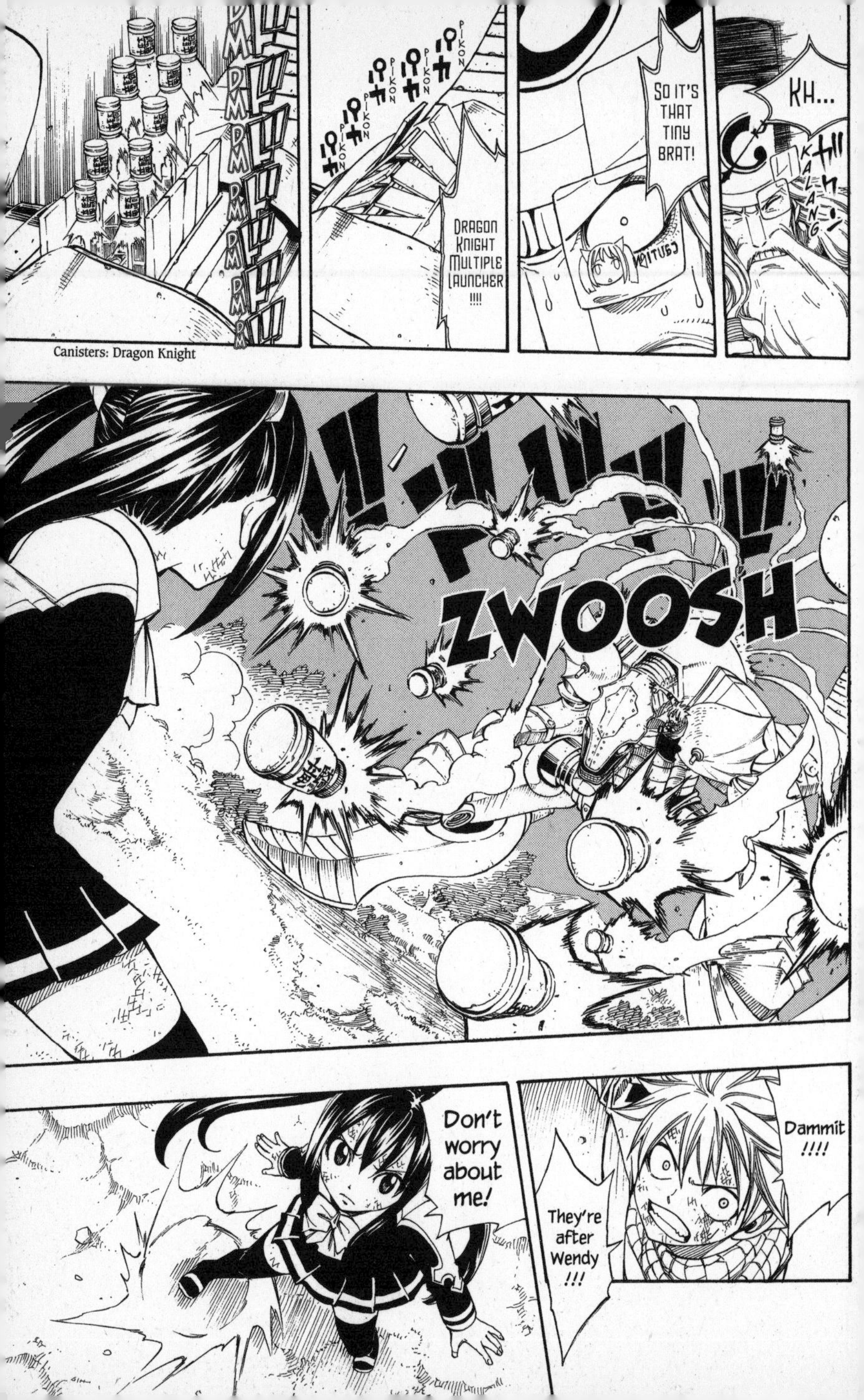
KH...
KALANG
So it's that tiny brat!
Dragon Knight Multiple Launcher!!!!
PIKON PIKON PIKON PIKON
DMDMDMDMDMDMDMDM
Canisters: Dragon Knight
ZWOOSH
Dammit!!!!
They're after Wendy!!!
Don't worry about me!

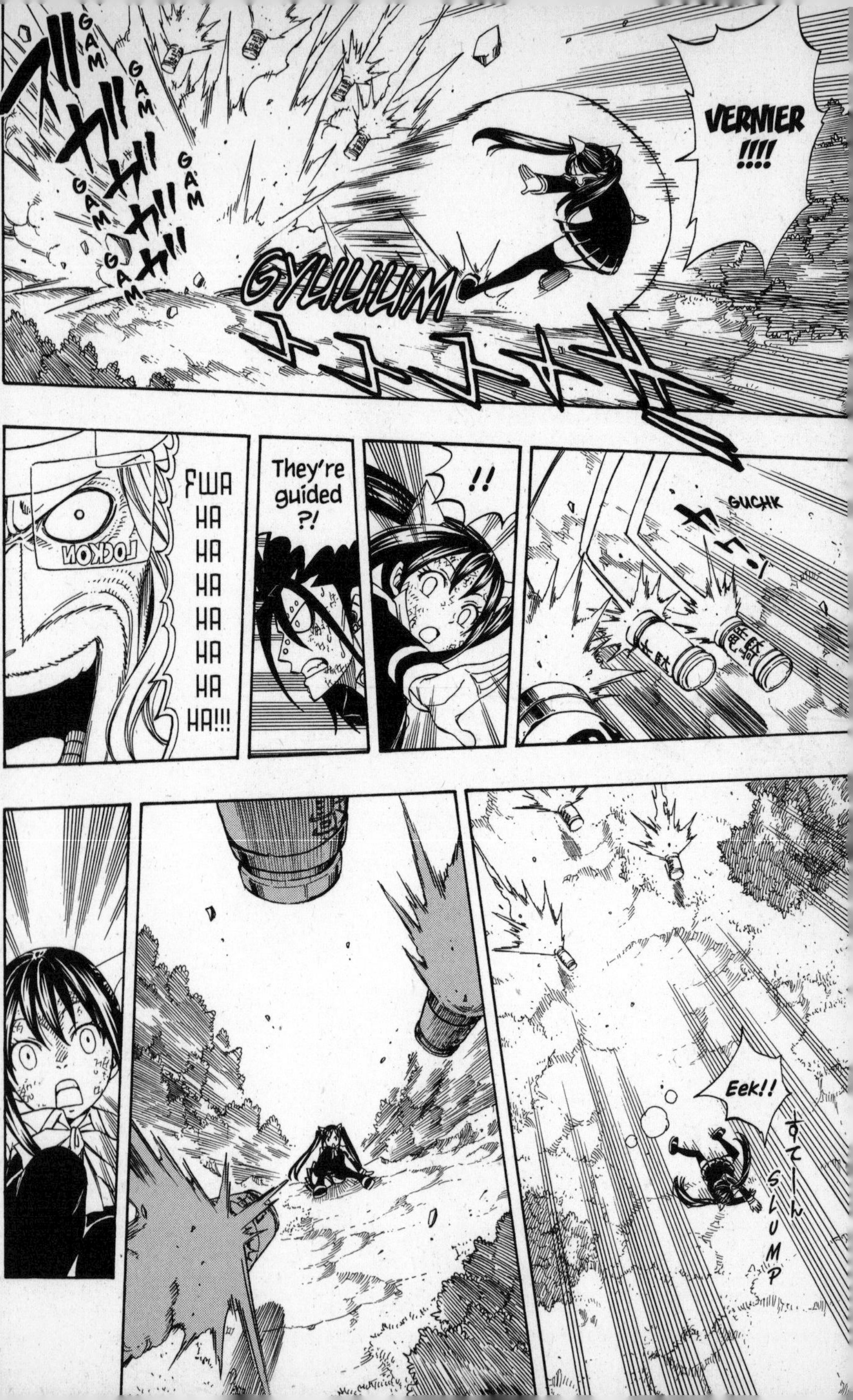
VERNIER !!!!
GAM GAM GAM
GAM GAM GAM
GYULLLLM
GUCHK
!!
They're guided ?!
FWA HA HA HA HA HA HA HA HA!!!
Eek!!
SLUMP

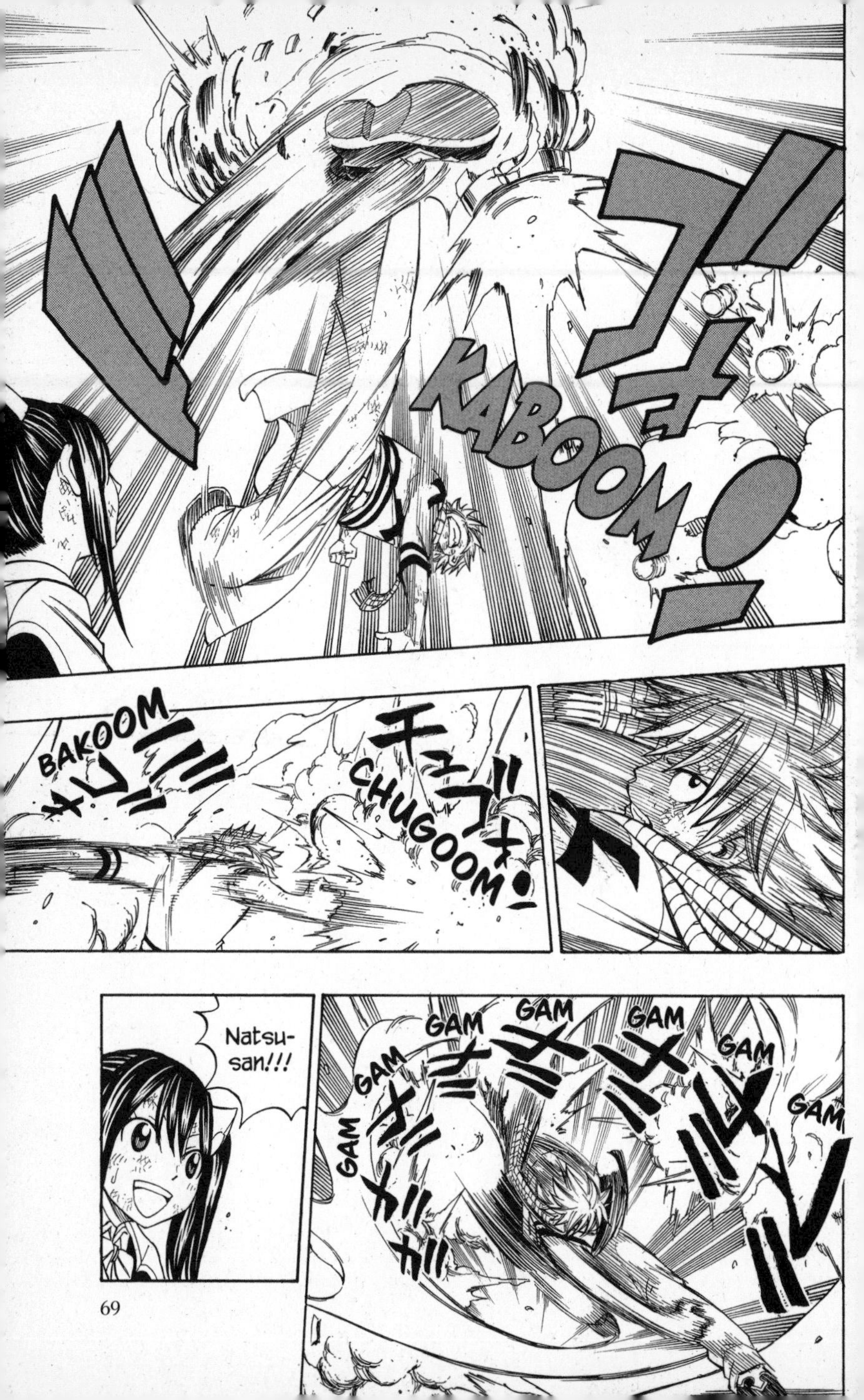
KABOOM!
CHUGOOM!
BAKOOM
GAM
GAM
GAM
GAM
GAM
GAM
GAM
GAM
Natsu-san!!!

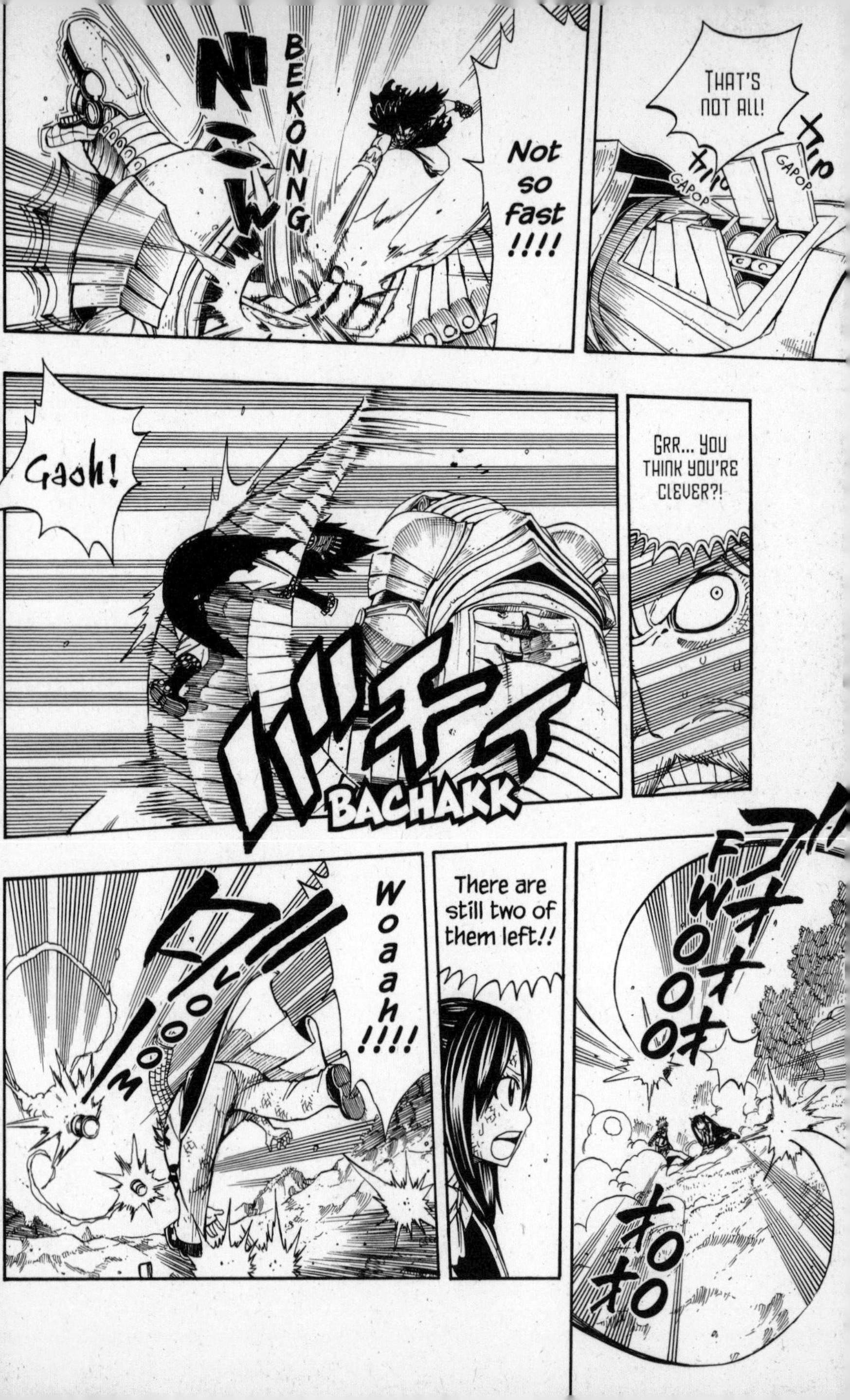
THAT'S NOT ALL!
GAPOP
GAPOP
Not so fast!!!!
BEKONNG
Grr... You think you're clever?!
Gaoh!
BACHAKK
FWOOO
There are still two of them left!!
Woaah!!!!
VOOOM

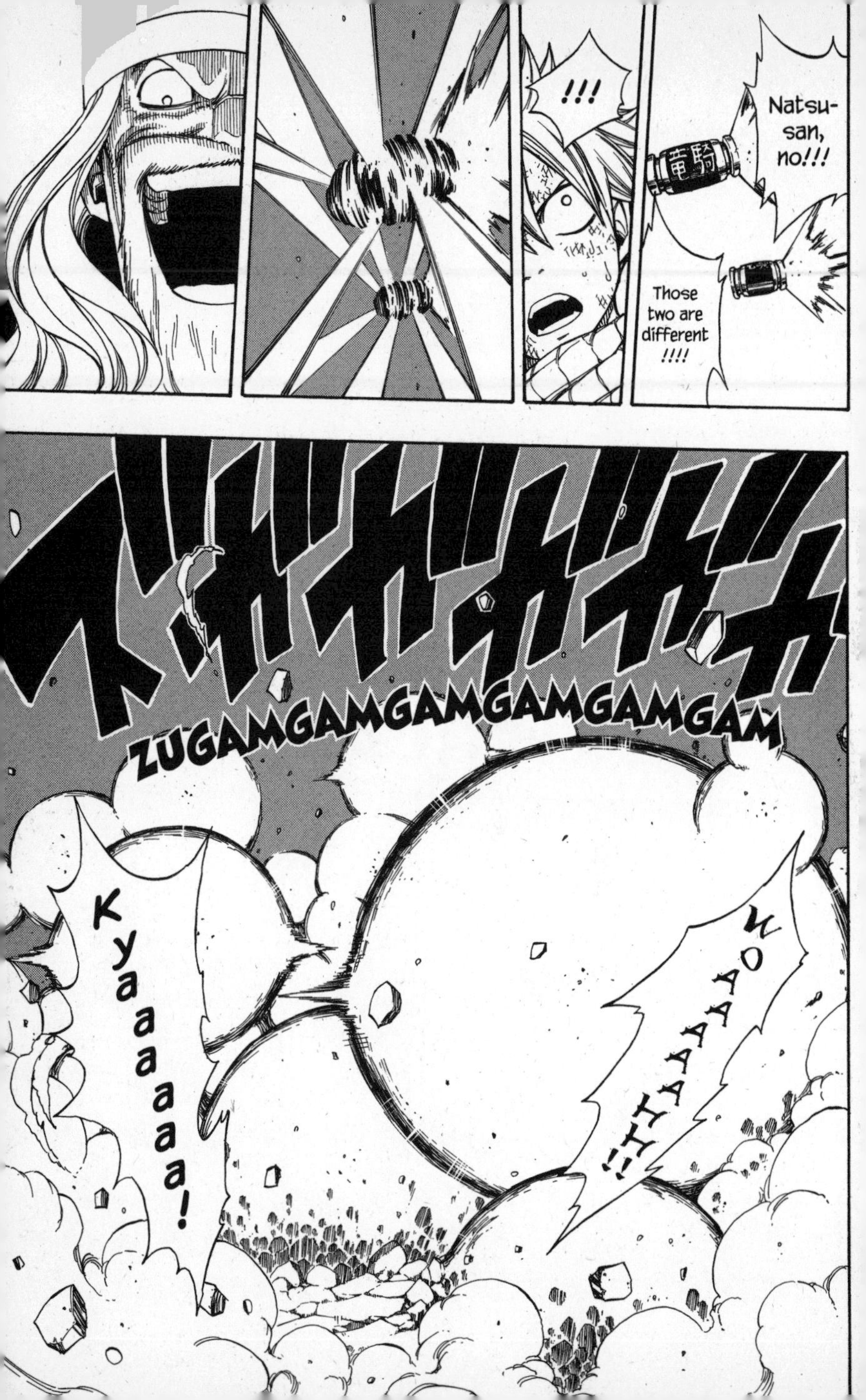

Natsu-san, no!!!
竜騎
Those two are different!!!!
!!!
ZUGAMGAMGAMGAMGAMGAM
WOAAAAAHH!!
Kyaaaaaa!

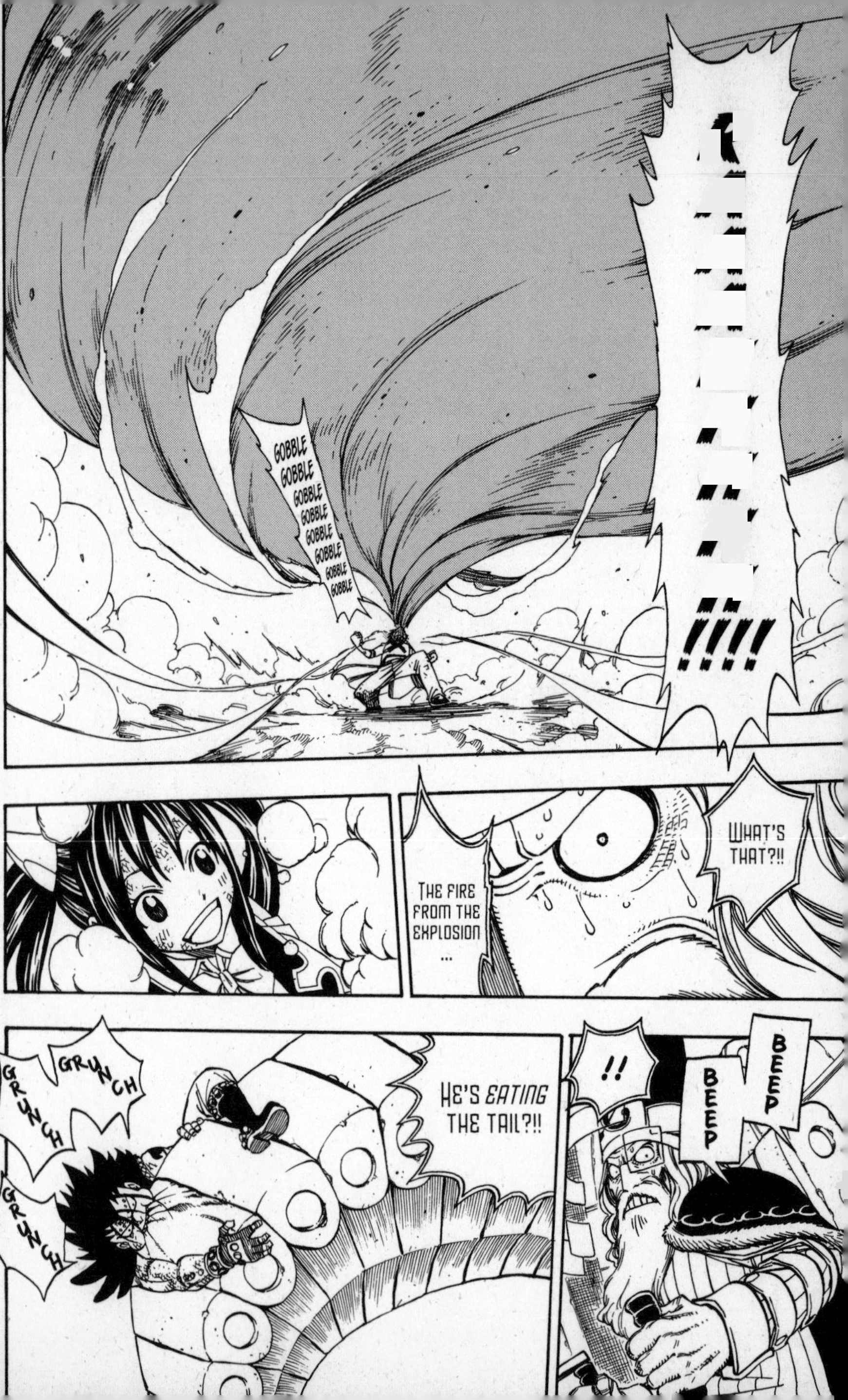
GOBBLE GOBBLE GOBBLE GOBBLE GOBBLE GOBBLE GOBBLE GOBBLE
WHAT'S THAT?!!
THE FIRE FROM THE EXPLOSION ...
!!
BEEP
BEEP
HE'S *EATING* THE TAIL?!!
GRUNCH
GRUNCH
GRUNCH

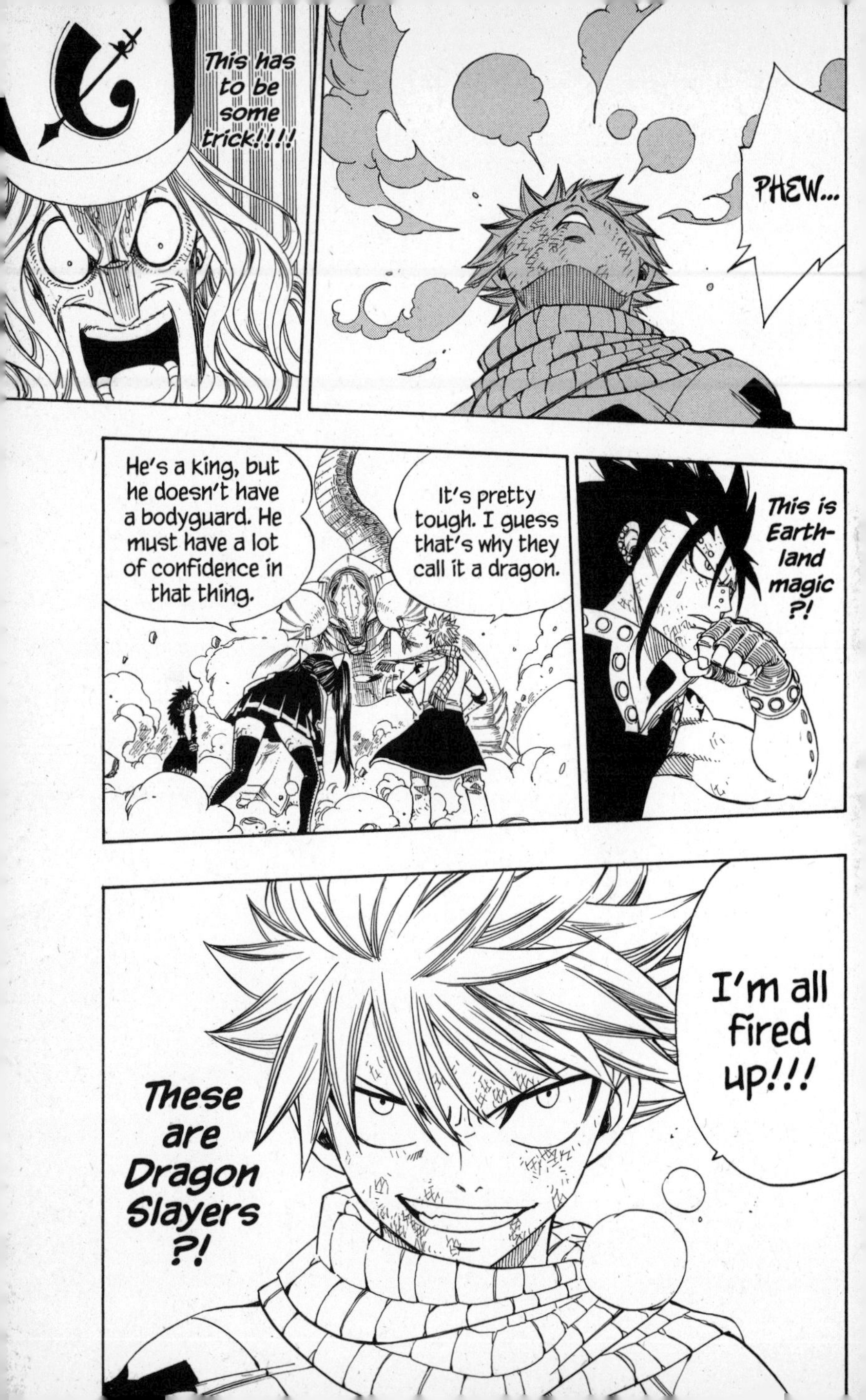
PHEW...
This has to be some trick!!!!
This is Earth-land magic?!
It's pretty tough. I guess that's why they call it a dragon.
He's a king, but he doesn't have a bodyguard. He must have a lot of confidence in that thing.
I'm all fired up!!!
These are Dragon Slayers?!

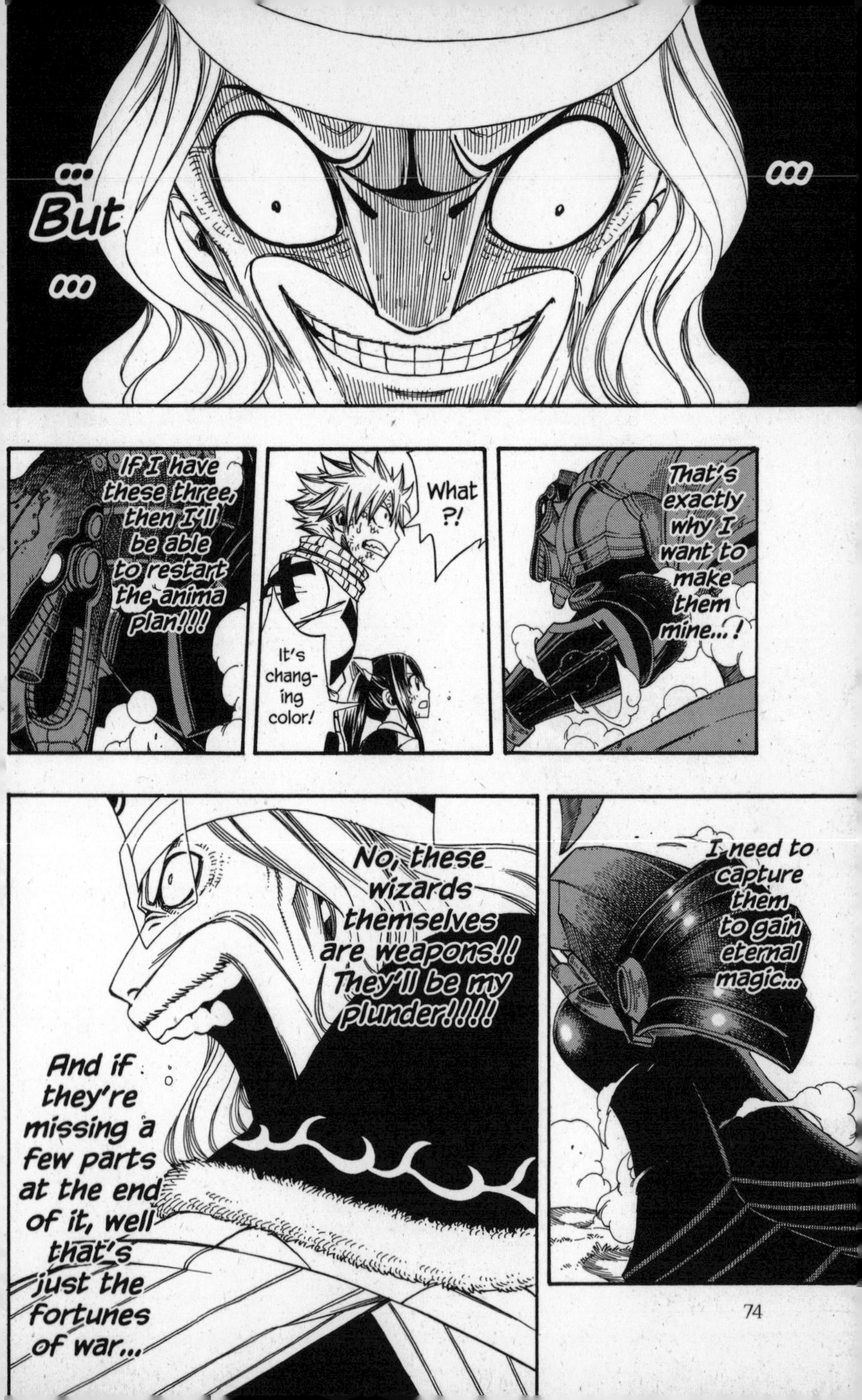
...
...But...
That's exactly why I want to make them mine...!
What ?!
It's changing color!
If I have these three, then I'll be able to restart the anima plan!!!
I need to capture them to gain eternal magic...
No, these wizards themselves are weapons!! They'll be my plunder!!!!
And if they're missing a few parts at the end of it, well that's just the fortunes of war...

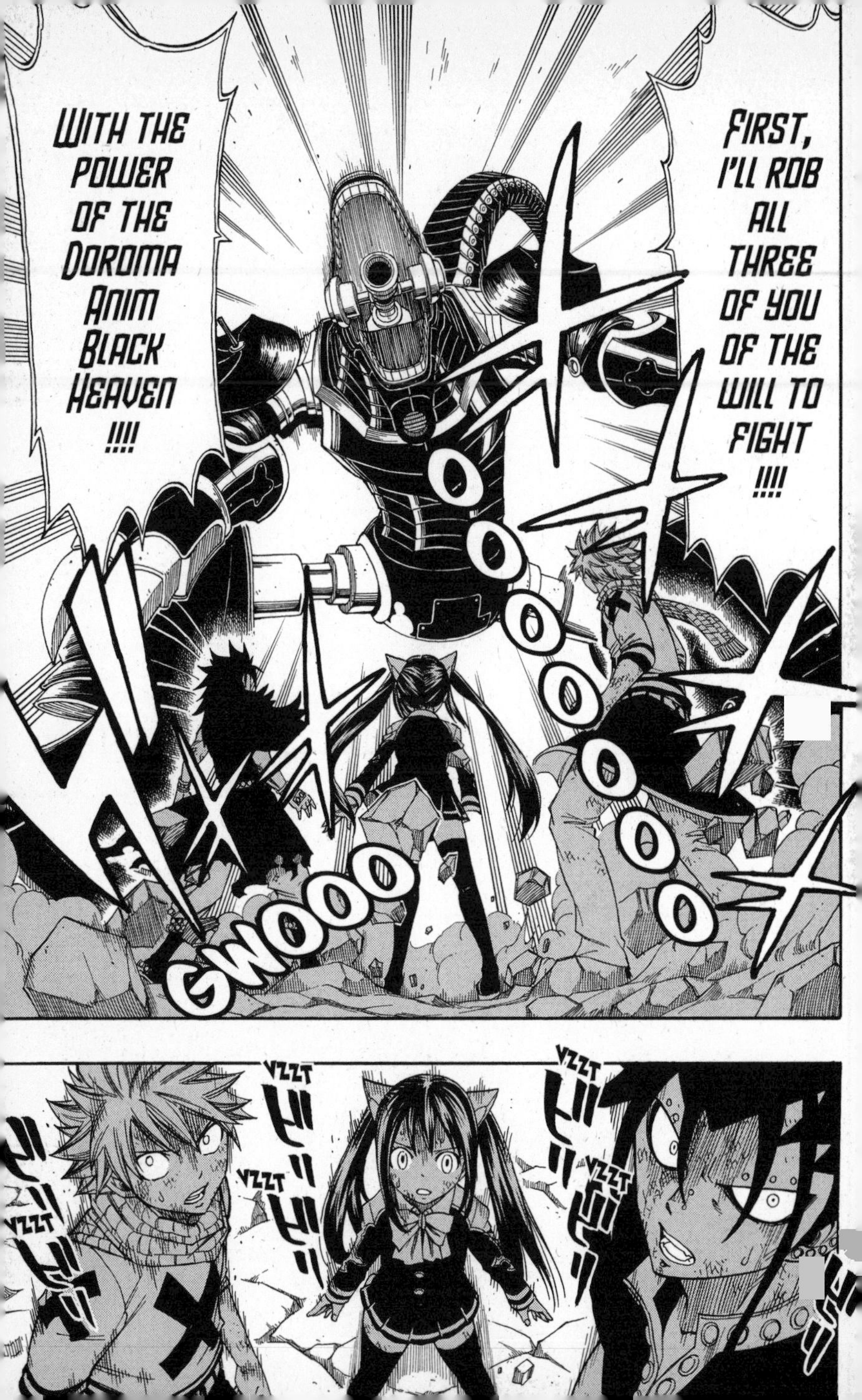
FIRST, I'LL ROB ALL THREE OF YOU OF THE WILL TO FIGHT !!!!
WITH THE POWER OF THE DOROMA ANIM BLACK HEAVEN !!!!
GWOOOOOOOOOOOOOOO
VZZT
VZZT
VZZT
VZZT
VZZT

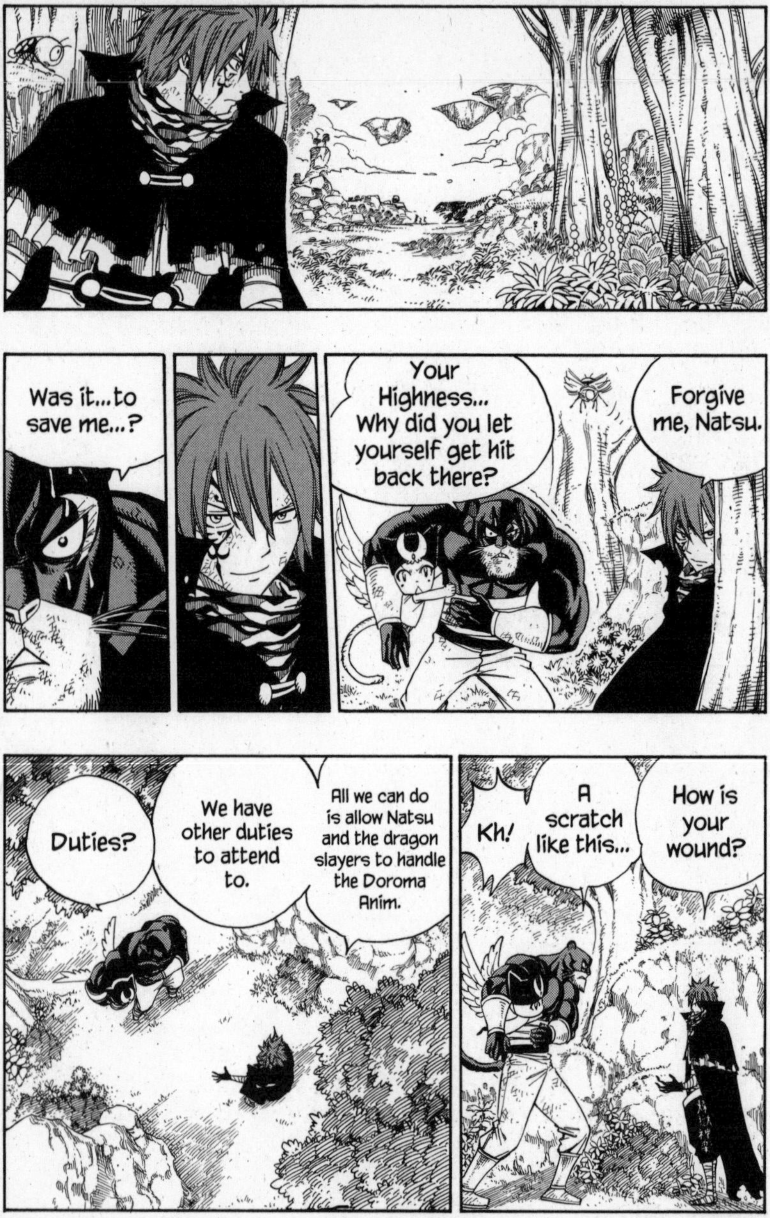
Forgive me, Natsu.
Your Highness... Why did you let yourself get hit back there?
Was it...to save me...?
How is your wound?
A scratch like this...
Kh!
All we can do is allow Natsu and the dragon slayers to handle the Doroma Anim.
We have other duties to attend to.
Duties?

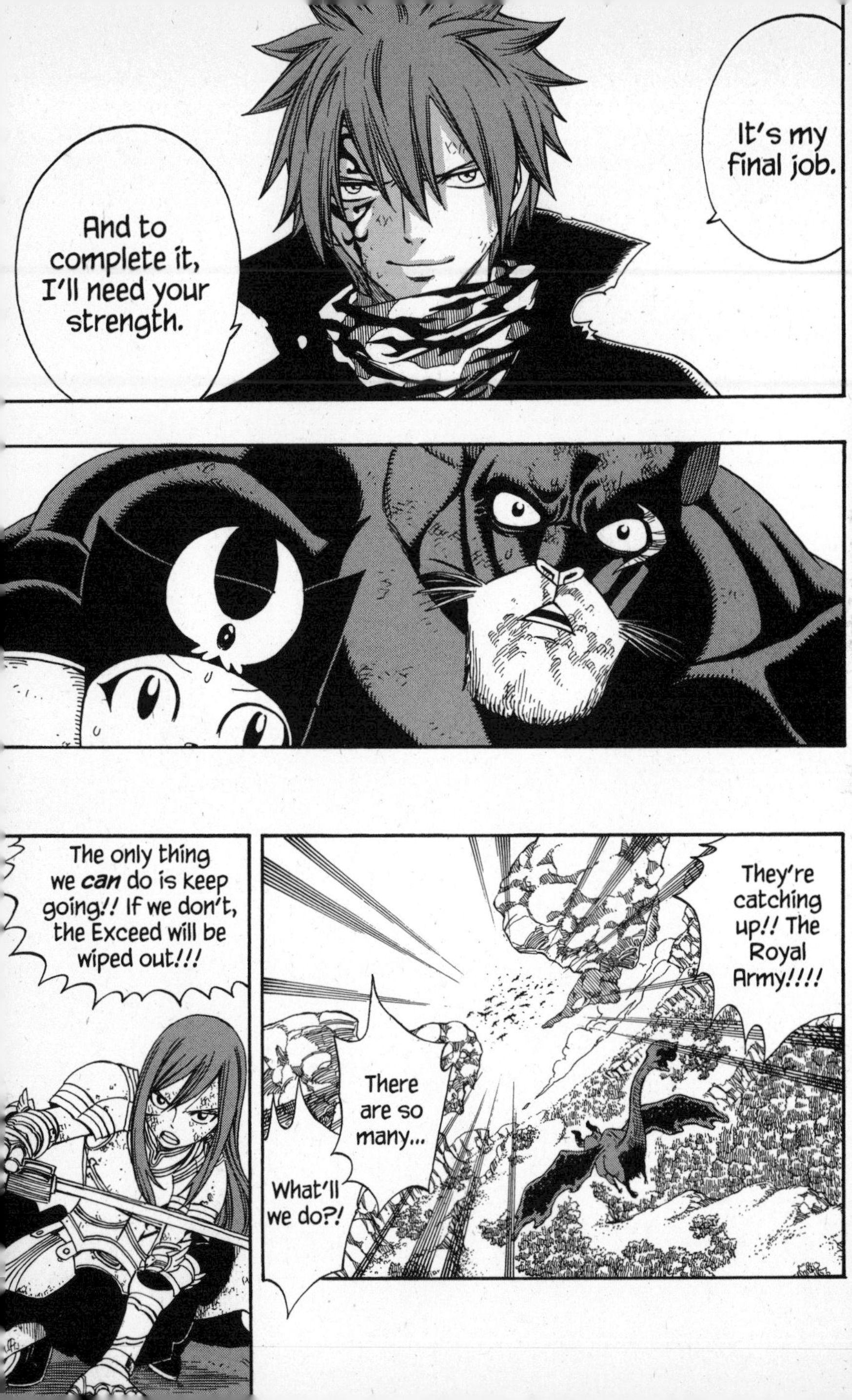
It's my final job.
And to complete it, I'll need your strength.
They're catching up!! The Royal Army!!!!
There are so many...
What'll we do?!
The only thing we *can* do is keep going!! If we don't, the Exceed will be wiped out!!!

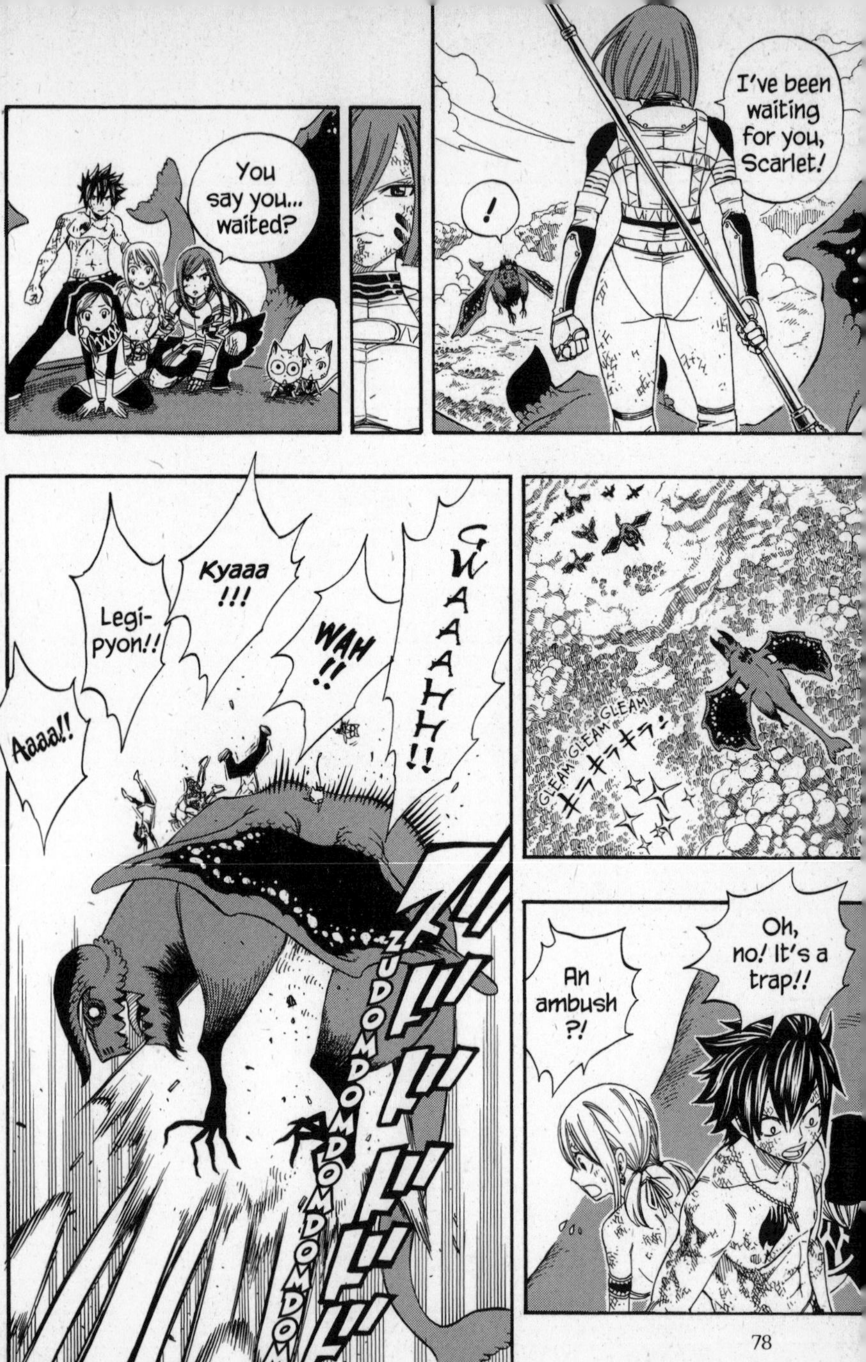
I've been waiting for you, Scarlet!
!
You say you... waited?
GLEAM GLEAM GLEAM
キラキラキラン
Oh, no! It's a trap!!
An ambush?!
GWAAAAHH!!
WAH!!
Kyaaa!!!
Legi-pyon!!
Aaaa!!
ZUDOMDOMDOMDOMDOMDOM

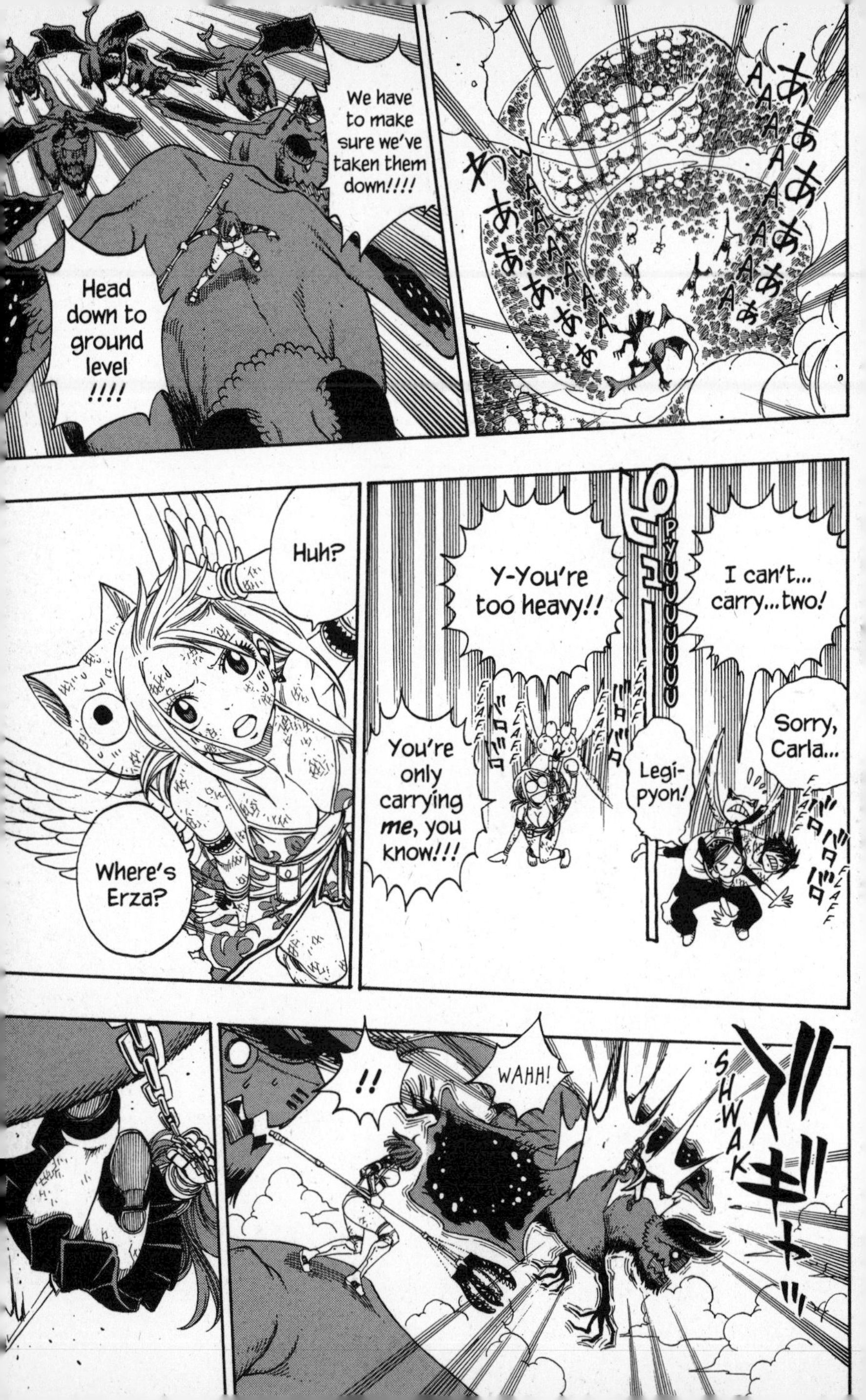

AAAAAAAAA
AAAAAAAA
We have to make sure we've taken them down!!!!
Head down to ground level!!!!
I can't... carry...two!
PYUUUUUUUU
Y-You're too heavy!!
FLAFF FLAFF
Sorry, Carla...
Legi-pyon!
You're only carrying *me*, you know!!!
FLAFF FLAFF
Huh?
Where's Erza?
SHWAK
WAHH!
!!

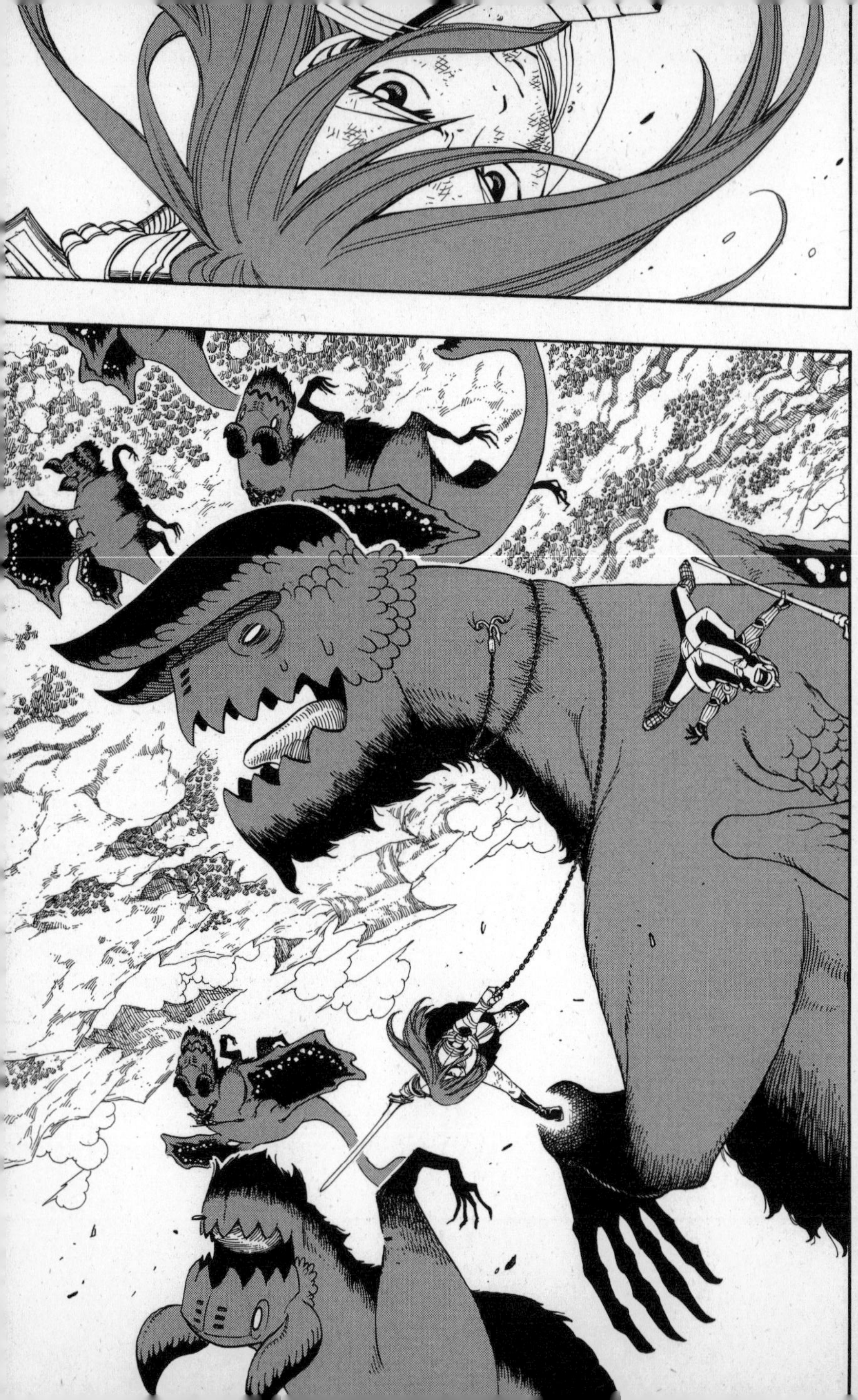

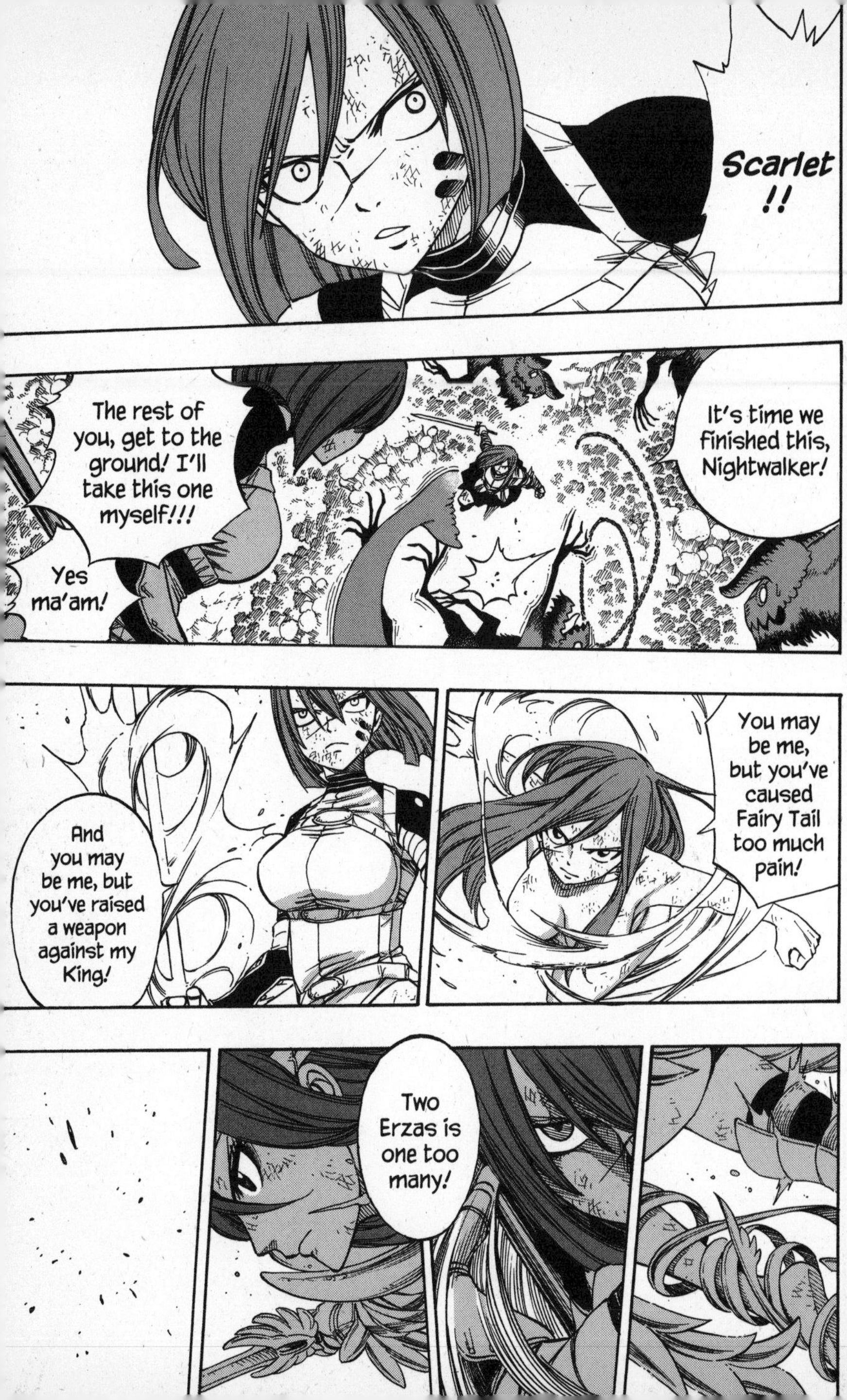
Scarlet !!
It's time we finished this, Nightwalker!
The rest of you, get to the ground! I'll take this one myself!!!
Yes ma'am!
You may be me, but you've caused Fairy Tail too much pain!
And you may be me, but you've raised a weapon against my King!
Two Erzas is one too many!

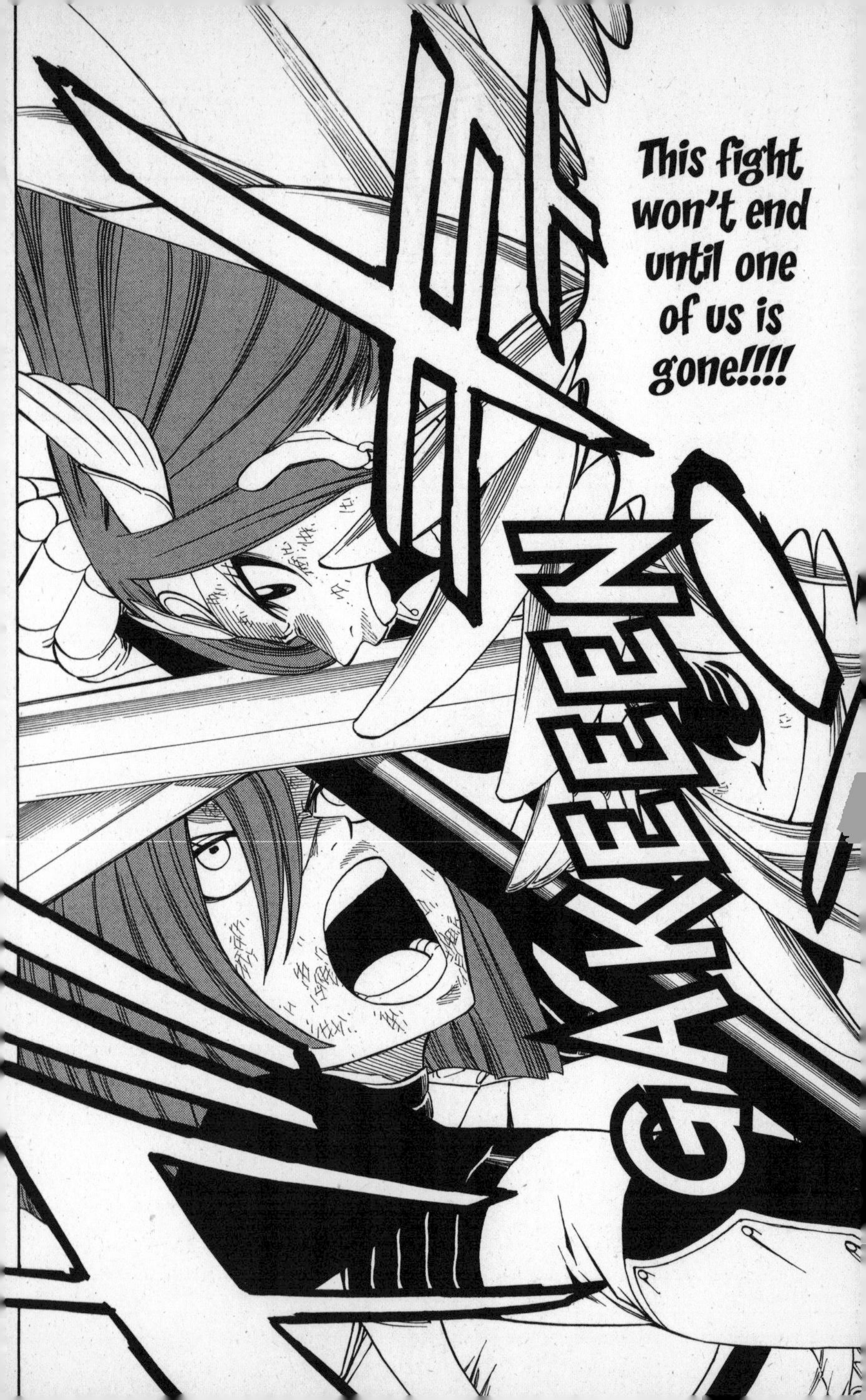
This fight won't end until one of us is gone!!!!
GAKEEEN

FAIRY TAIL
フェアリーテイル

Chapter 192: Won't Run Anymore

BONY'S

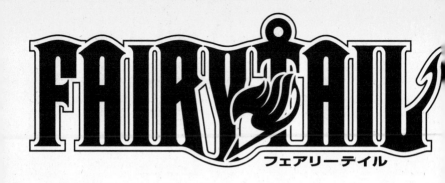

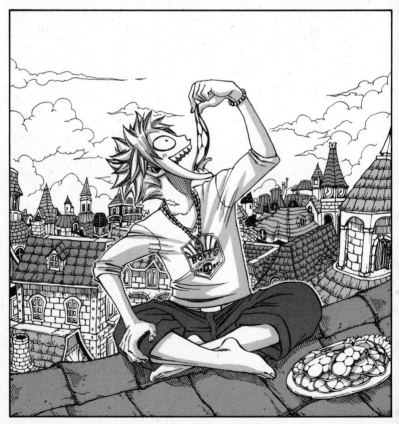

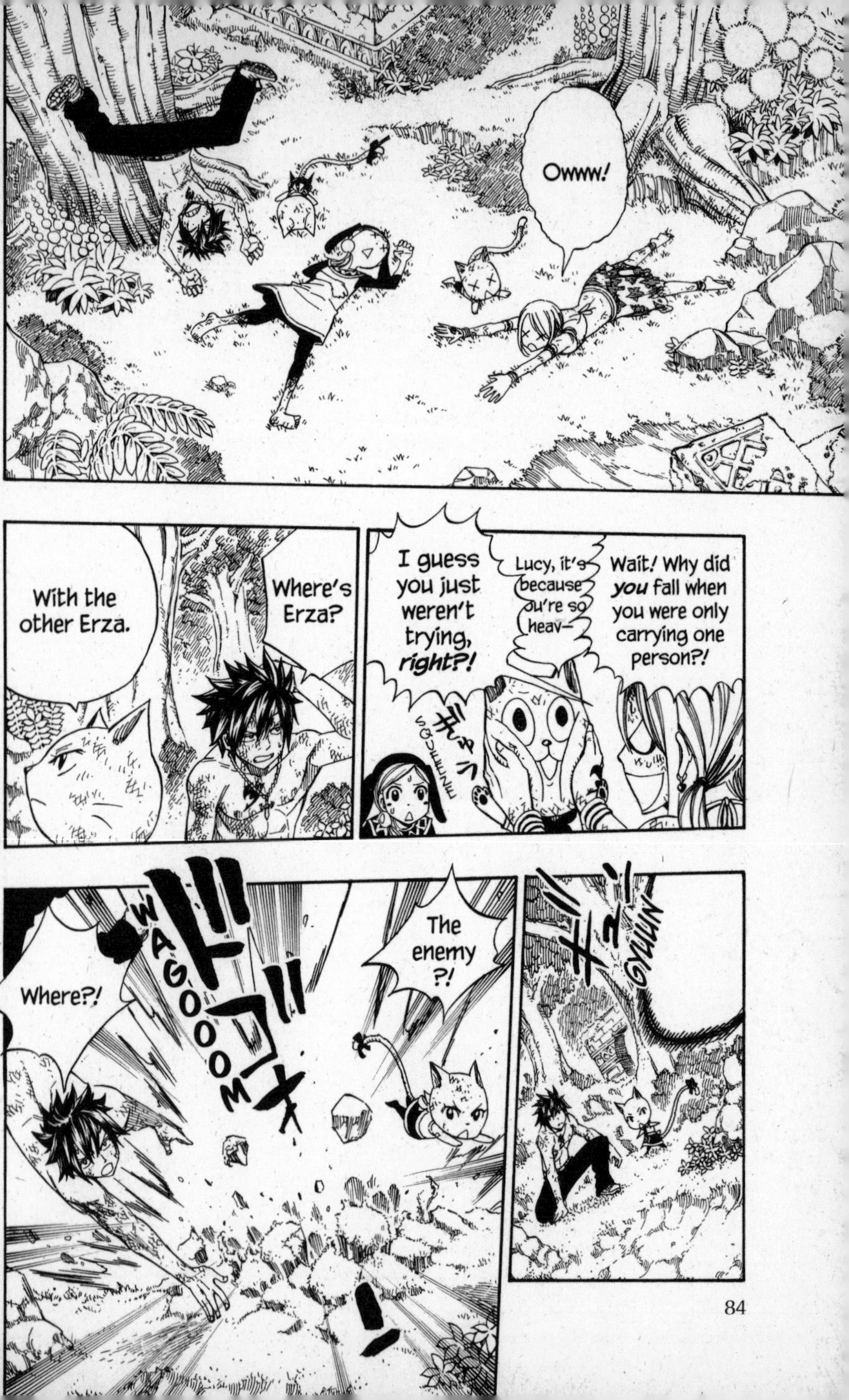
Owww!
Wait! Why did you fall when you were only carrying one person?!
Lucy, it's because ou're so heav—
I guess you just weren't trying, right?!
SQUEEZE
Where's Erza?
With the other Erza.
GYUUN
The enemy?!
WAGOOOM
Where?!

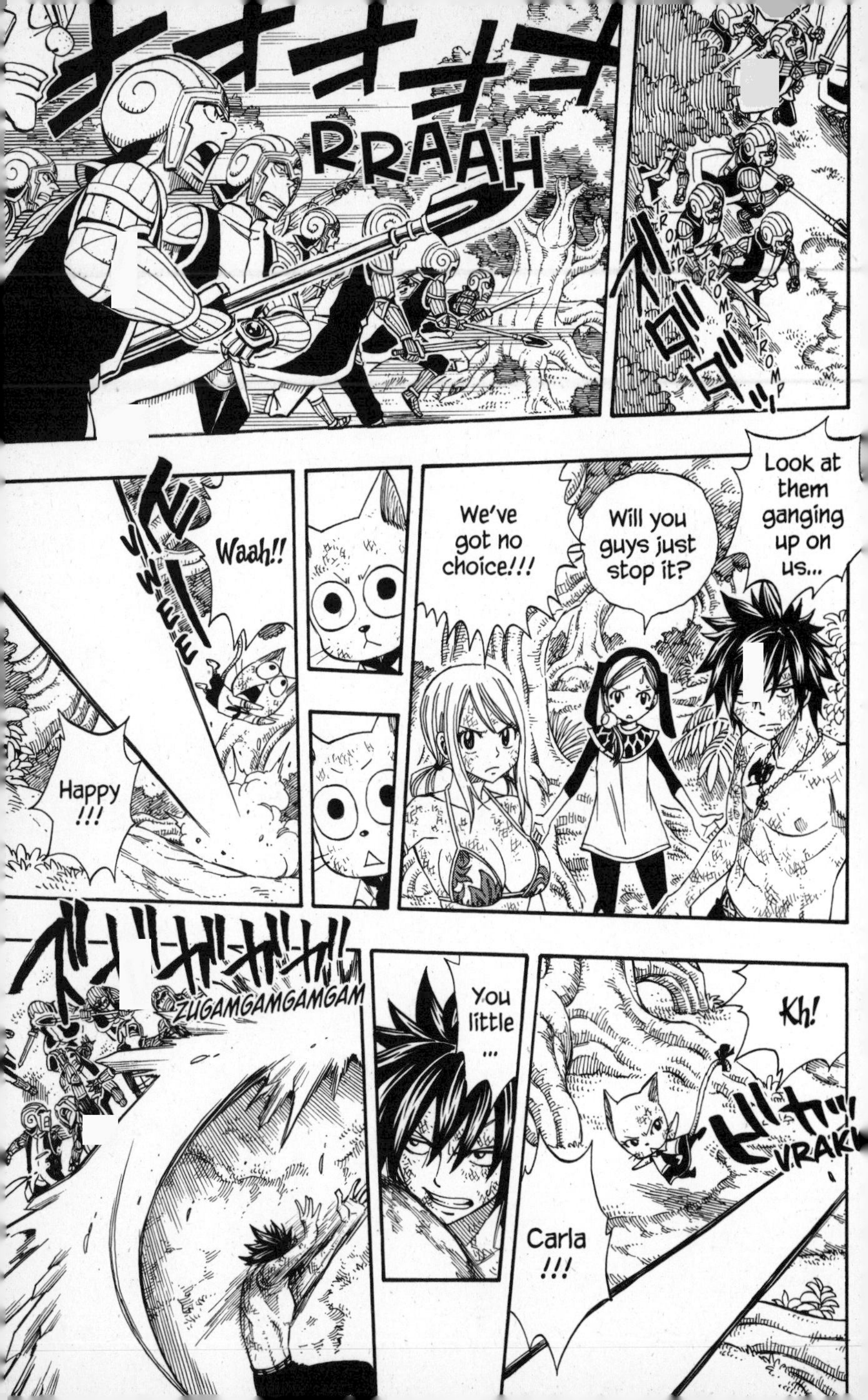
TROMP TROMP TROMP TROMP
RRAAH
Look at them ganging up on us...
Will you guys just stop it?
We've got no choice!!!
Waah!!
WHEEE
Happy !!!
Kh!
VRAK
Carla !!!
You little ...
ZUGAMGAMGAMGAM

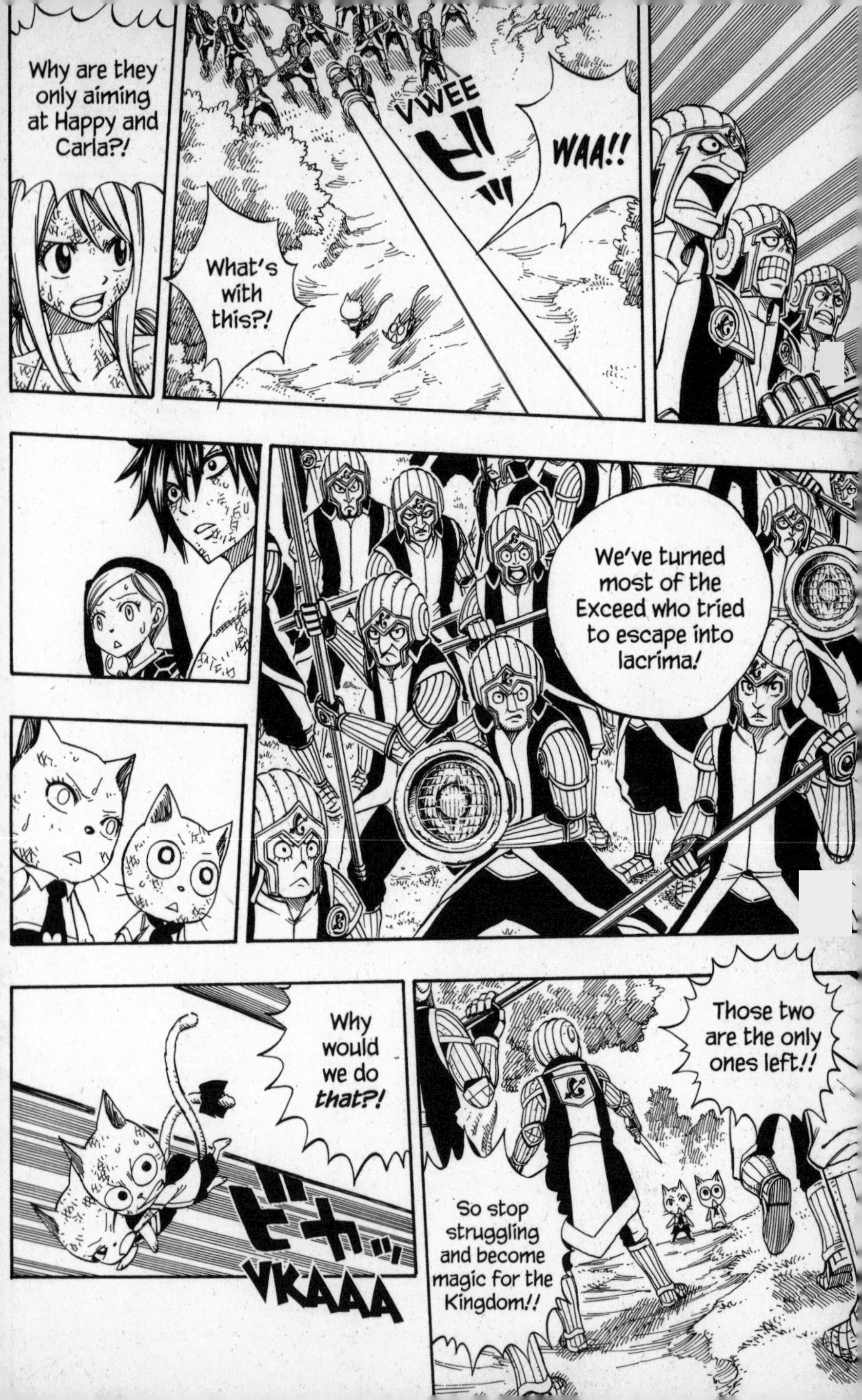
WAA!!
VWEE
ビ
What's with this?!
Why are they only aiming at Happy and Carla?!
We've turned most of the Exceed who tried to escape into lacrima!
Those two are the only ones left!!
So stop struggling and become magic for the Kingdom!!
Why would we do *that*?!
ビカ
VKAAA

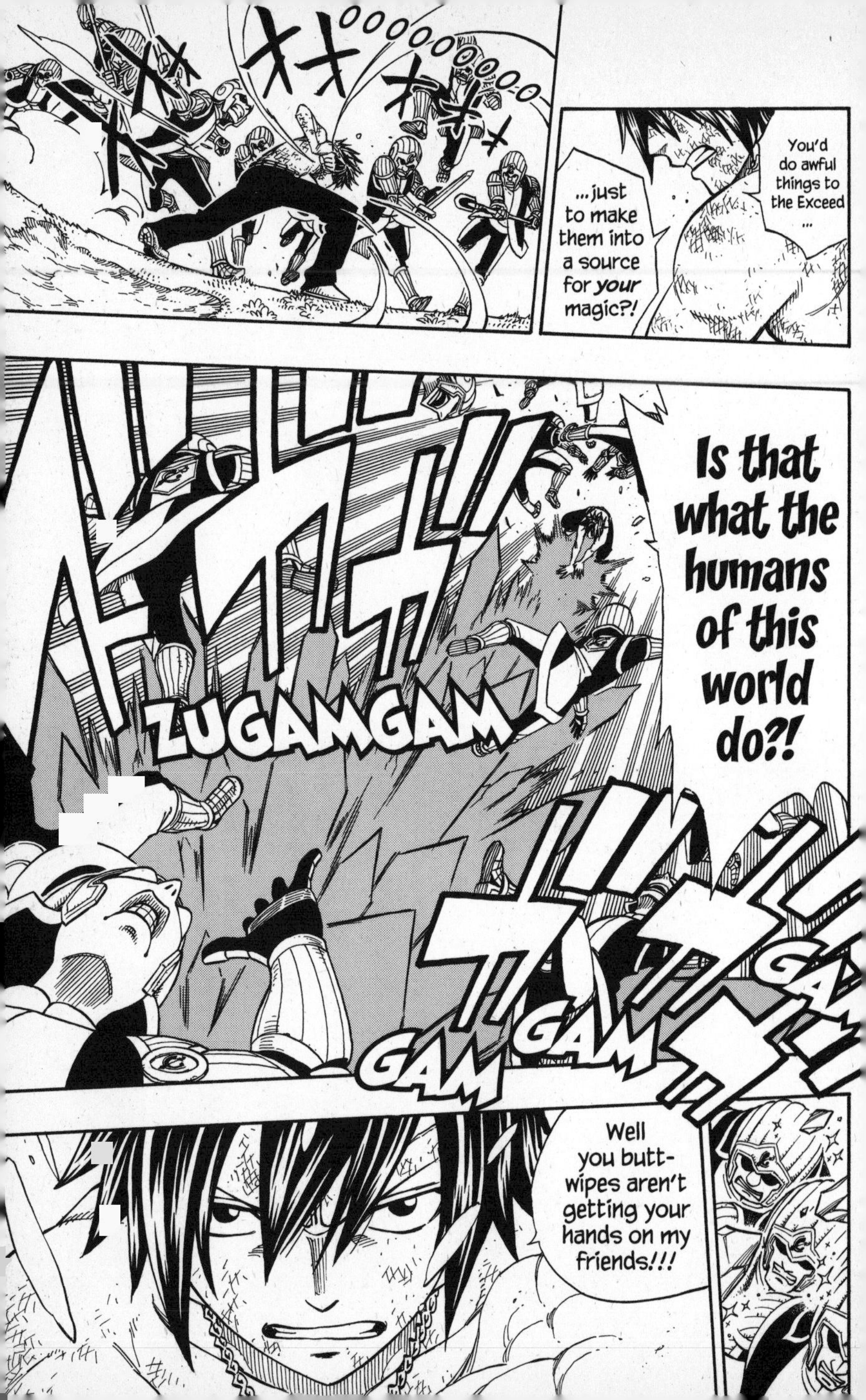
You'd do awful things to the Exceed...
...just to make them into a source for *your* magic?!
Is that what the humans of this world do?!
ZUGAMGAM
GAM
GAM
Well you butt-wipes aren't getting your hands on my friends!!!

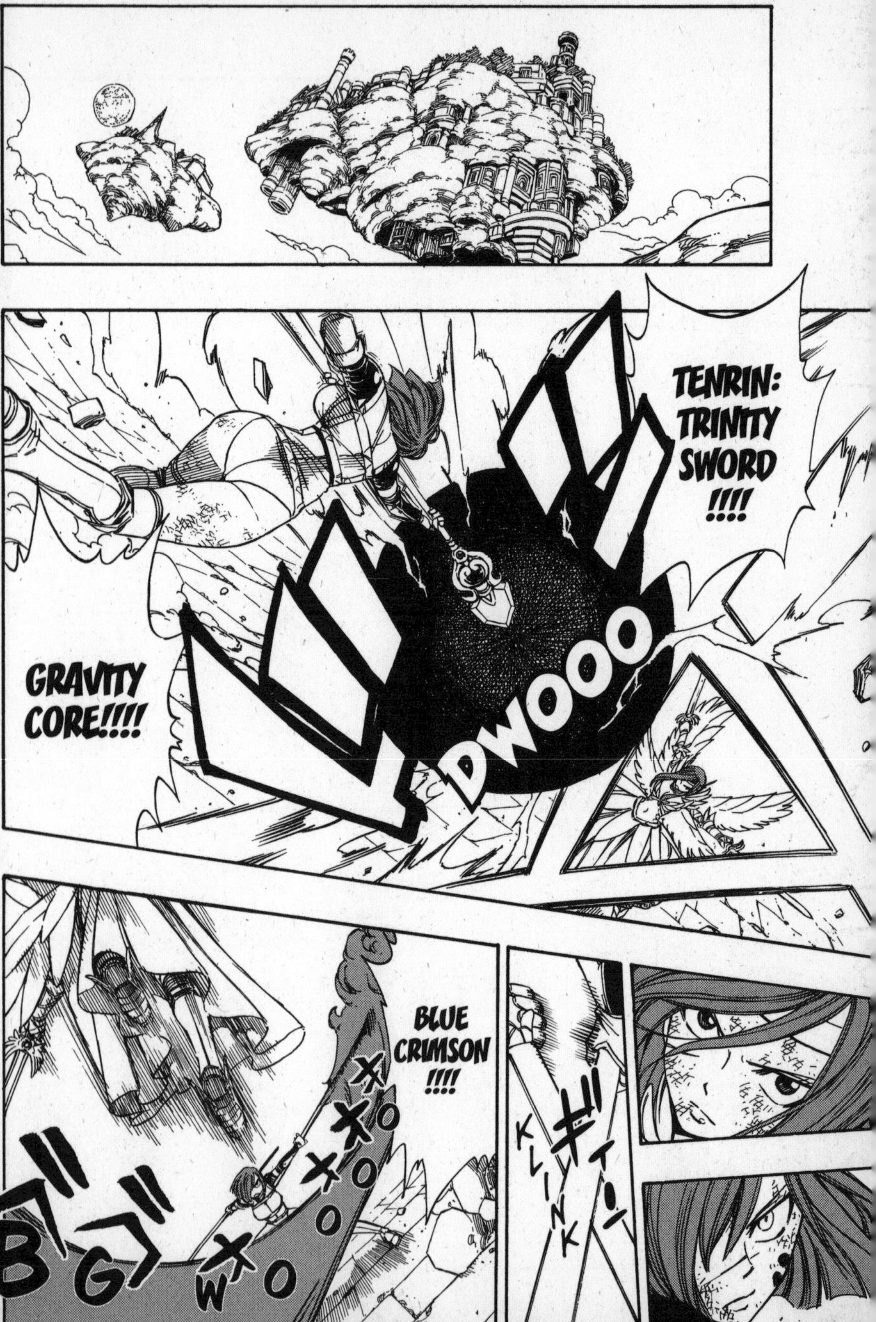
TENRIN: TRINITY SWORD!!!!
DWOOO
GRAVITY CORE!!!!
KLINK
BLUE CRIMSON!!!!
WOOOO
BGG

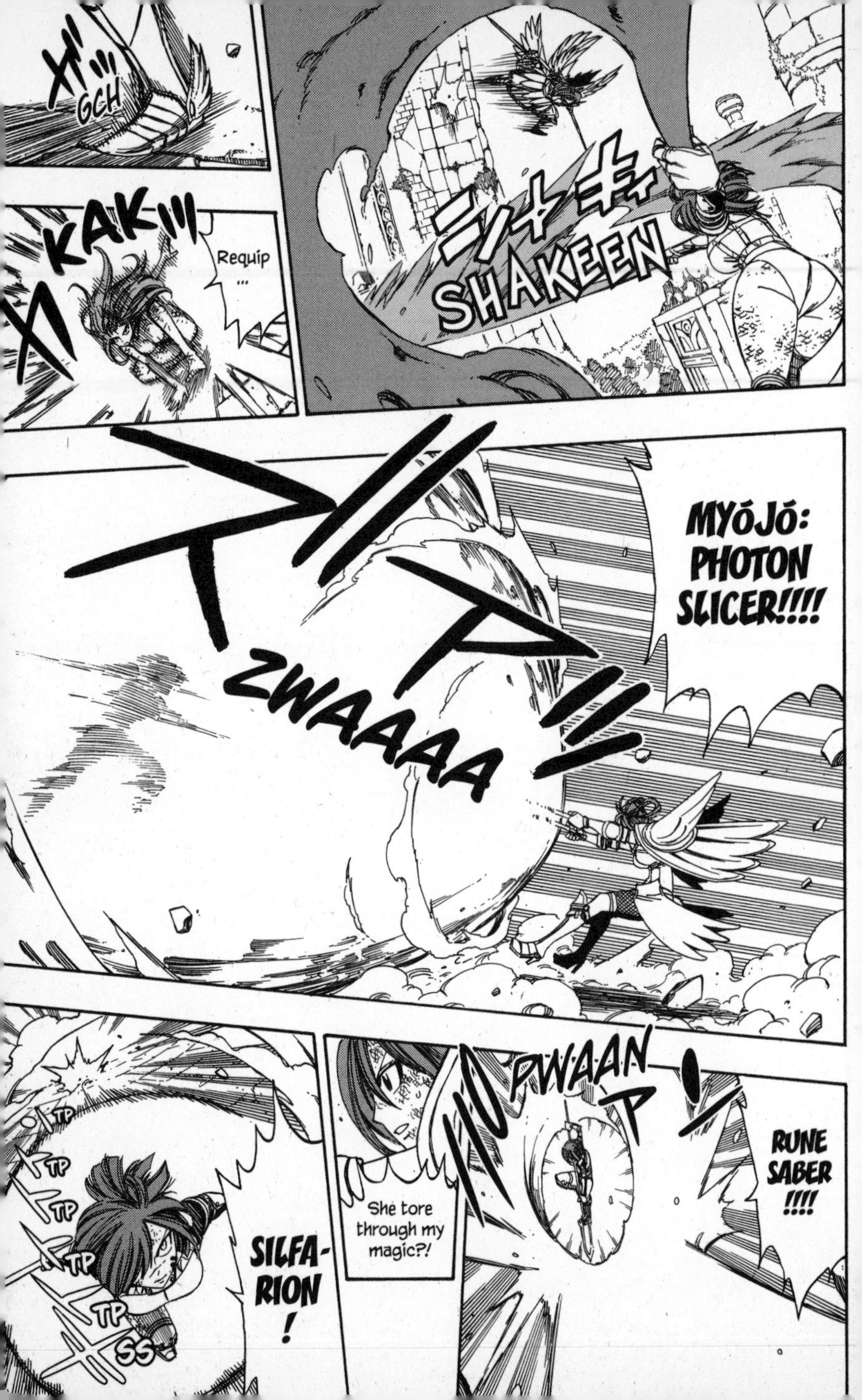
SHAKEEN
GCH
KAK
Requip ...
MYŌJŌ: PHOTON SLICER!!!!
ZWAAAAA
PWAAN
RUNE SABER!!!!
She tore through my magic?!
TP
TP
TP
TP
TP
SILFA-RION!
SS

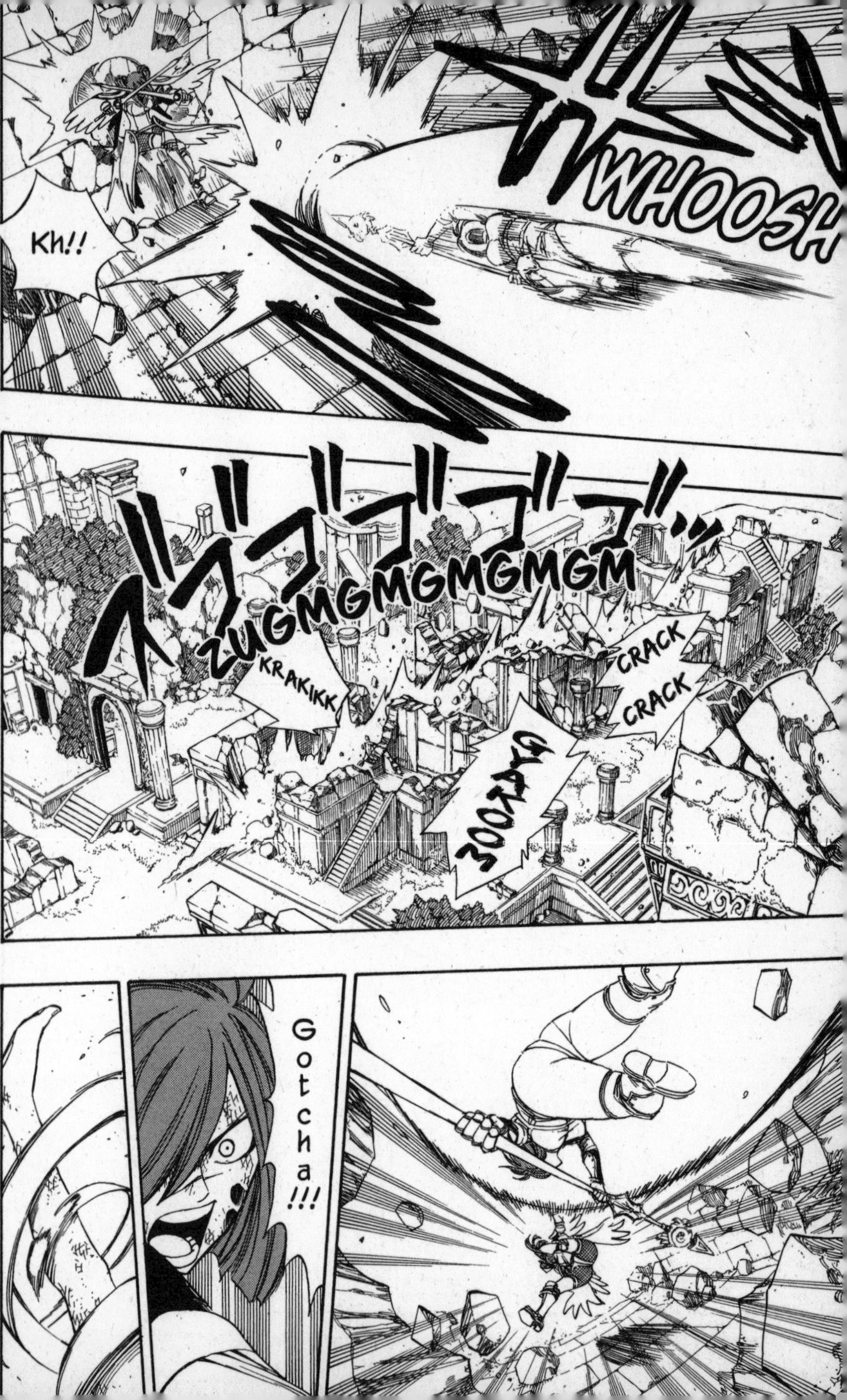
WHOOSH
Kh!!
ZUGMGMGMGMGM
CRACK
CRACK
KRAKIKK
GLAKOOM
Gotcha!!!

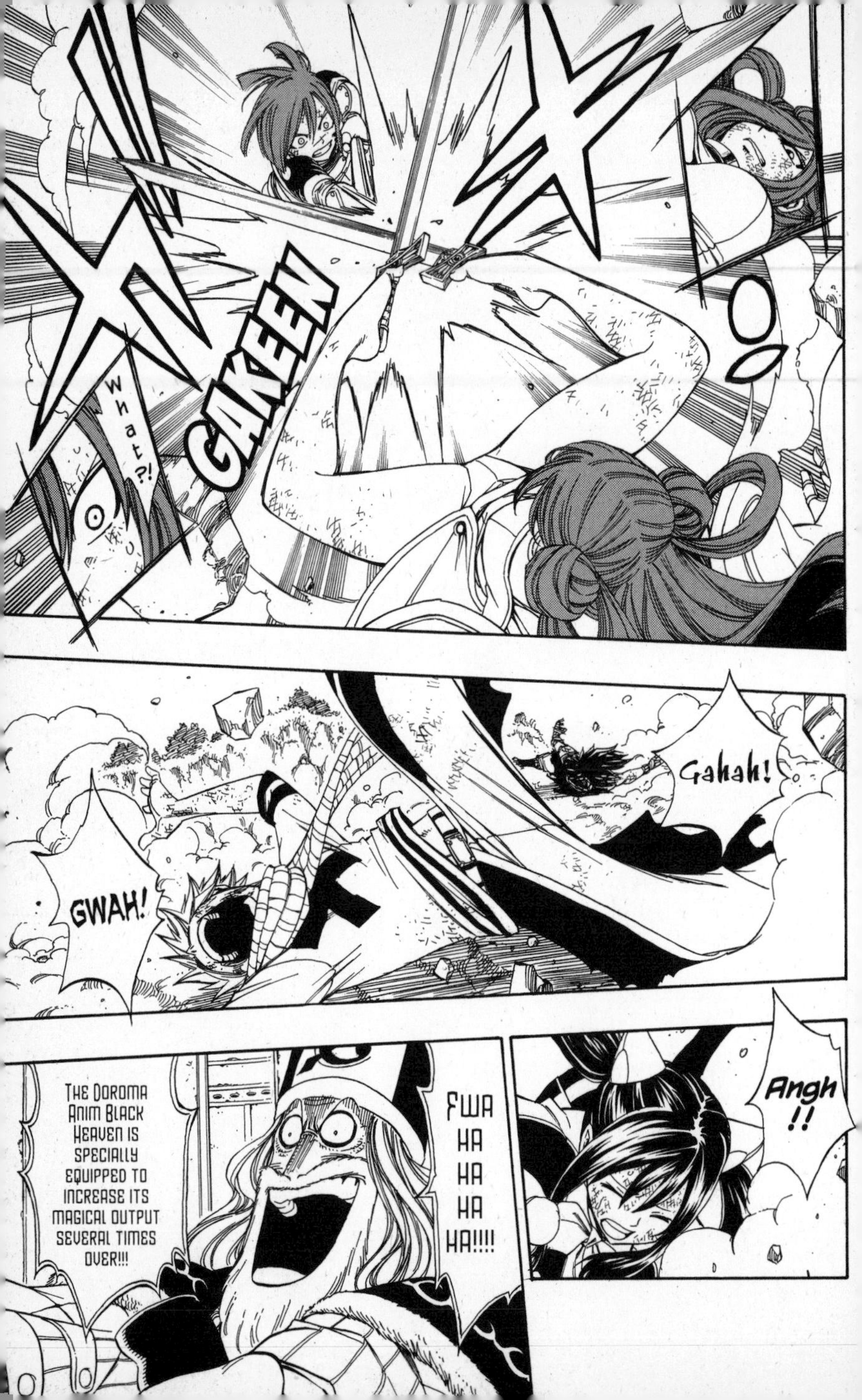
GAKEEN
What?!
Gahah!
GWAH!
Angh!!
FWA HA HA HA HA!!!!
The Doroma Anim Black Heaven is specially equipped to increase its magical output several times over!!!

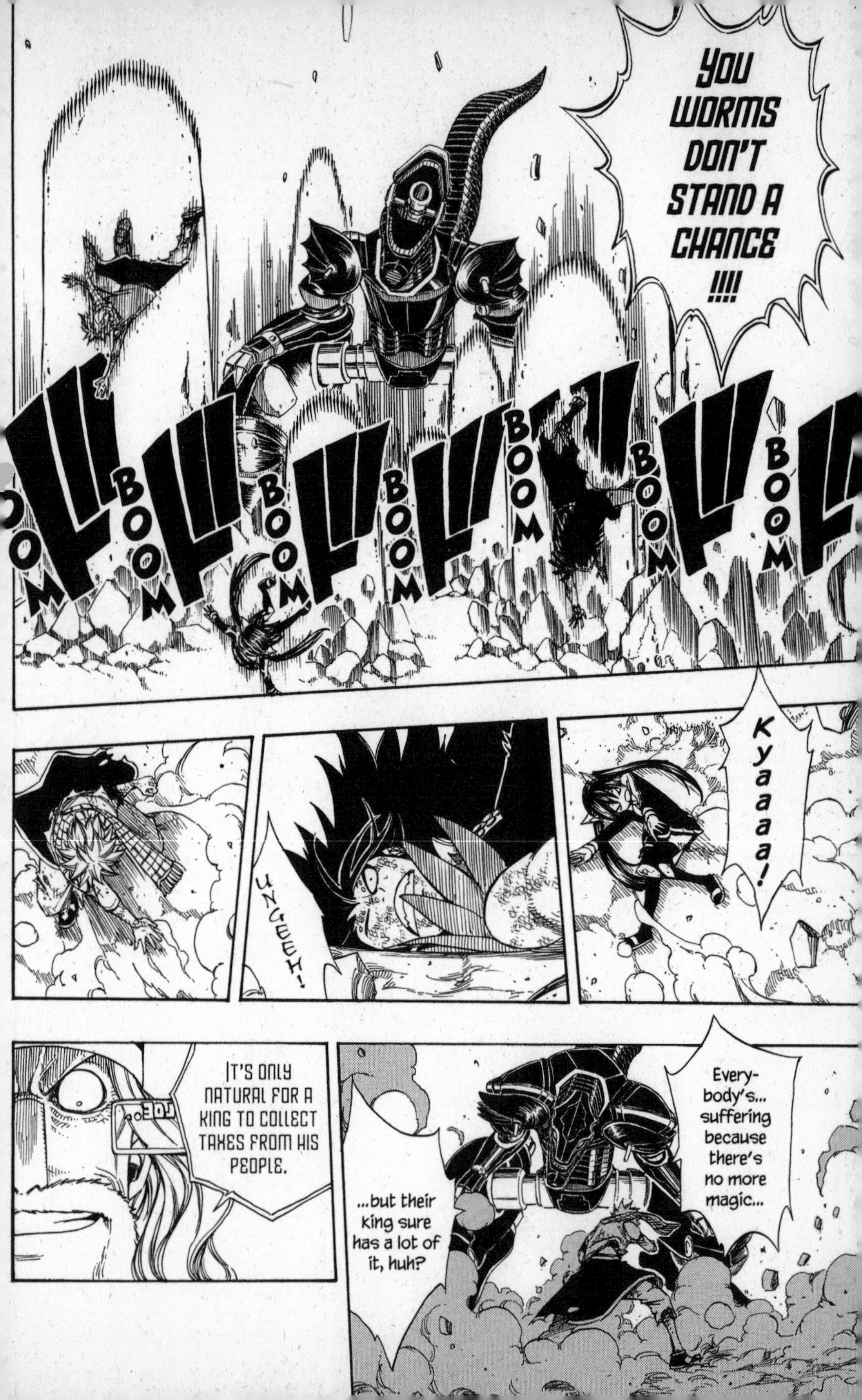

YOU WORMS DON'T STAND A CHANCE!!!!
BOOM
BOOM
BOOM
BOOM
BOOM
BOOM
BOOM
Kyaaaa!
UNGEEEH!
Every-body's... suffering because there's no more magic...
...but their king sure has a lot of it, huh?
It's only natural for a king to collect taxes from his people.

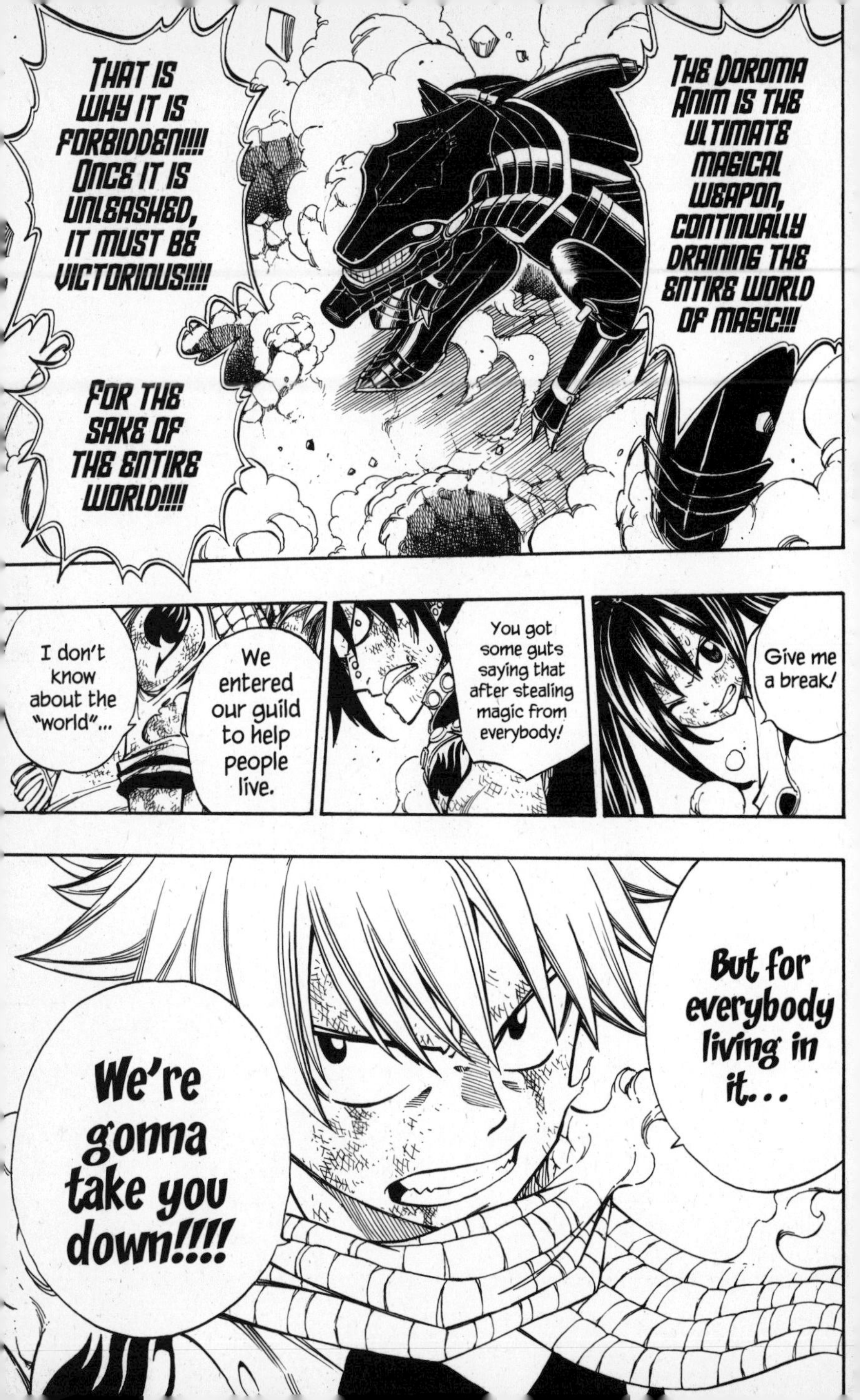
THE DOROMA ANIM IS THE ULTIMATE MAGICAL WEAPON, CONTINUALLY DRAINING THE ENTIRE WORLD OF MAGIC!!!
THAT IS WHY IT IS FORBIDDEN!!!! ONCE IT IS UNLEASHED, IT MUST BE VICTORIOUS!!!!
FOR THE SAKE OF THE ENTIRE WORLD!!!!
Give me a break!
You got some guts saying that after stealing magic from everybody!
We entered our guild to help people live.
I don't know about the "world"...
But for everybody living in it...
We're gonna take you down!!!!

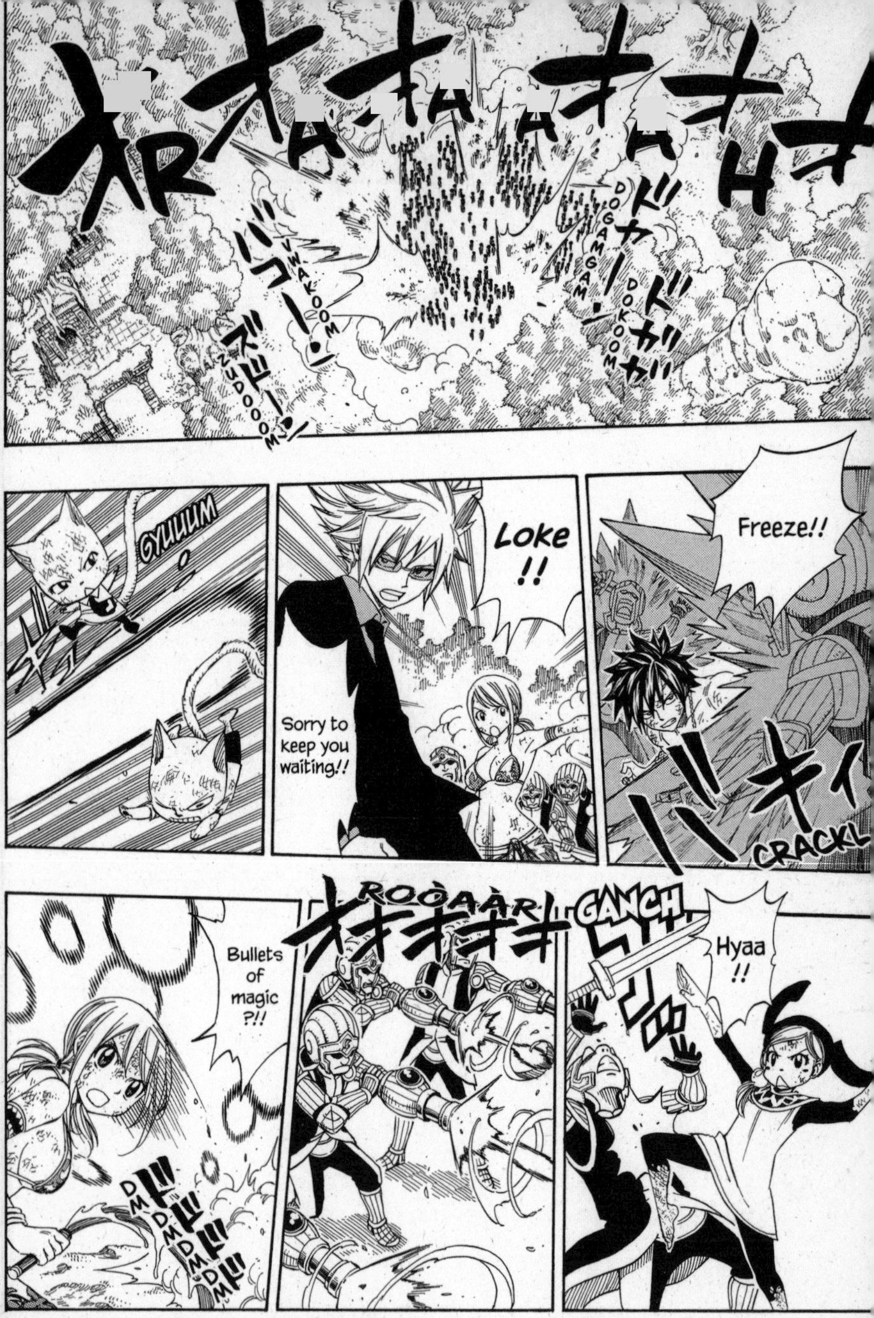
DOGAMGAM
DOKOOOM
VWAKOOOM
ZUDOOOOM
Freeze!!
CRACKL
Loke!!
Sorry to keep you waiting!!
GYUUUM
Hyaa!!
GANCH
ROOAAR
Bullets of magic?!!
DMDMDMDM

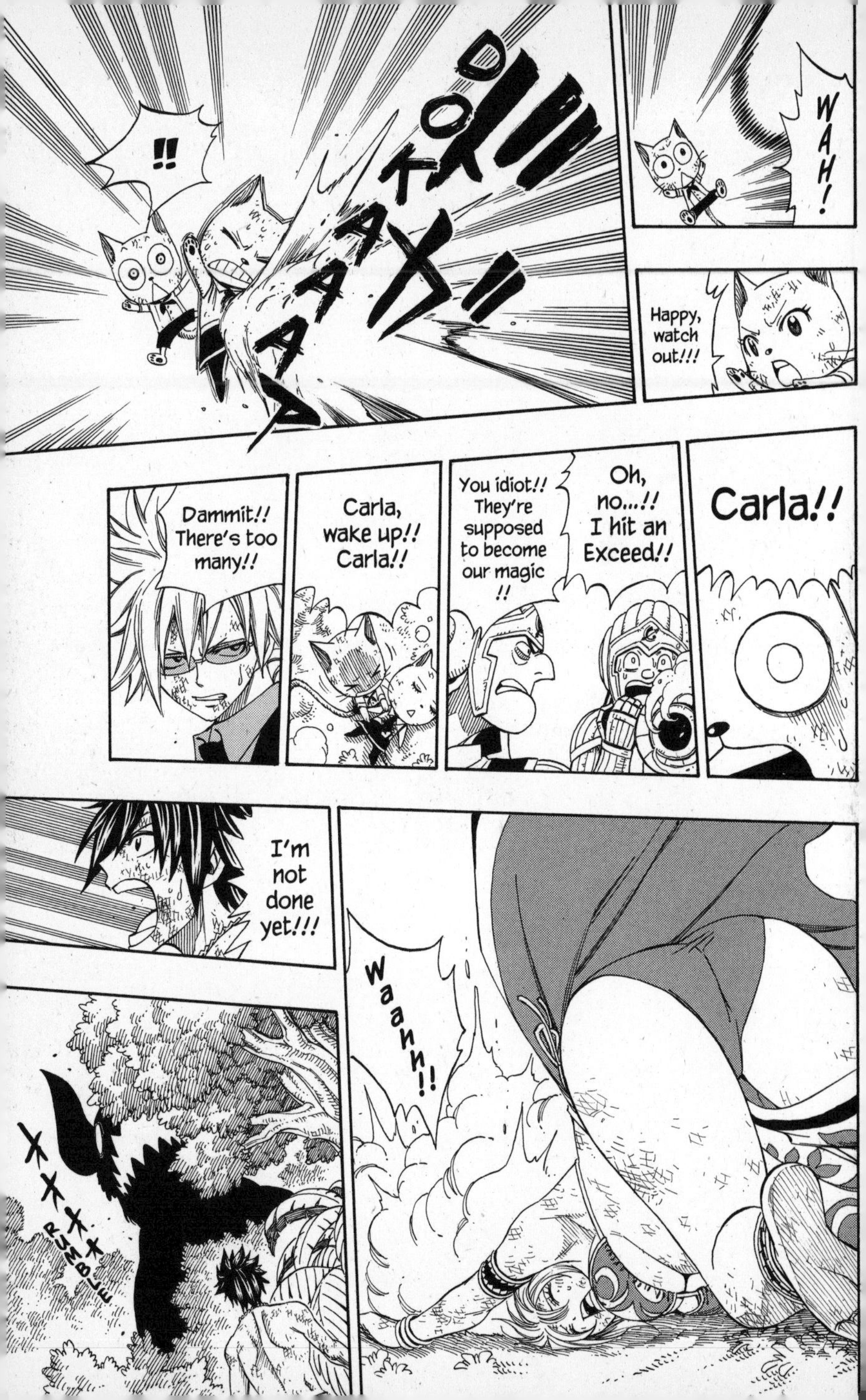
WAH!
Happy, watch out!!!
!!
DOKAAAA
Carla!!
Oh, no...!! I hit an Exceed!!
You idiot!! They're supposed to become our magic!!
Carla, wake up!! Carla!!
Dammit!! There's too many!!
Waanh!!
I'm not done yet!!!
RUMBLE

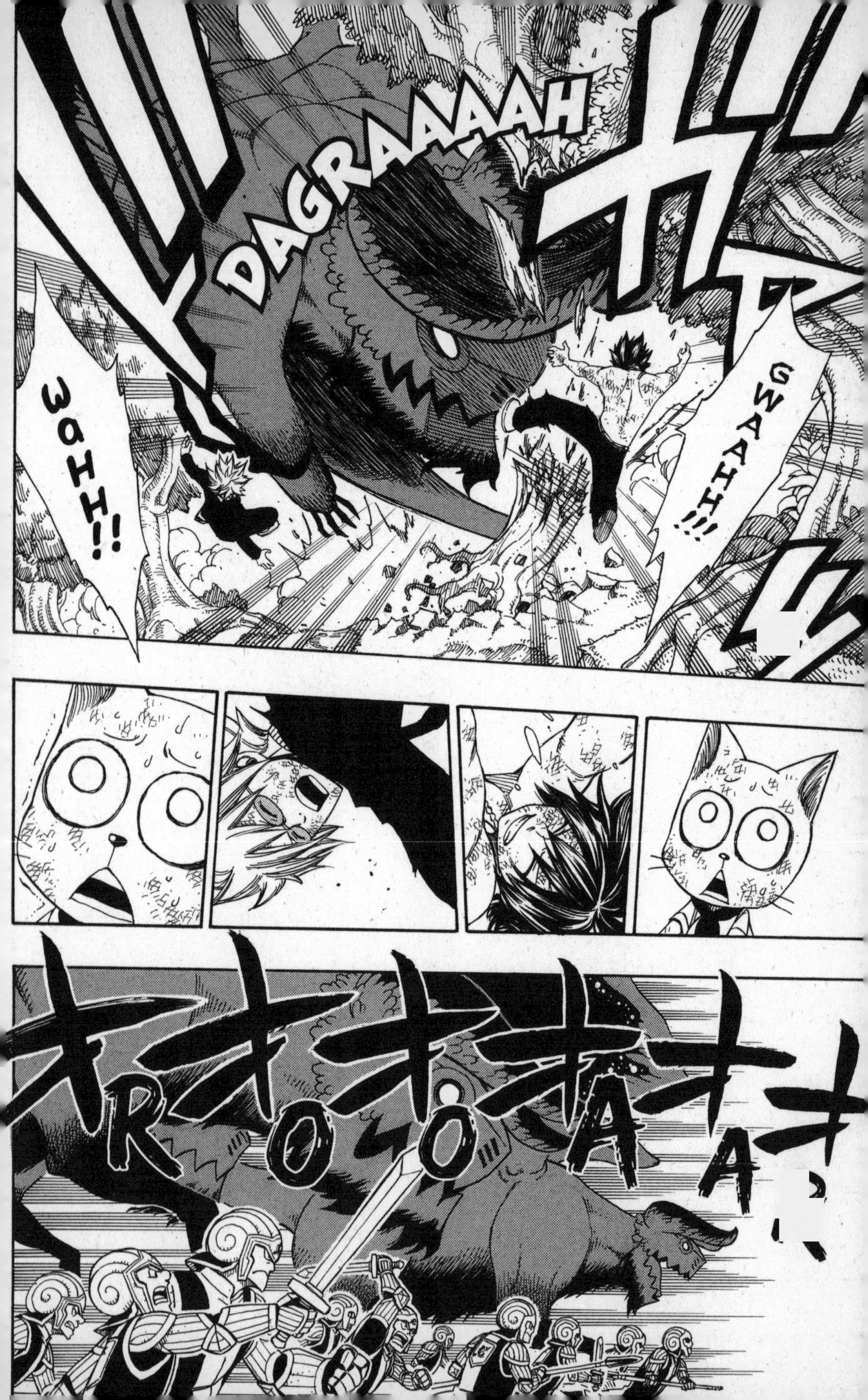
DAGRAAAAAH
GWAAHH!!!
WAHH!!
ROOAA

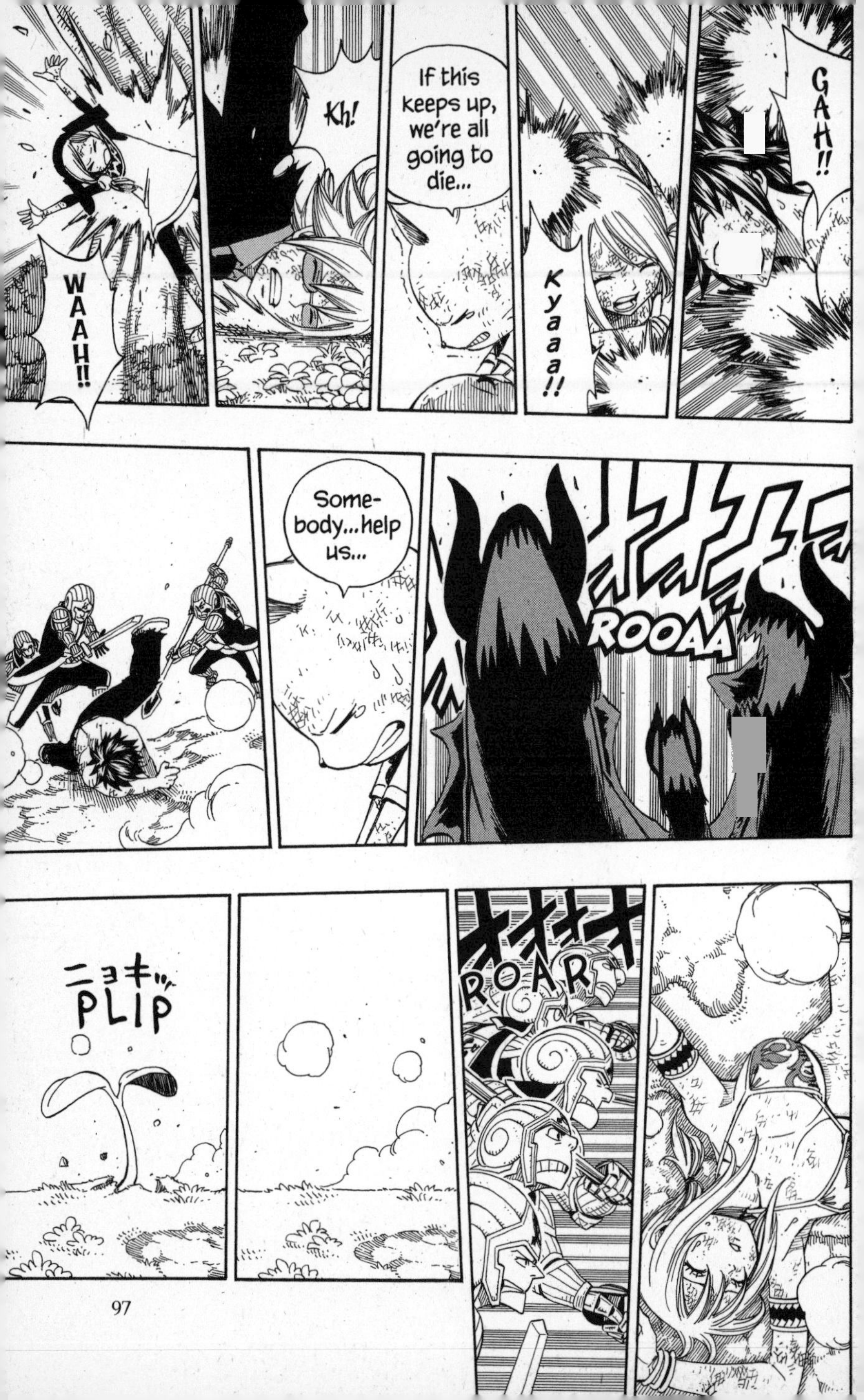
GAH!!
Kyaaa!!
If this keeps up, we're all going to die...
Kh!
WAAAH!!
ROOAA
Some-body...help us...
ROAR
ニョキッ
PLIP

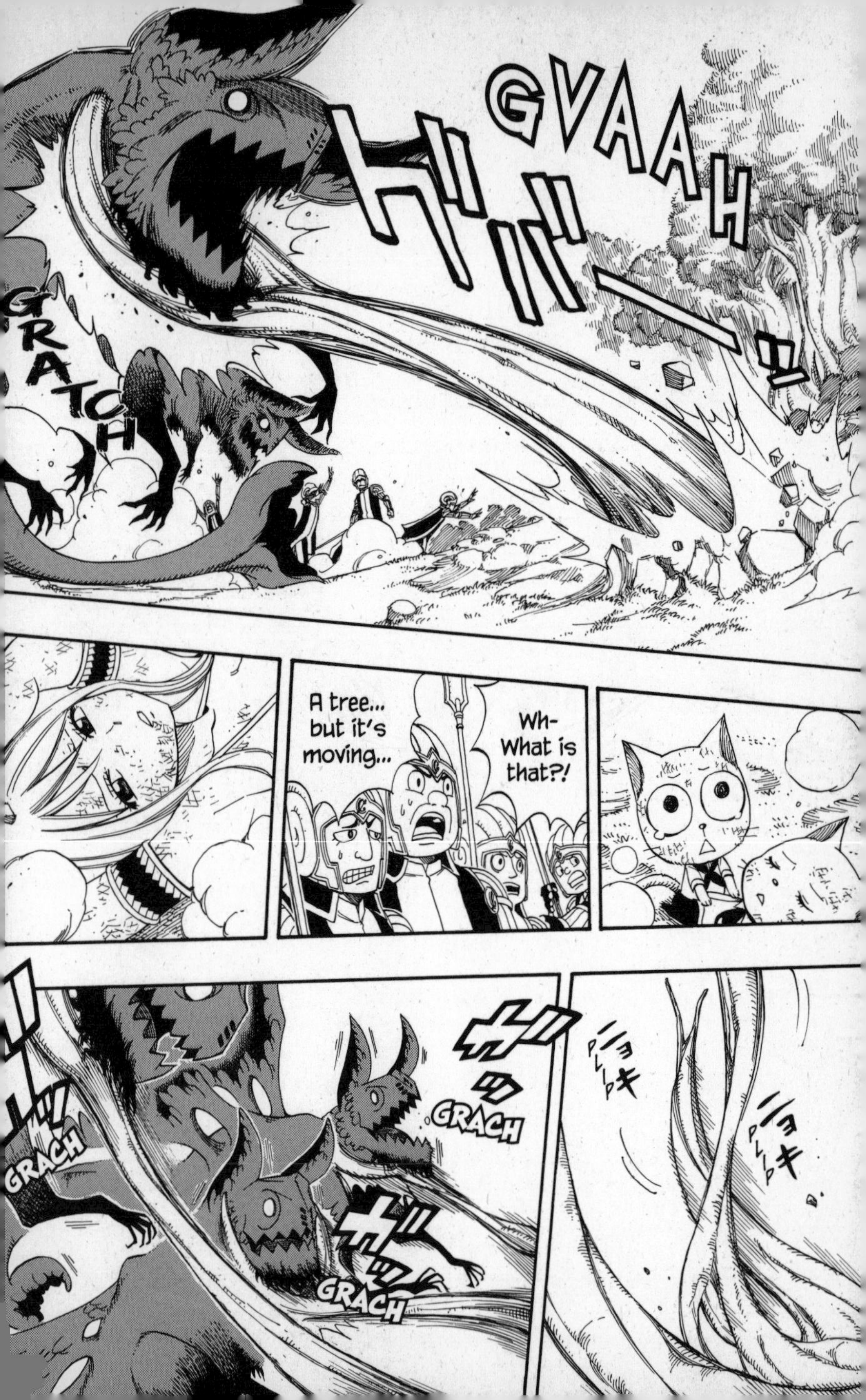
GVAAH
GRATCH
Wh- What is that?!
A tree... but it's moving...
PLIP
PLIP
GRACH
GRACH
GRACH

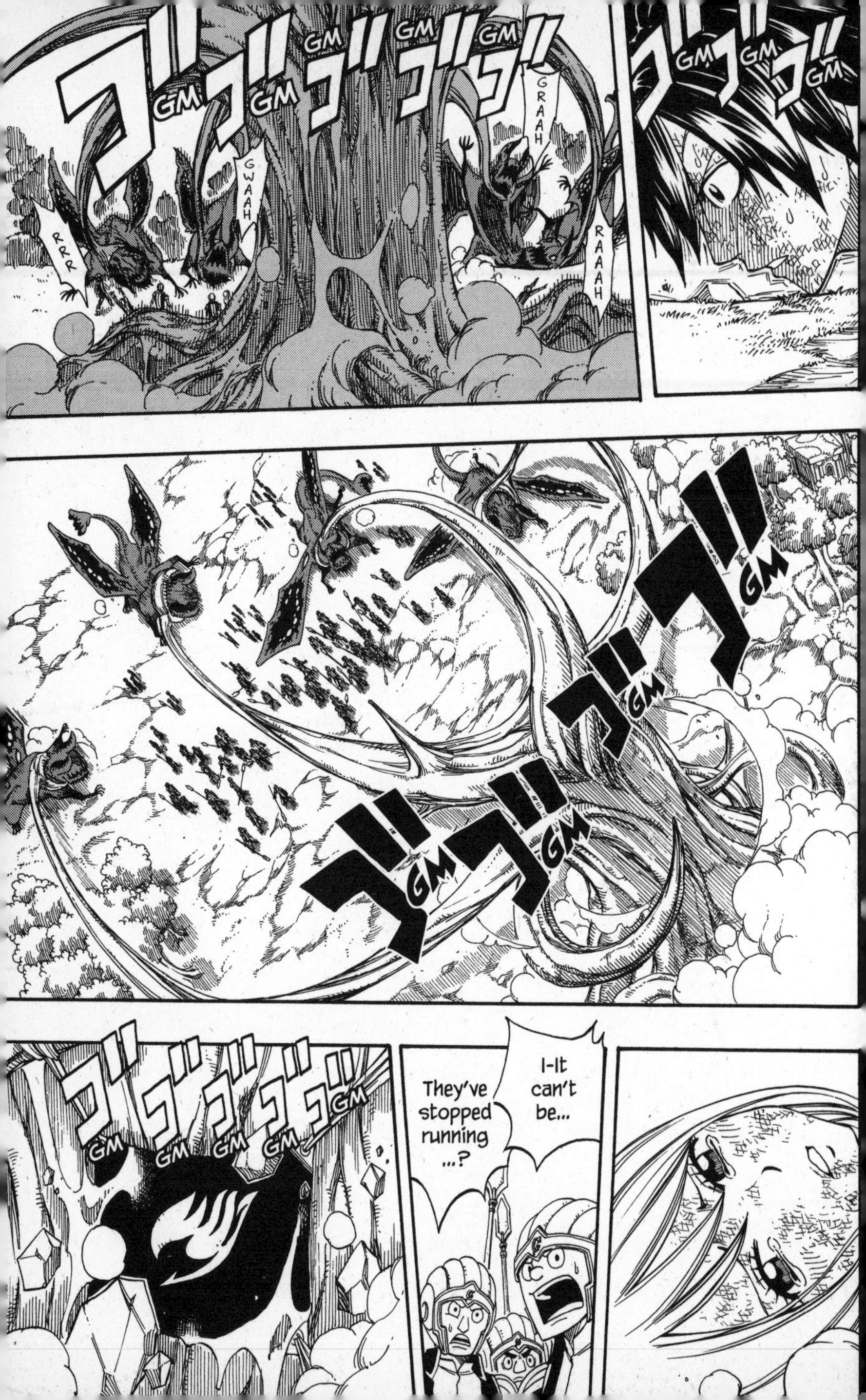

GM GM GM
GM GM GM GM
GRAAH
RAAAH
GWAAH
RRR
GM GM GM GM
I-It can't be...
They've stopped running ...?
GM GM GM GM GM

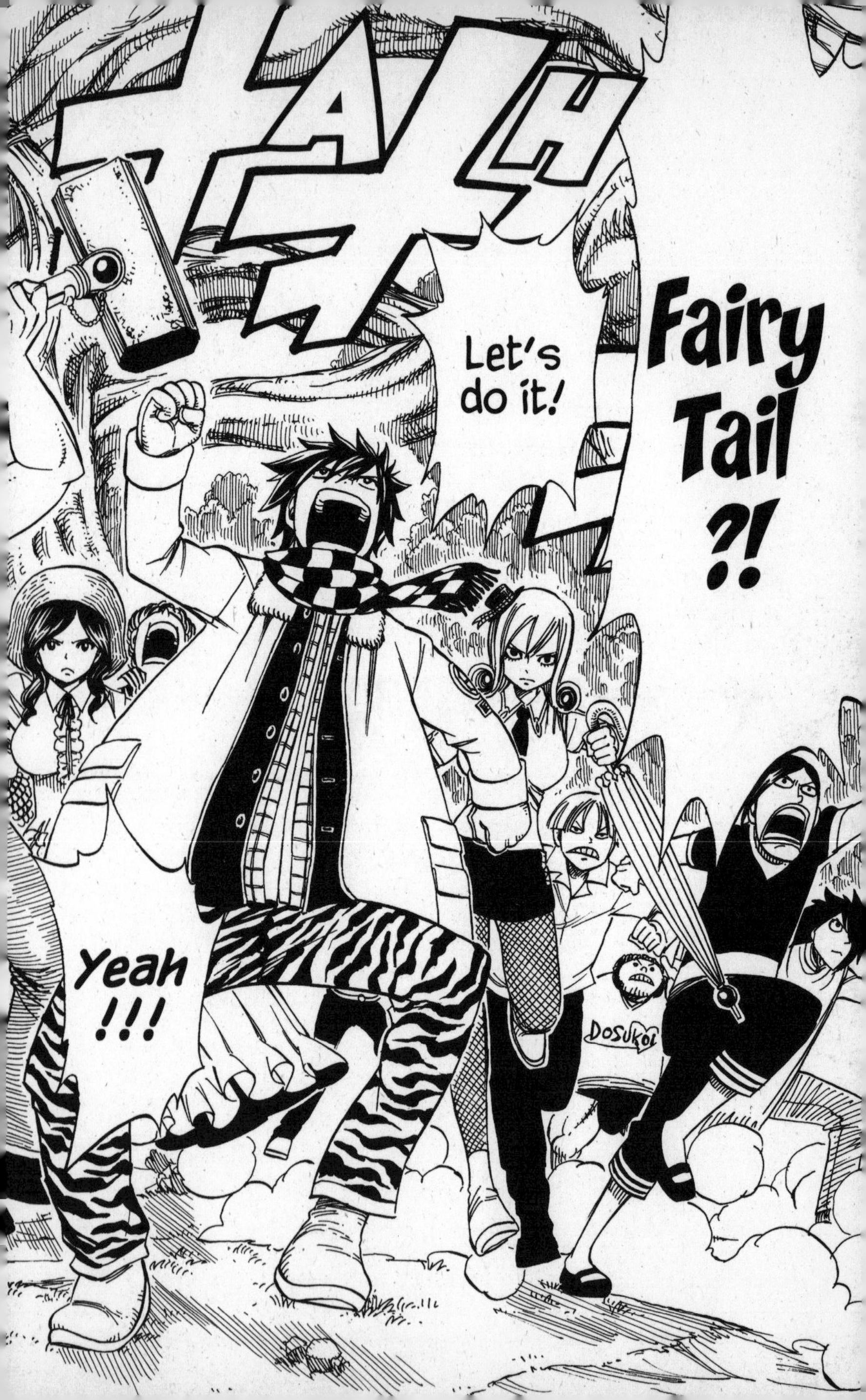
Fairy Tail ?!
Let's do it!
Yeah !!!
DOSUKOI

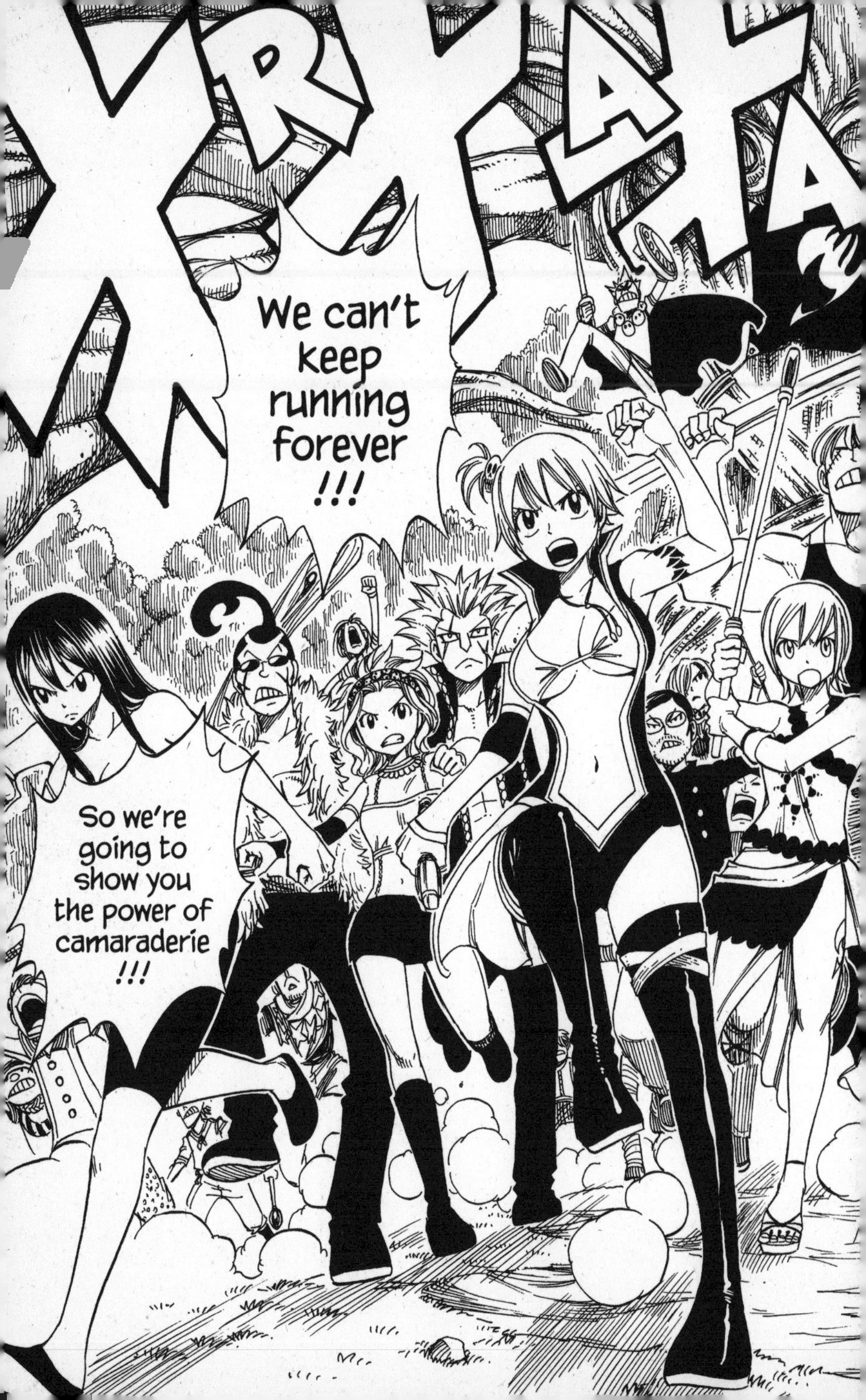
We can't keep running forever !!!
So we're going to show you the power of camaraderie !!!

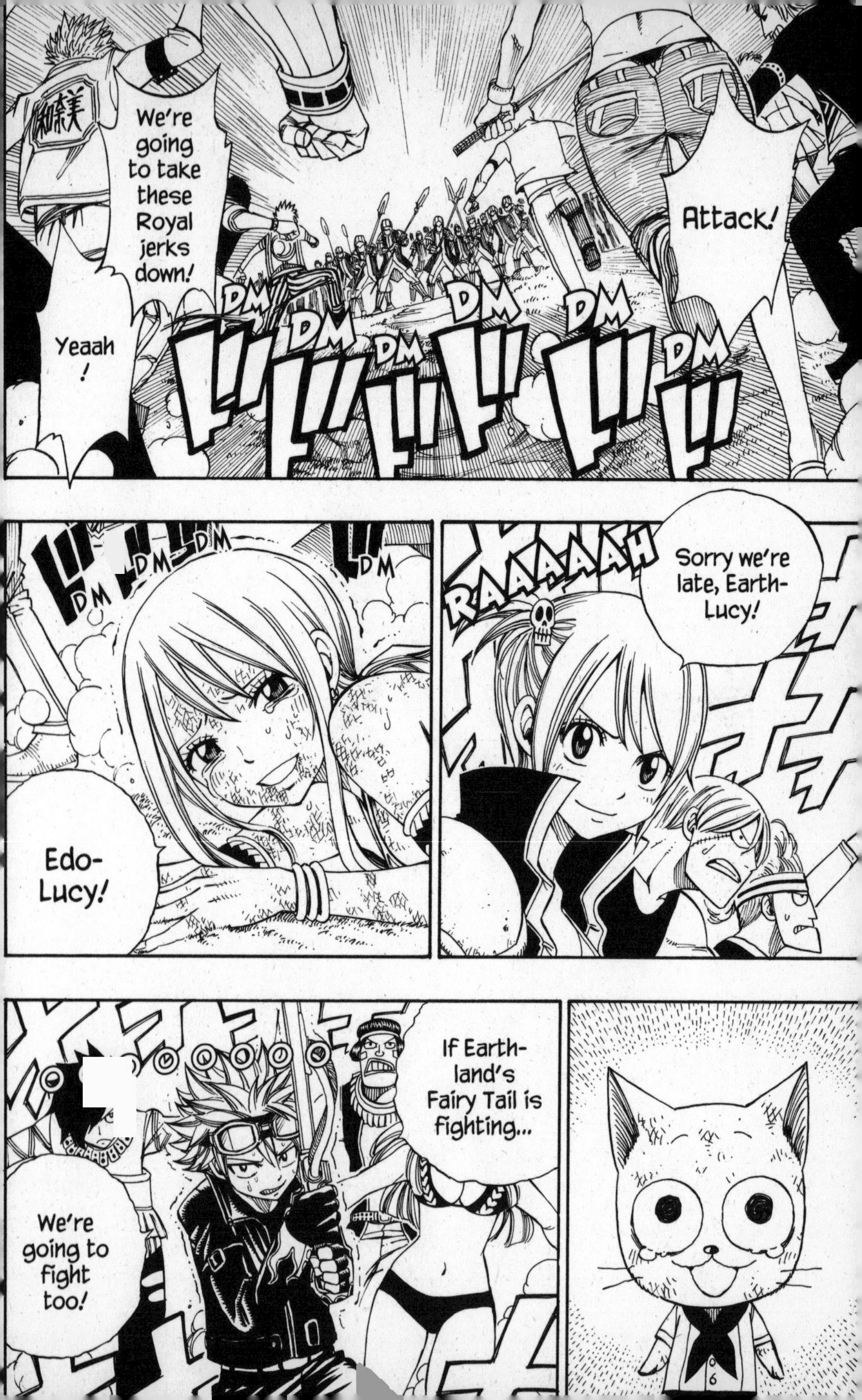
Attack!
We're going to take these Royal jerks down!
DM DM DM DM DM DM
Yeaah!
RAAAAAH
Sorry we're late, Earth-Lucy!
DM DM DM
DM
Edo-Lucy!
If Earth-land's Fairy Tail is fighting...
We're going to fight too!

FAIRY TAIL
フェアリーテイル

Chapter 193: To Be Alive

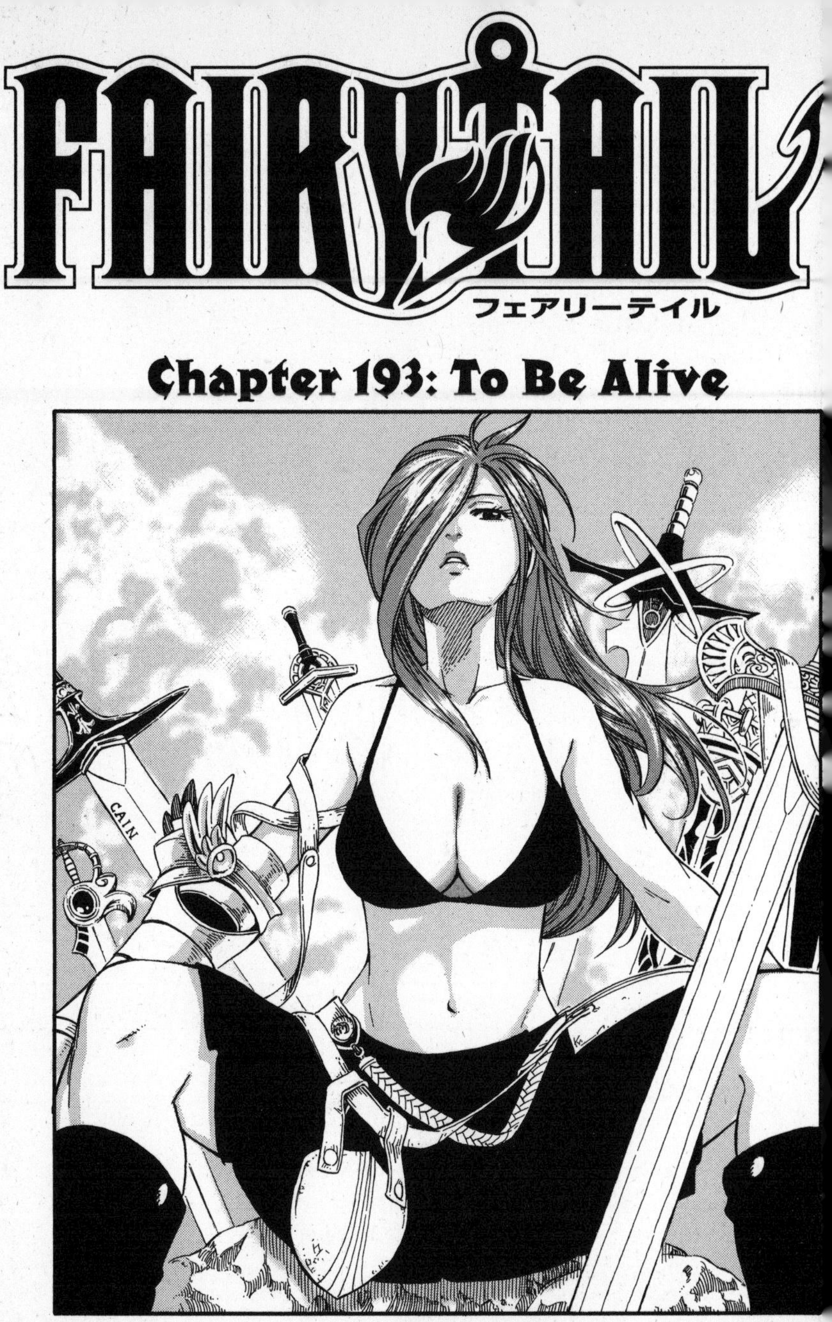
CAIN

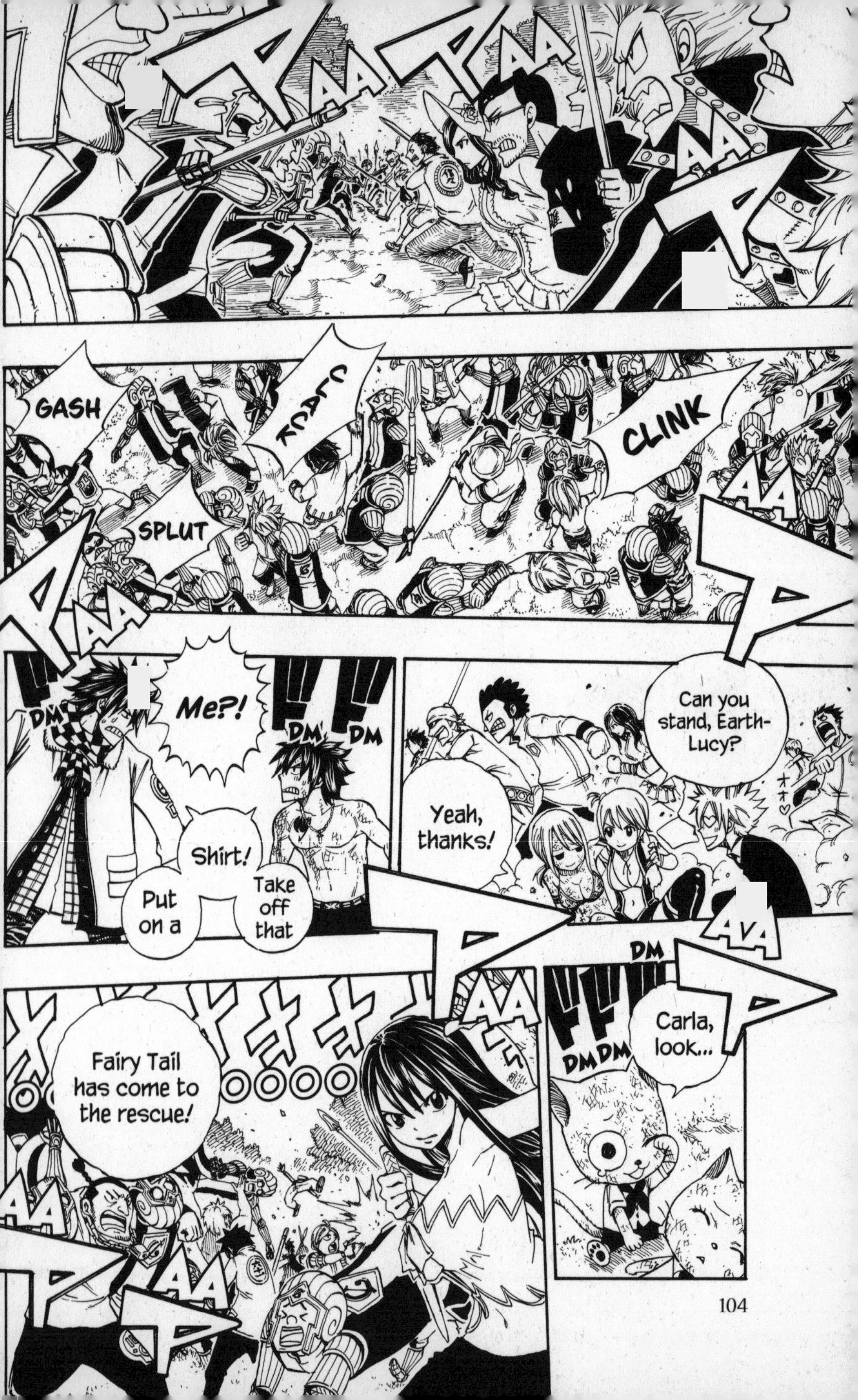
CLINK
CLACK
GASH
SPLUT
Can you stand, Earth-Lucy?
Yeah, thanks!
DM DM
Me?!
DM
Shirt!
Take off that
Put on a
DM
DM DM
Carla, look...
Fairy Tail has come to the rescue!

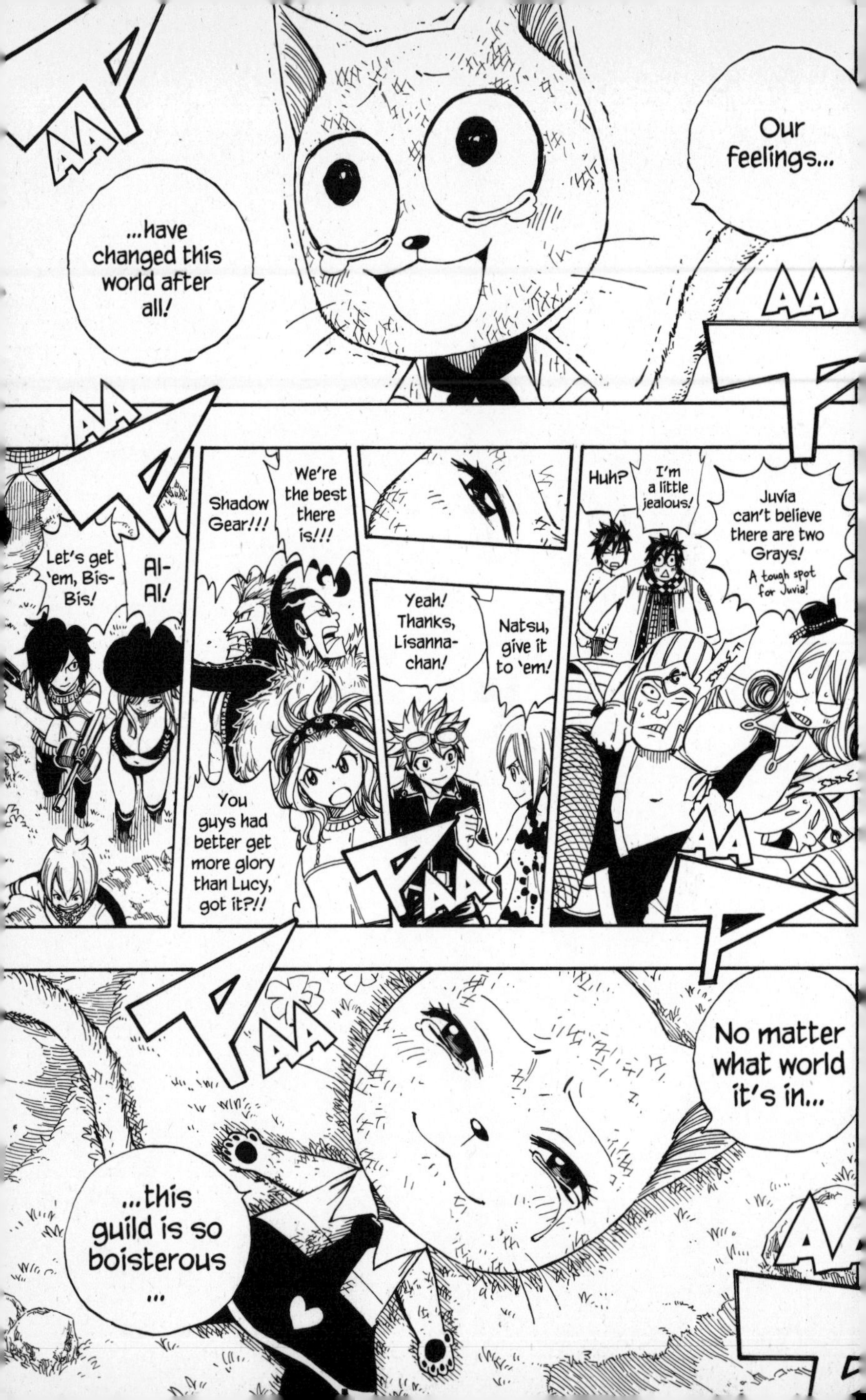
Our feelings...
...have changed this world after all!
Juvia can't believe there are two Grays!
A tough spot for Juvia!
I'm a little jealous!
Huh?
Natsu, give it to 'em!
Yeah! Thanks, Lisanna-chan!
We're the best there is!!!
Shadow Gear!!!
You guys had better get more glory than Lucy, got it?!!
Al-Al!
Let's get 'em, Bis-Bis!
No matter what world it's in...
...this guild is so boisterous...

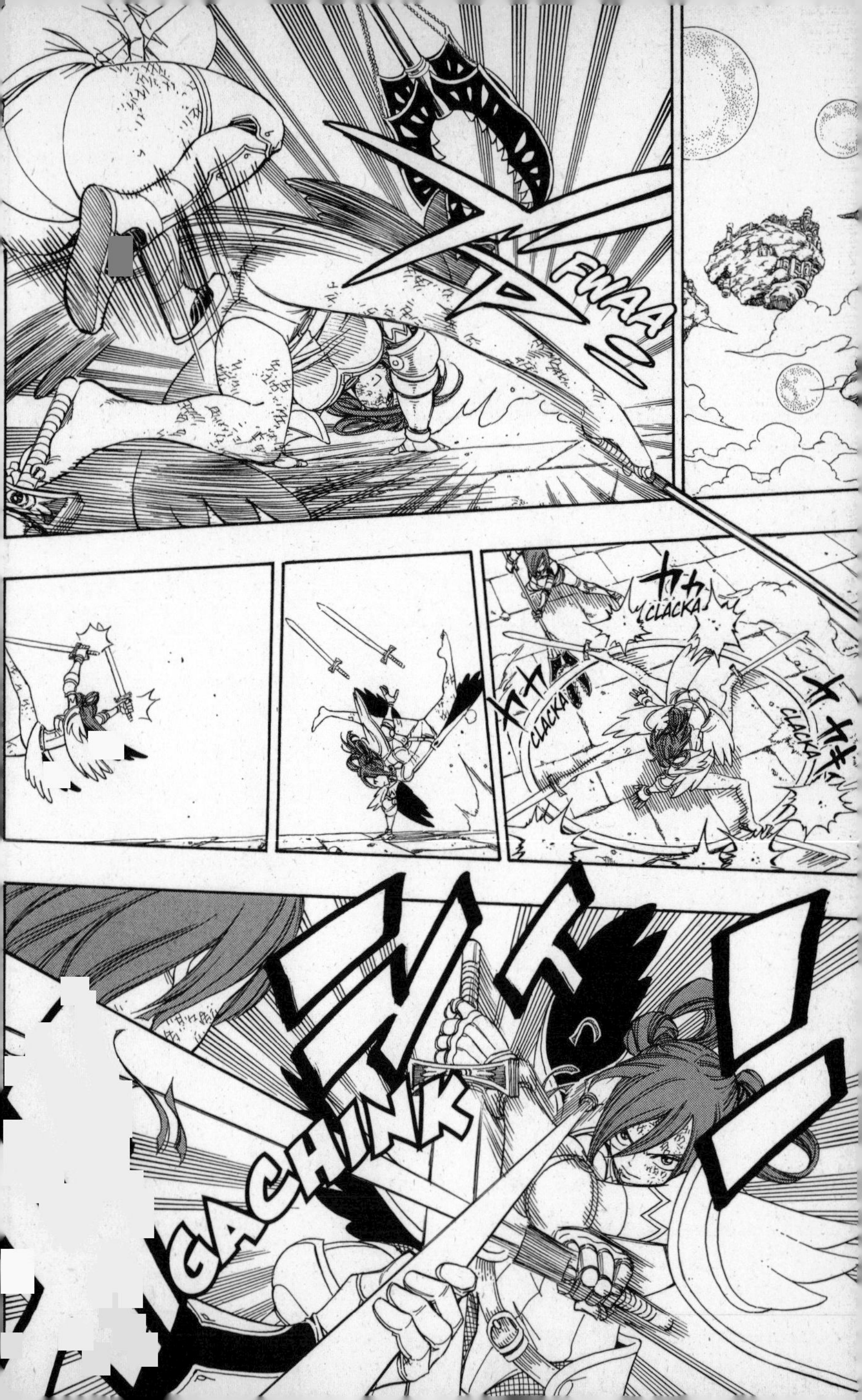
FWAA
CLACKA
CLACKA
CLACKA
GACHINK

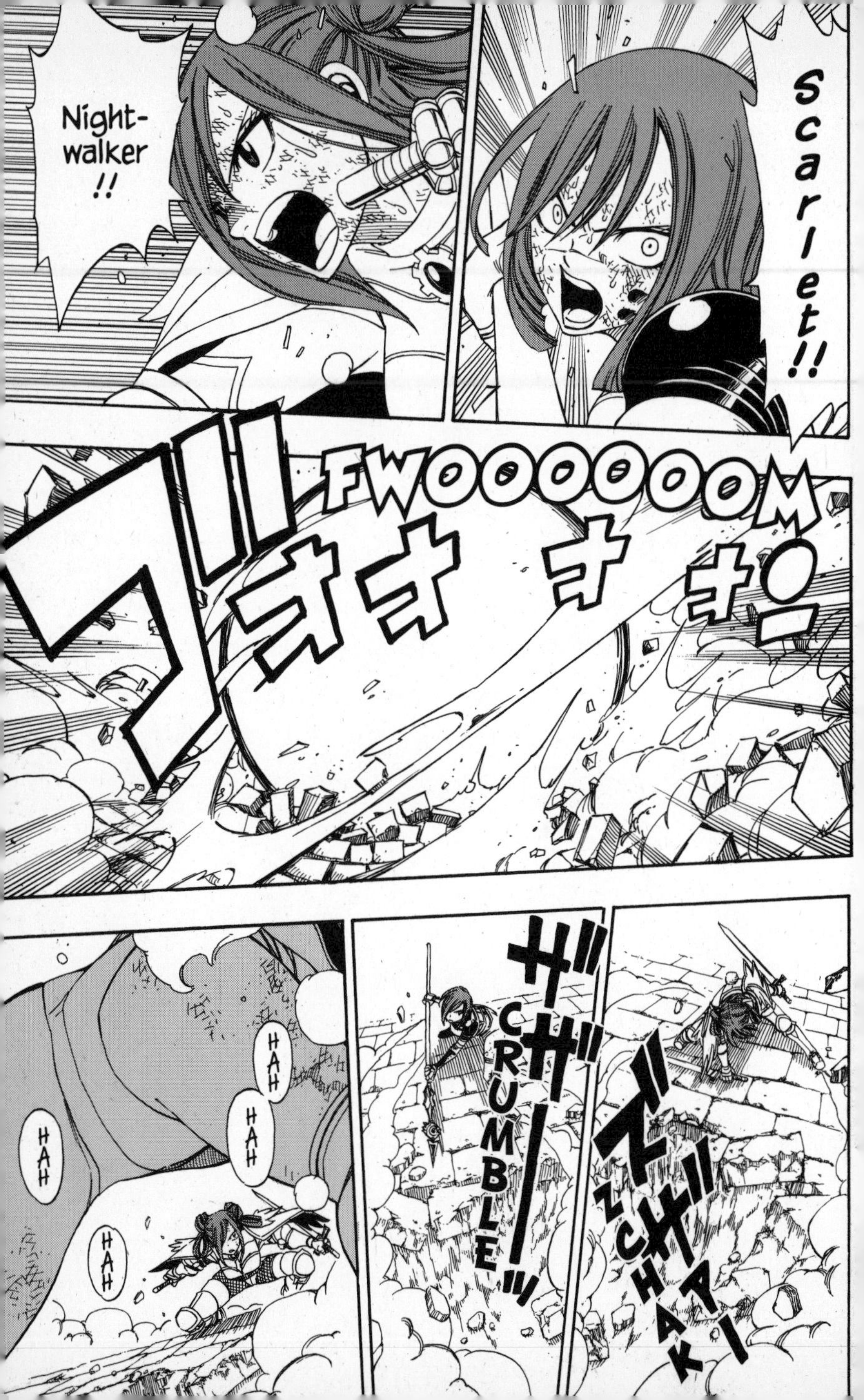
Scarlet!!
Night-walker!!
FWOOOOOOM
ZCHAK!
CRUMBLE
HAH
HAH
HAH
HAH

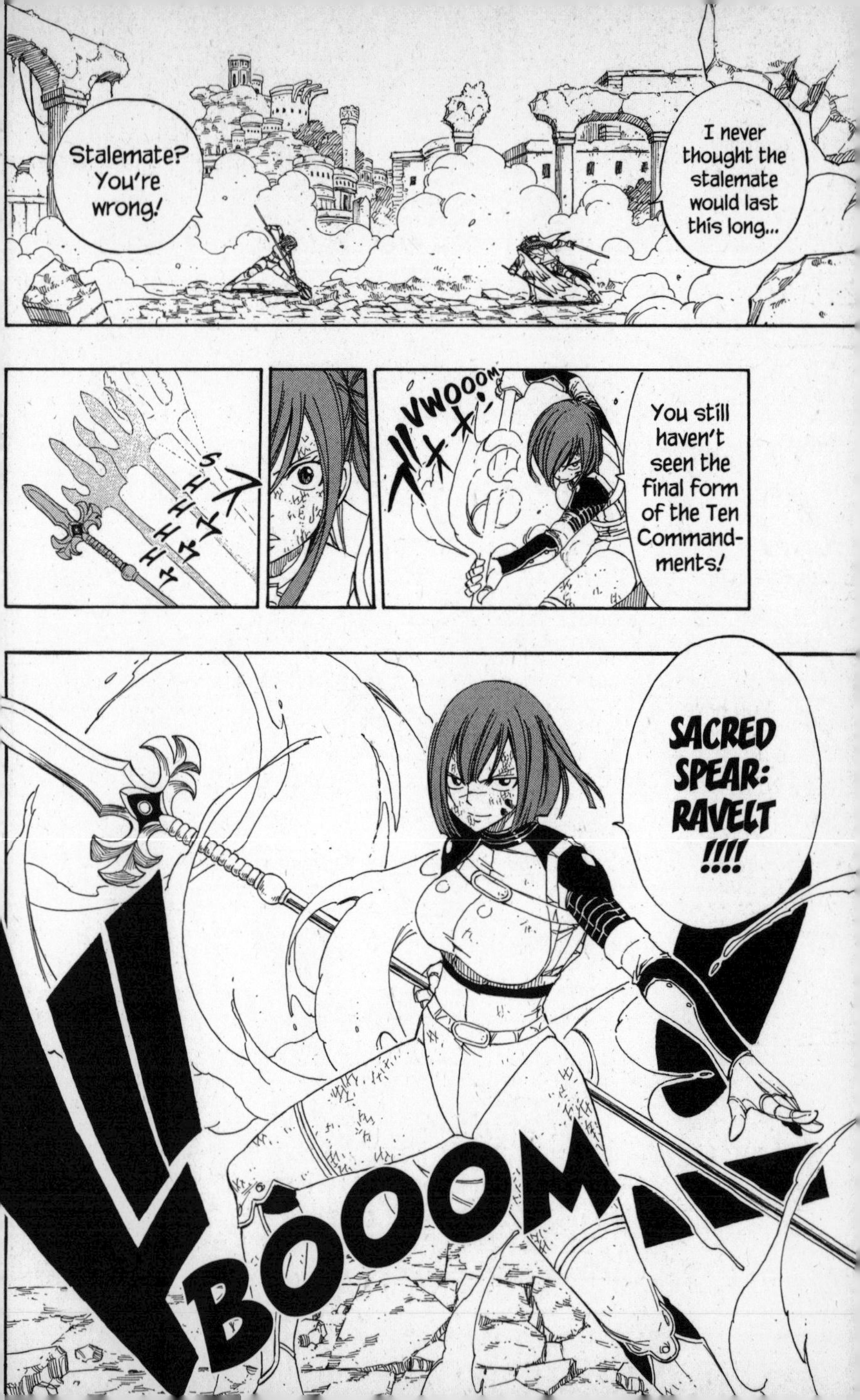
I never thought the stalemate would last this long...
Stalemate? You're wrong!
VWOOOM
You still haven't seen the final form of the Ten Commandments!
SHHHHH
SACRED SPEAR: RAVELT!!!!
BOOOM

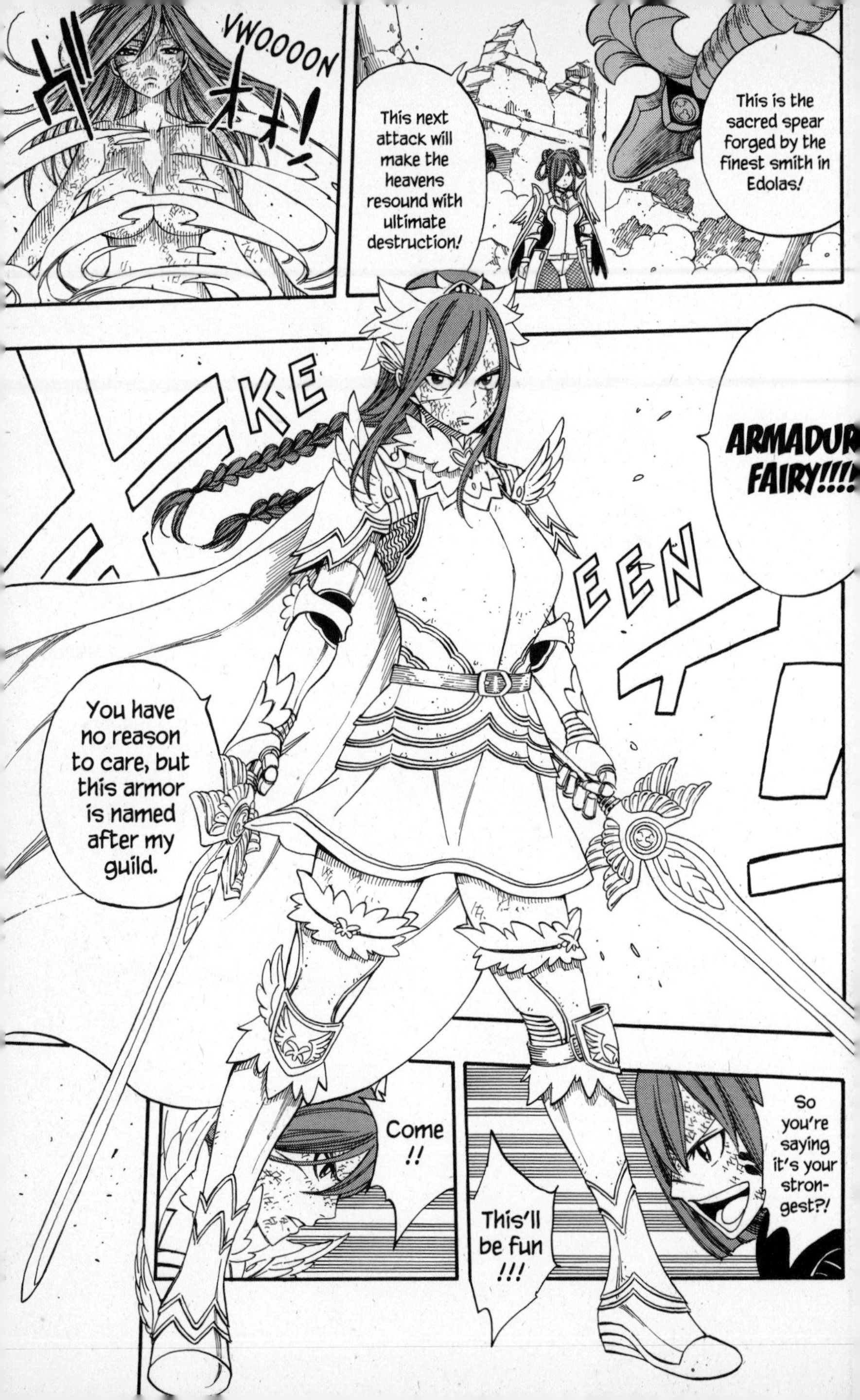
This is the sacred spear forged by the finest smith in Edolas!
This next attack will make the heavens resound with ultimate destruction!
VWOOOON
ARMADUR FAIRY!!!!
KE
EEN
You have no reason to care, but this armor is named after my guild.
So you're saying it's your strongest?!
This'll be fun!!!
Come!!

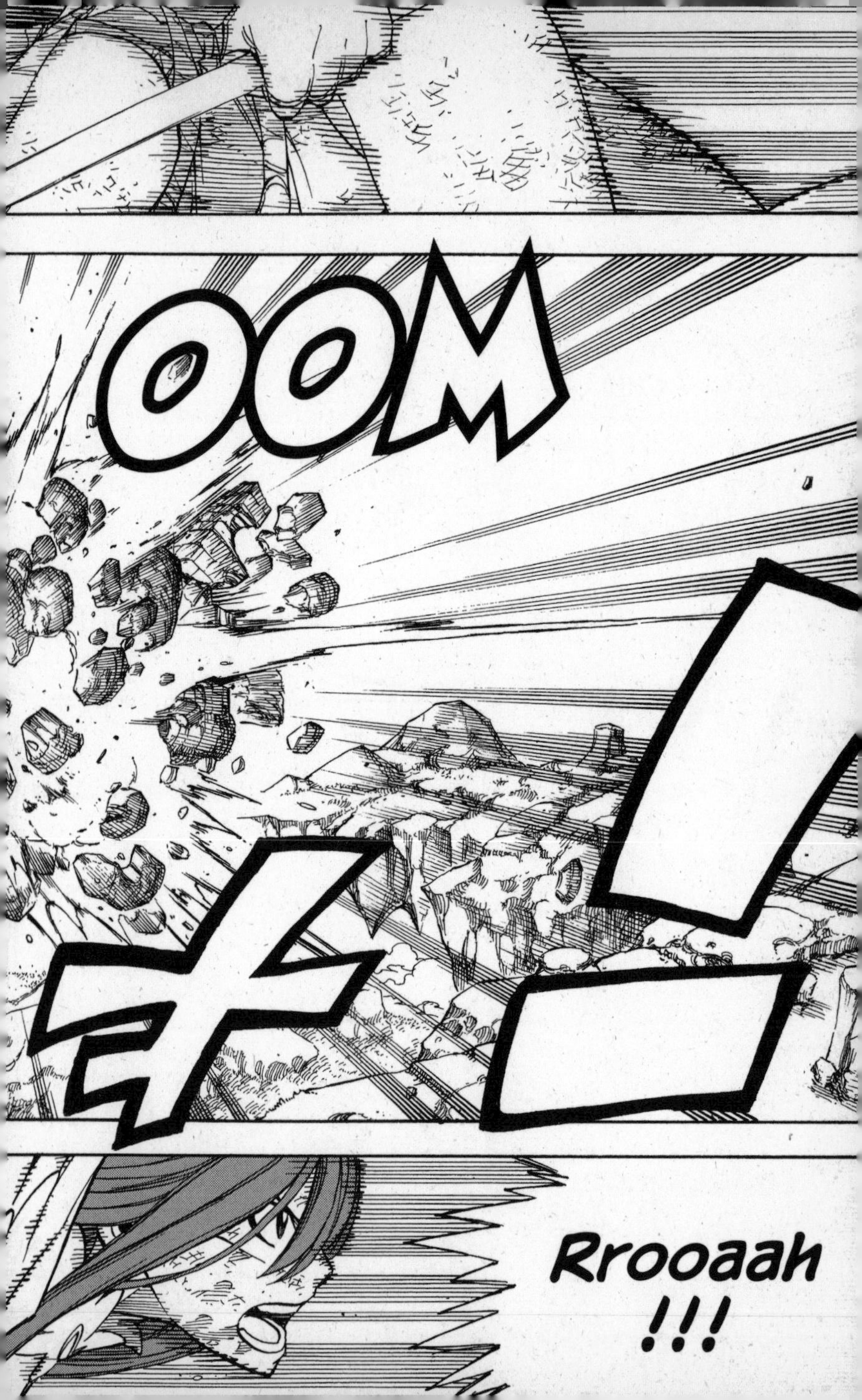
OOM
Rrooaah !!!

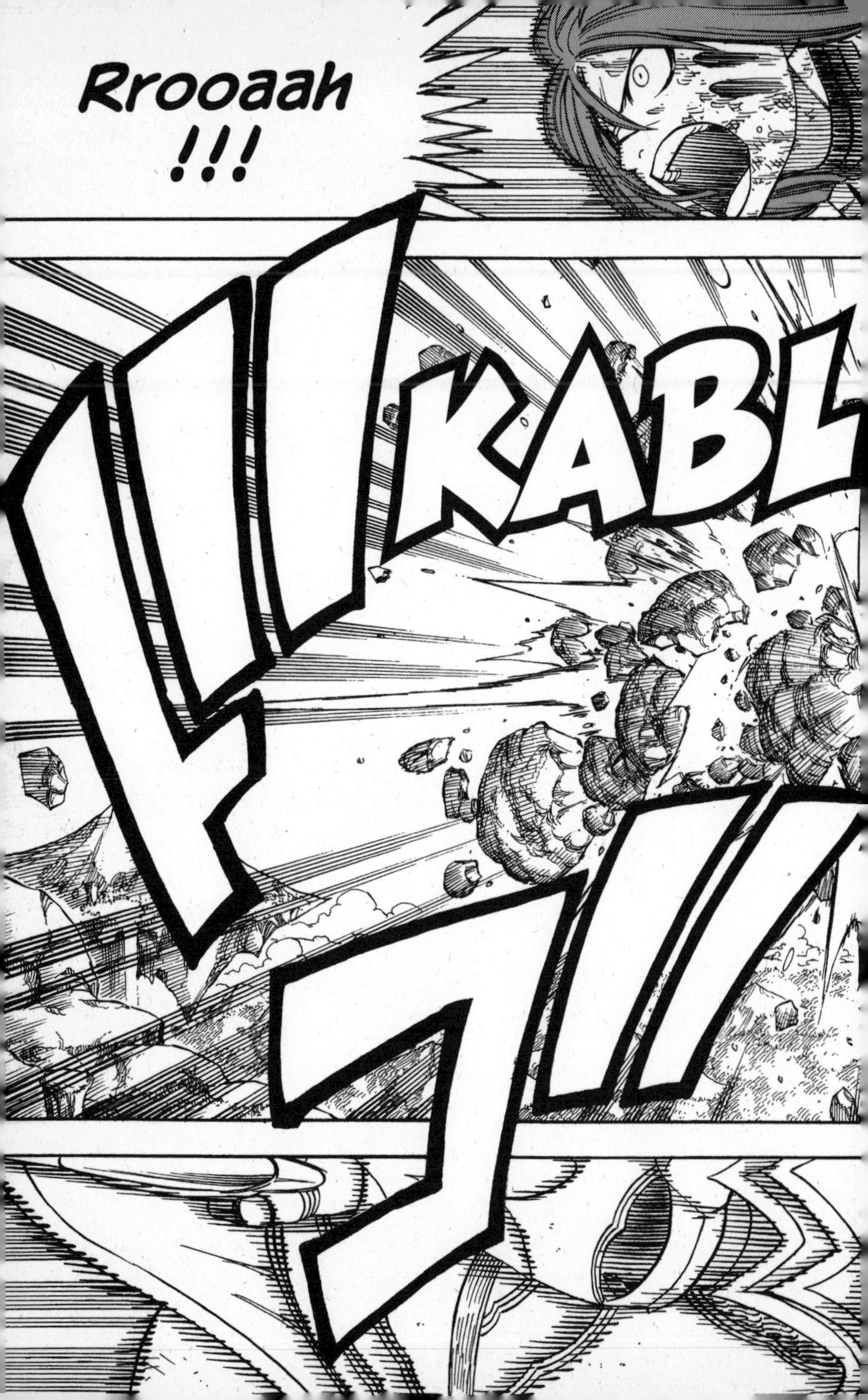
Rrooaah
!!!
KABL

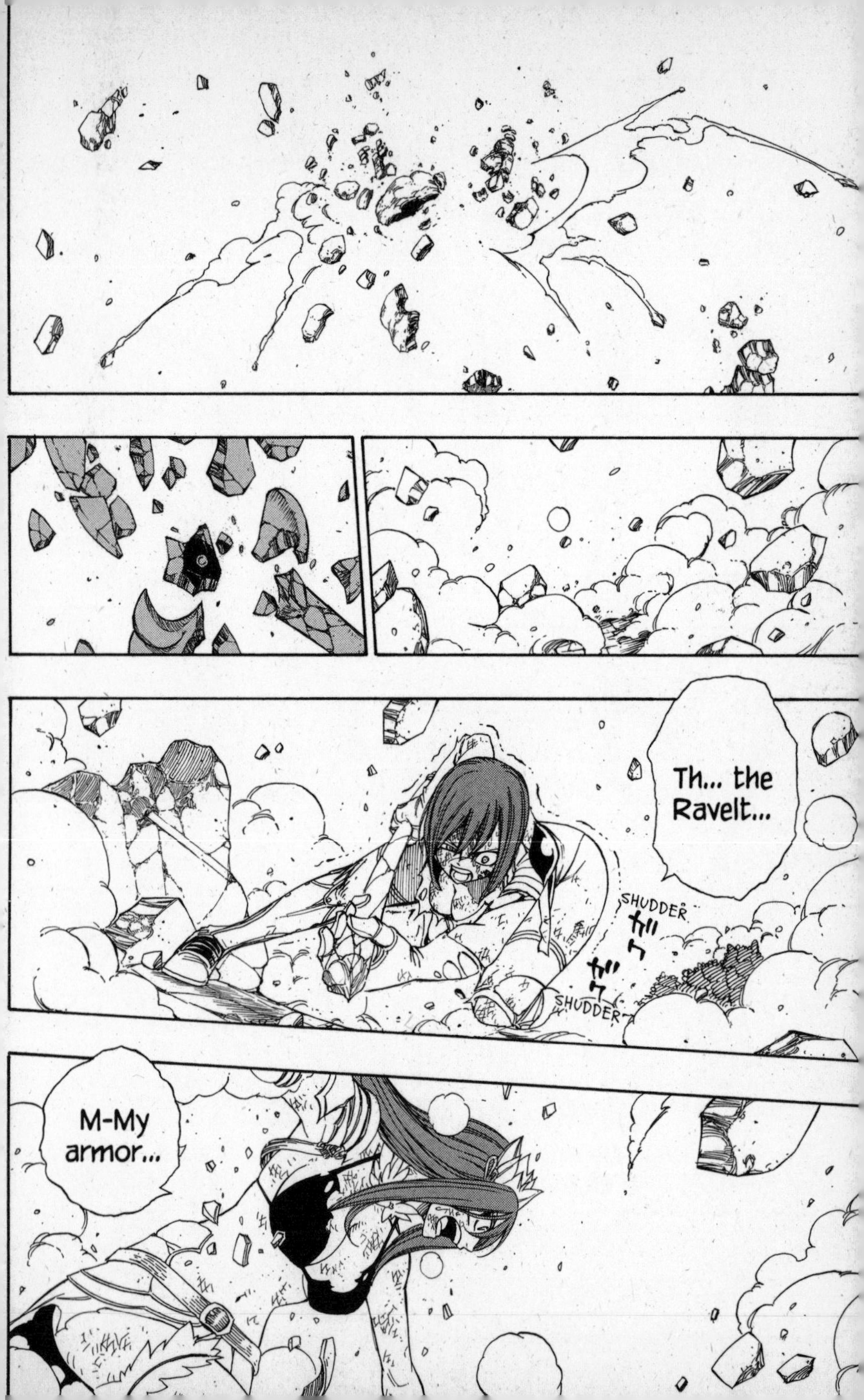

Th... the Ravelt...
SHUDDER
SHUDDER
M-My armor...

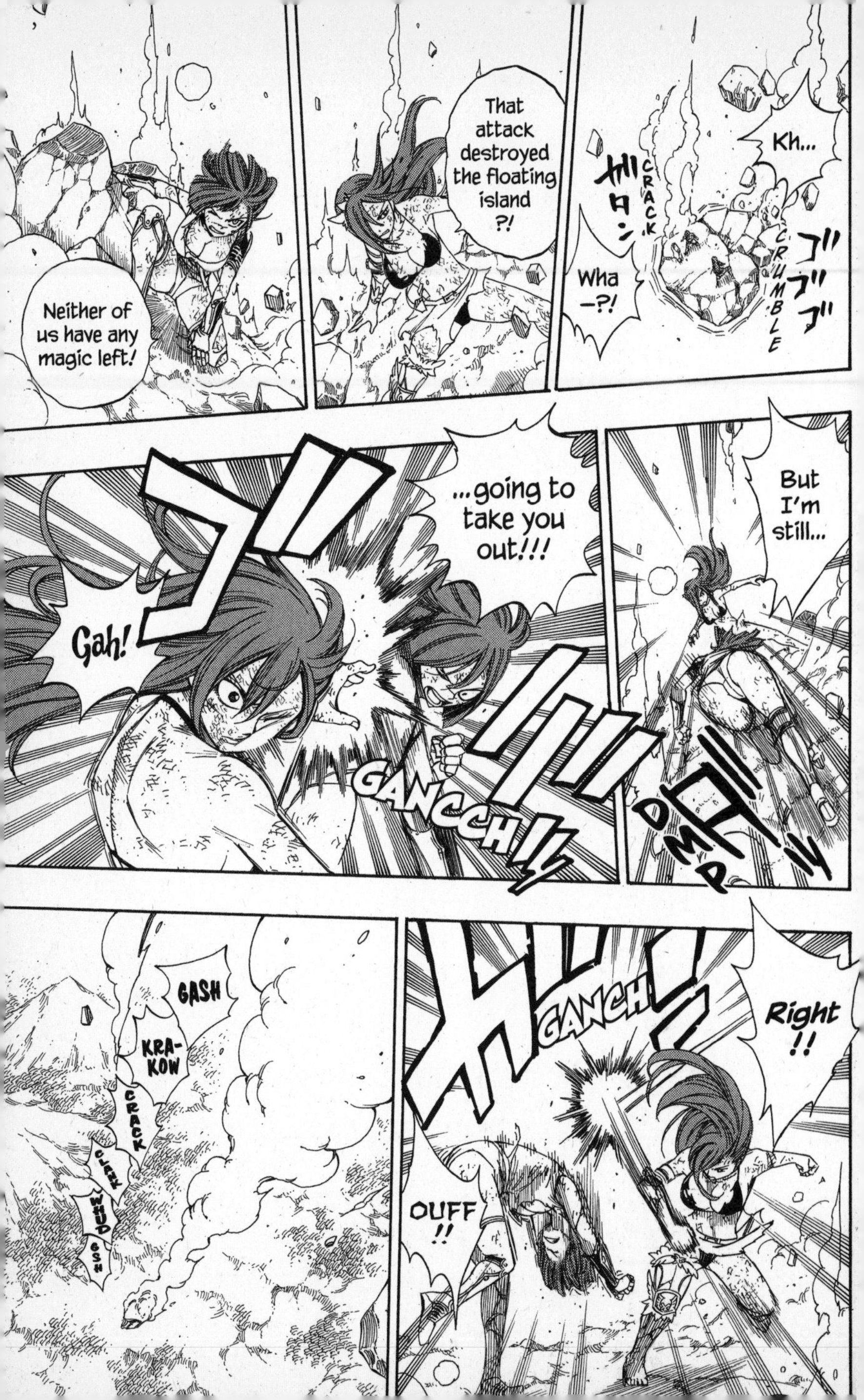
Kh...
ゴゴゴ
CRUMBLE
CRACK
Wha—?!
That attack destroyed the floating island ?!
Neither of us have any magic left!
But I'm still...
DMP
...going to take you out!!!
Gah!
GANCCH!!
Right!!
GANCH
OUFF!!
GASH
KRA-KOW
CRACK
CLANK
WHUD
GSH

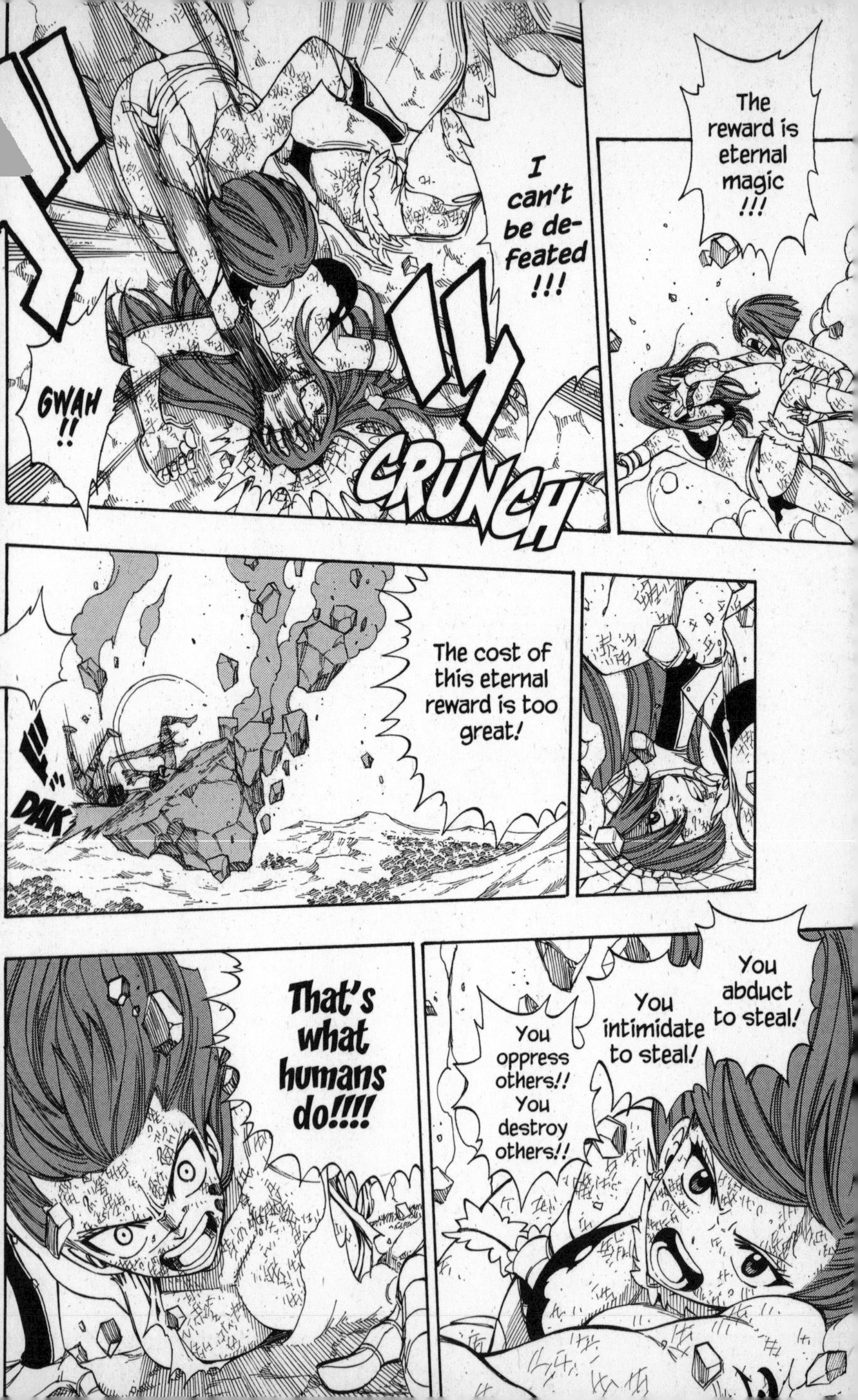
The reward is eternal magic!!!
I can't be de-feated!!!
CRUNCH
GWAH!!
The cost of this eternal reward is too great!
DAK
You abduct to steal!
You intimidate to steal!
You oppress others!! You destroy others!!
That's what humans do!!!!

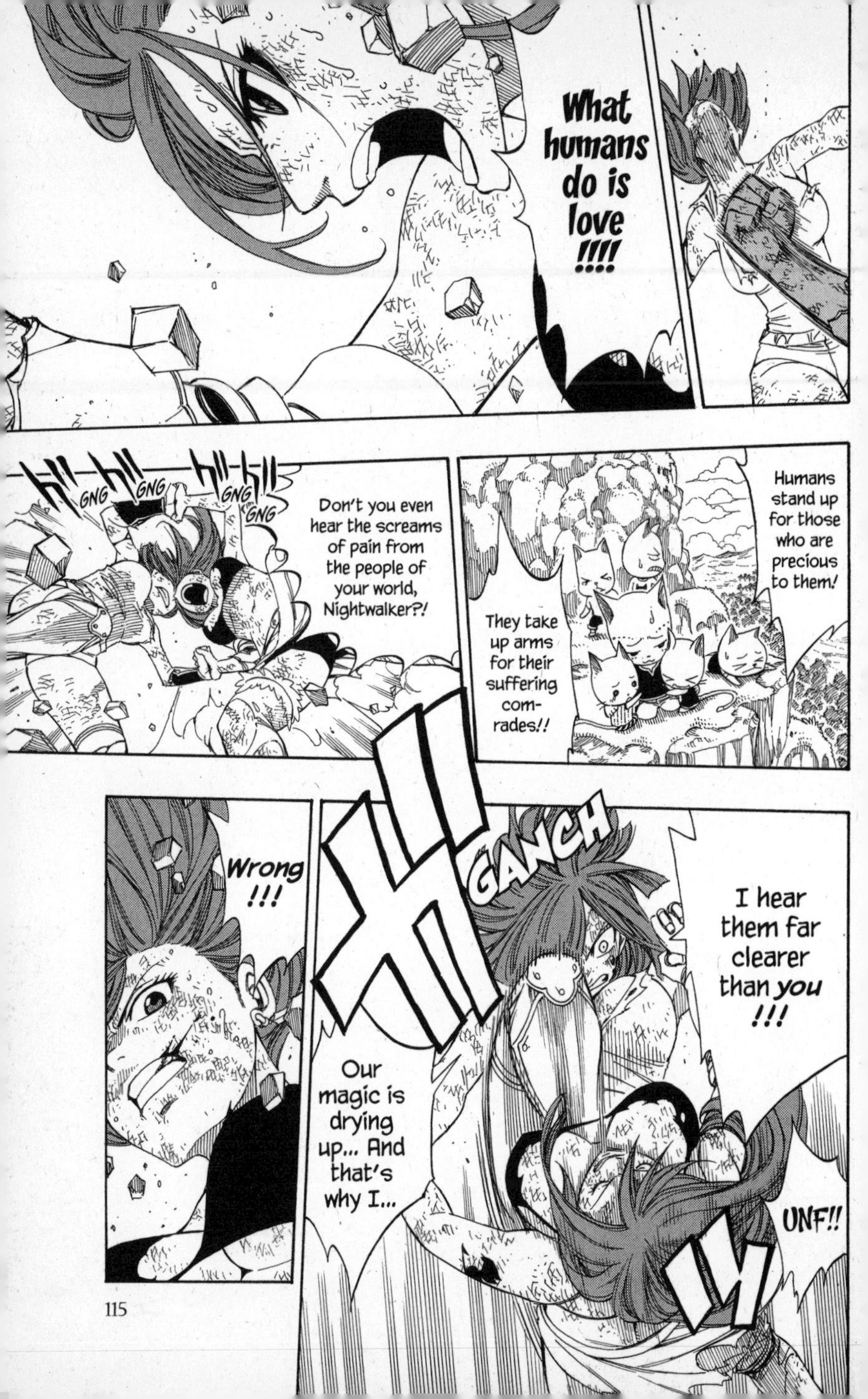

What humans do is love!!!!
Humans stand up for those who are precious to them!
They take up arms for their suffering com-rades!!
GNG GNG GNG GNG
Don't you even hear the screams of pain from the people of your world, Nightwalker?!
GANCH
I hear them far clearer than *you*!!!
Our magic is drying up... And that's why I...
UNF!!
Wrong!!!

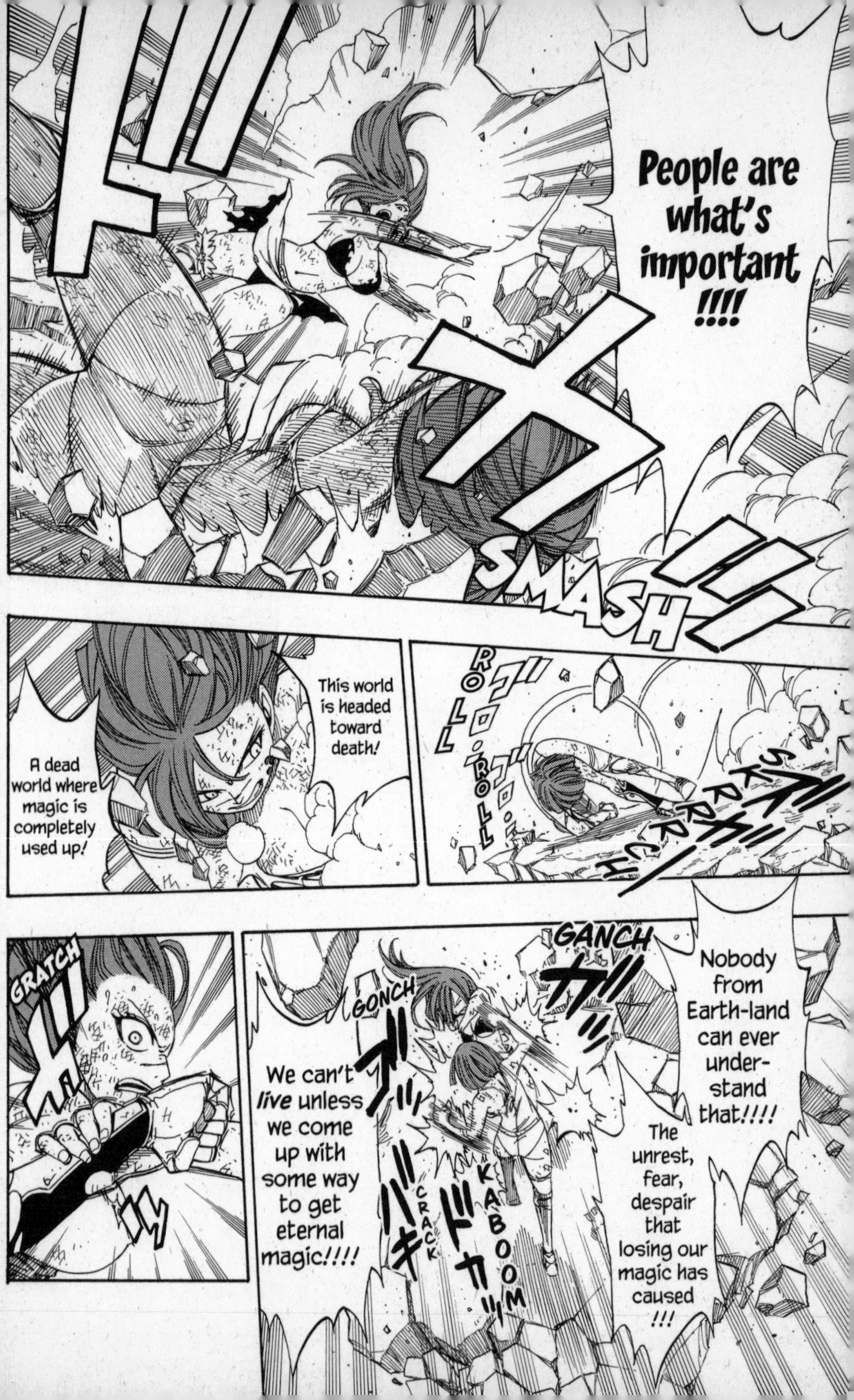
People are what's important!!!!
SMASH
ROLL ROLL
SKRRCH
This world is headed toward death!
A dead world where magic is completely used up!
GANCH
Nobody from Earth-land can ever under-stand that!!!!
The unrest, fear, despair that losing our magic has caused!!!
GONCH
We can't *live* unless we come up with some way to get eternal magic!!!!
CRACK
KABOOM
GRATCH

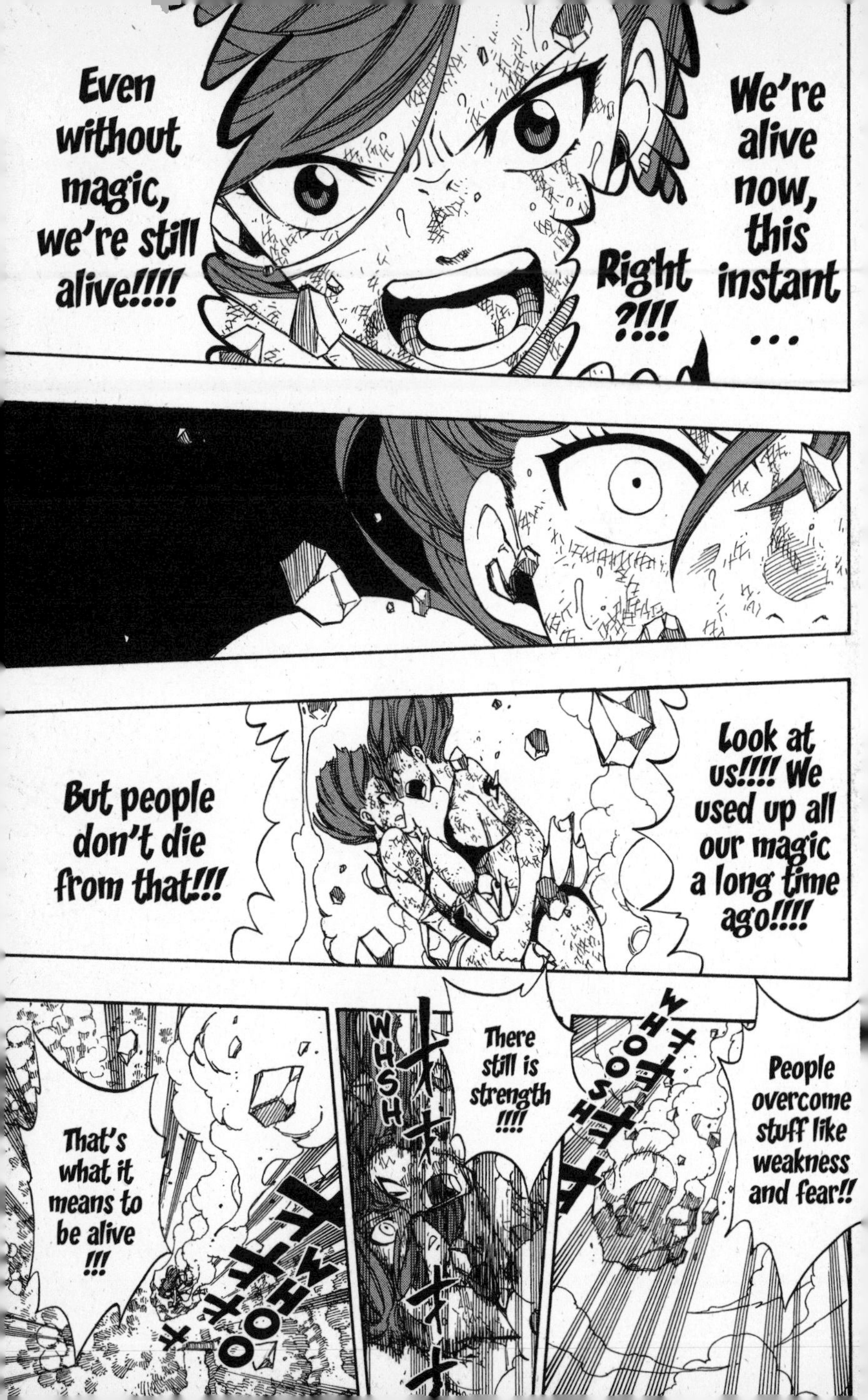
We're alive now, this instant...
Right?!!!
Even without magic, we're still alive!!!!
Look at us!!!! We used up all our magic a long time ago!!!!
But people don't die from that!!!
People overcome stuff like weakness and fear!!
WHOOSH
There still is strength!!!!
WHSH
That's what it means to be alive!!!
WHOOOSH

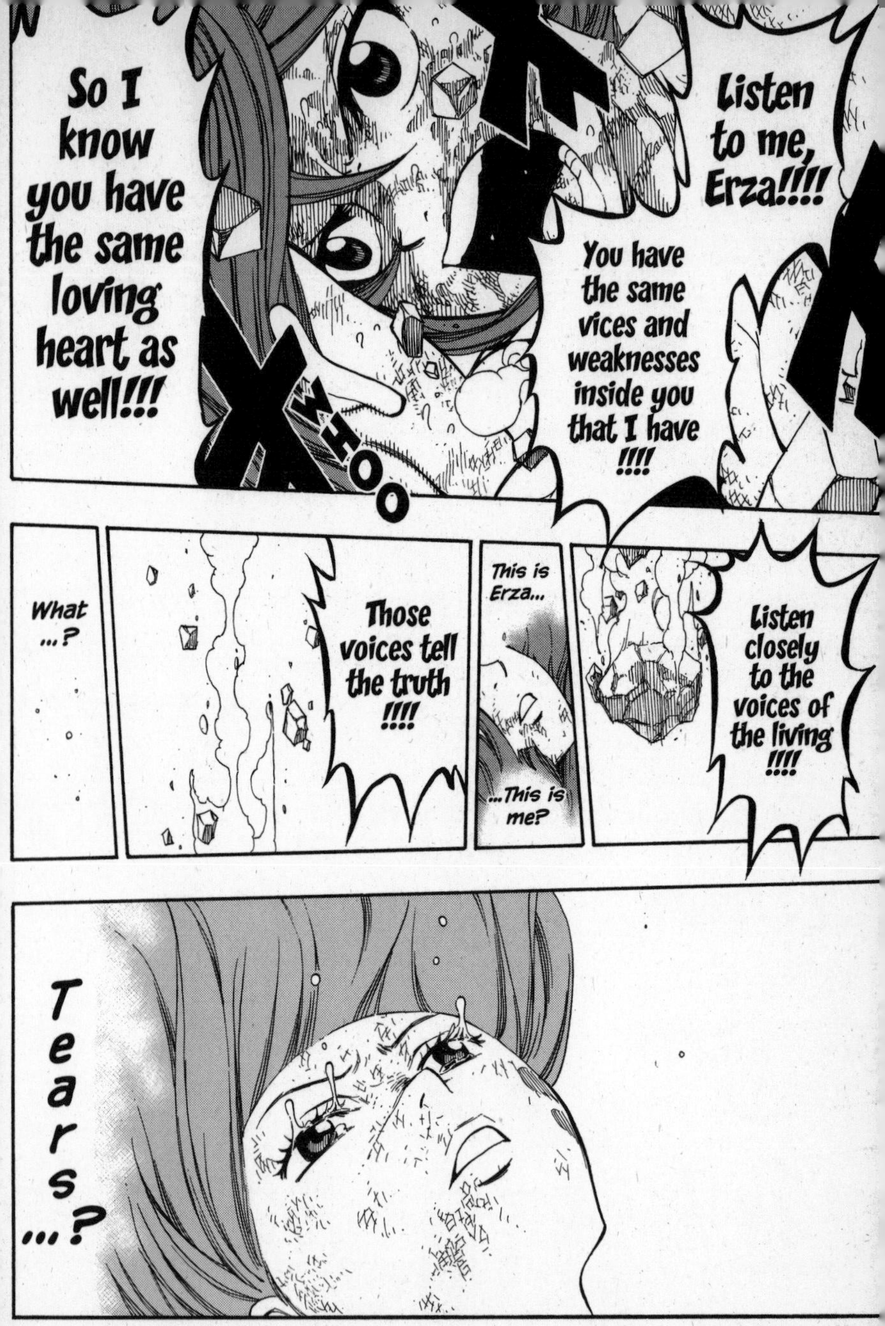
Listen to me, Erza!!!!
You have the same vices and weaknesses inside you that I have !!!!
WHOO
So I know you have the same loving heart as well!!!
Listen closely to the voices of the living !!!!
This is Erza...
...This is me?
Those voices tell the truth !!!!
What ...?
Tears ...?

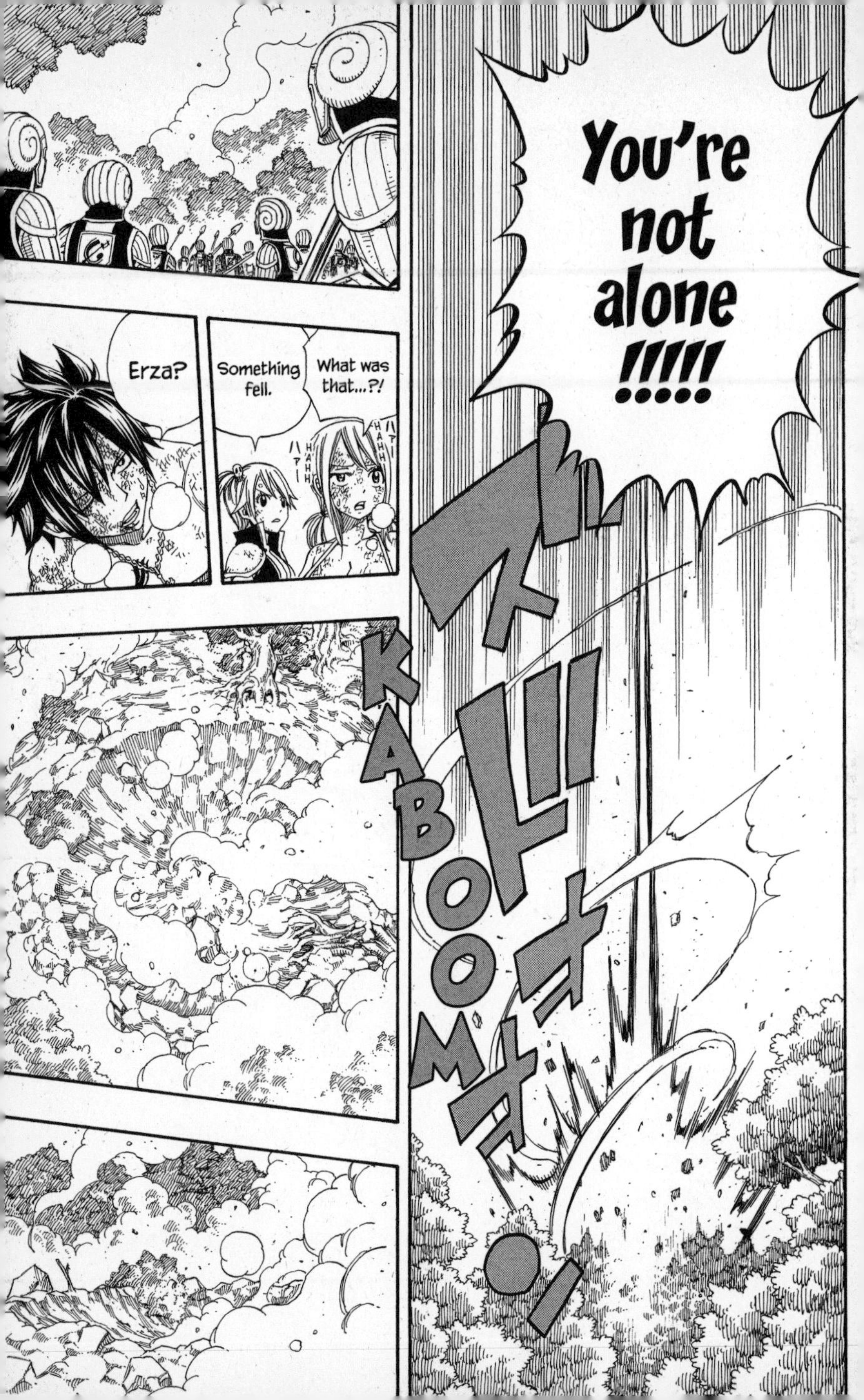
You're not alone!!!!!
KABOOM
What was that...?!
Something fell.
Erza?

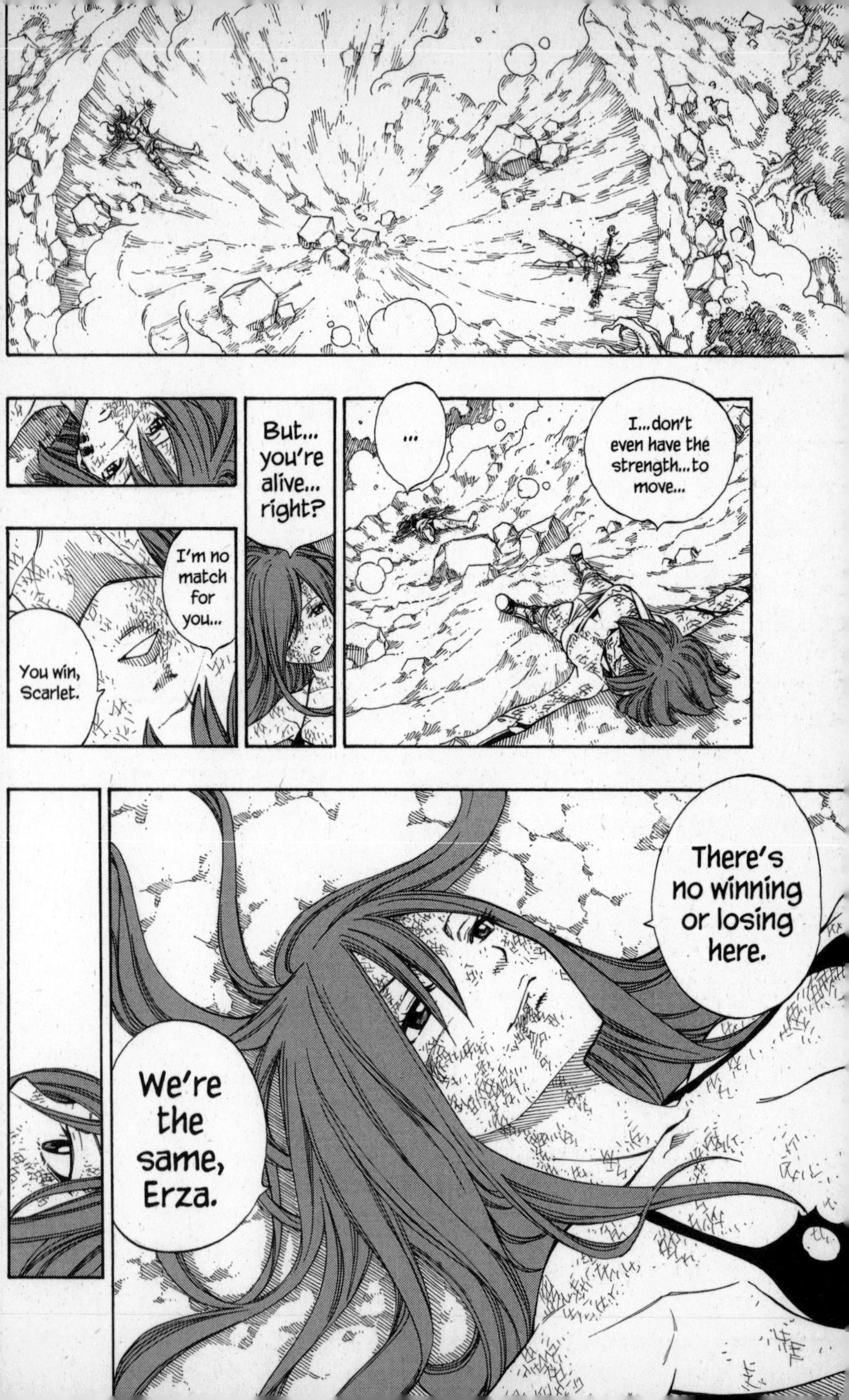
I...don't even have the strength...to move...
...
But... you're alive... right?
I'm no match for you...
You win, Scarlet.
There's no winning or losing here.
We're the same, Erza.

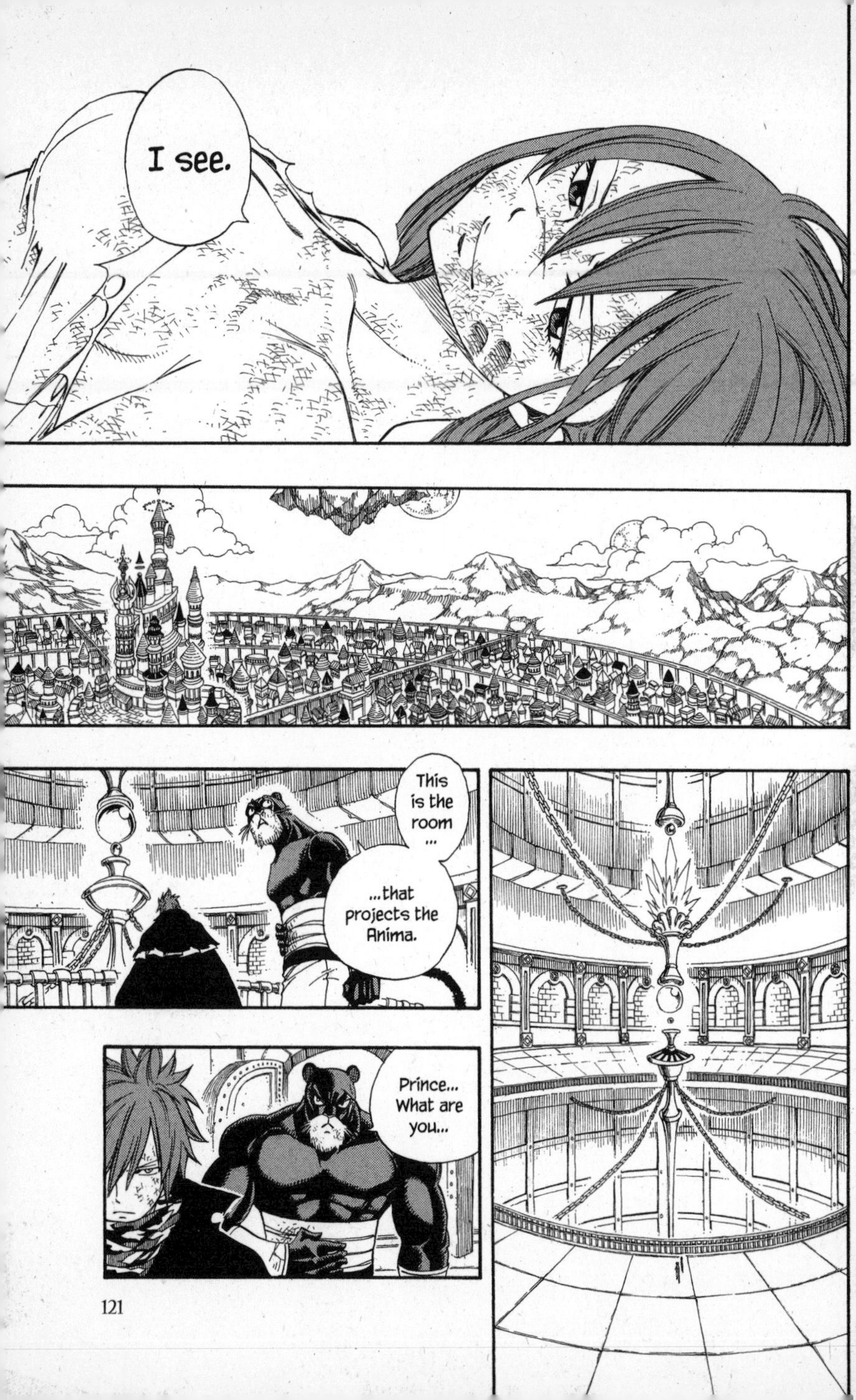
I see.
This is the room ...
...that projects the Anima.
Prince... What are you...

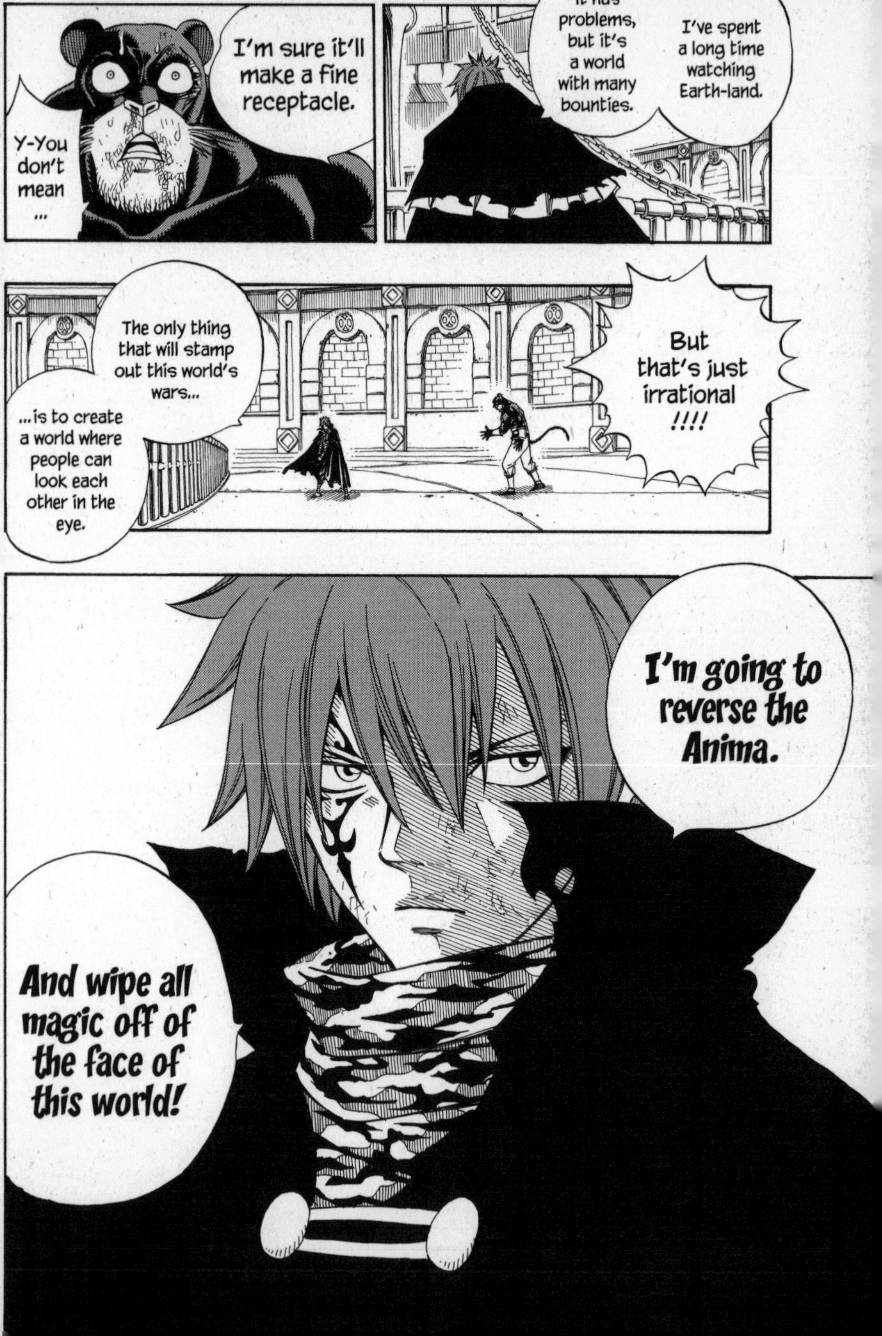
I've spent a long time watching Earth-land.
It has problems, but it's a world with many bounties.
I'm sure it'll make a fine receptacle.
Y-You don't mean ...
But that's just irrational !!!!
The only thing that will stamp out this world's wars...
...is to create a world where people can look each other in the eye.
I'm going to reverse the Anima.
And wipe all magic off of the face of this world!

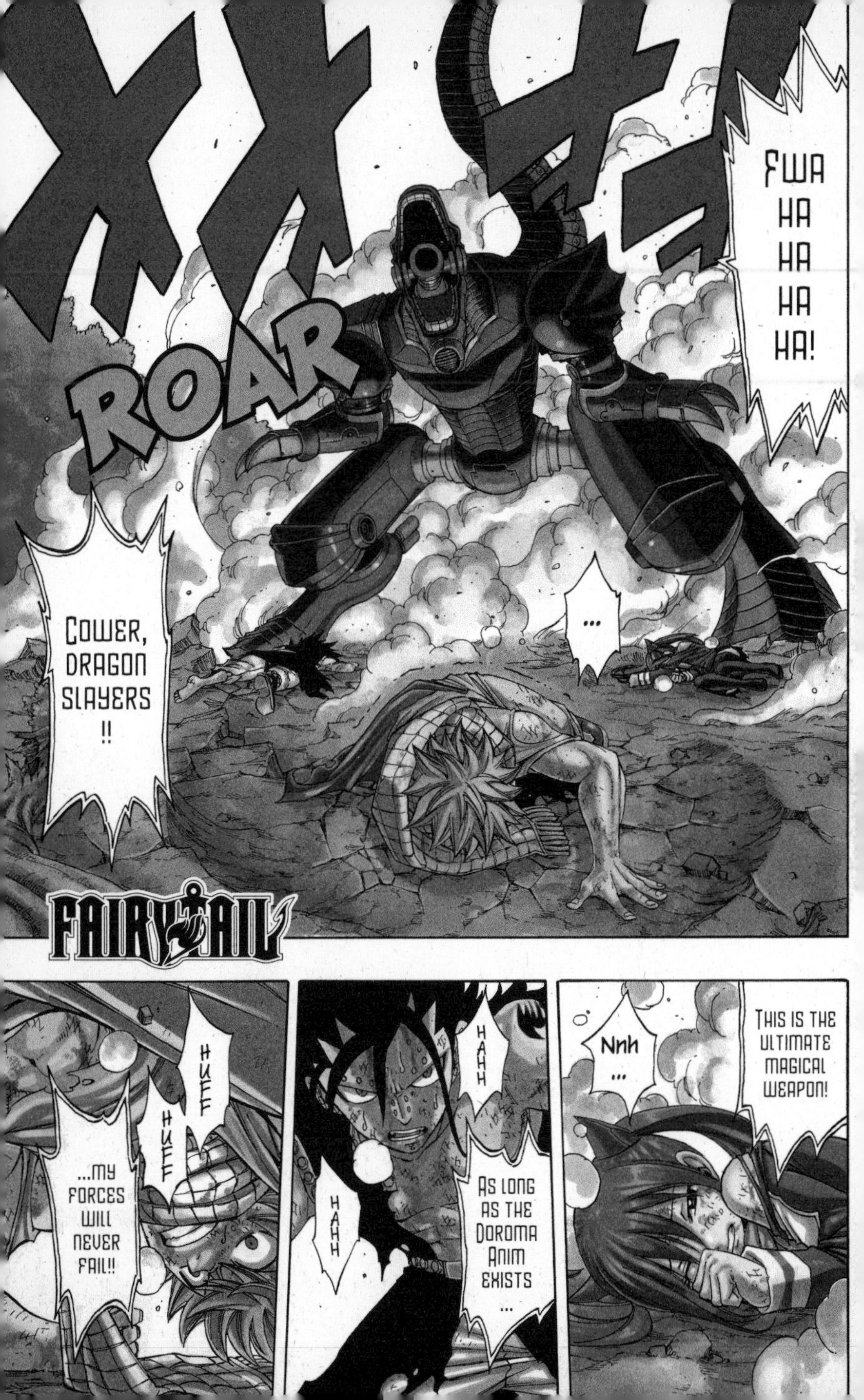
FWA HA HA HA HA!
ROAR
...
COWER, DRAGON SLAYERS !!
THIS IS THE ULTIMATE MAGICAL WEAPON!
Nnh ...
HAHH
AS LONG AS THE DOROMA ANIM EXISTS ...
HAHH
HUFF
HUFF
...MY FORCES WILL NEVER FAIL!!

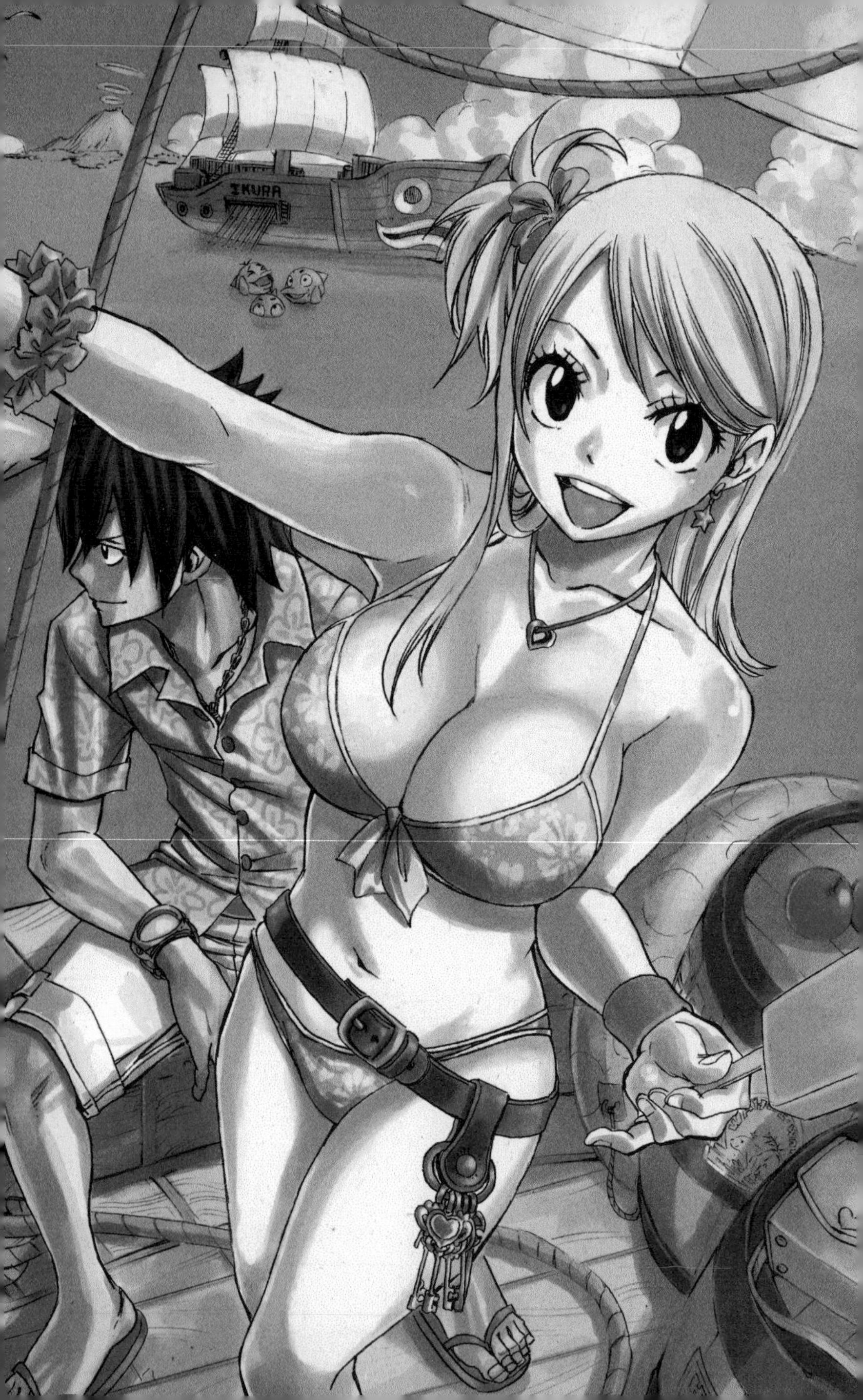
IKURA

Chapter 194: I'm Standing Right Here

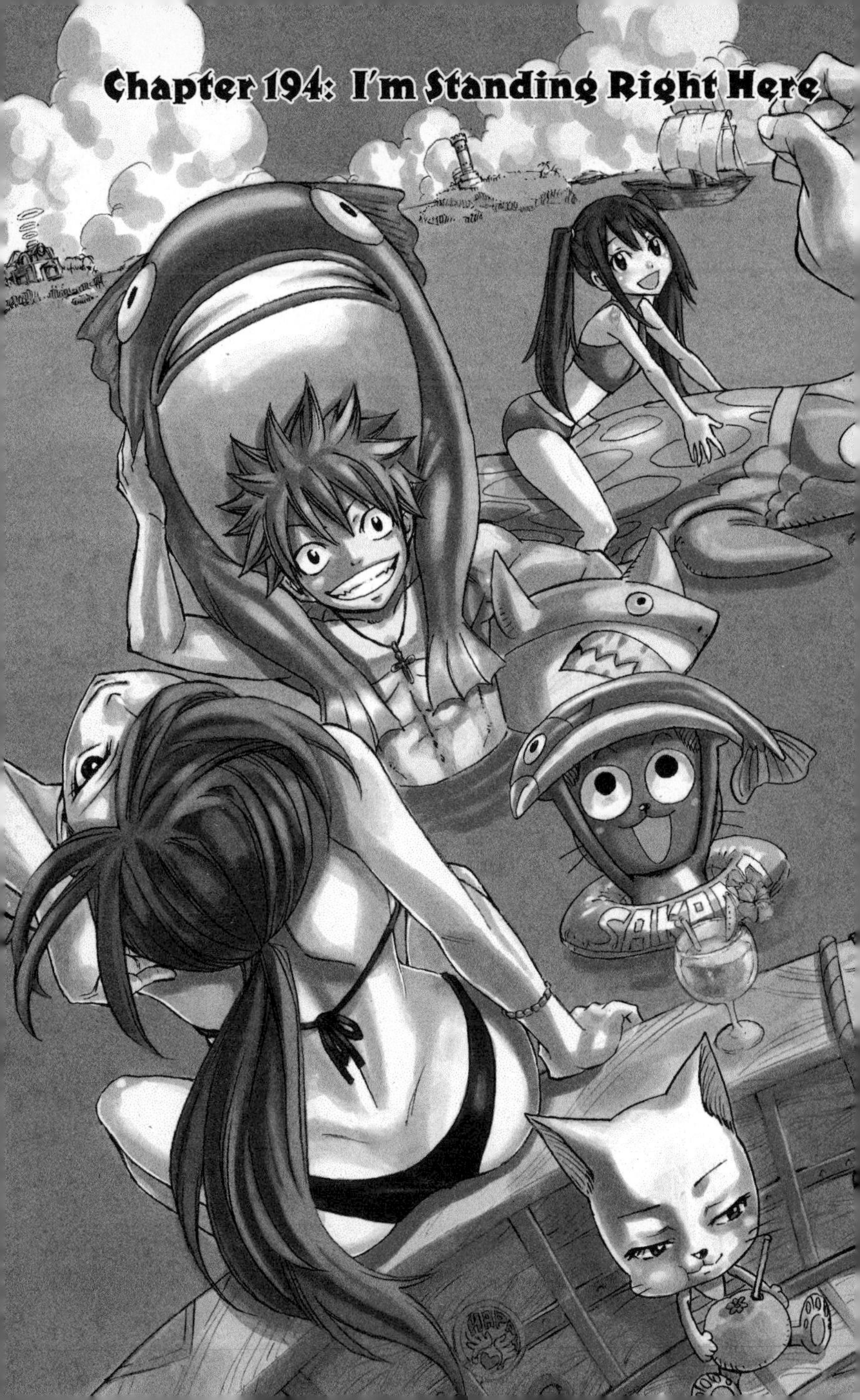

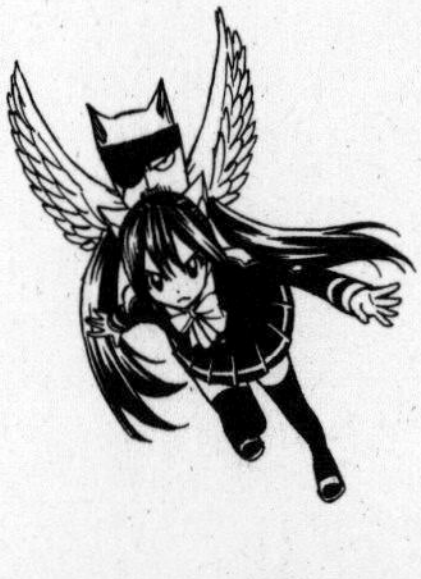

FAIRY TAIL

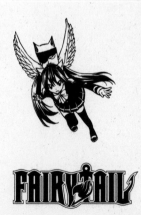

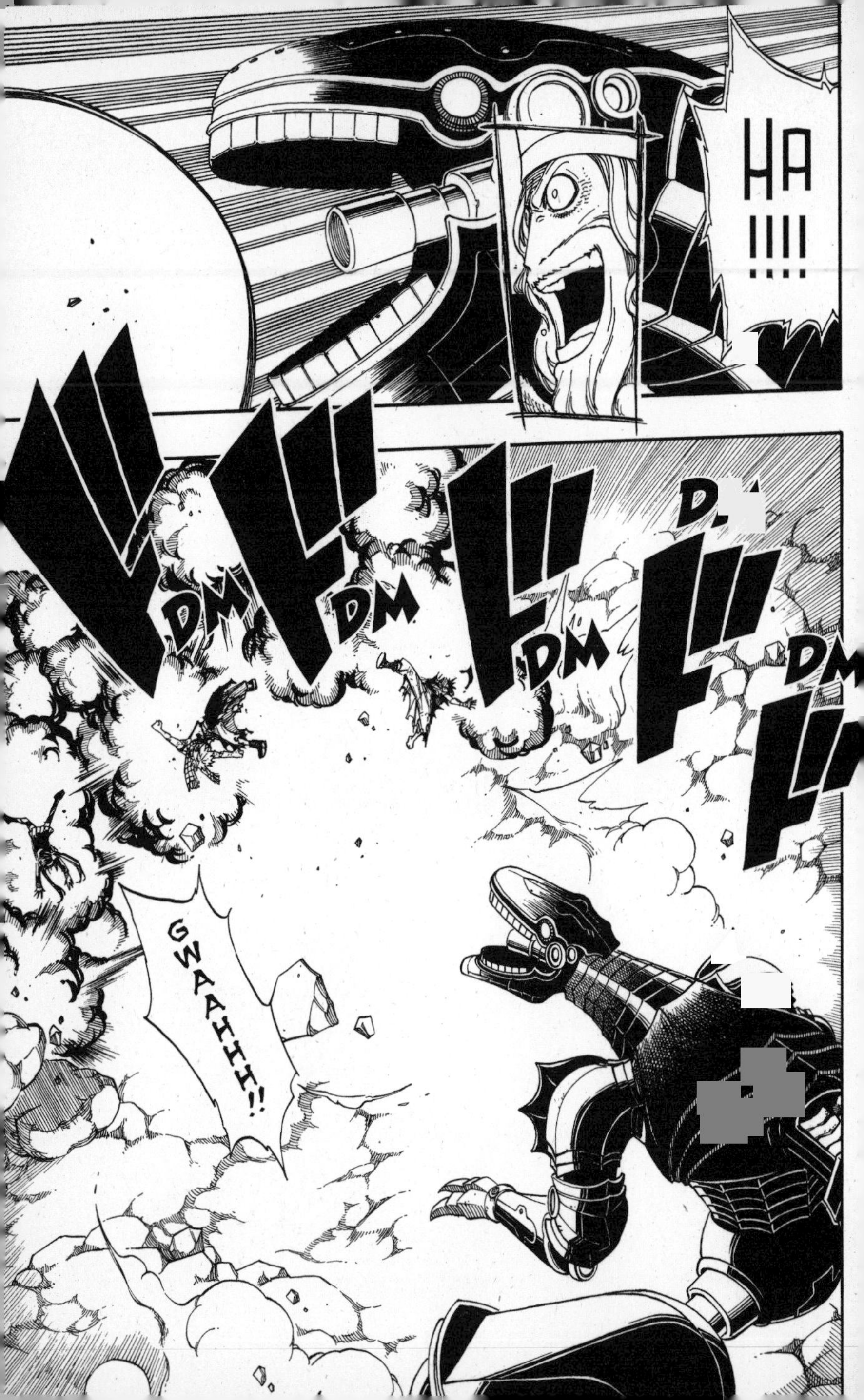
HA!!!!
DM
DM
DM
DM
DM
GWAAHHH!!

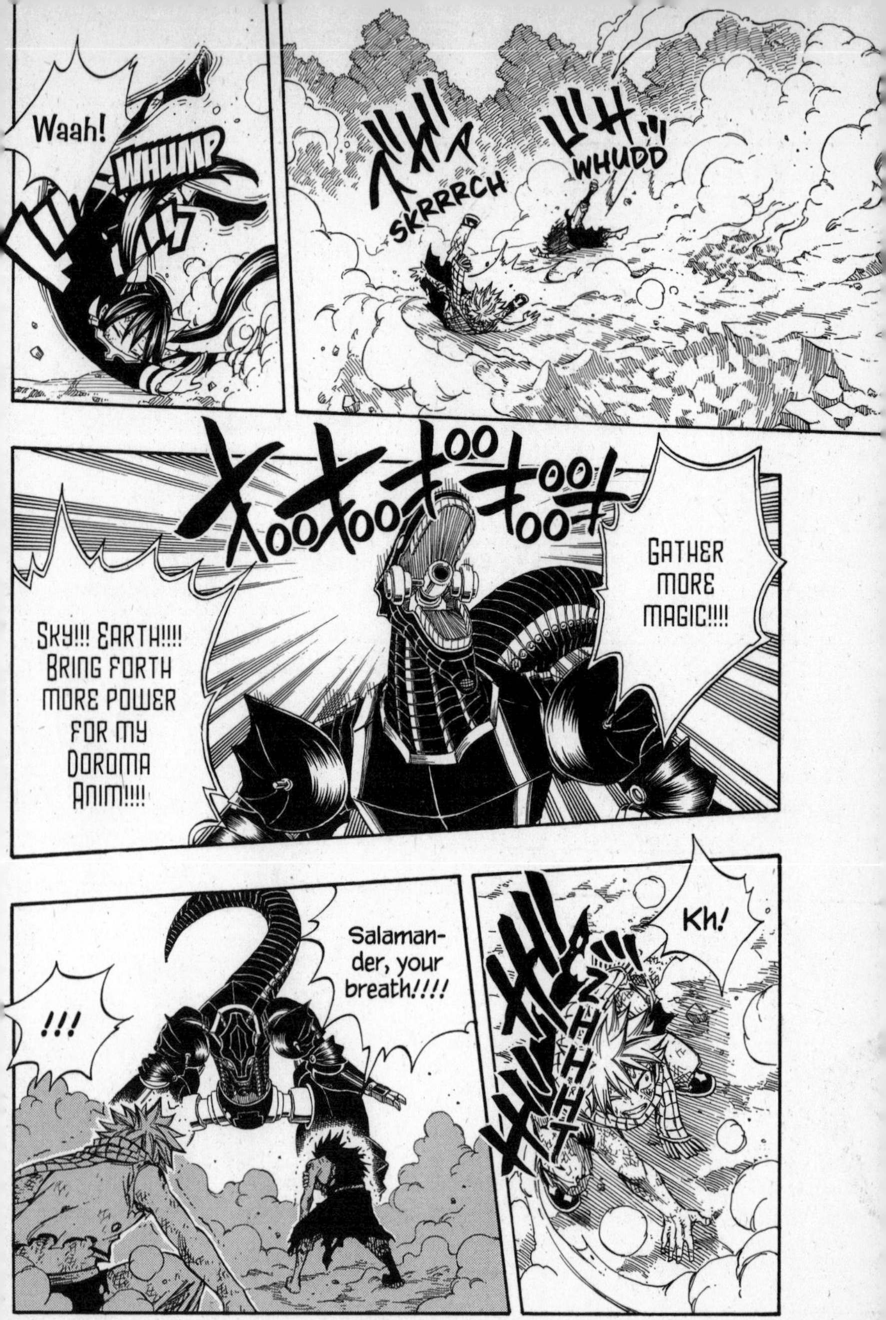
WHUDD
SKRRRCH
Waah!
WHUMP
GATHER MORE MAGIC!!!!
SKY!!! EARTH!!!! BRING FORTH MORE POWER FOR MY DOROMA ANIM!!!!
Kh!
Salamander, your breath!!!!
!!!

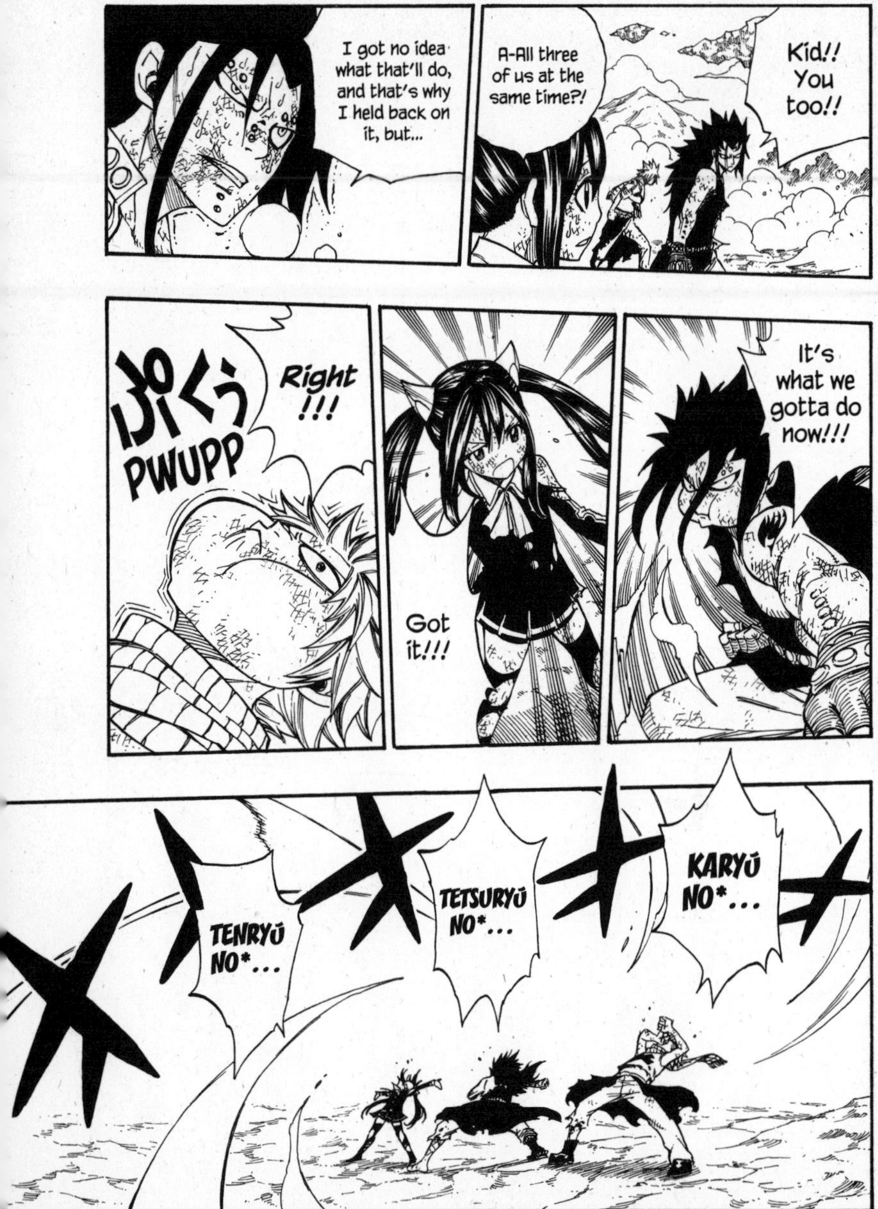
Kid!! You too!!
A-All three of us at the same time?!
I got no idea what that'll do, and that's why I held back on it, but...
It's what we gotta do now!!!
Got it!!!
Right!!!
ぷくぅ PWUPP
KARYŪ NO*...
TETSURYŪ NO*...
TENRYŪ NO*...

*Sky Dragon's... *Iron Dragon's... *Fire Dragon's...

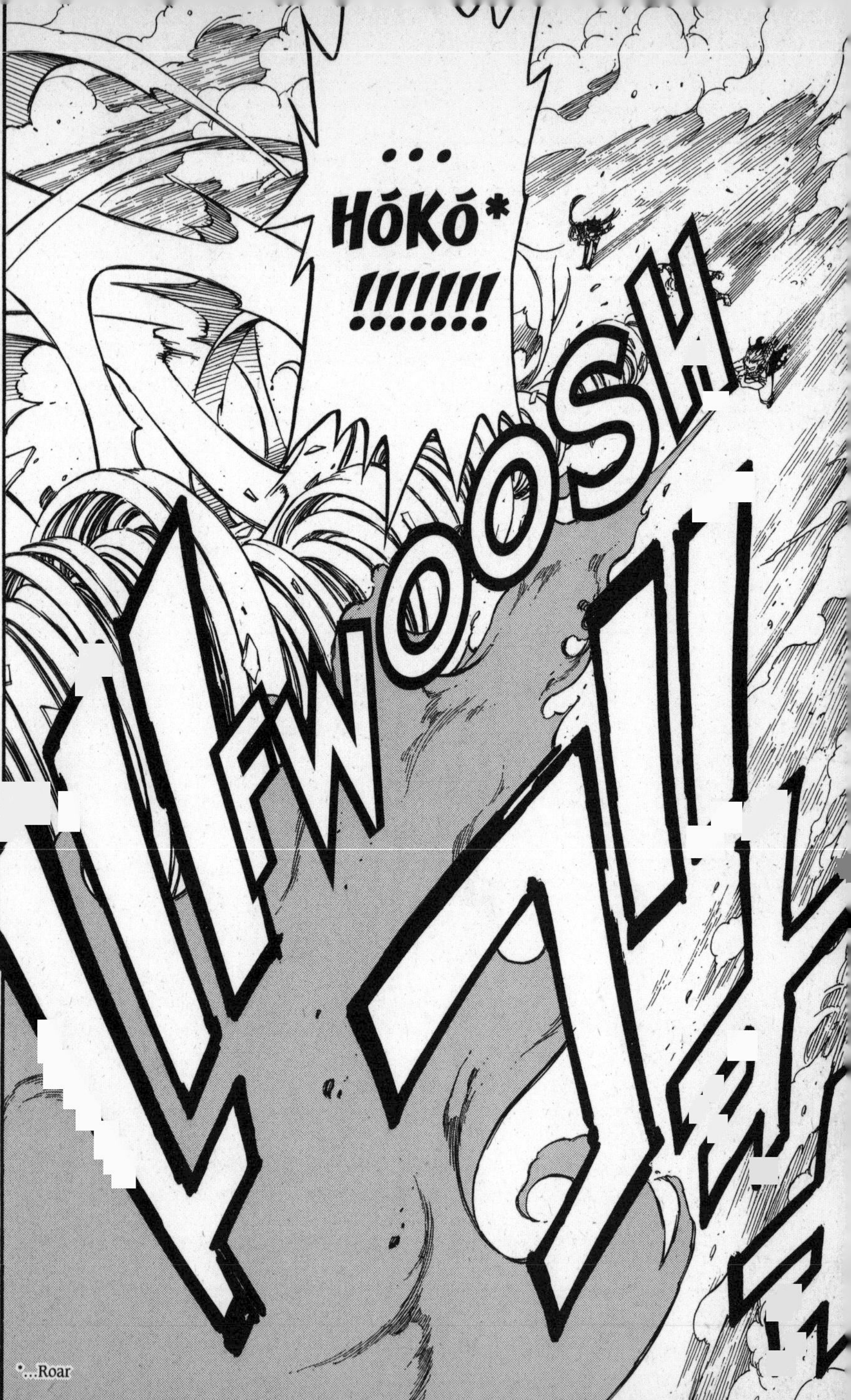
...HŌKŌ*!!!!!!!
FWOOSH

*...Roar

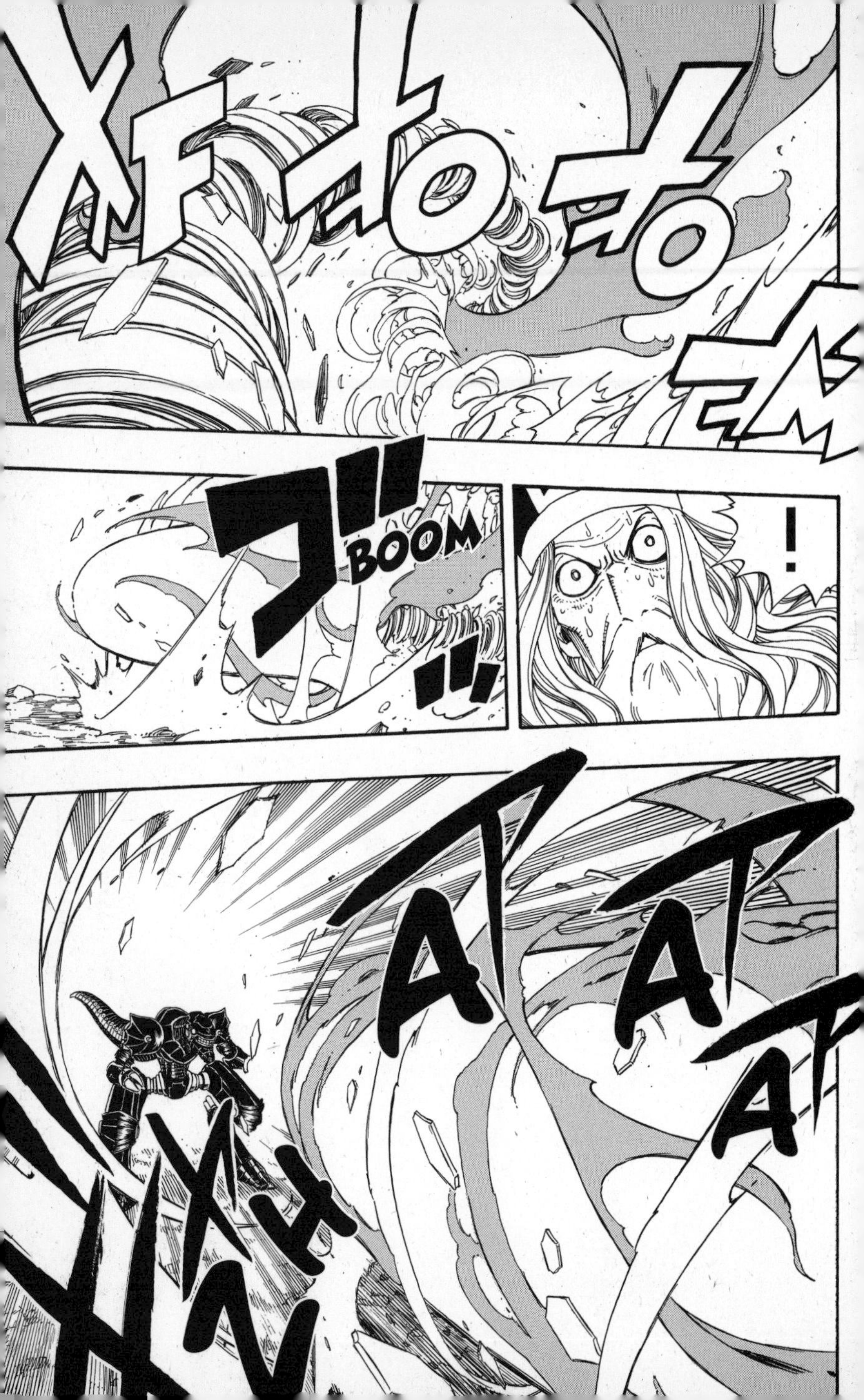

!
BOOM
AAAA

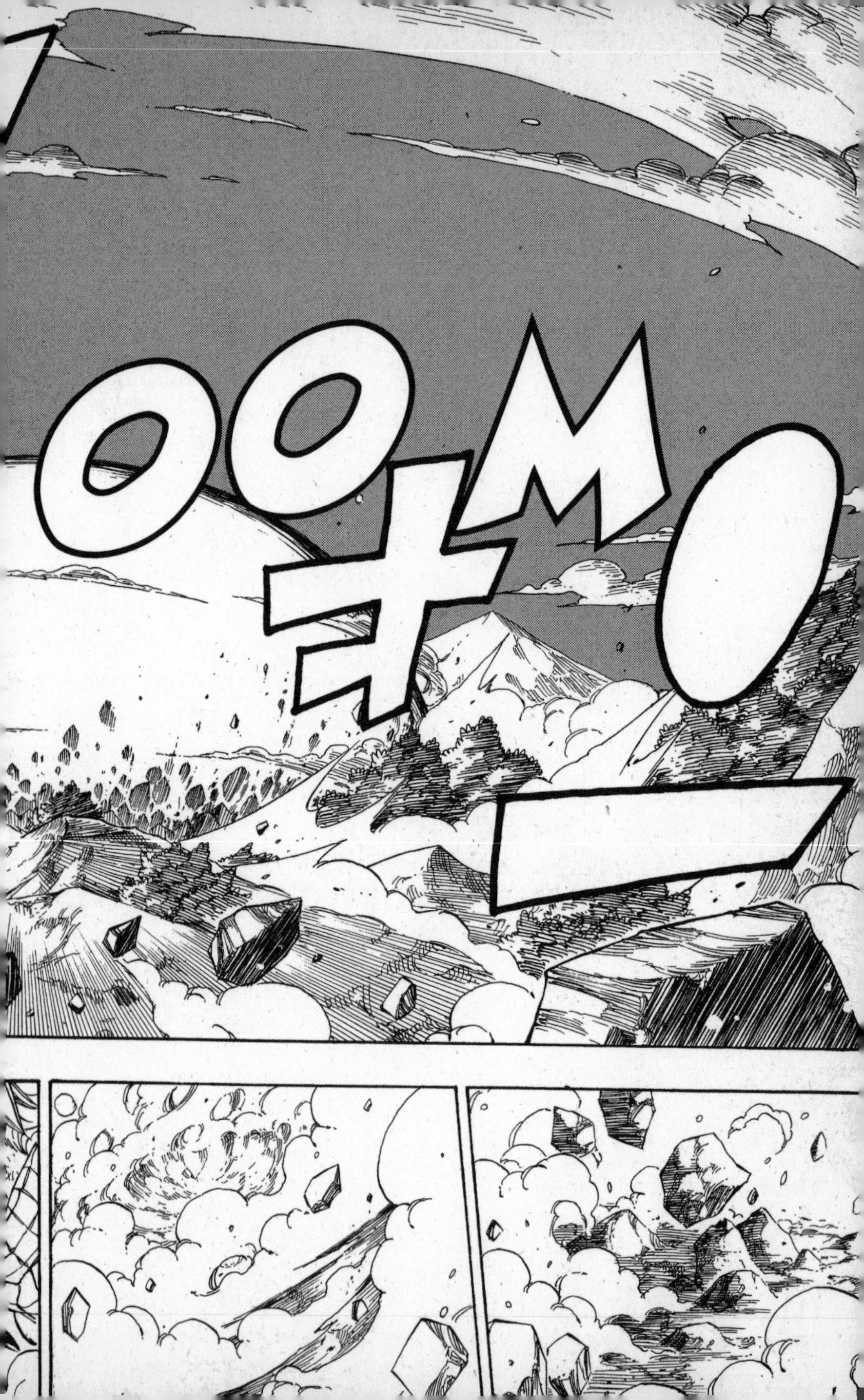

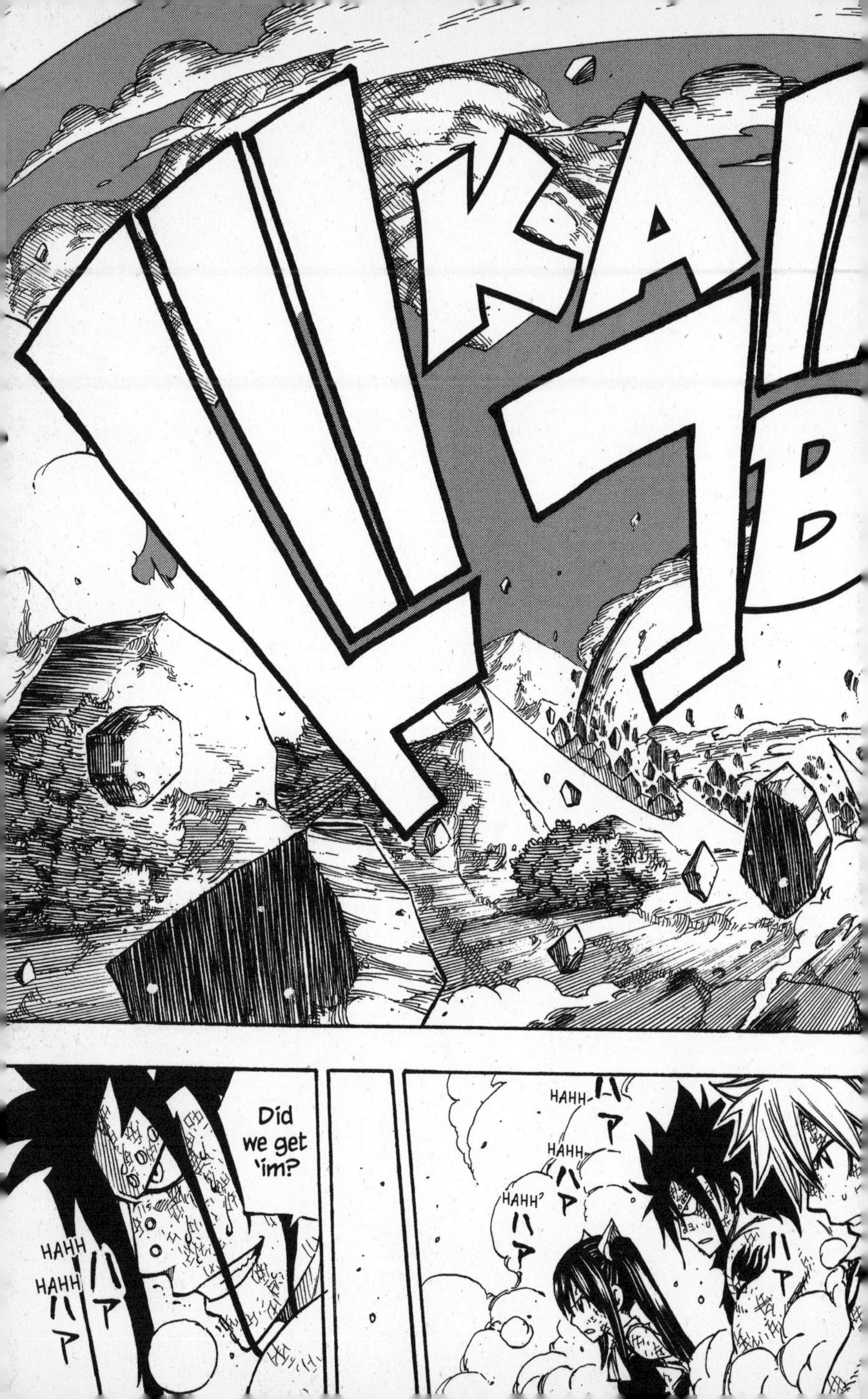
HAHH- ハァ
HAHH- ハァ
HAHH ハァ
ハァ
Did we get 'im?
HAHH ハァ
HAHH ハァ

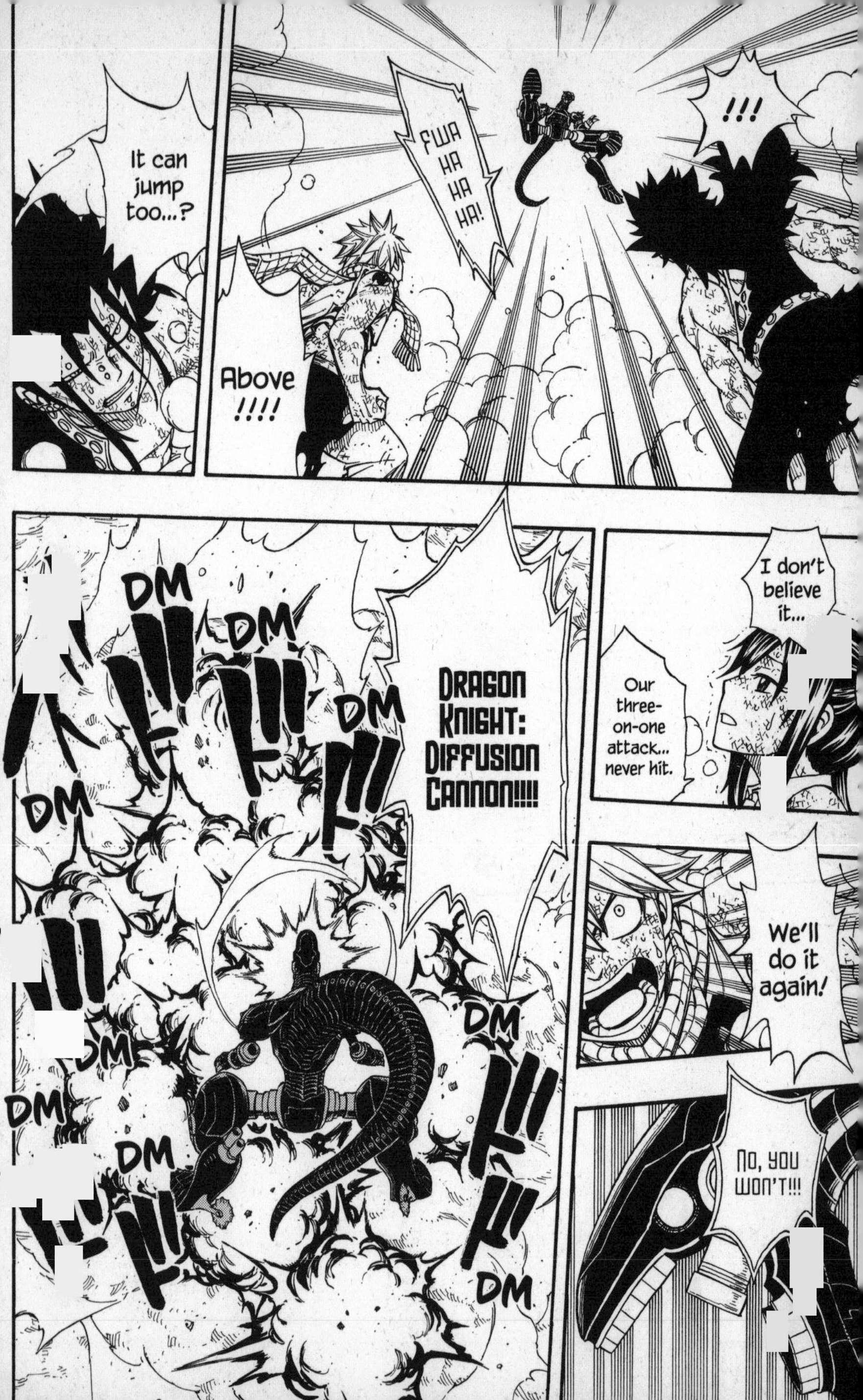
!!!
FWA HA HA HA!
Above !!!!
It can jump too...?
I don't believe it...
Our three-on-one attack... never hit.
We'll do it again!
No, YOU WON'T!!!
DRAGON KNIGHT: DIFFUSION CANNON!!!!!
DM
DM
DM
DM
DM
DM
DM
DM
DM

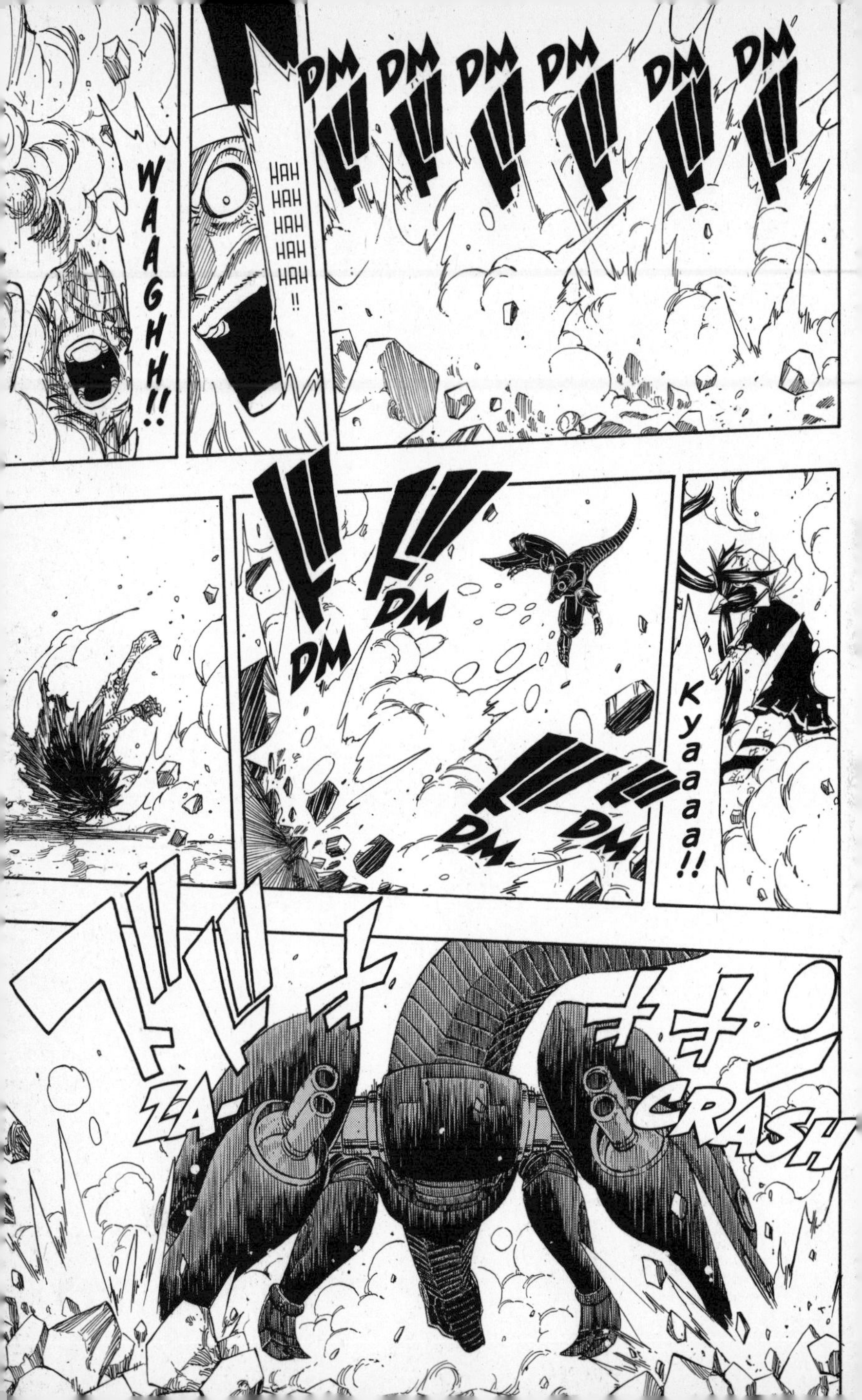

DM DM DM DM DM DM
HAH HAH HAH HAH HAH !!
WAAAGHH!!
Kyaaaaa!!
DM DM
DM DM
ZA-
CRASH

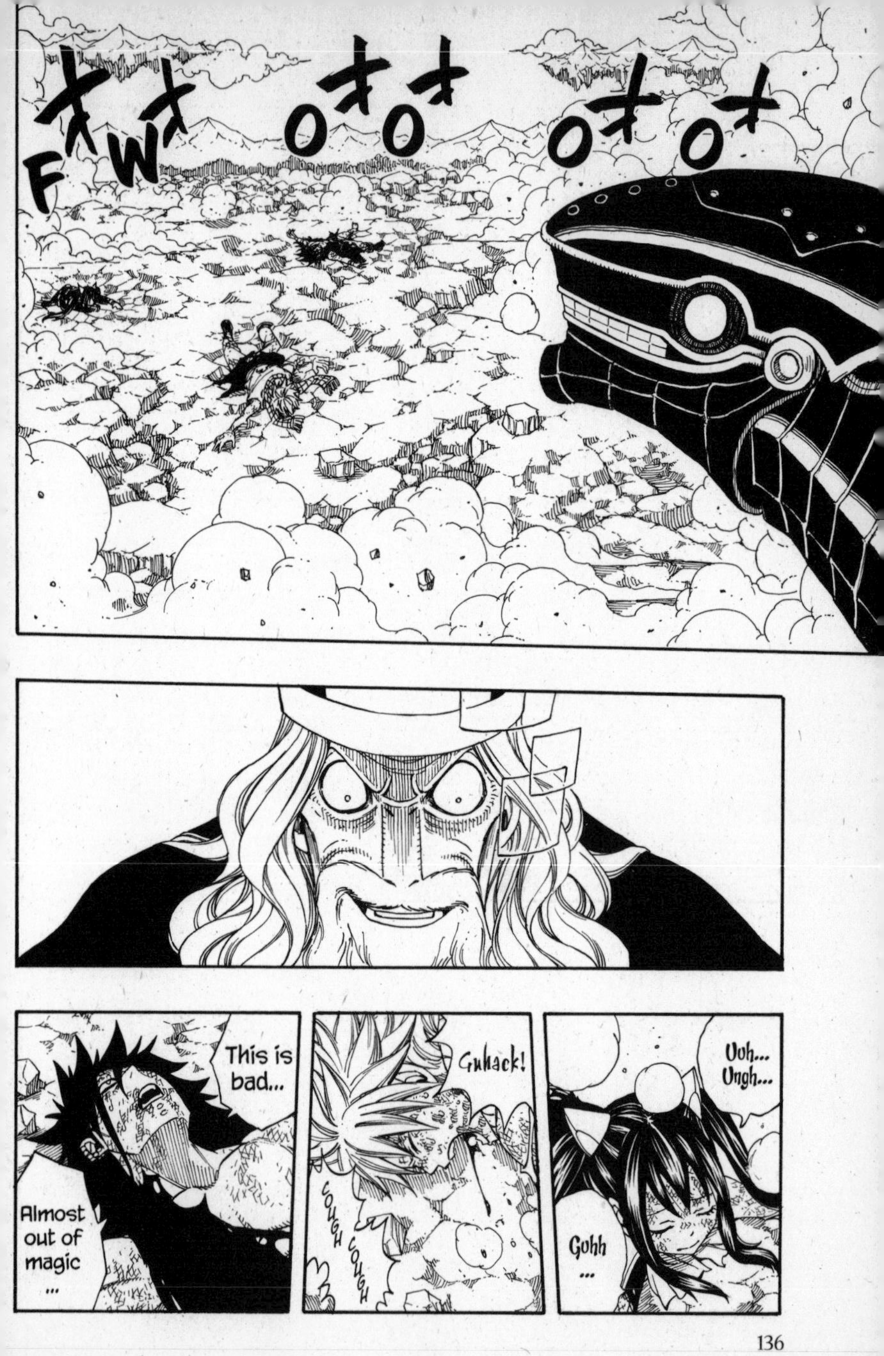
FWOOOO
Uoh... Ungh...
Guhh ...
Guhack!
COUGH COUGH
This is bad...
Almost out of magic ...

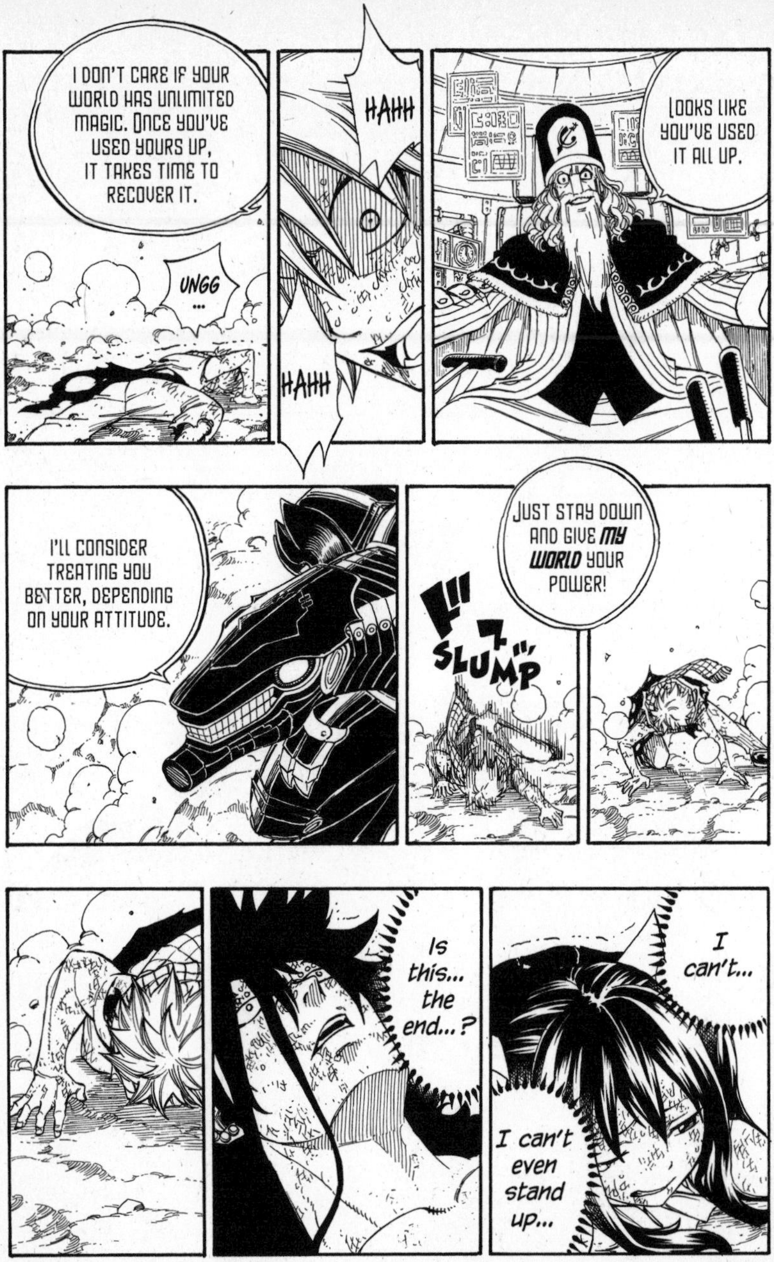
LOOKS LIKE YOU'VE USED IT ALL UP.
HAHH
HAHH
I DON'T CARE IF YOUR WORLD HAS UNLIMITED MAGIC. ONCE YOU'VE USED YOURS UP, IT TAKES TIME TO RECOVER IT.
UNGG...
JUST STAY DOWN AND GIVE ***MY WORLD*** YOUR POWER!
SLUMP
I'LL CONSIDER TREATING YOU BETTER, DEPENDING ON YOUR ATTITUDE.
I can't...
I can't even stand up...
Is this... the end...?

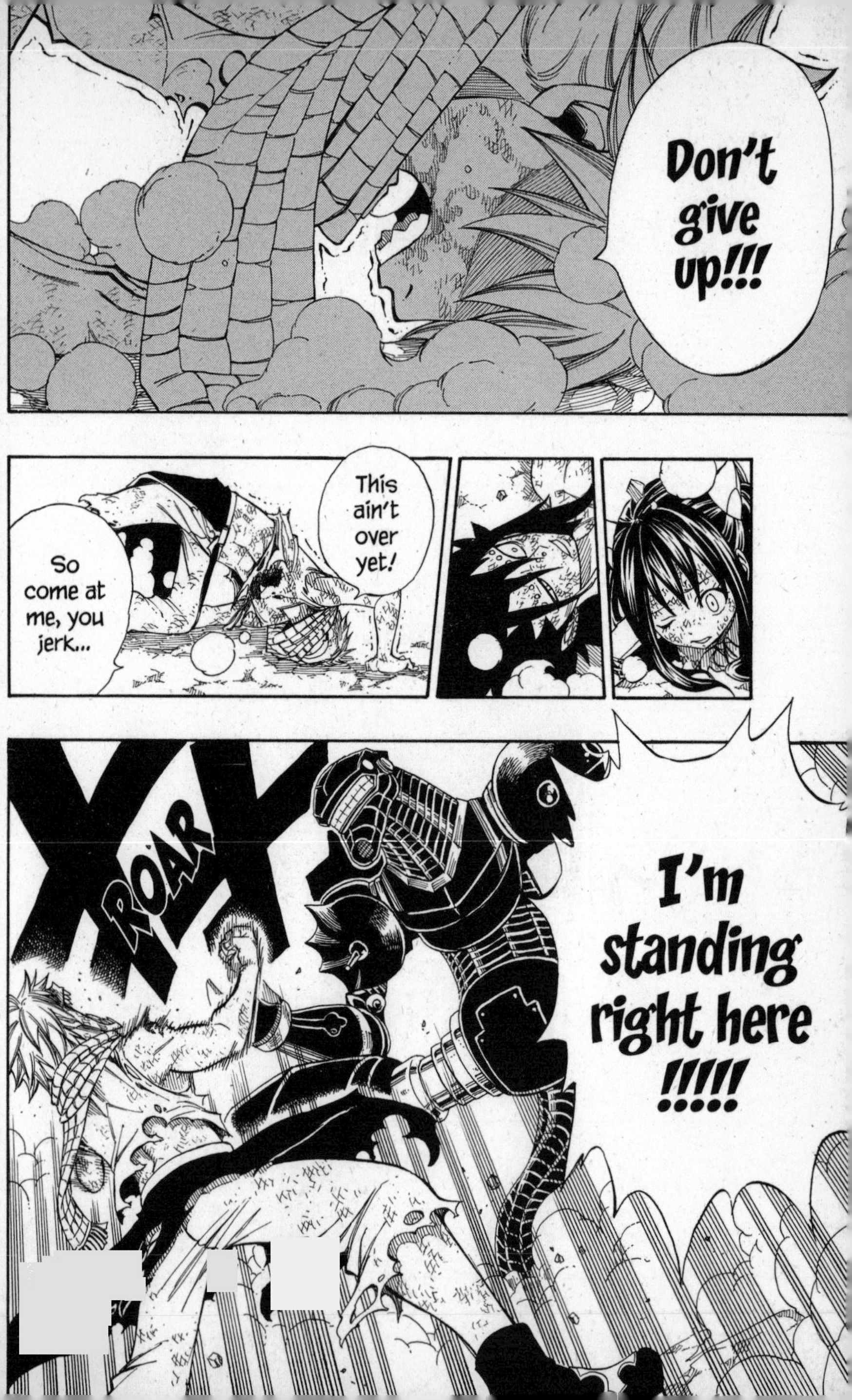
Don't give up!!!
This ain't over yet!
So come at me, you jerk...
I'm standing right here!!!!!
ROAR

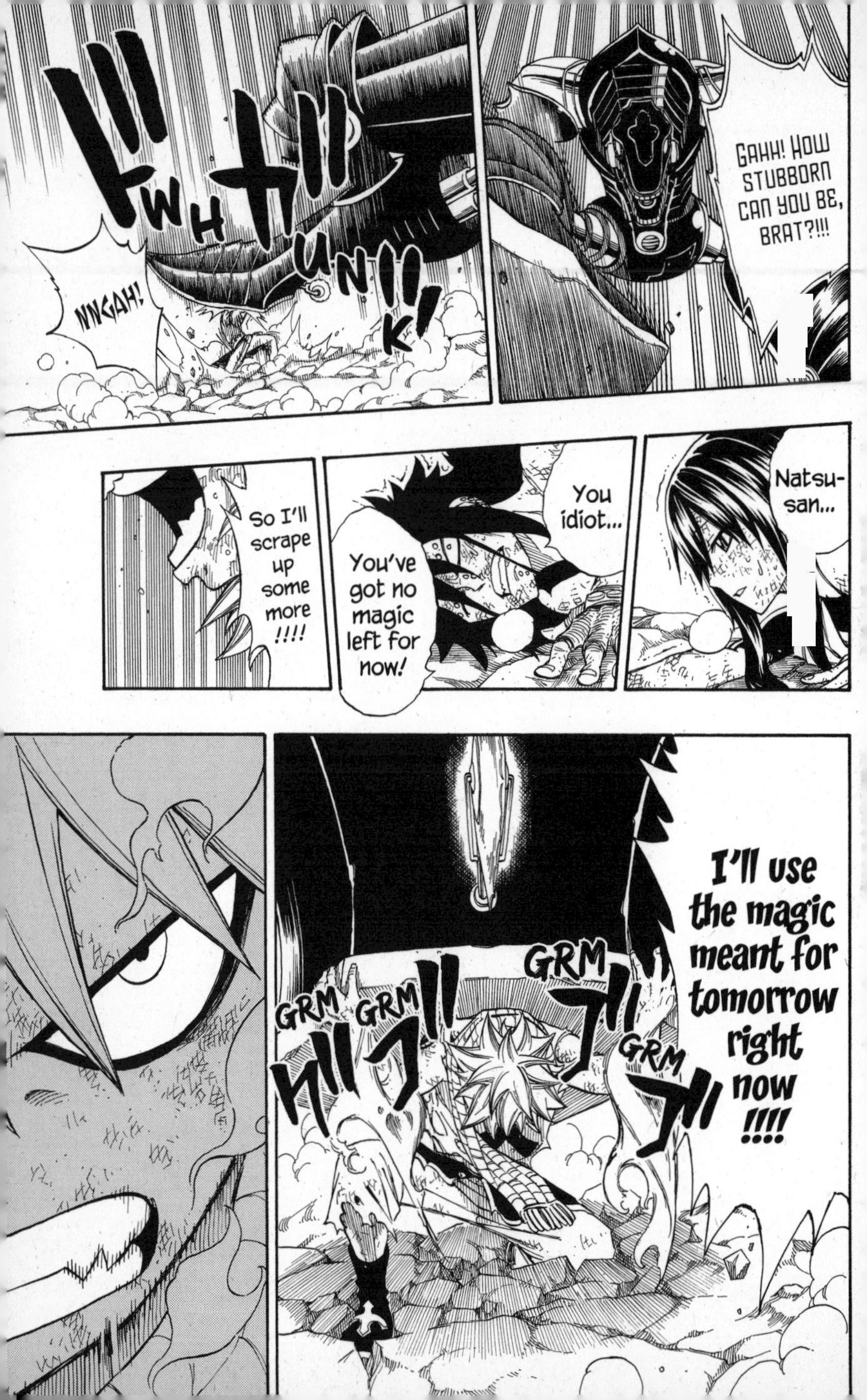
GAHH! HOW STUBBORN CAN YOU BE, BRAT?!!!
WHUNK!!
NNGAH!
Natsu-san...
You idiot...
You've got no magic left for now!
So I'll scrape up some more !!!!
I'll use the magic meant for tomorrow right now !!!!
GRM GRM
GRM
GRM

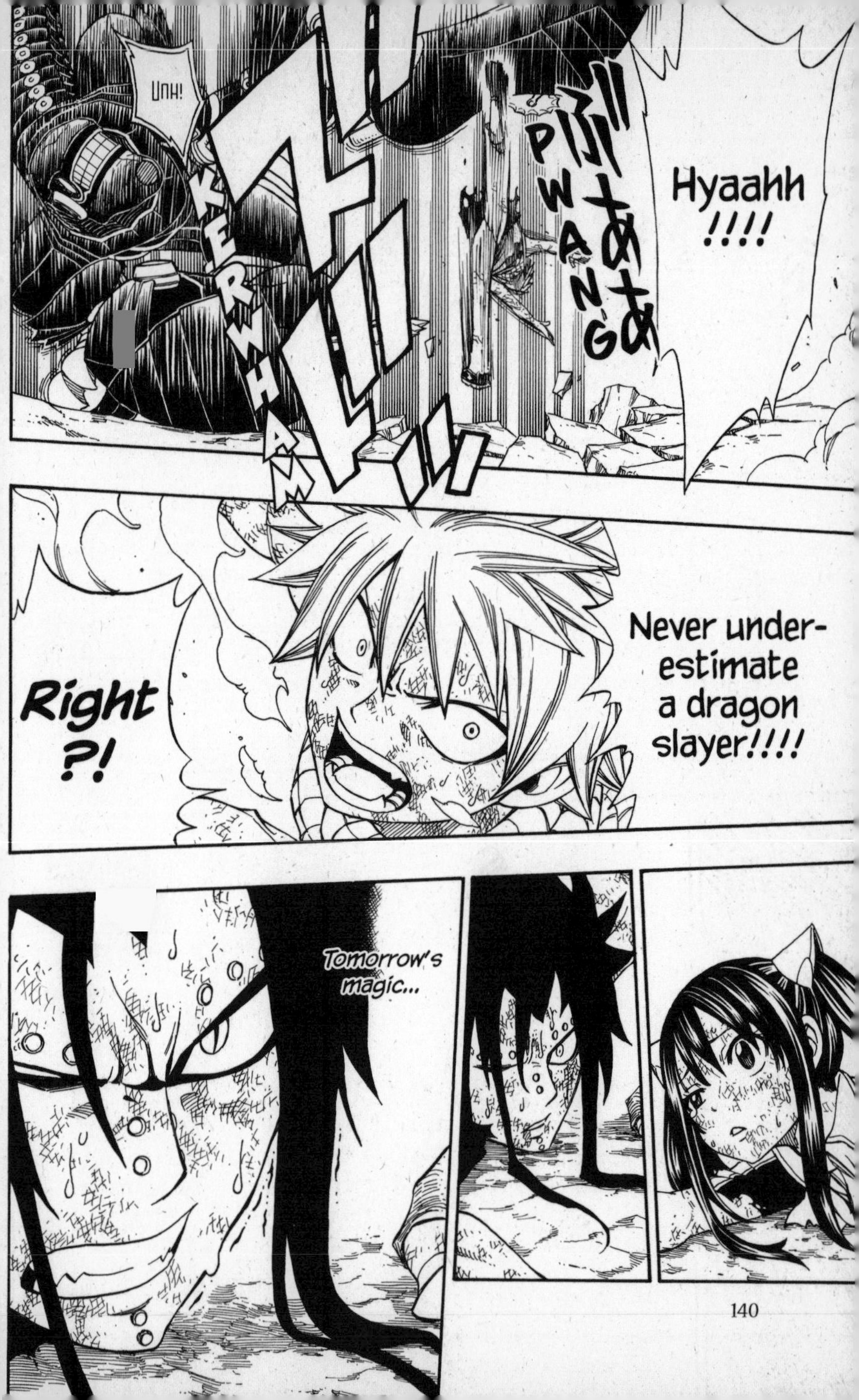
Hyaaahh!!!!
PIWANG
KERWHAM
Unh!
Never under-estimate a dragon slayer!!!!
Right?!
Tomorrow's magic...

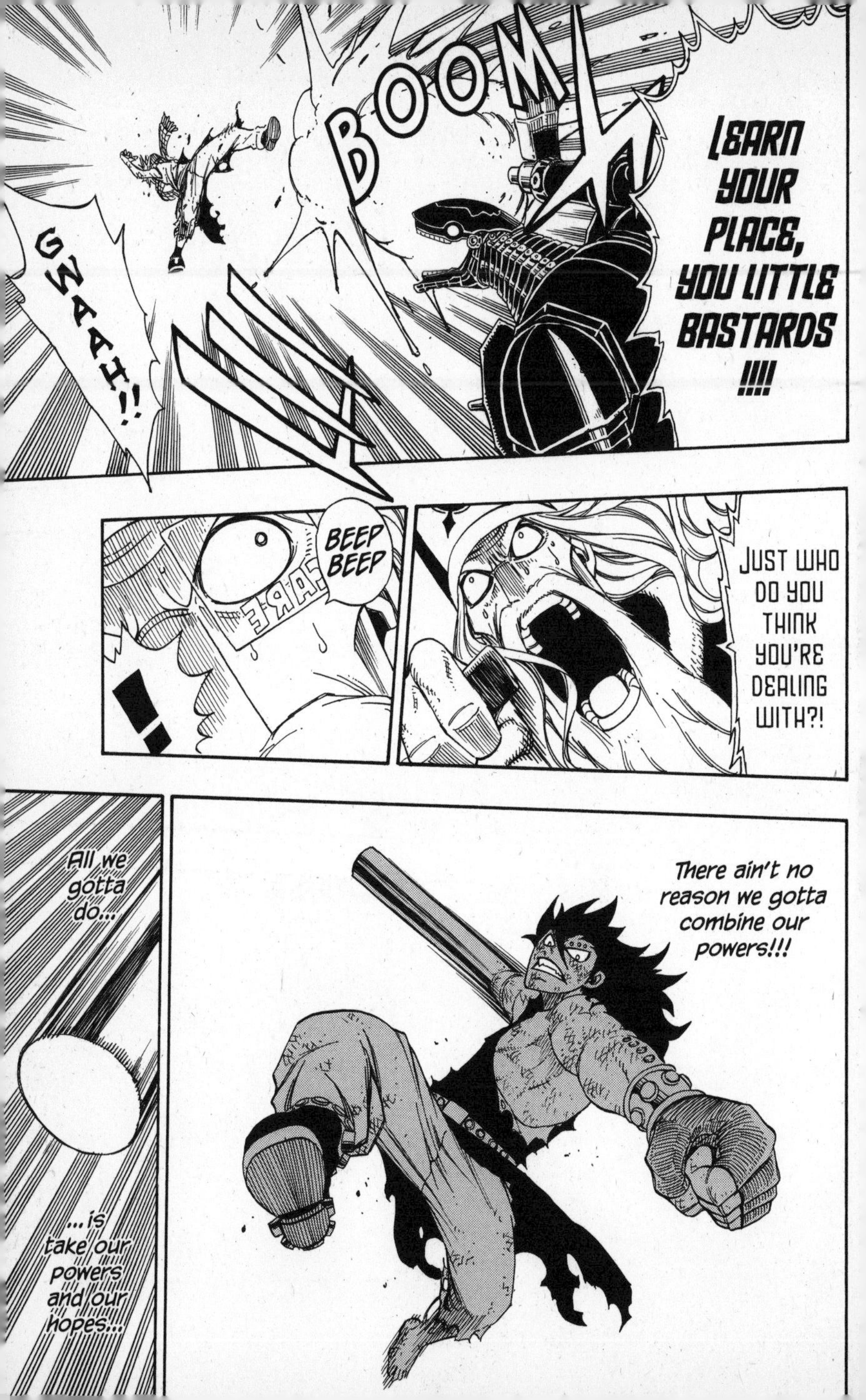
LEARN YOUR PLACE, YOU LITTLE BASTARDS!!!!
BOOM
GWAAH!!
JUST WHO DO YOU THINK YOU'RE DEALING WITH?!
BEEP BEEP
!
There ain't no reason we gotta combine our powers!!!
All we gotta do...
...is take our powers and our hopes...

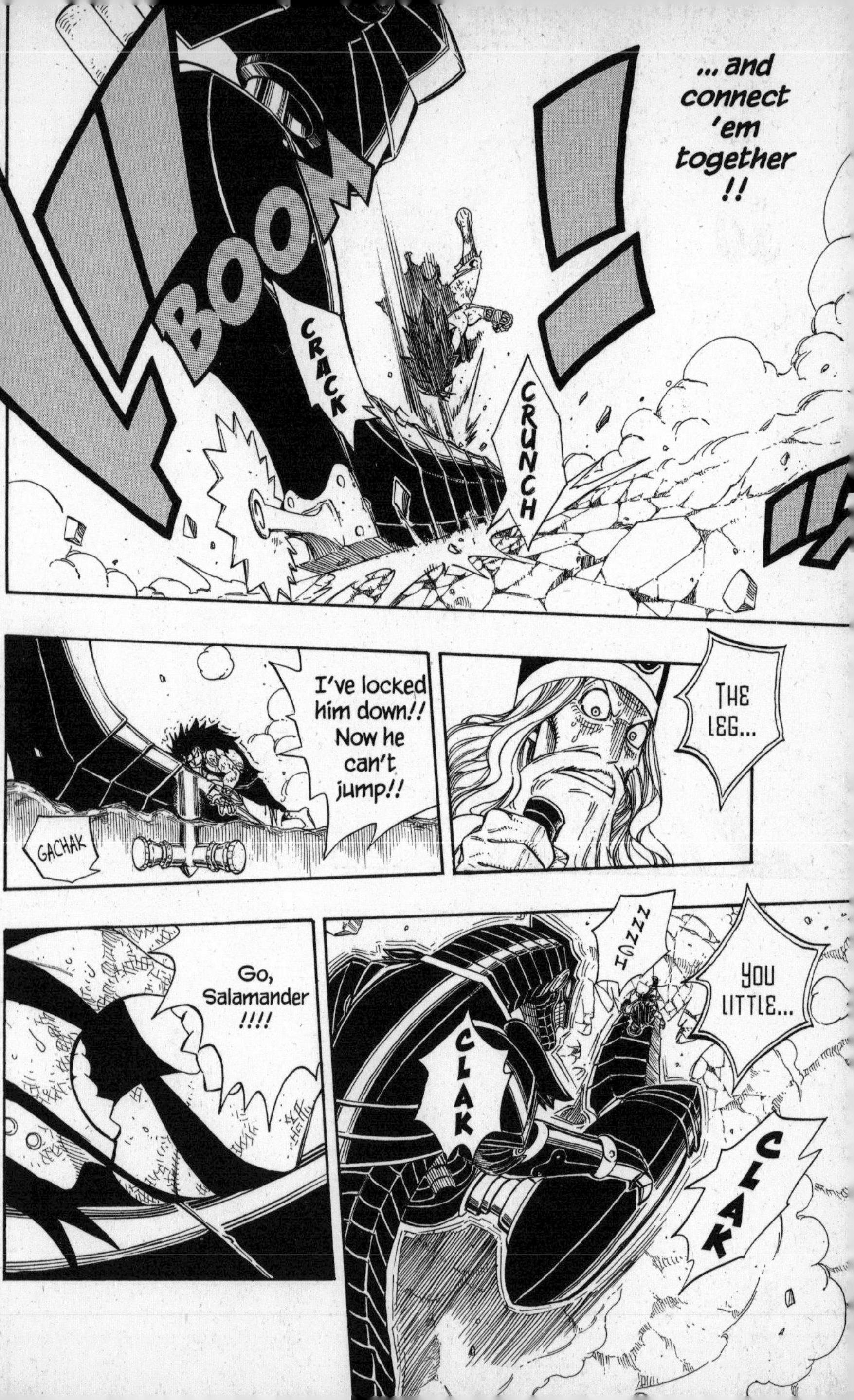
...and connect 'em together !!
BOOOM
CRACK
CRUNCH
THE LEG...
I've locked him down!! Now he can't jump!!
GACHAK
YOU LITTLE...
NNNGH
CLAK
CLAK
Go, Salamander !!!!

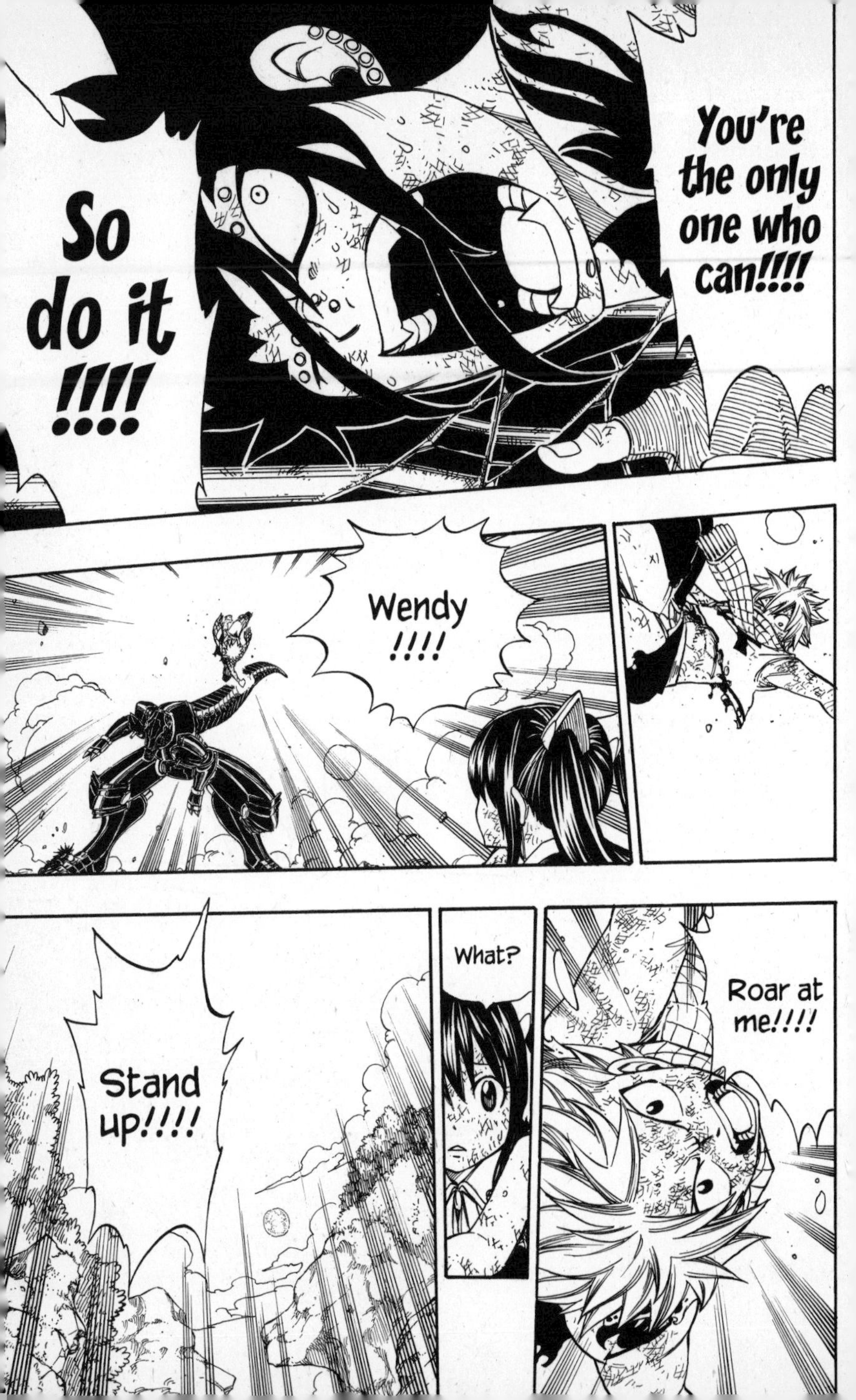
You're the only one who can!!!!
So do it!!!!
Wendy!!!!
Roar at me!!!!
What?
Stand up!!!!

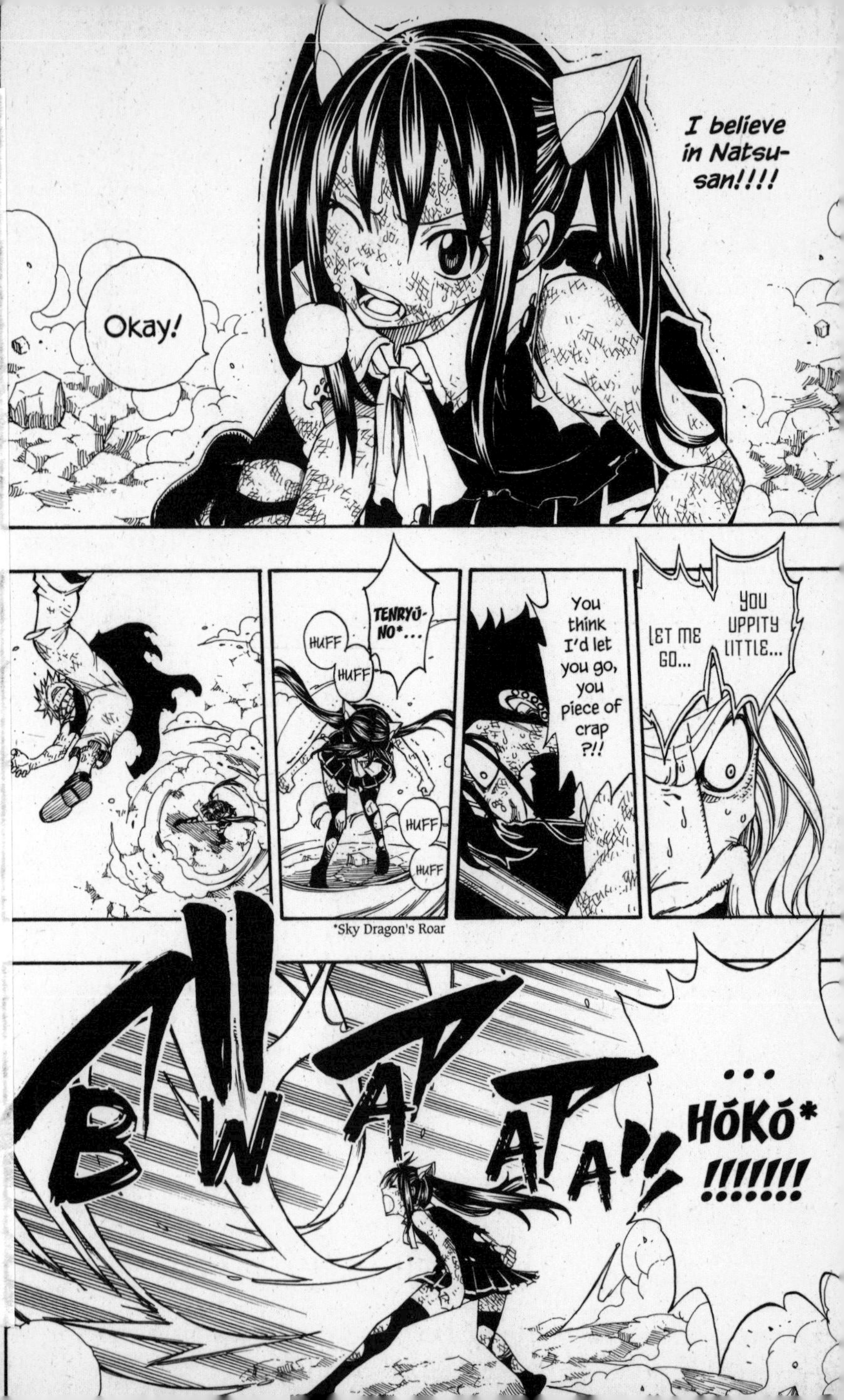
I believe in Natsu-san!!!!
Okay!
YOU UPPITY LITTLE...
LET ME GO...
You think I'd let you go, you piece of crap?!!
TENRYŪ-NO*...
HUFF
HUFF
HUFF
HUFF
...HŌKŌ* !!!!!!!
BWAAAA!!
*Sky Dragon's Roar

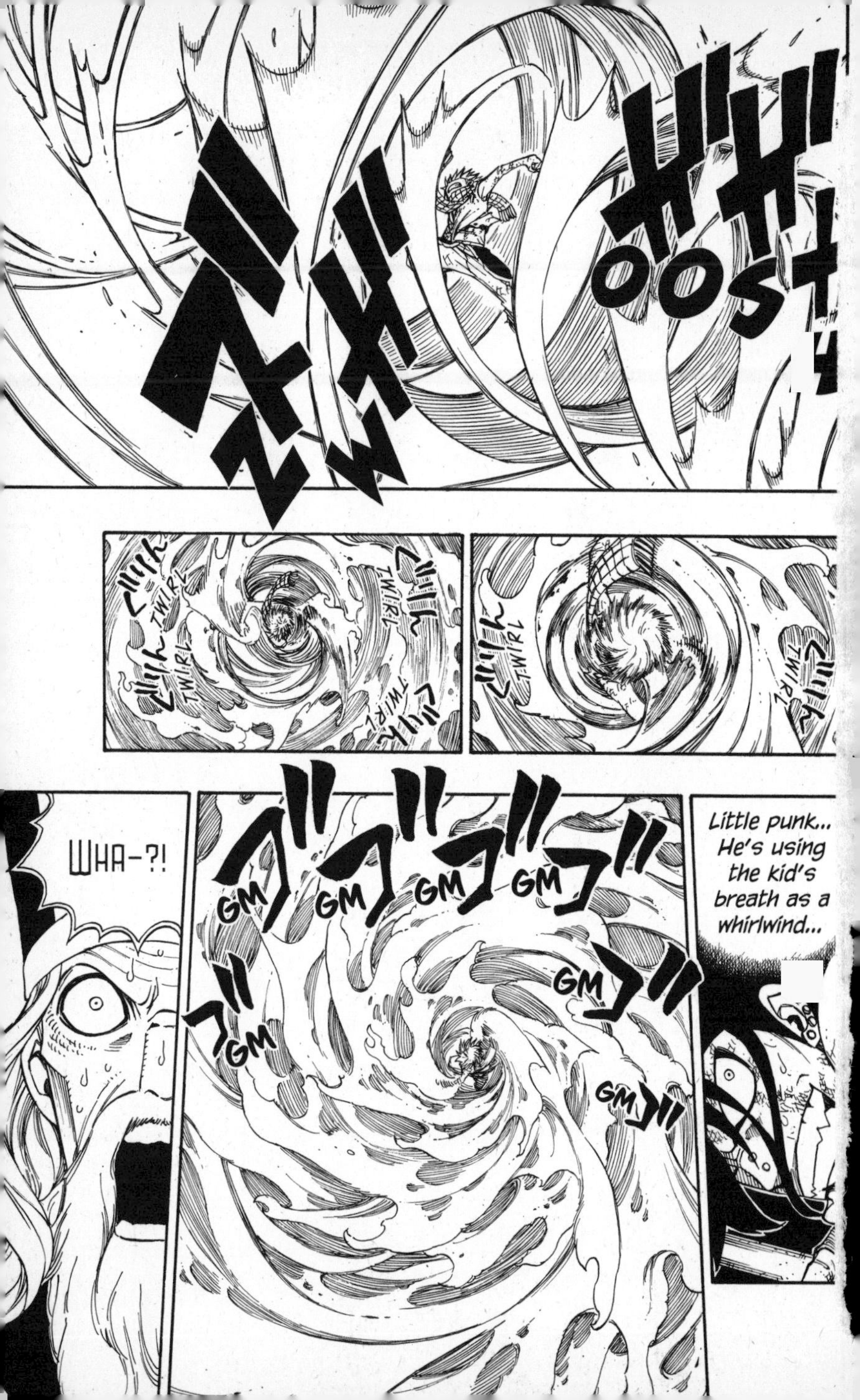
TWIRL
TWIRL
TWIRL
TWIRL
TWIRL
TWIRL
Little punk... He's using the kid's breath as a whirlwind...
GM
GM
GM
GM
GM
GM
GM
WHA-?!

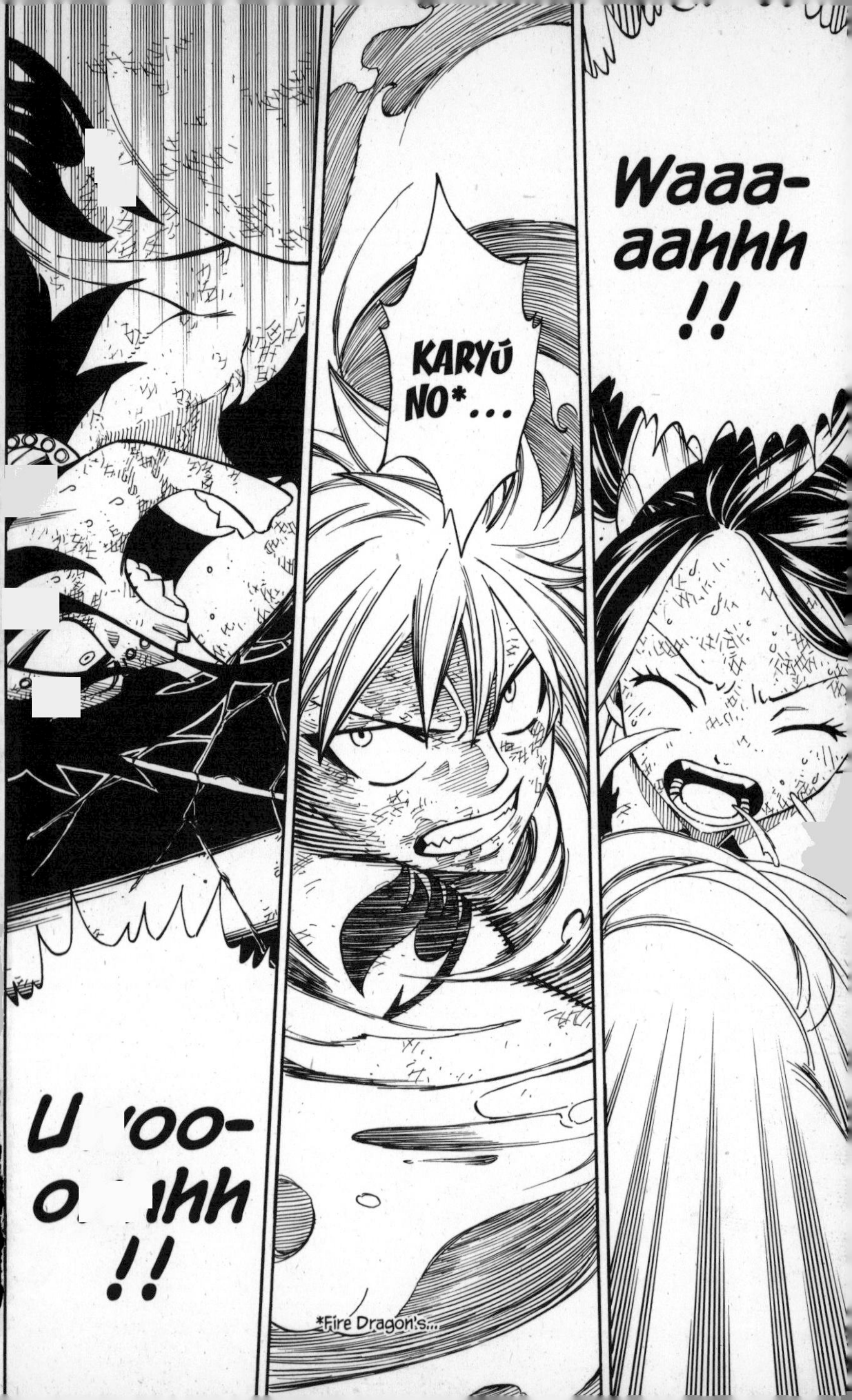
Waaa-aahhh!!
KARYŪ NO*...
U oo- o hh !!
*Fire Dragon's...

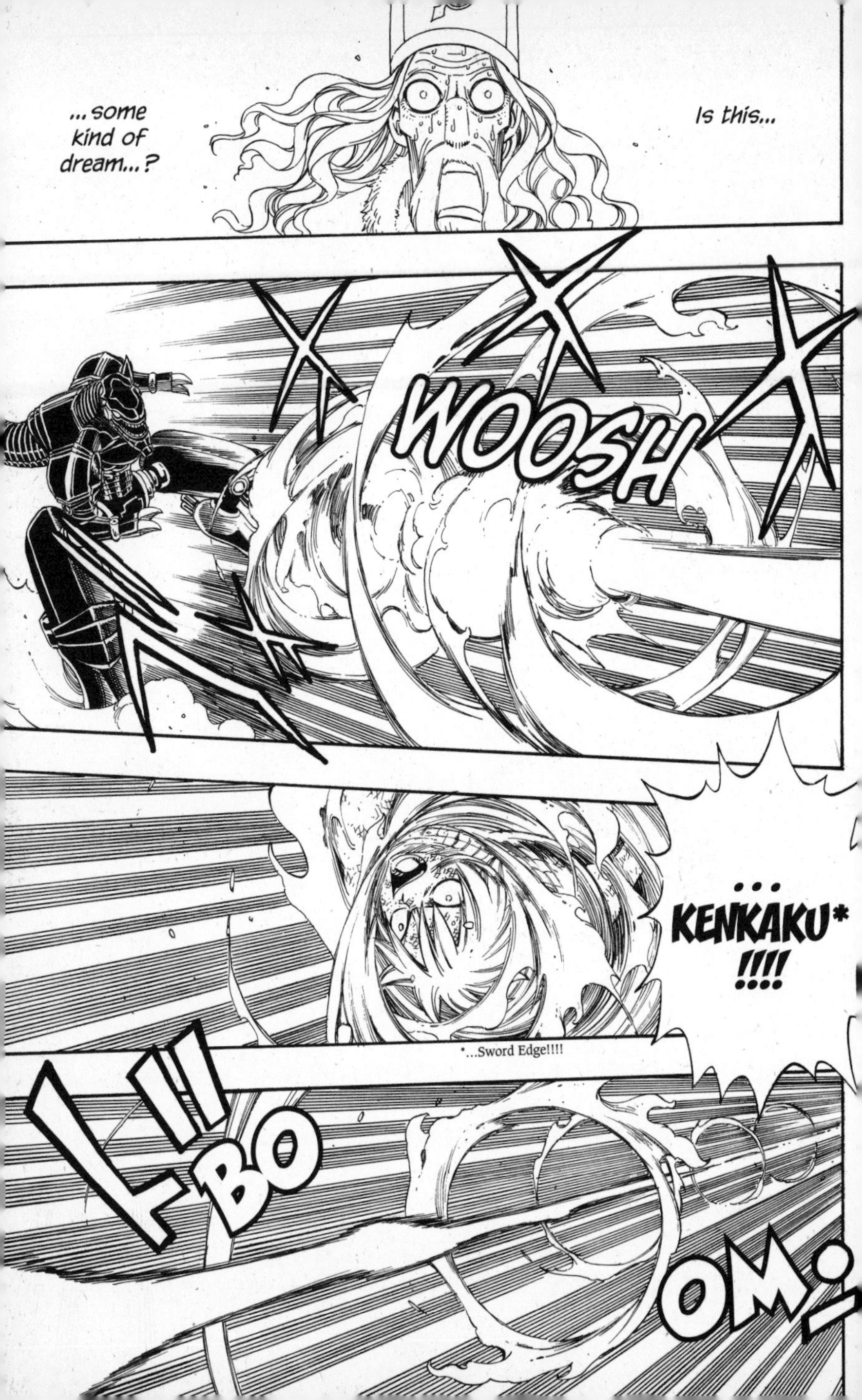
Is this...
...some kind of dream...?
WOOSH
...KENKAKU* !!!!
BO
OM!
*...Sword Edge!!!!

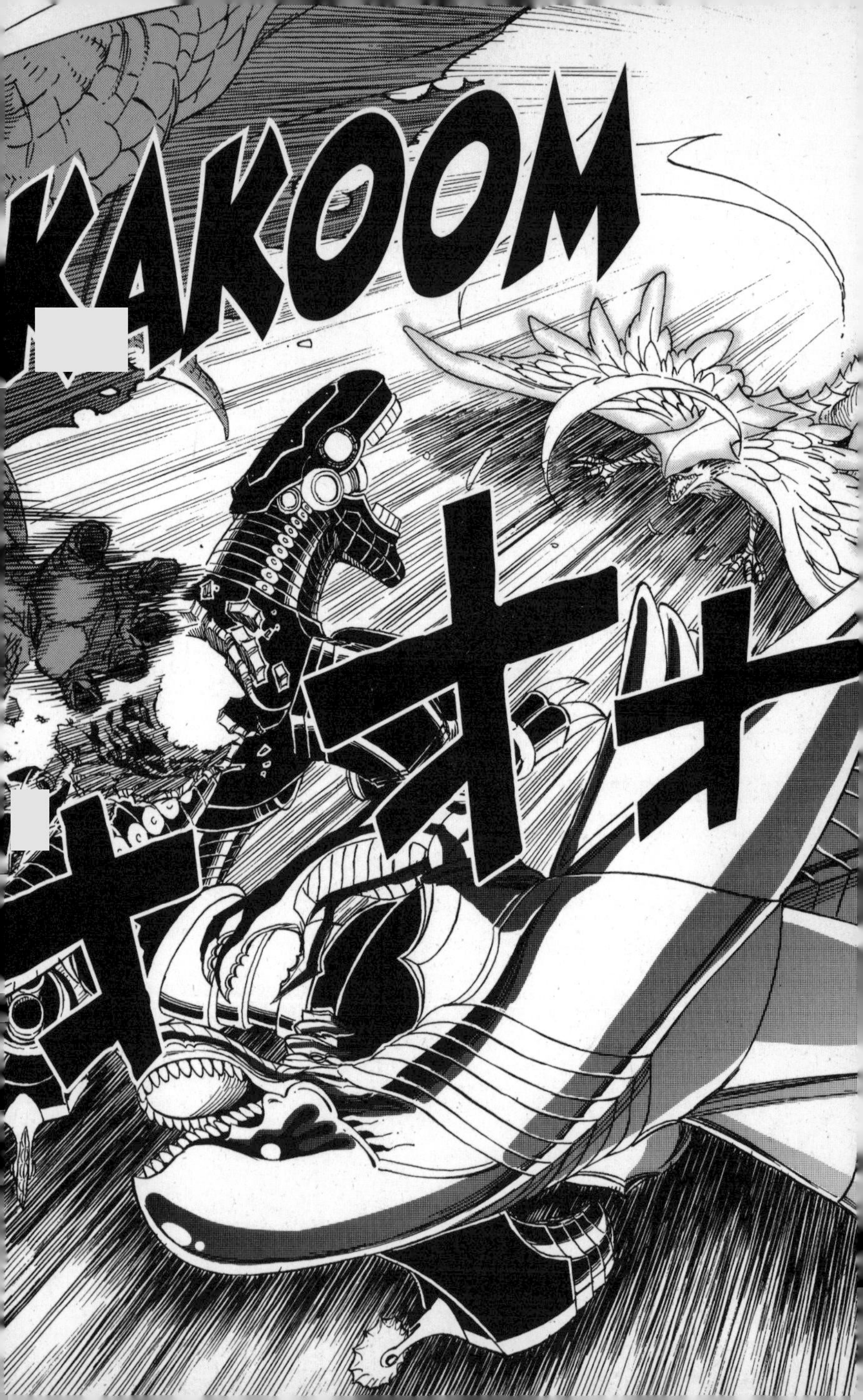
KAKOOM

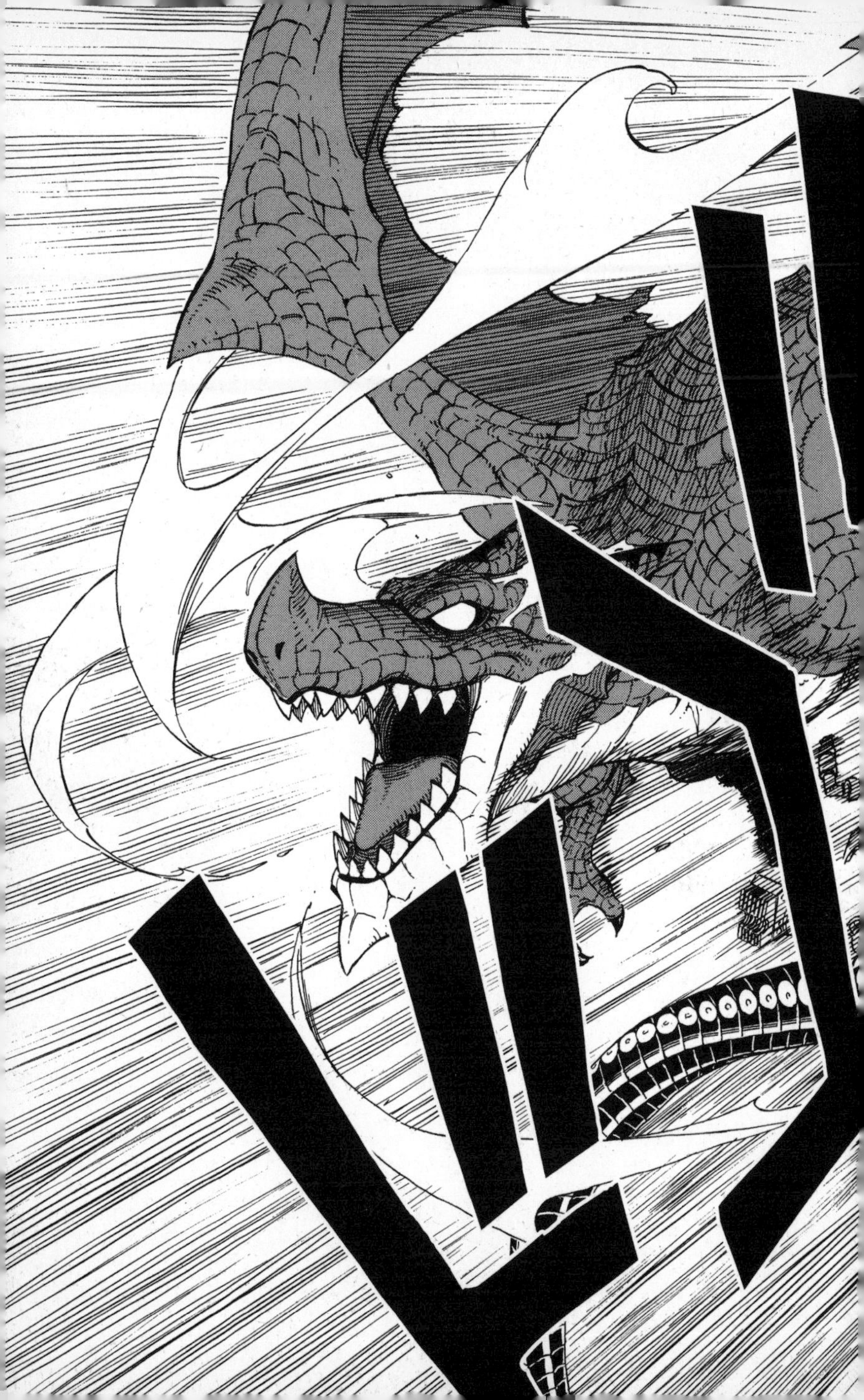

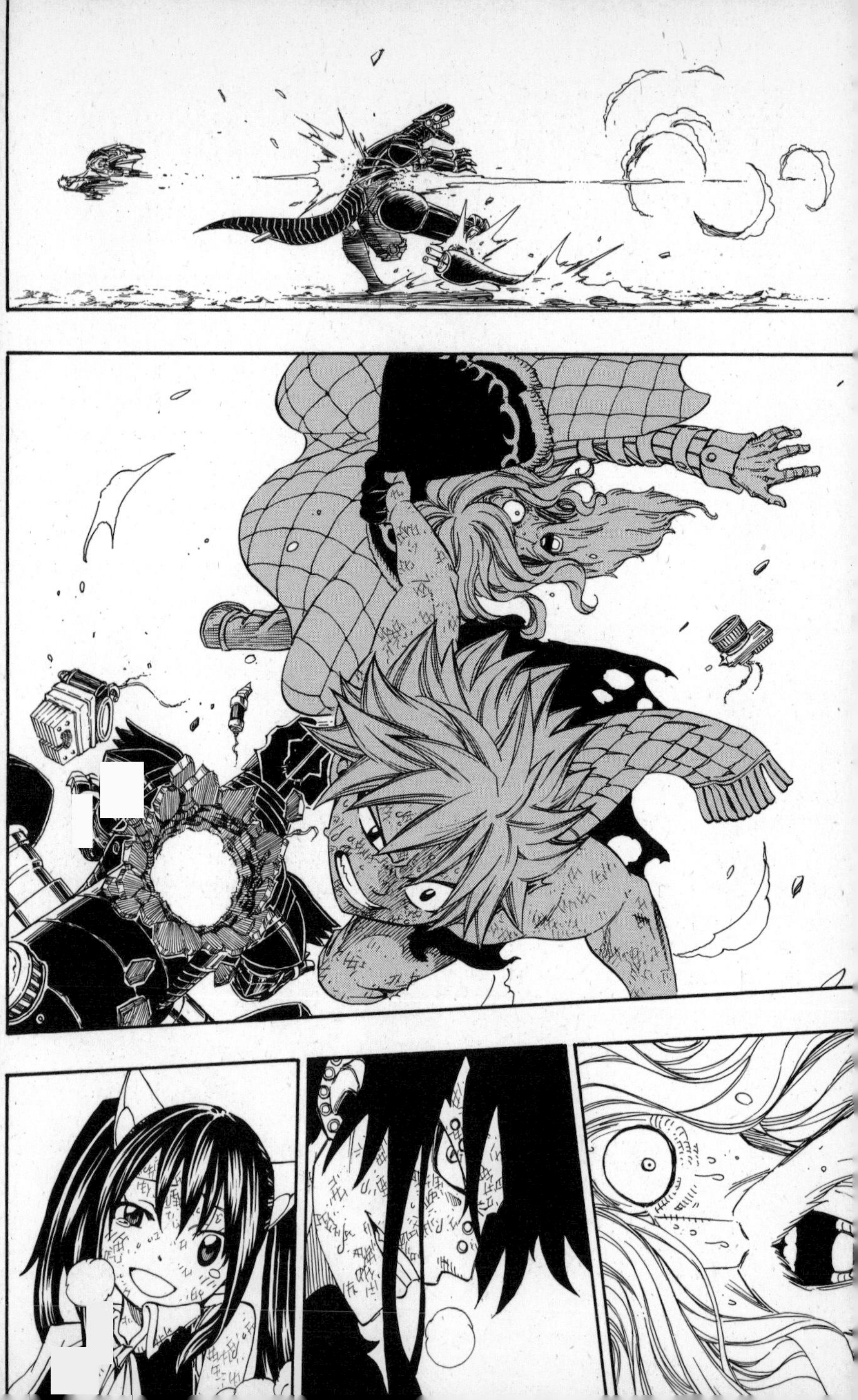

FAIRY TAIL

フェアリーテイル

Chapter 195: King of a New World

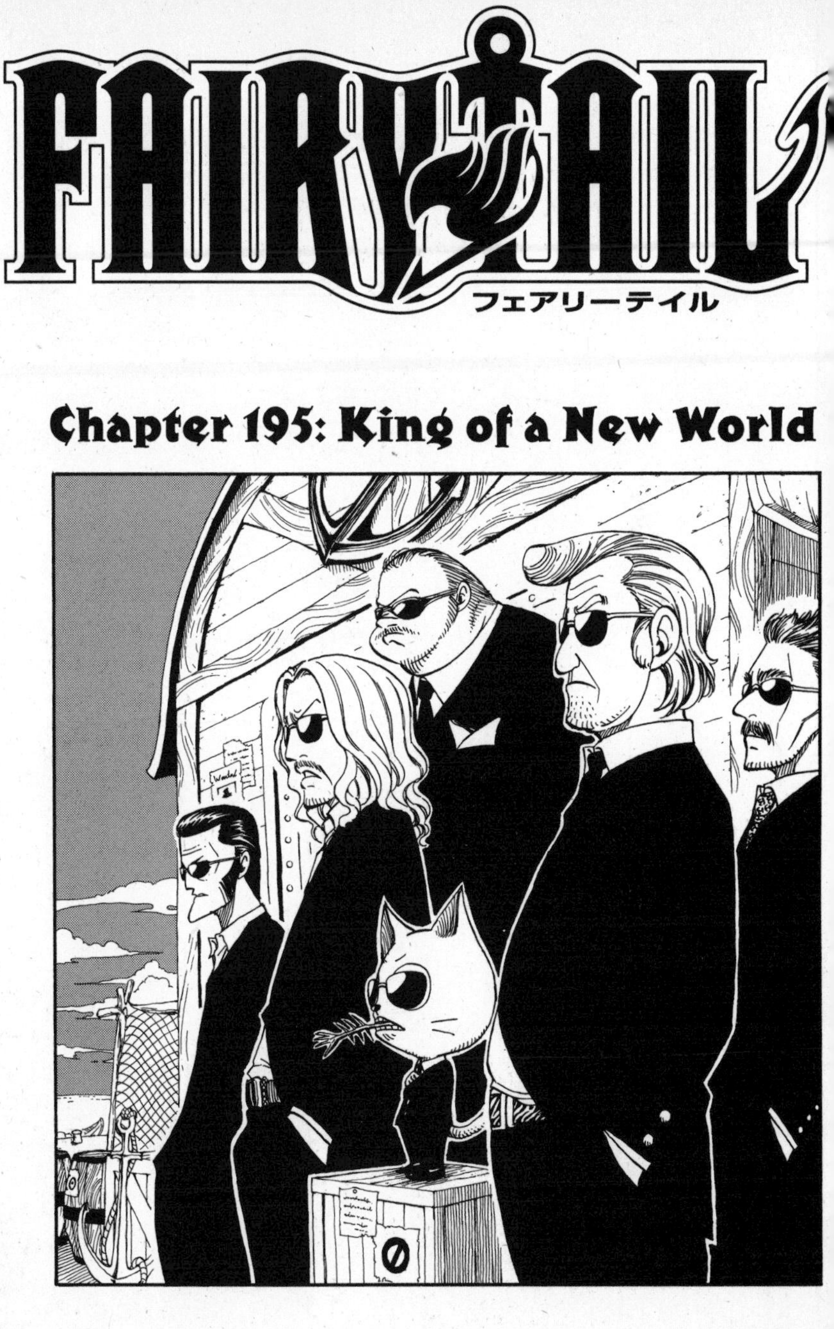

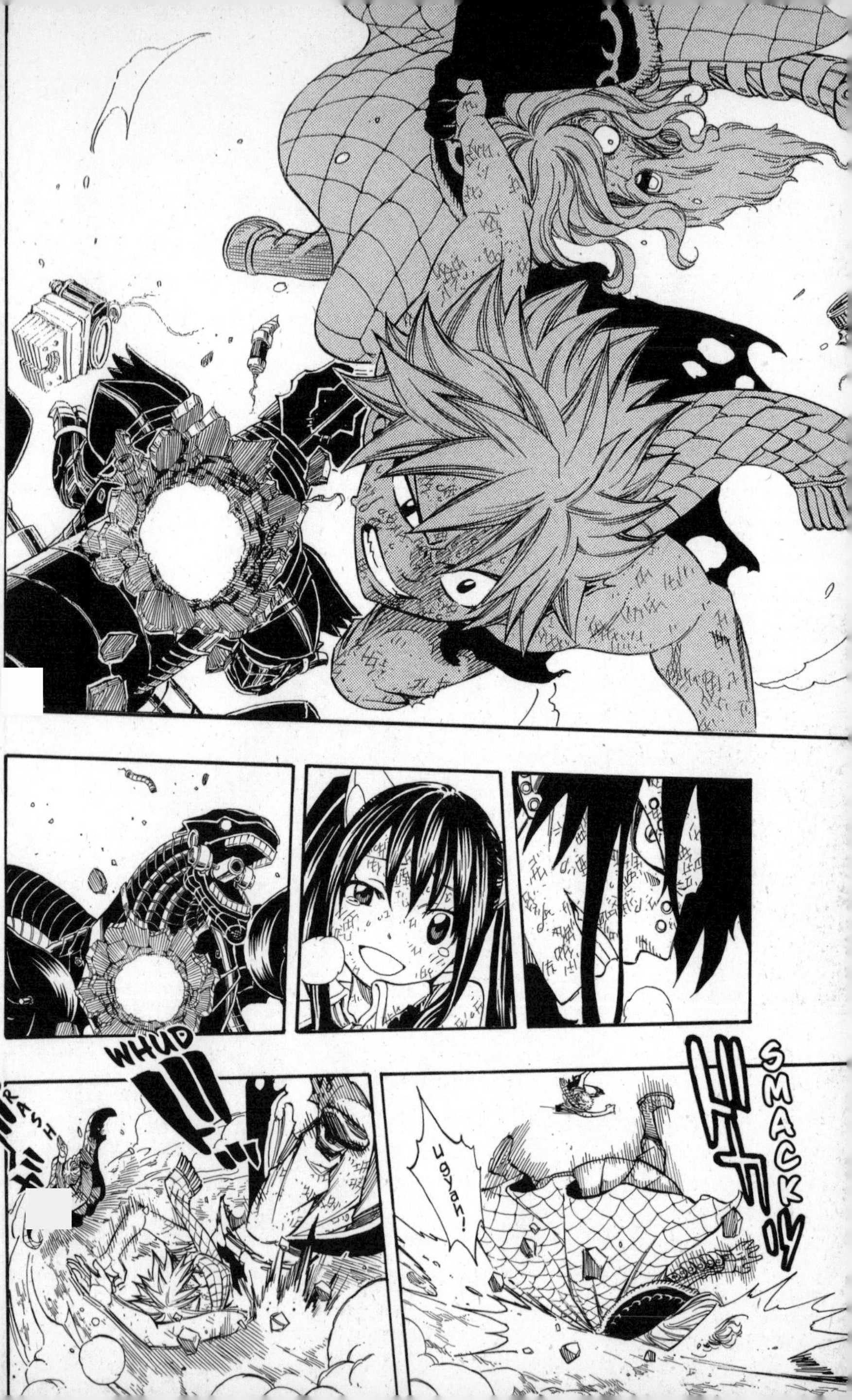
SMACK!!
Ugyah!
WHUD!!
RASH

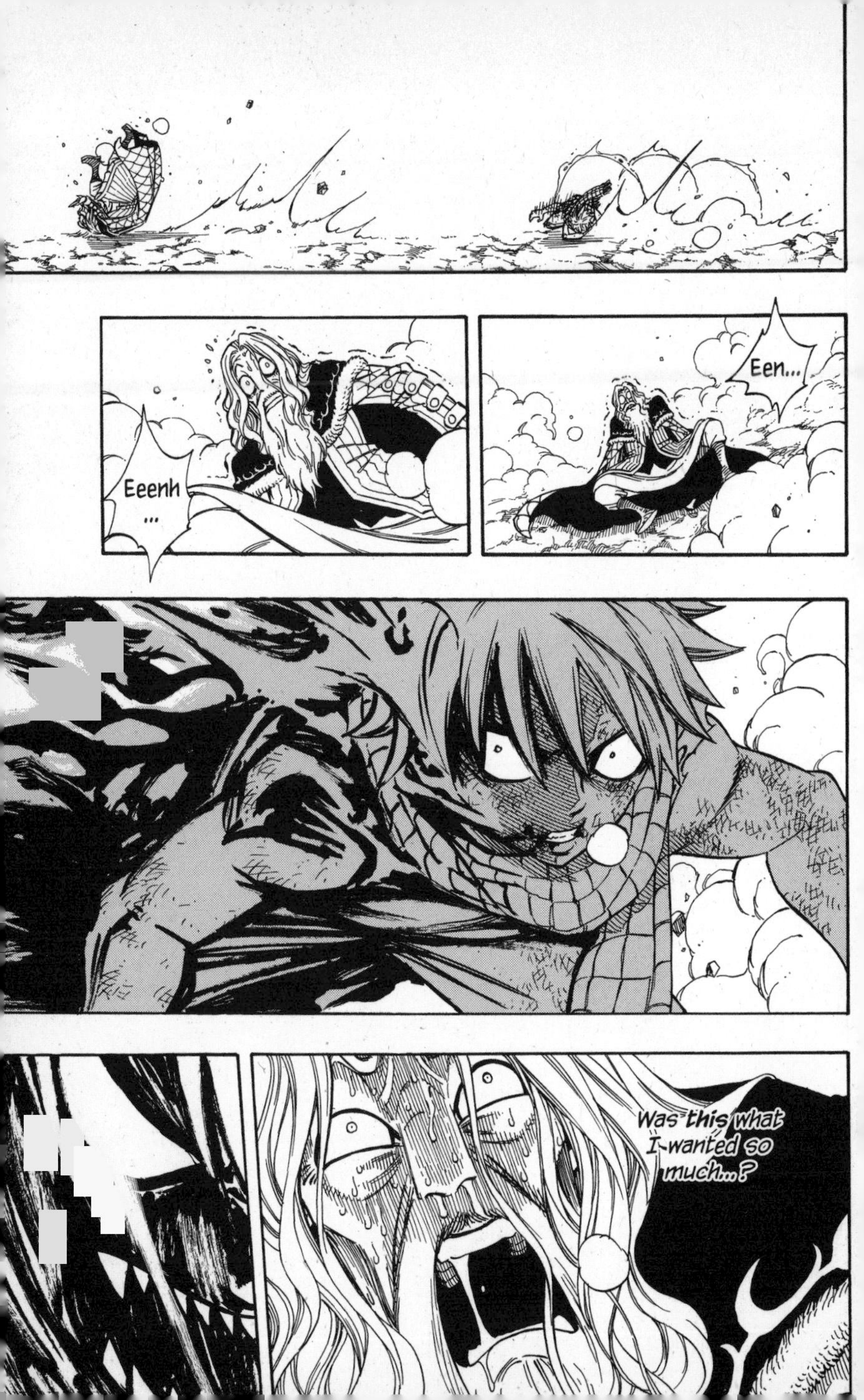
Een...
Eeenh ...
Was this what I wanted so much...?

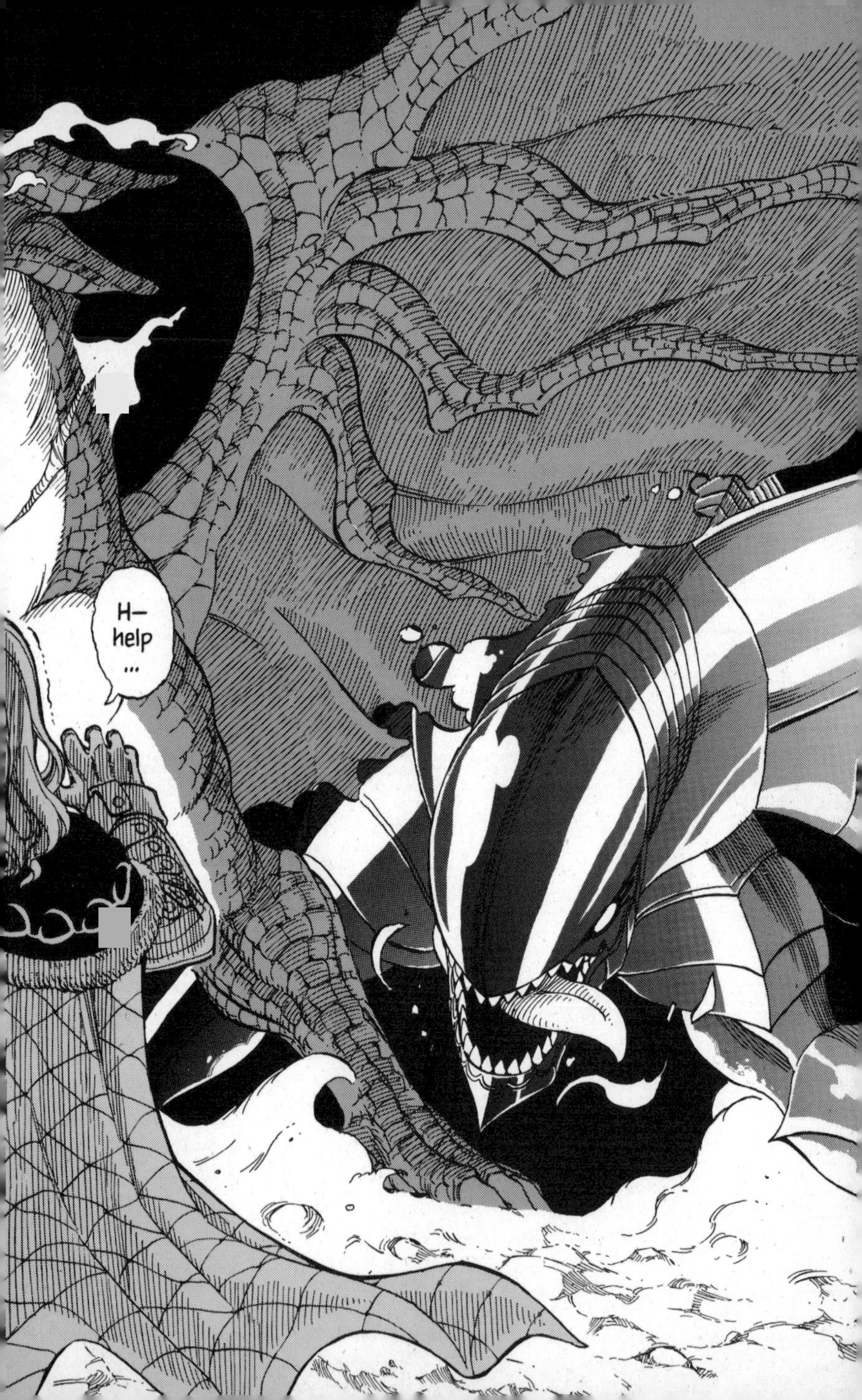
H—help ...

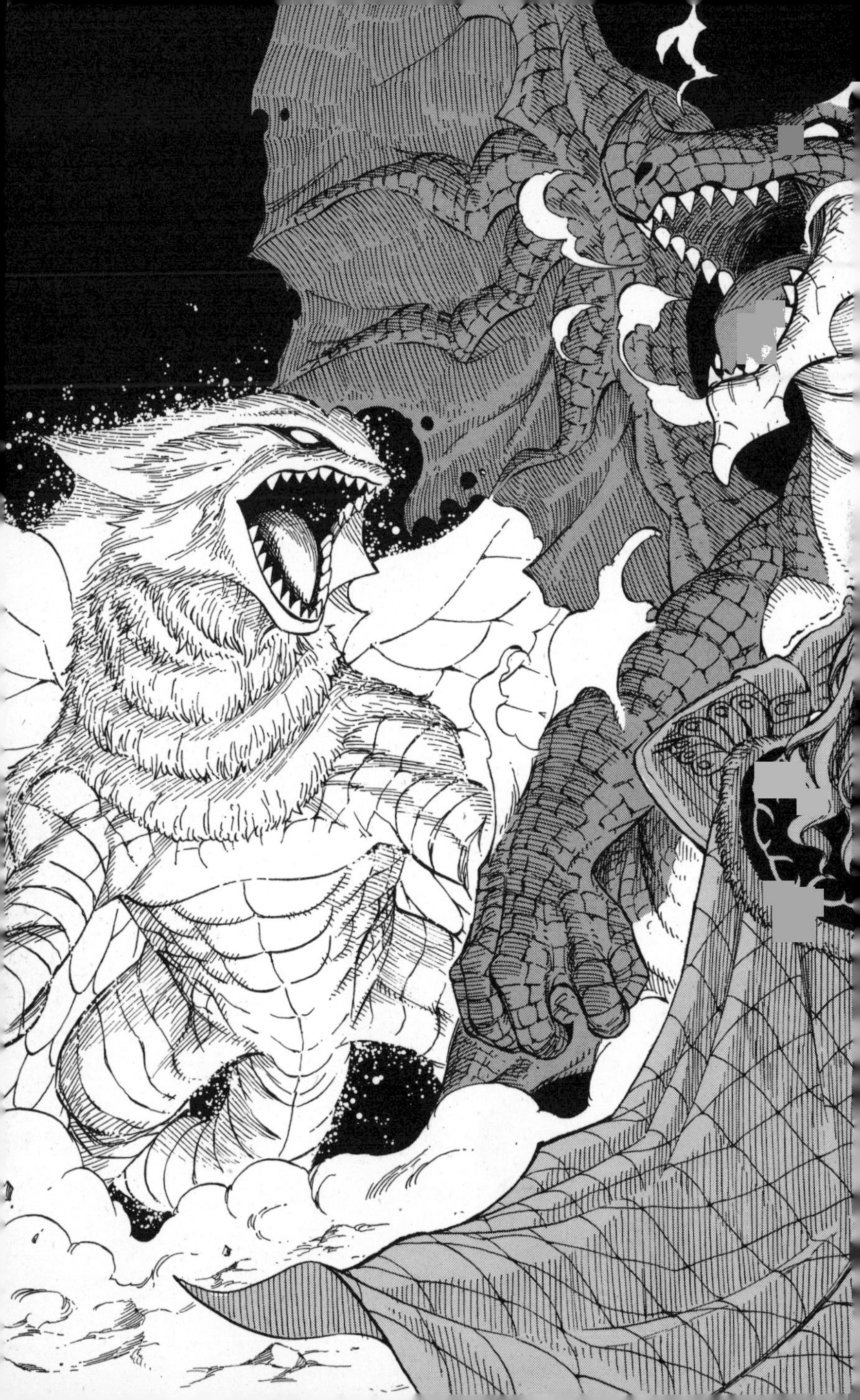

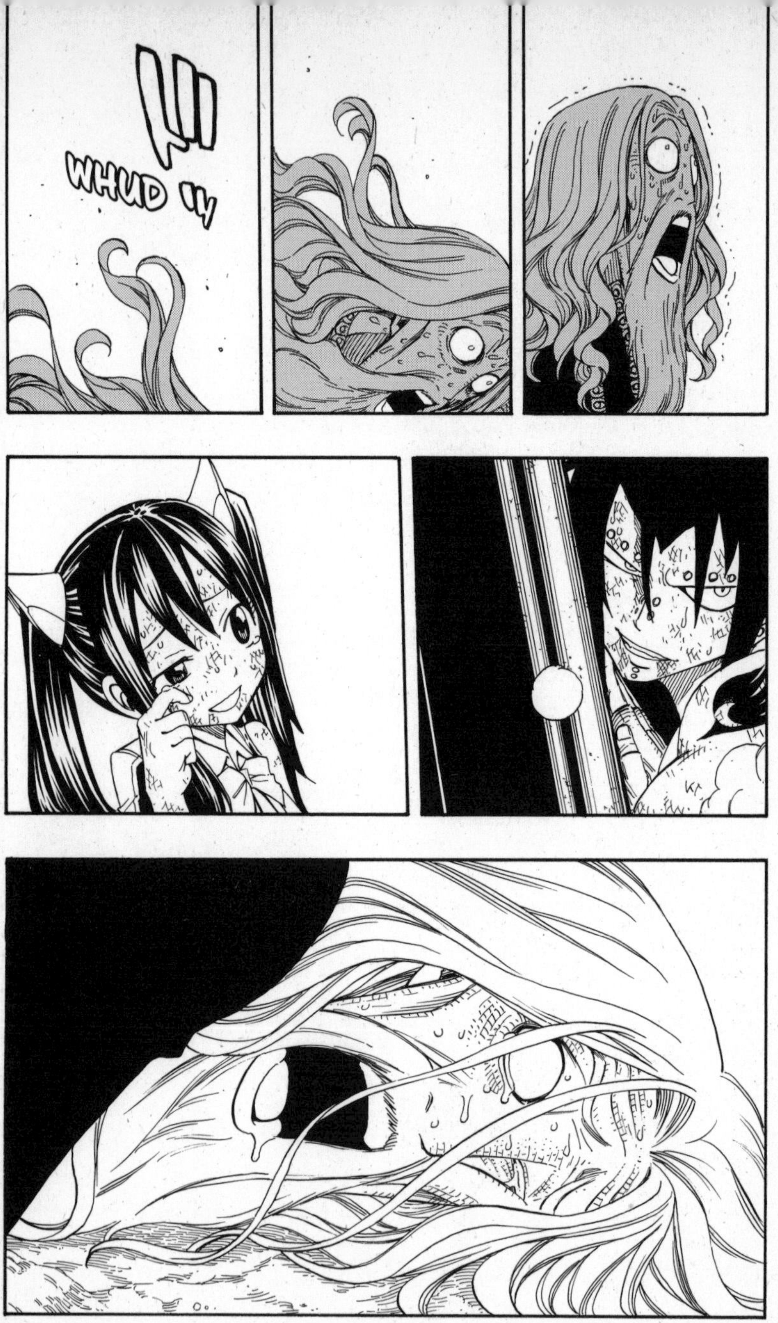
!!!
WHUD

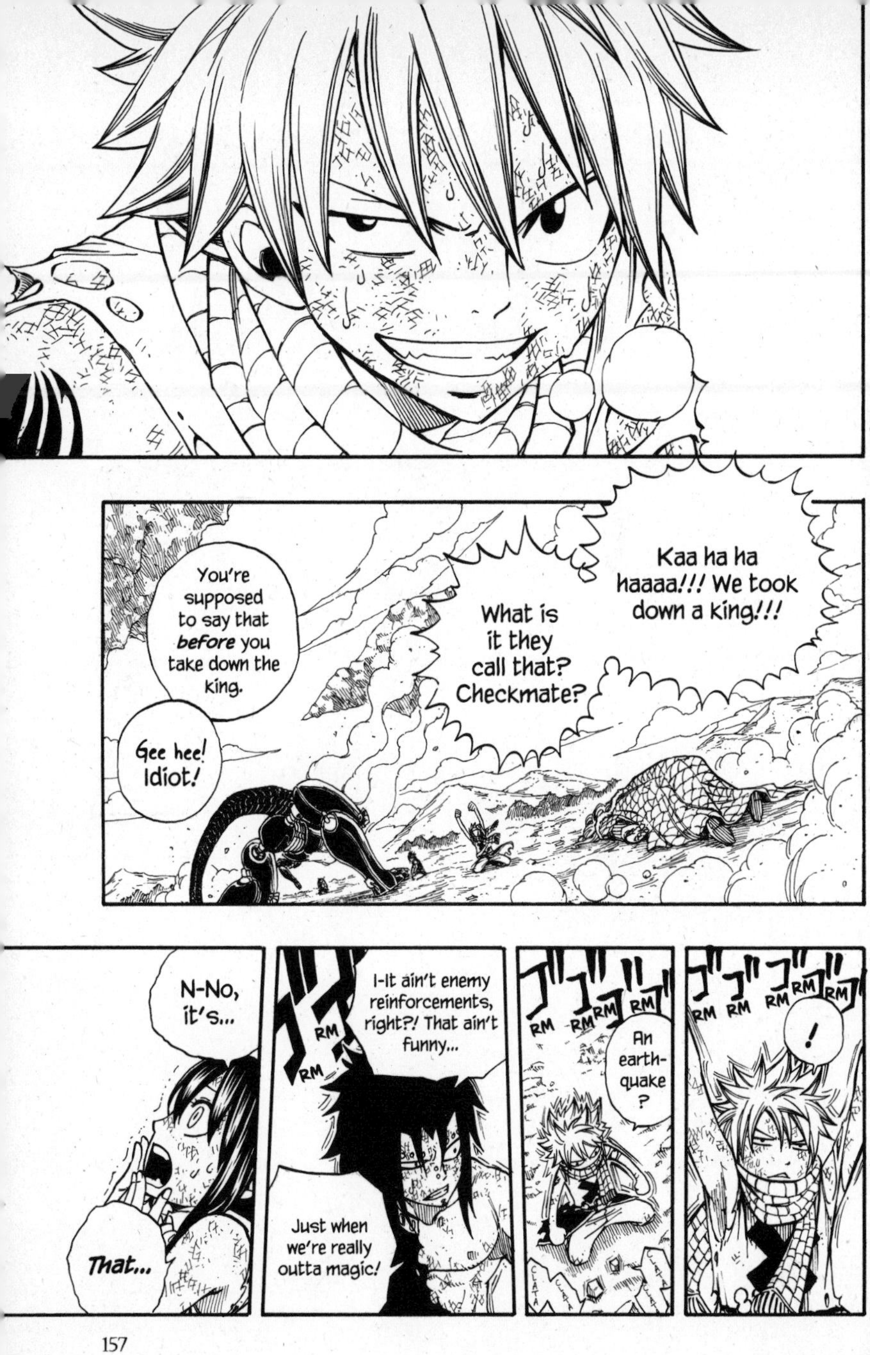
Kaa ha ha haaaa!!! We took down a king!!!
What is it they call that? Checkmate?
You're supposed to say that *before* you take down the king.
Gee hee! Idiot!
RM RM RM RM RM
!
RM RM RM RM
An earth-quake?
CLATA CLATA CLATA
RM RM
I-It ain't enemy reinforcements, right?! That ain't funny...
Just when we're really outta magic!
N-No, it's...
That...

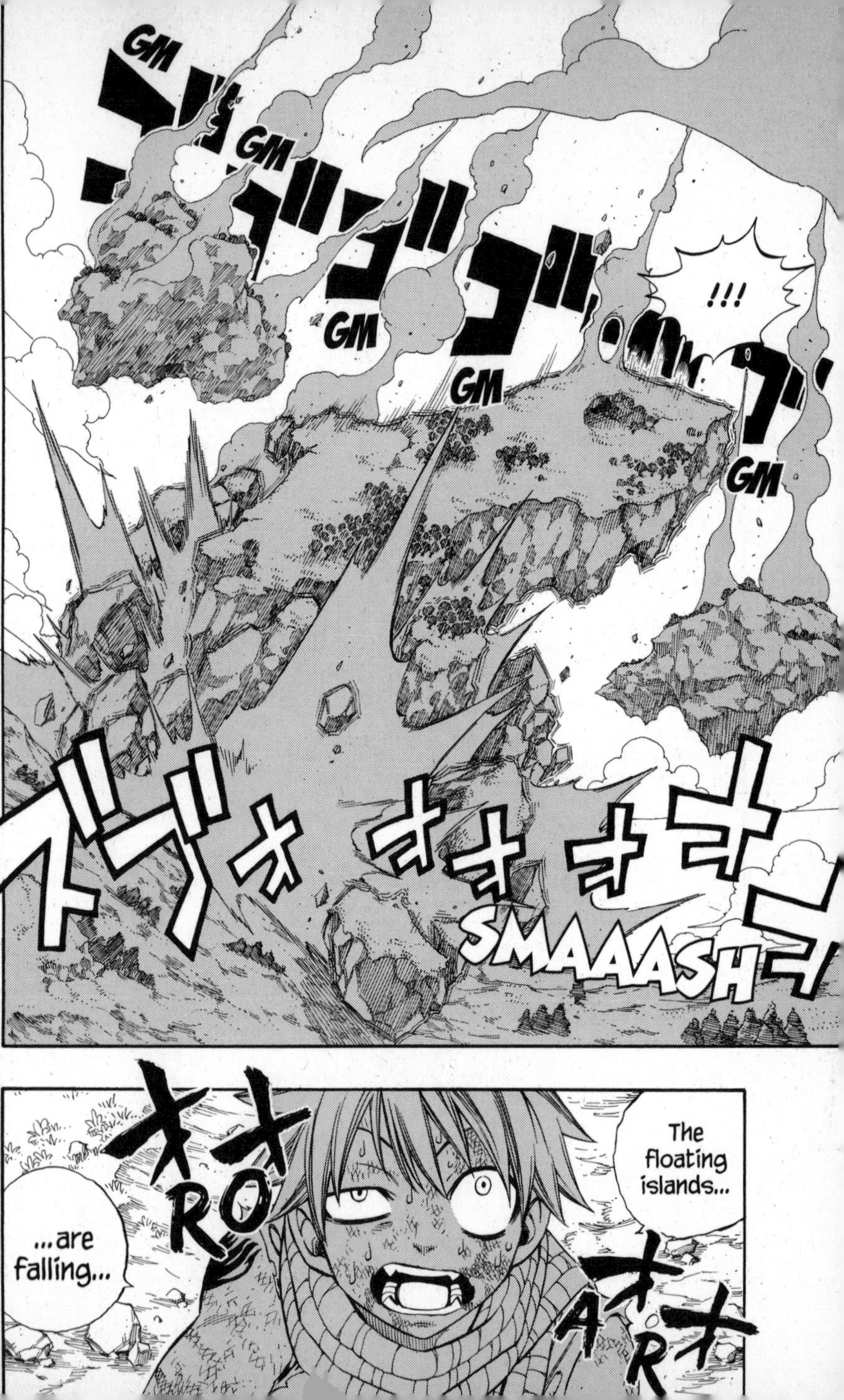
GM
GM
GM
GM
GM
!!!
SMAAASH
The floating islands...
ROAR
...are falling...

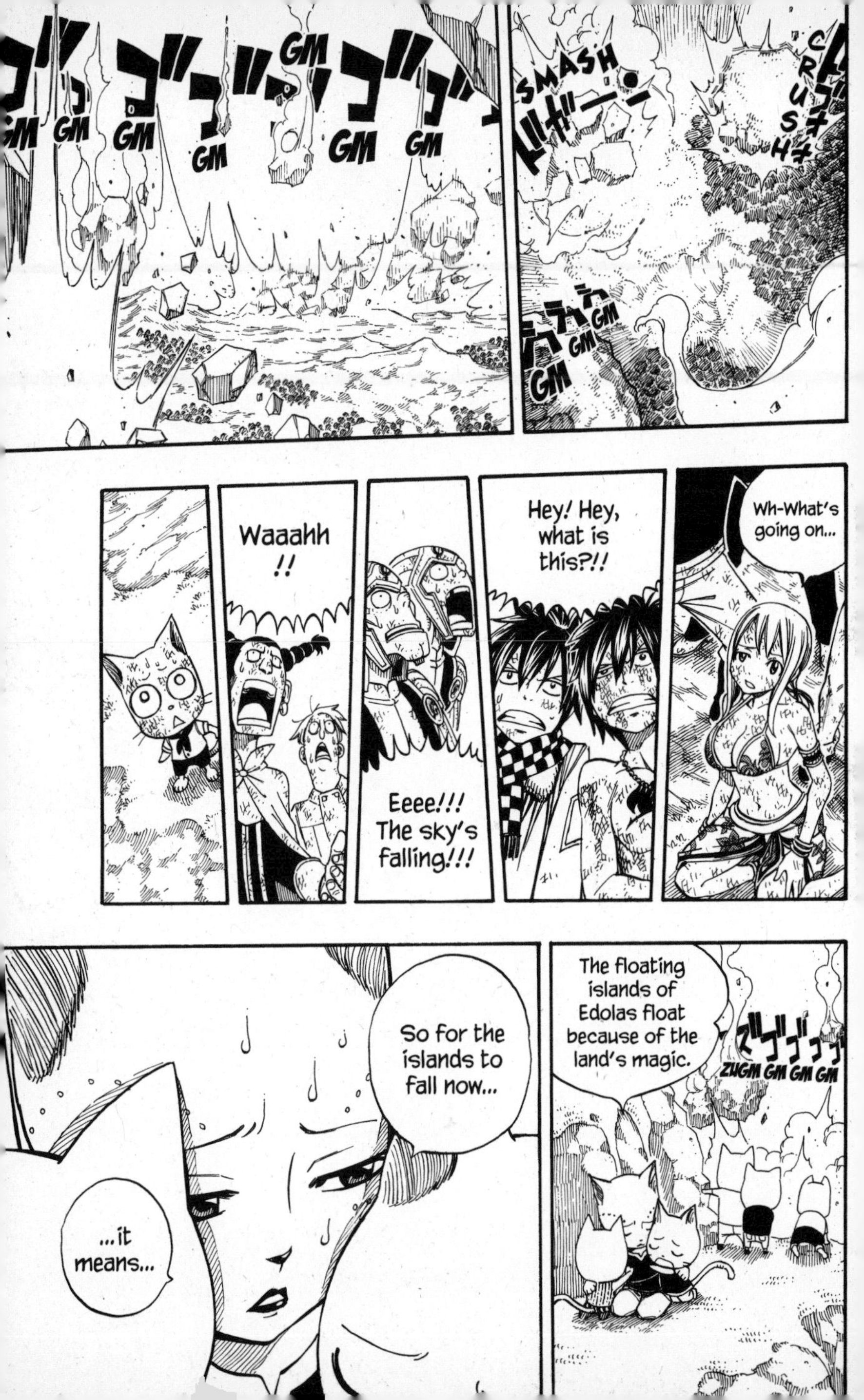
SMASH
CRUSH
GM GM GM
GM GM GM GM GM GM GM GM
Wh-What's going on...
Hey! Hey, what is this?!!
Eeee!!! The sky's falling!!!
Waaahh !!
The floating islands of Edolas float because of the land's magic.
ZUGM GM GM GM
So for the islands to fall now...
...it means...

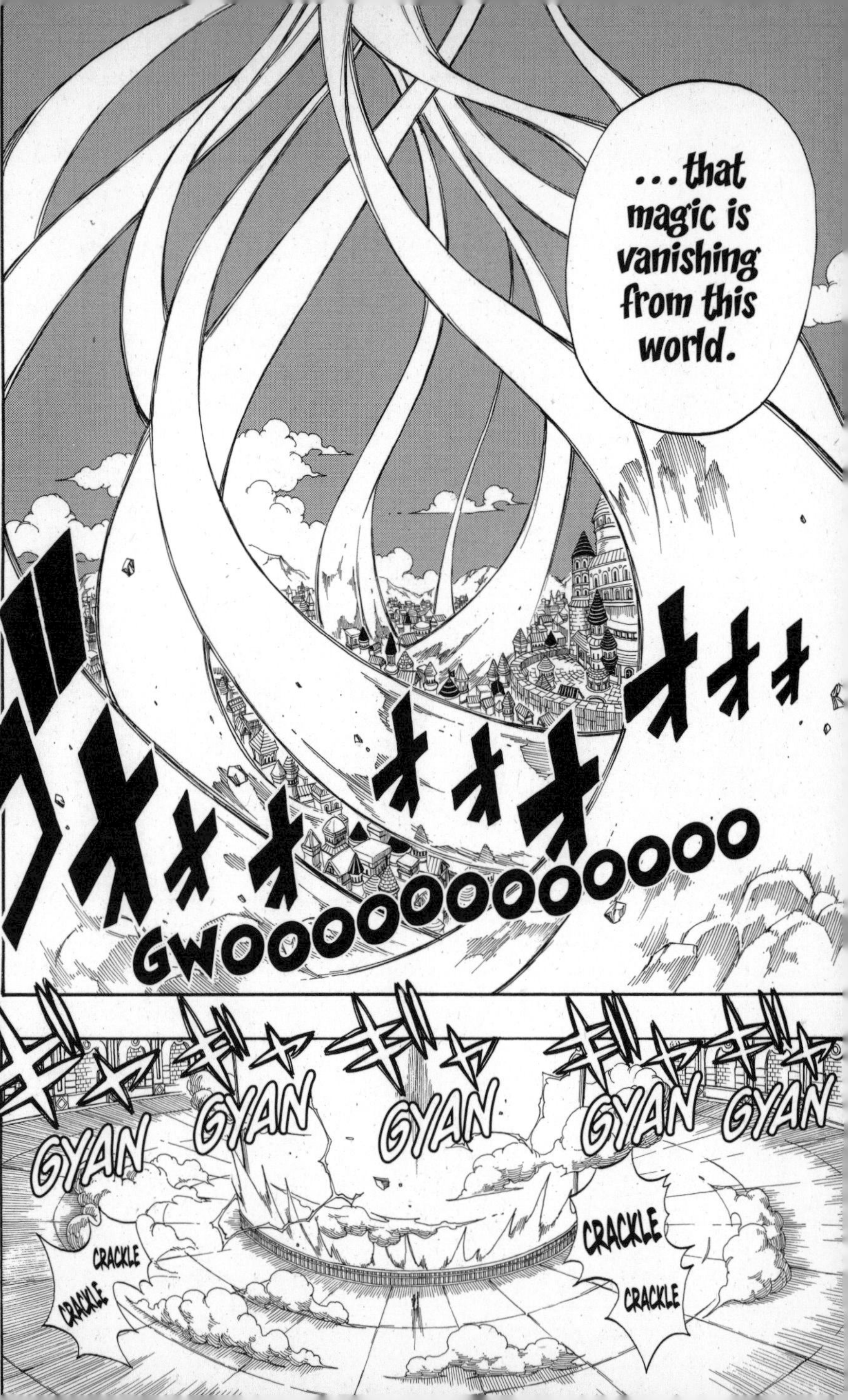
...that magic is vanishing from this world.
GWOOOOOOOOOOOO
GYAN
GYAN
CRACKLE
CRACKLE
GYAN
GYAN
GYAN
CRACKLE
CRACKLE

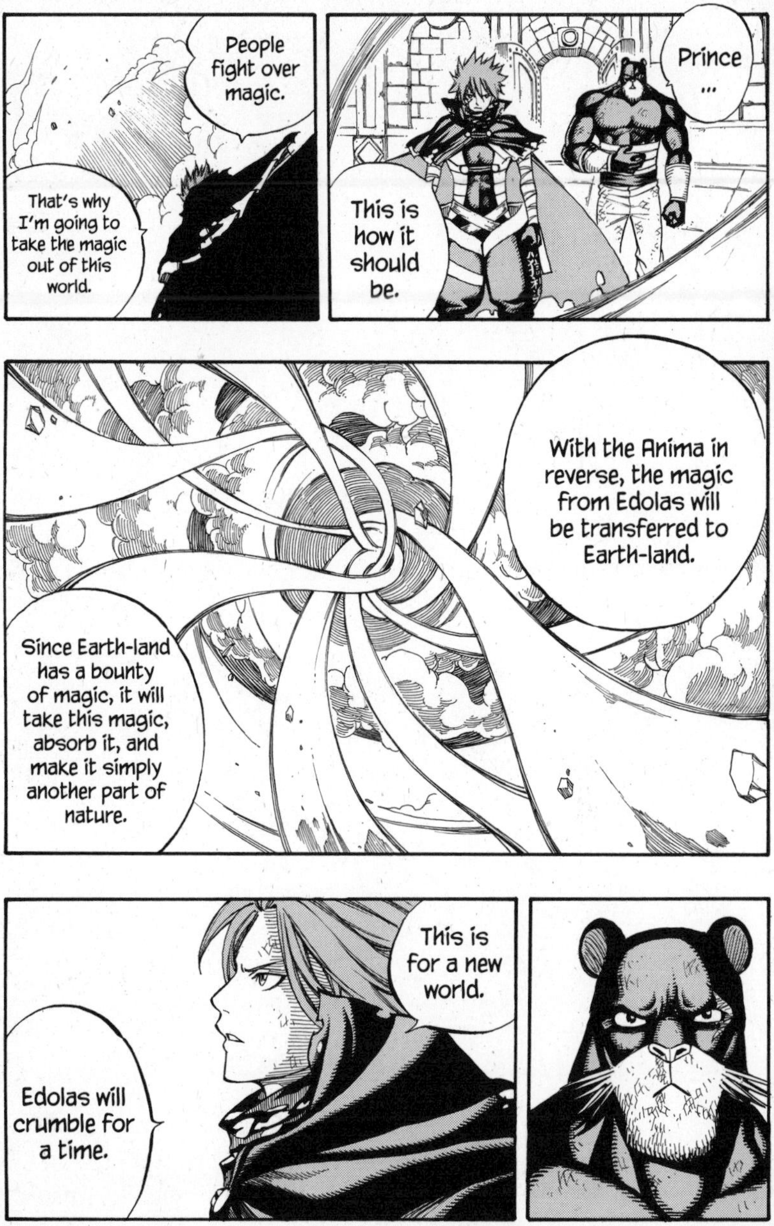
Prince ...
This is how it should be.
People fight over magic.
That's why I'm going to take the magic out of this world.
With the Anima in reverse, the magic from Edolas will be transferred to Earth-land.
Since Earth-land has a bounty of magic, it will take this magic, absorb it, and make it simply another part of nature.
This is for a new world.
Edolas will crumble for a time.

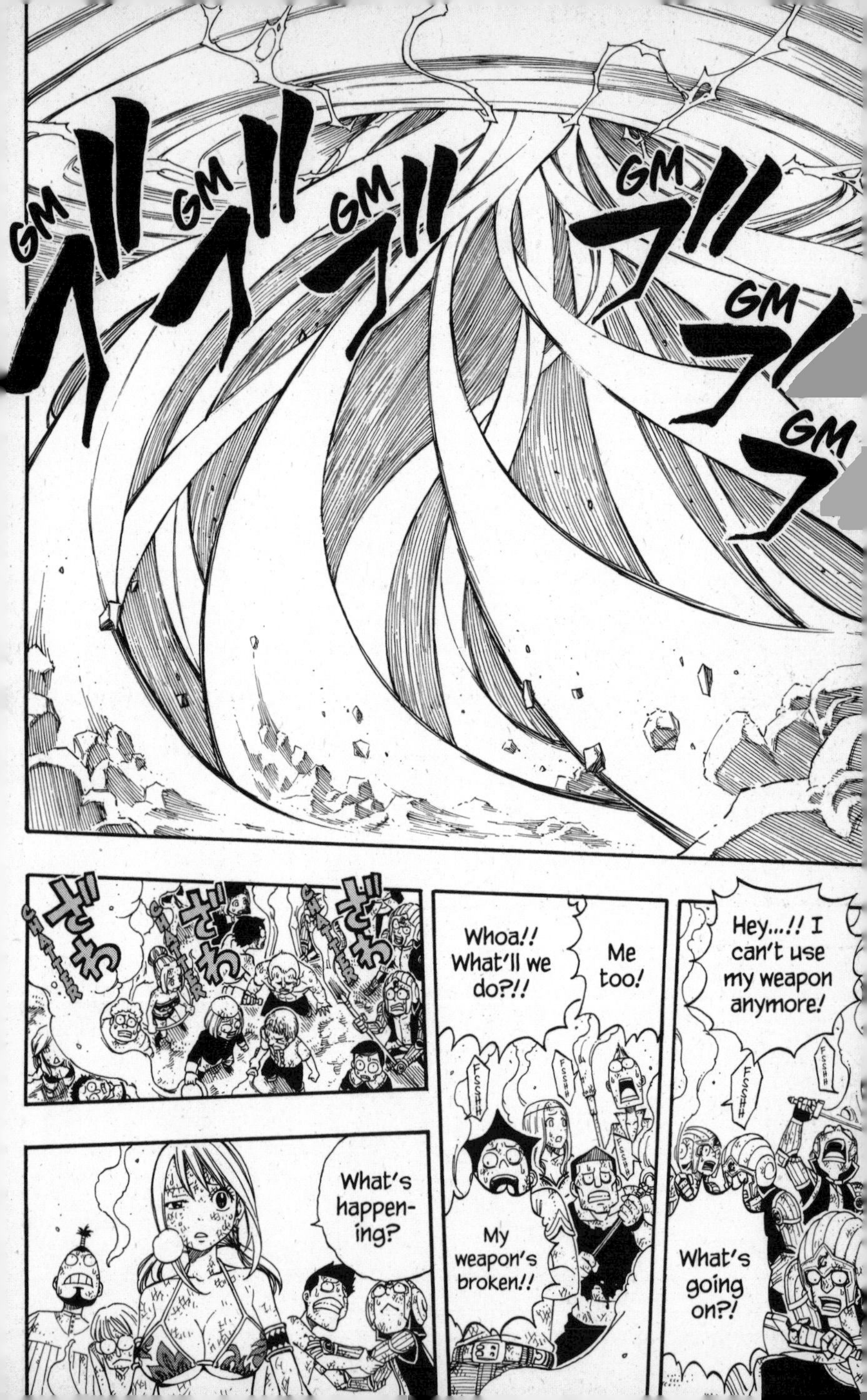

GM
GM
GM
GM
GM
GM
Hey...!! I can't use my weapon anymore!
FSSHH
What's going on?!
Me too!
Whoa!! What'll we do?!!
FSSHH
FSSHH
FSSHH
My weapon's broken!!
ざわ
ざわ
ざわ
What's happening?

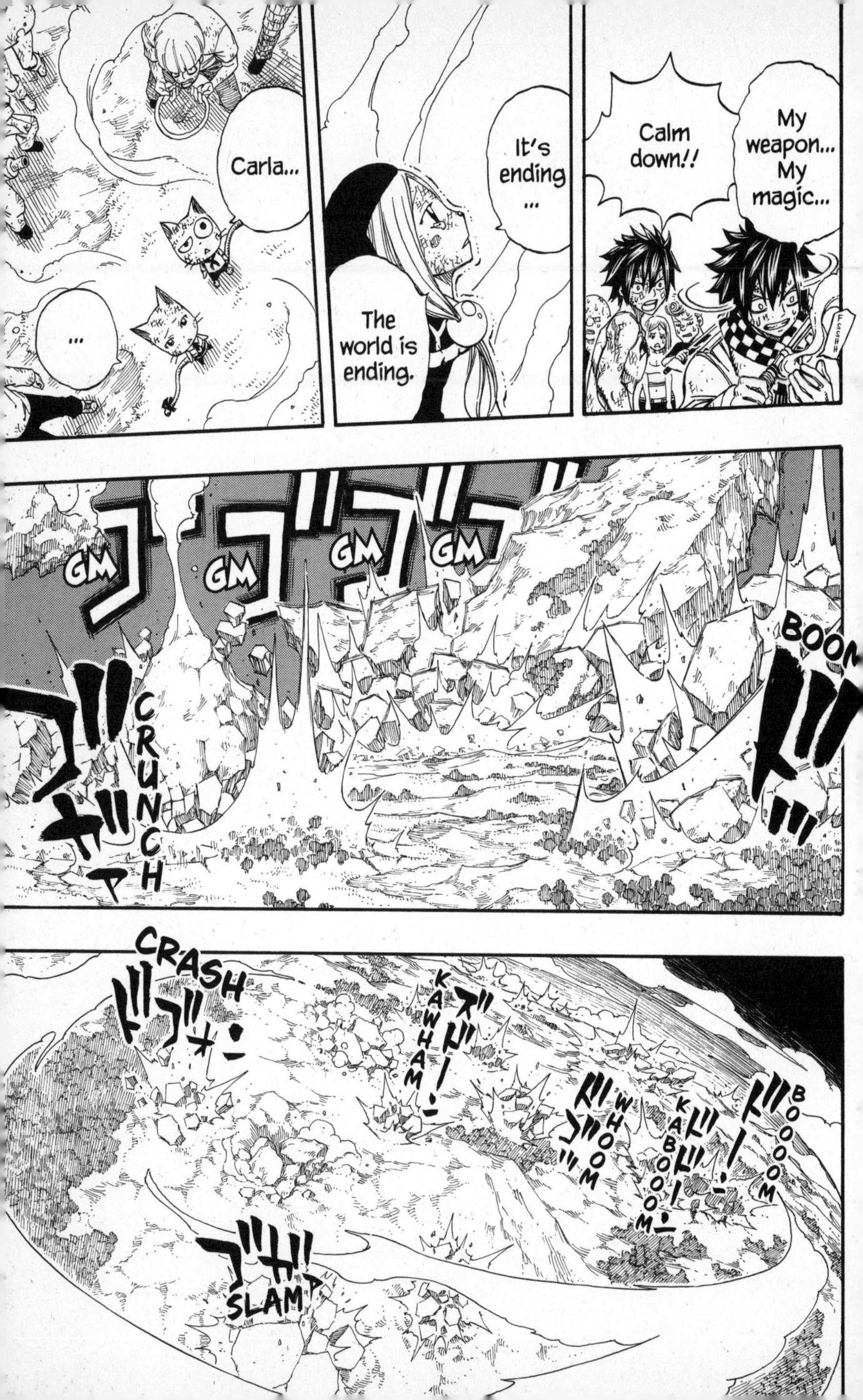
My weapon... My magic...
Calm down!!
It's ending ...
The world is ending.
Carla...
...
BOOM
GM
GM
GM
GM
CRUNCH
BOOOOOM
KABOOOOM
WHOOOM
KAWHAM
CRASH
SLAM

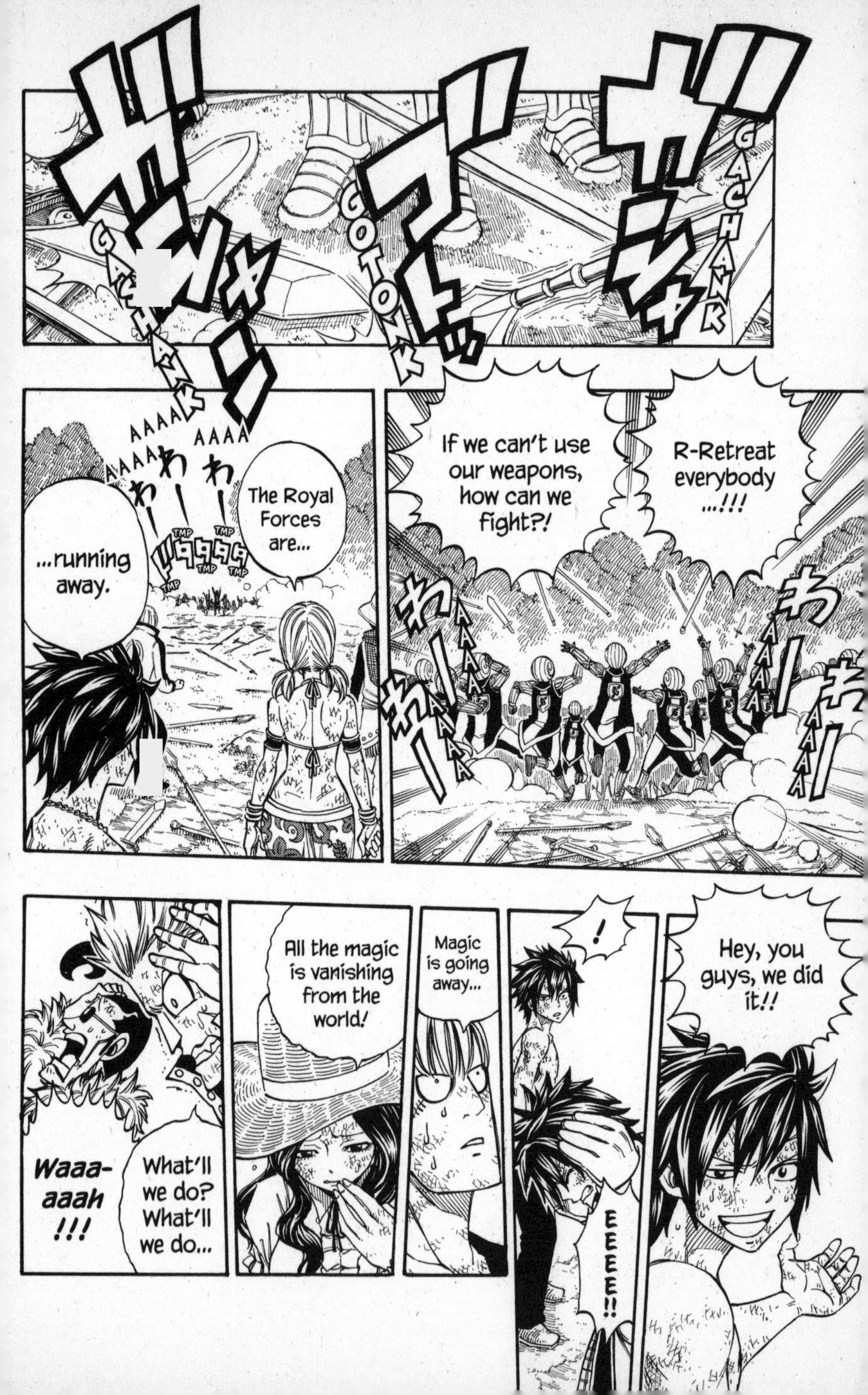
GACHANK
GOTONK
GACHANK
R-Retreat everybody ...!!!
If we can't use our weapons, how can we fight?!
The Royal Forces are...
...running away.
AAAA
AAAA
AAAA
TMP
TMP
TMP
TMP
Hey, you guys, we did it!!
!
EEEEE!!
Magic is going away...
All the magic is vanishing from the world!
What'll we do? What'll we do...
Waaa-aaah!!!

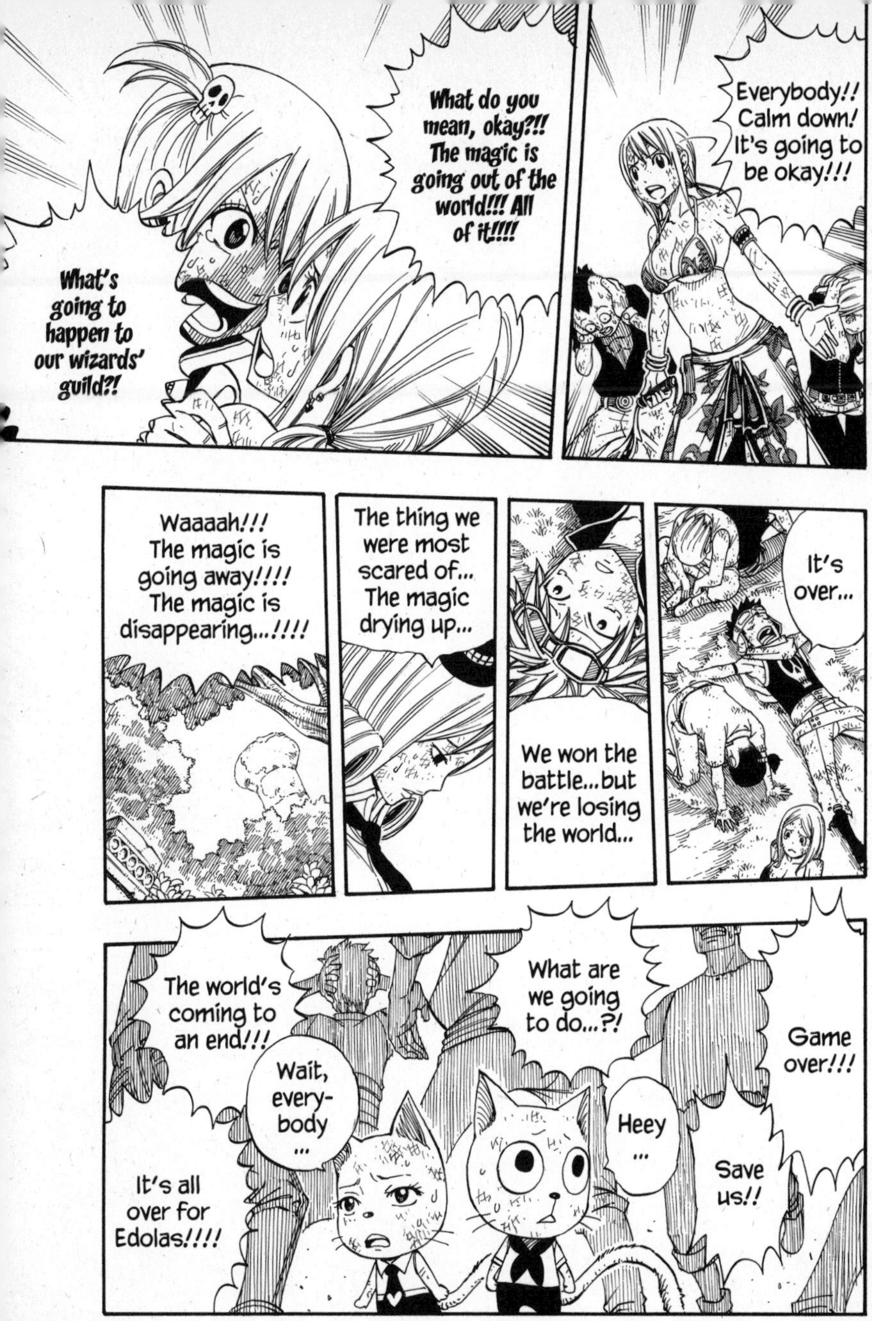

Everybody!! Calm down! It's going to be okay!!!
What do you mean, okay?!! The magic is going out of the world!!! All of it!!!!
What's going to happen to our wizards' guild?!
It's over...
We won the battle...but we're losing the world...
The thing we were most scared of... The magic drying up...
Waaaah!!! The magic is going away!!!! The magic is disappearing...!!!!
Game over!!!
What are we going to do...?!
Save us!!
Heey ...
The world's coming to an end!!!
Wait, every-body ...
It's all over for Edolas!!!!

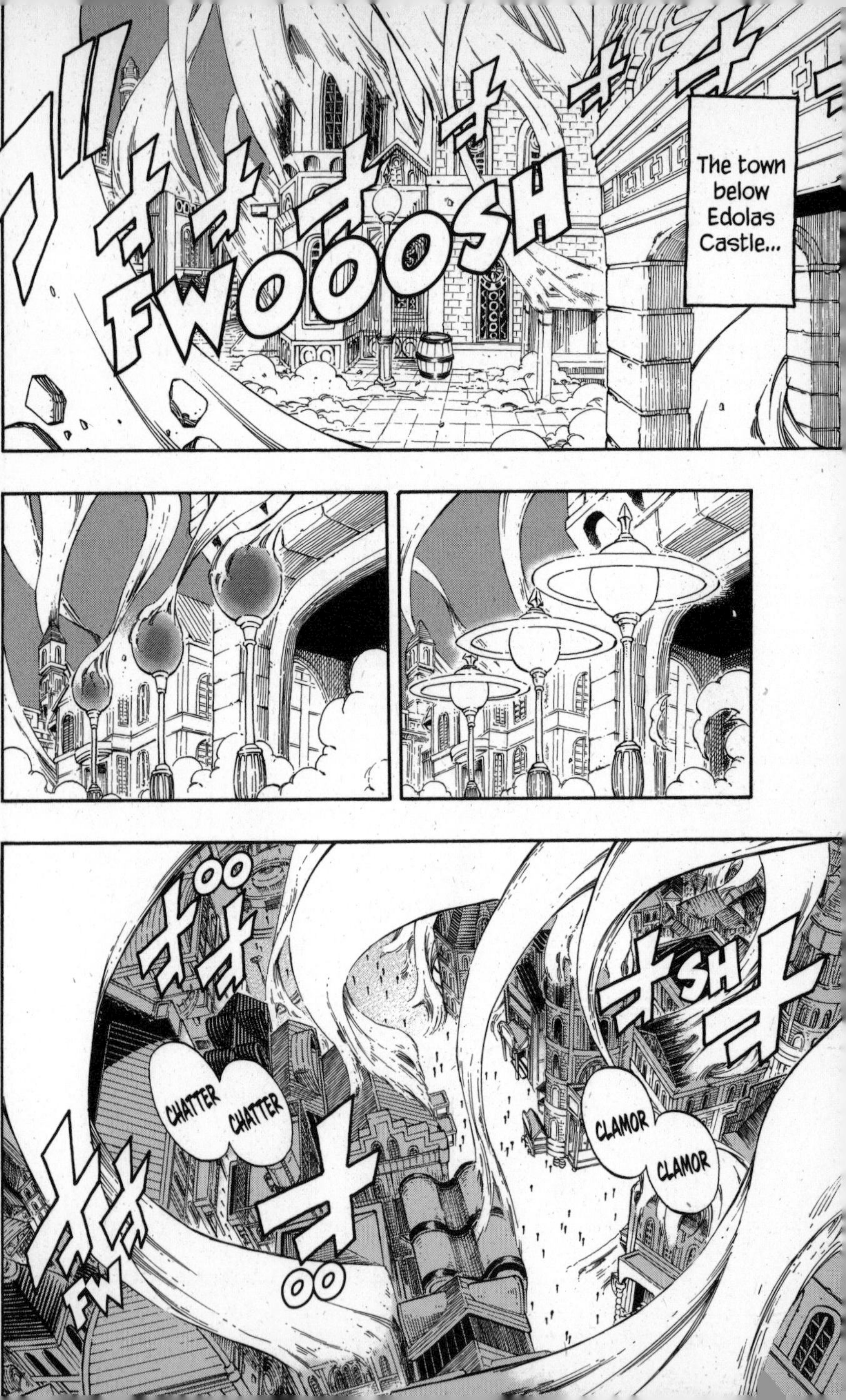
The town below Edolas Castle...
FWOOOSH
SH
CLAMOR CLAMOR
CHATTER CHATTER
FW

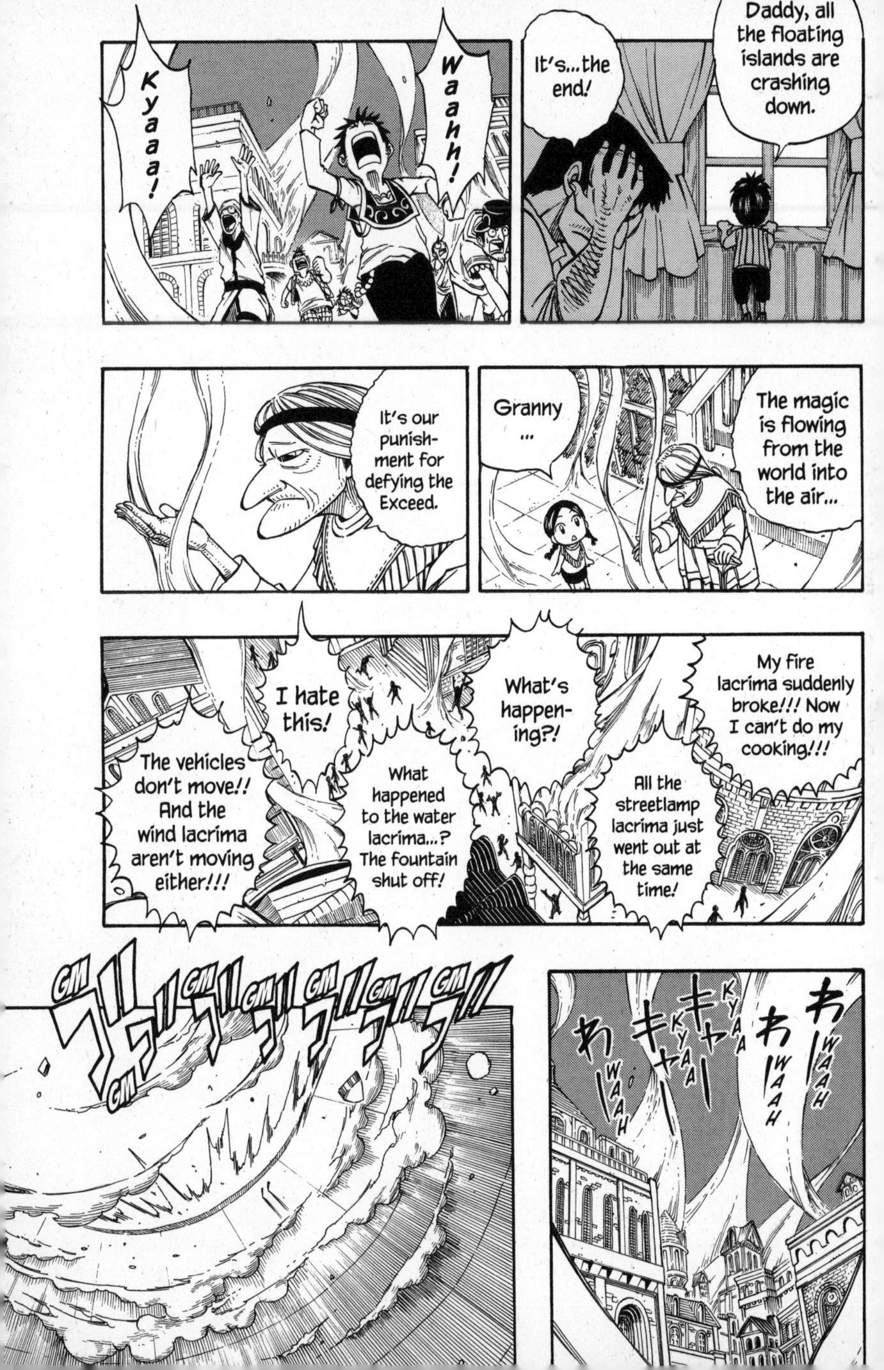

Daddy, all the floating islands are crashing down.
It's...the end!
Waahh!
Kyaaa!
The magic is flowing from the world into the air...
Granny ...
It's our punishment for defying the Exceed.
My fire lacrima suddenly broke!!! Now I can't do my cooking!!!
What's happening?!
All the streetlamp lacrima just went out at the same time!
I hate this!
What happened to the water lacrima...? The fountain shut off!
The vehicles don't move!! And the wind lacrima aren't moving either!!!
WAAH
WAAH
KYAA
KYAA
WAAH
GM
GM
GM
GM
GM
GM
GM

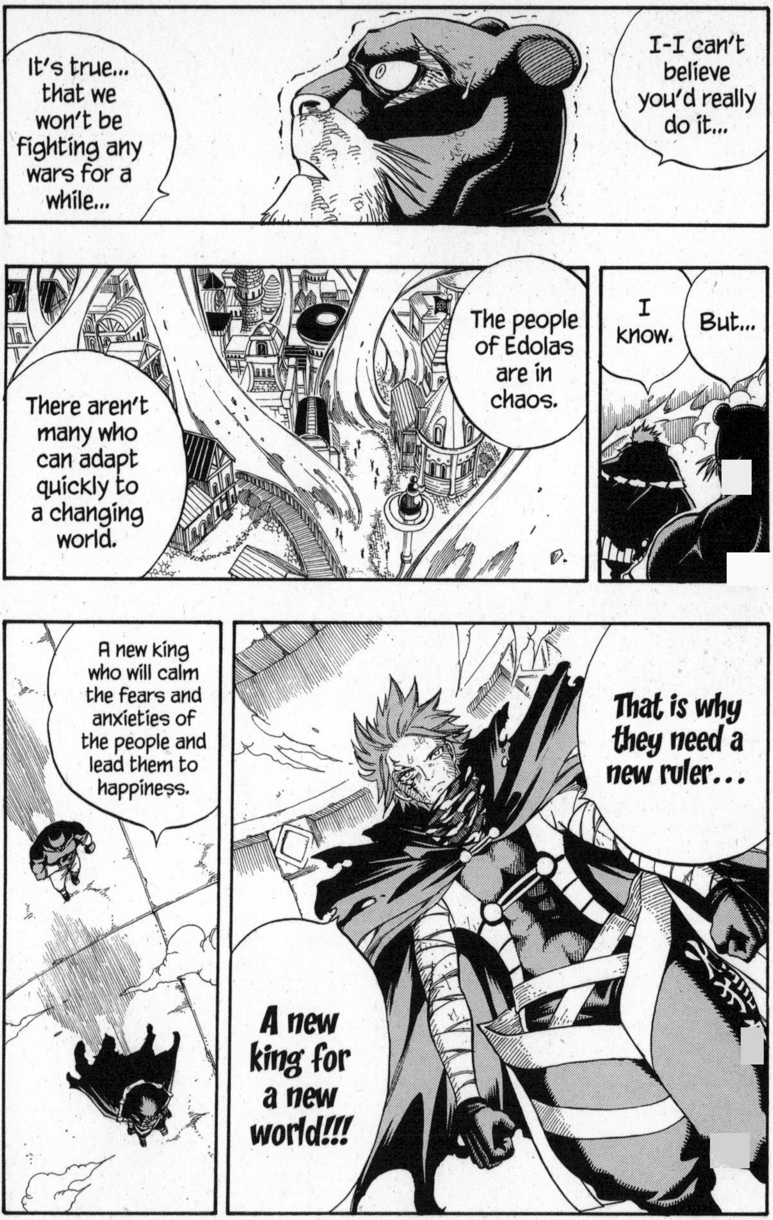
I-I can't believe you'd really do it...
It's true... that we won't be fighting any wars for a while...
But...
I know.
The people of Edolas are in chaos.
There aren't many who can adapt quickly to a changing world.
That is why they need a new ruler...
A new king for a new world!!!
A new king who will calm the fears and anxieties of the people and lead them to happiness.

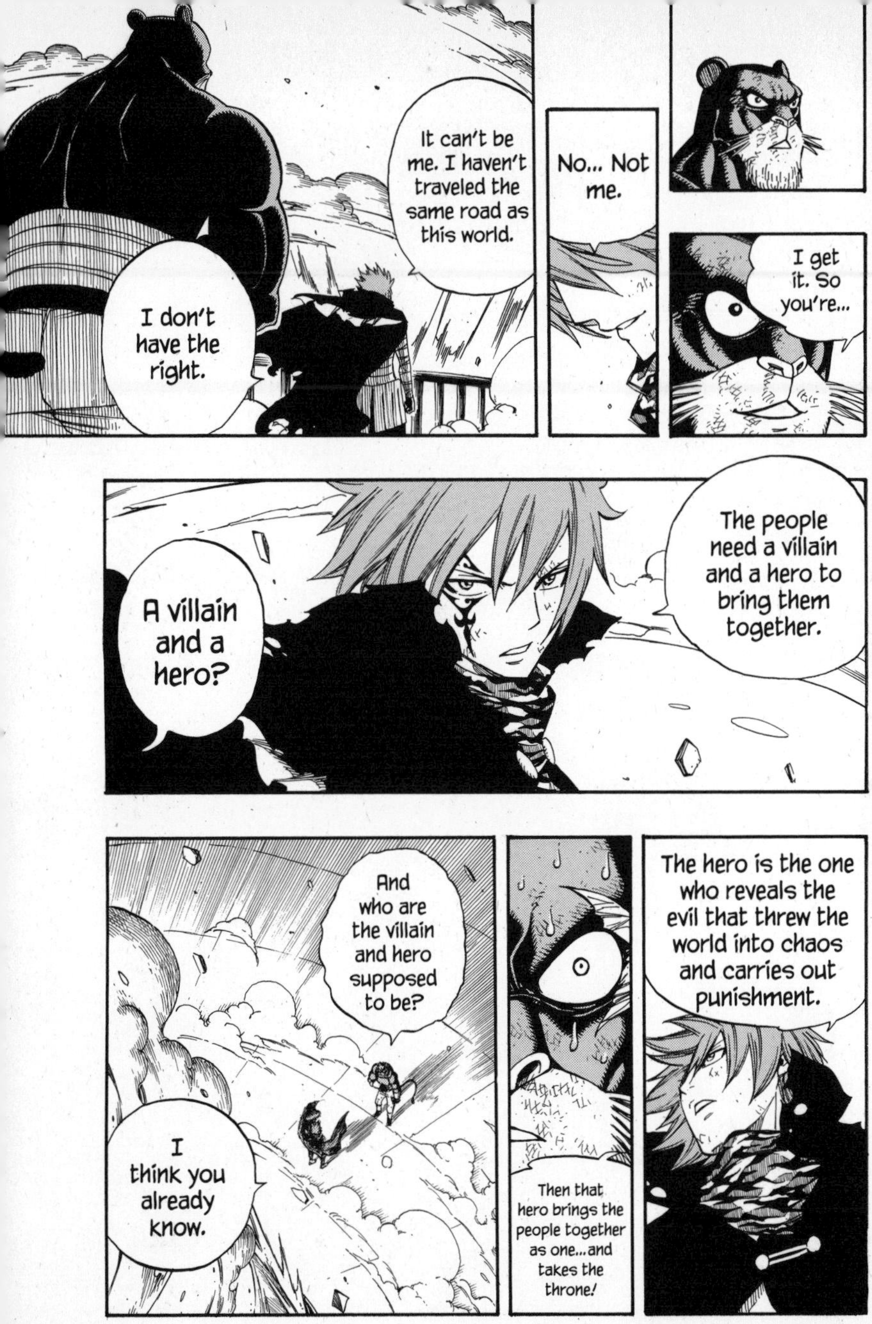
I get it. So you're...
No... Not me.
It can't be me. I haven't traveled the same road as this world.
I don't have the right.
The people need a villain and a hero to bring them together.
A villain and a hero?
The hero is the one who reveals the evil that threw the world into chaos and carries out punishment.
Then that hero brings the people together as one...and takes the throne!
And who are the villain and hero supposed to be?
I think you already know.

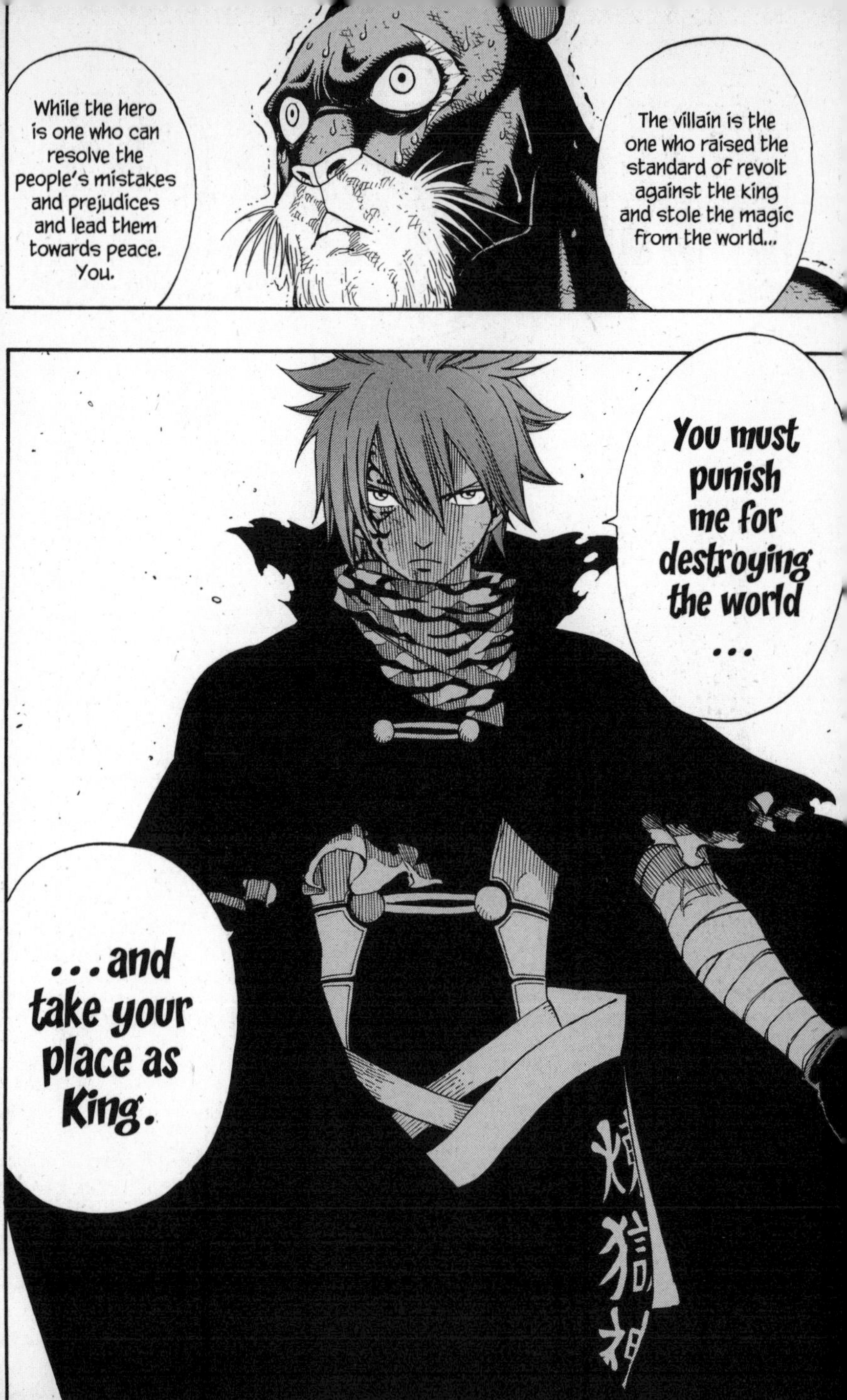
The villain is the one who raised the standard of revolt against the king and stole the magic from the world...
While the hero is one who can resolve the people's mistakes and prejudices and lead them towards peace. You.
You must punish me for destroying the world ...
...and take your place as King.

FAIRY TAIL
フェアリーテイル

Chapter 196: Demon God Dragneel

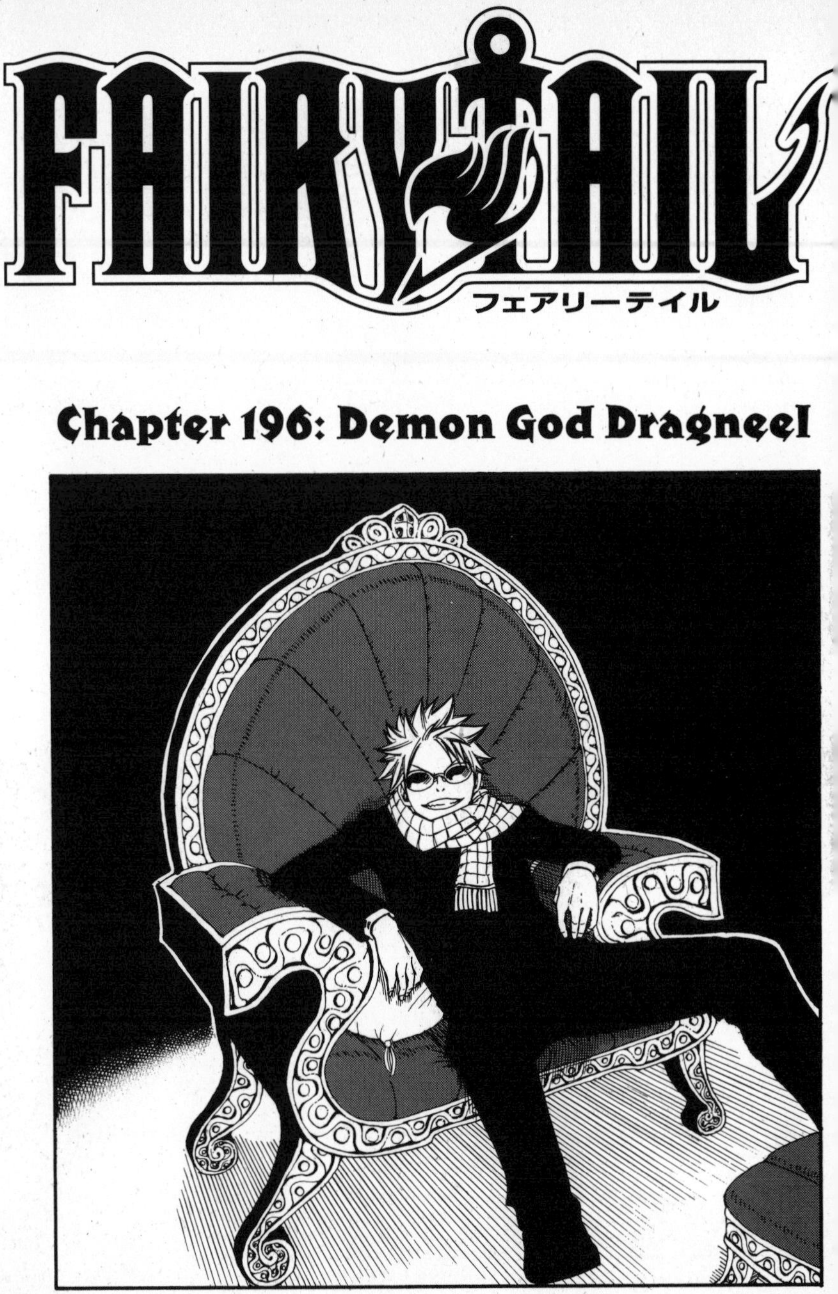

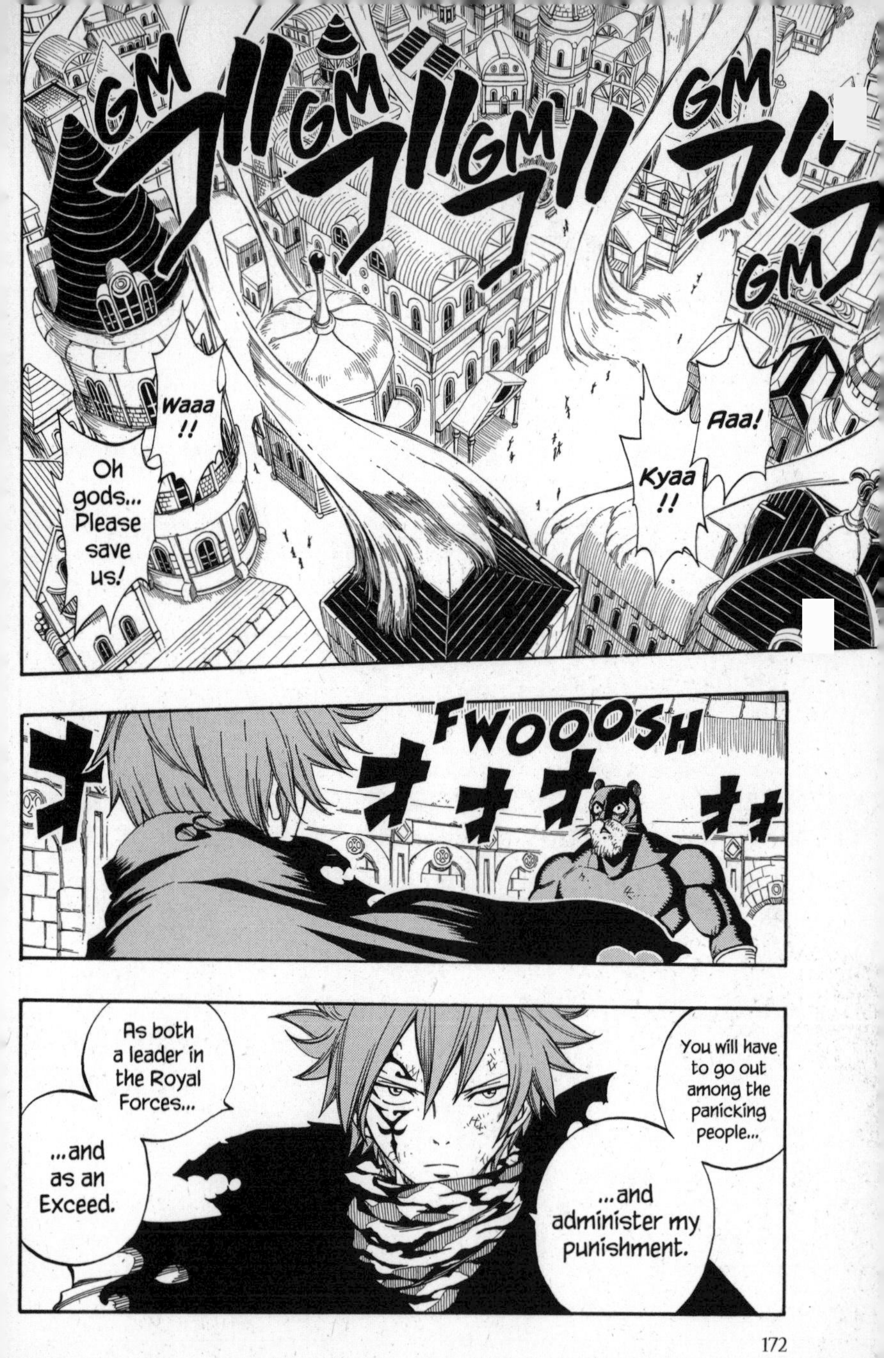
GM GM GM GM GM GM
Aaa!
Kyaa!!
Waaa!!
Oh gods... Please save us!
FWOOOSH
You will have to go out among the panicking people...
...and administer my punishment.
As both a leader in the Royal Forces...
...and as an Exceed.

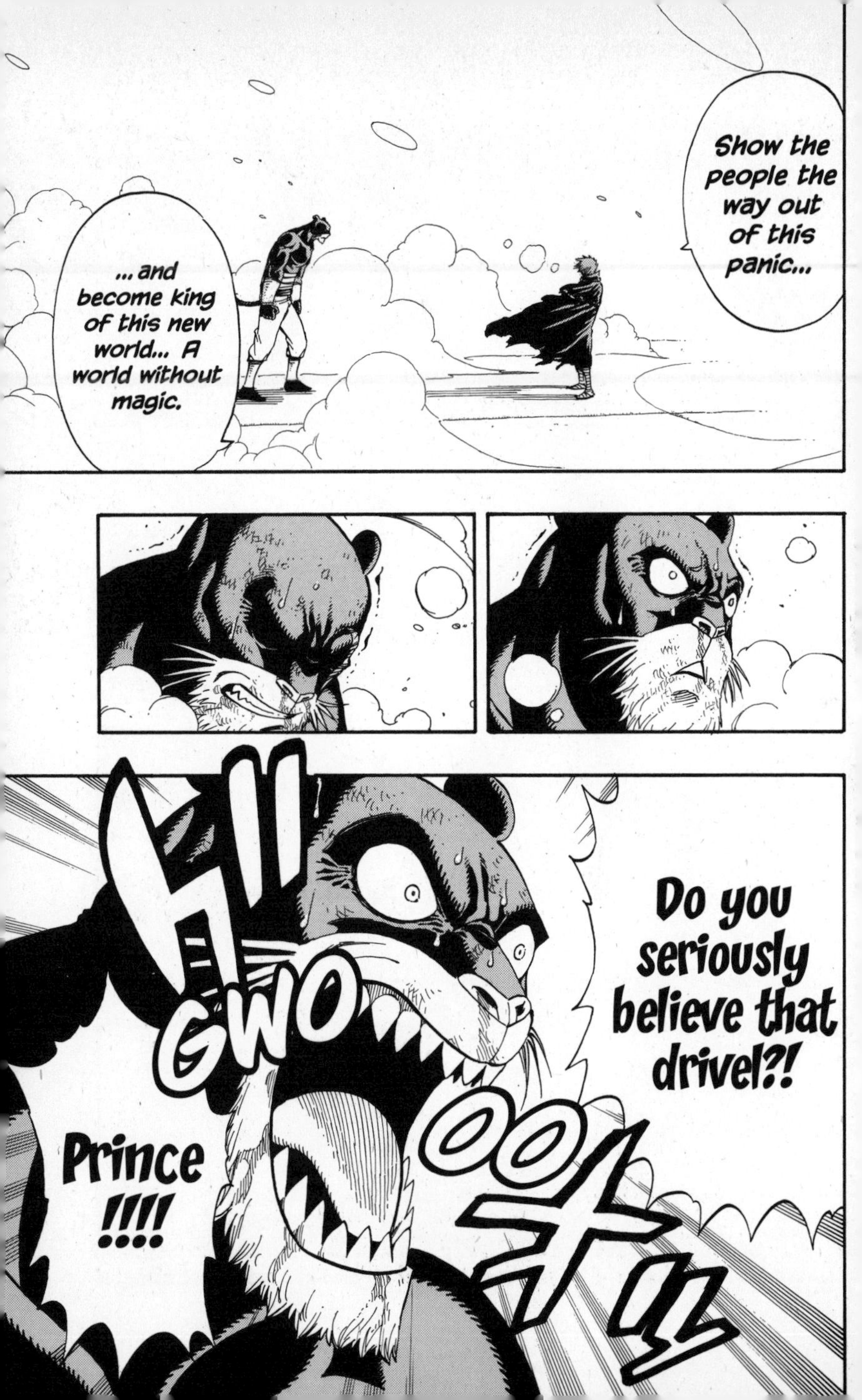

Show the people the way out of this panic...
...and become king of this new world... A world without magic.
Do you seriously believe that drivel?!
GWOOO
Prince!!!!

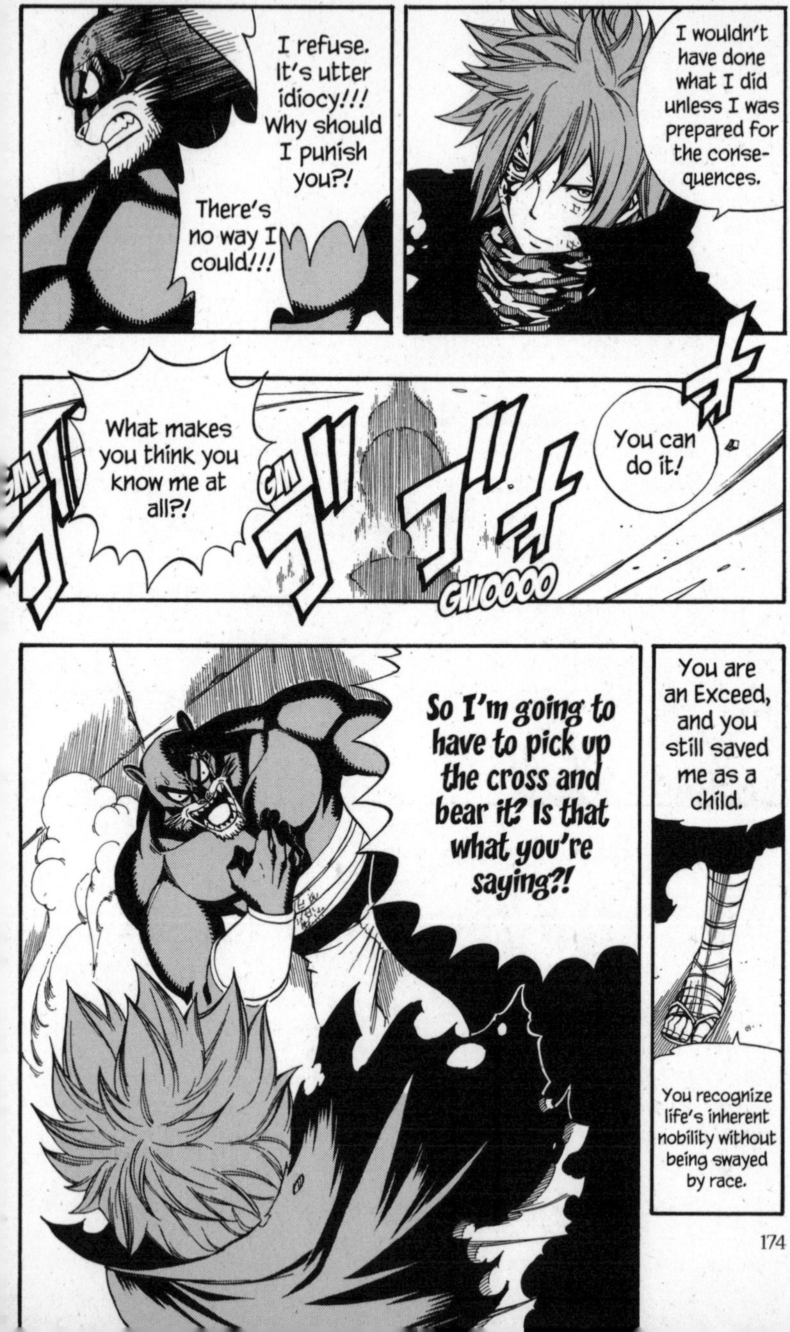
I wouldn't have done what I did unless I was prepared for the conse- quences.
I refuse. It's utter idiocy!!! Why should I punish you?!
There's no way I could!!!
You can do it!
GWOOOO
GM
What makes you think you know me at all?!
GM
You are an Exceed, and you still saved me as a child.
You recognize life's inherent nobility without being swayed by race.
So I'm going to have to pick up the cross and bear it? Is that what you're saying?!

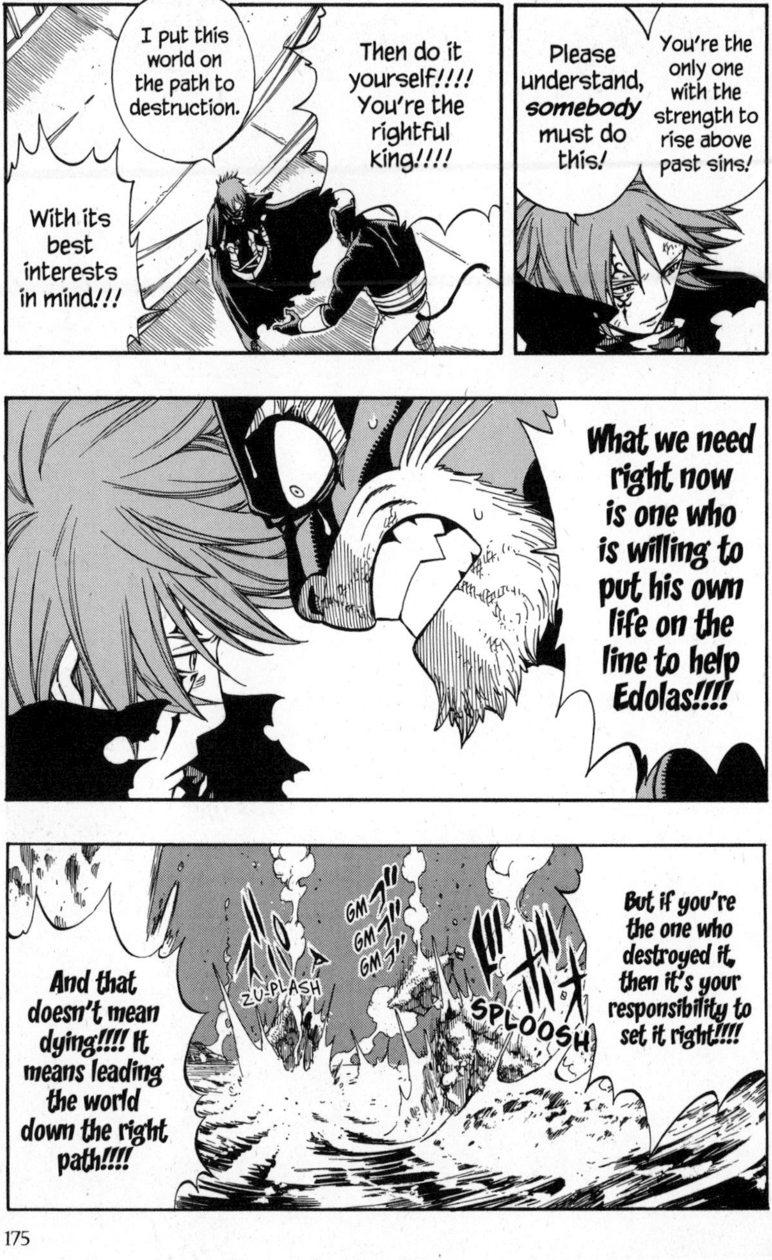
You're the only one with the strength to rise above past sins!
Please understand, *somebody* must do this!
Then do it yourself!!!! You're the rightful king!!!!
I put this world on the path to destruction.
With its best interests in mind!!!
What we need right now is one who is willing to put his own life on the line to help Edolas!!!!
But if you're the one who destroyed it, then it's your responsibility to set it right!!!!
GM GM GM
SPLOOSH
ZU-PLASH
And that doesn't mean dying!!!! It means leading the world down the right path!!!!

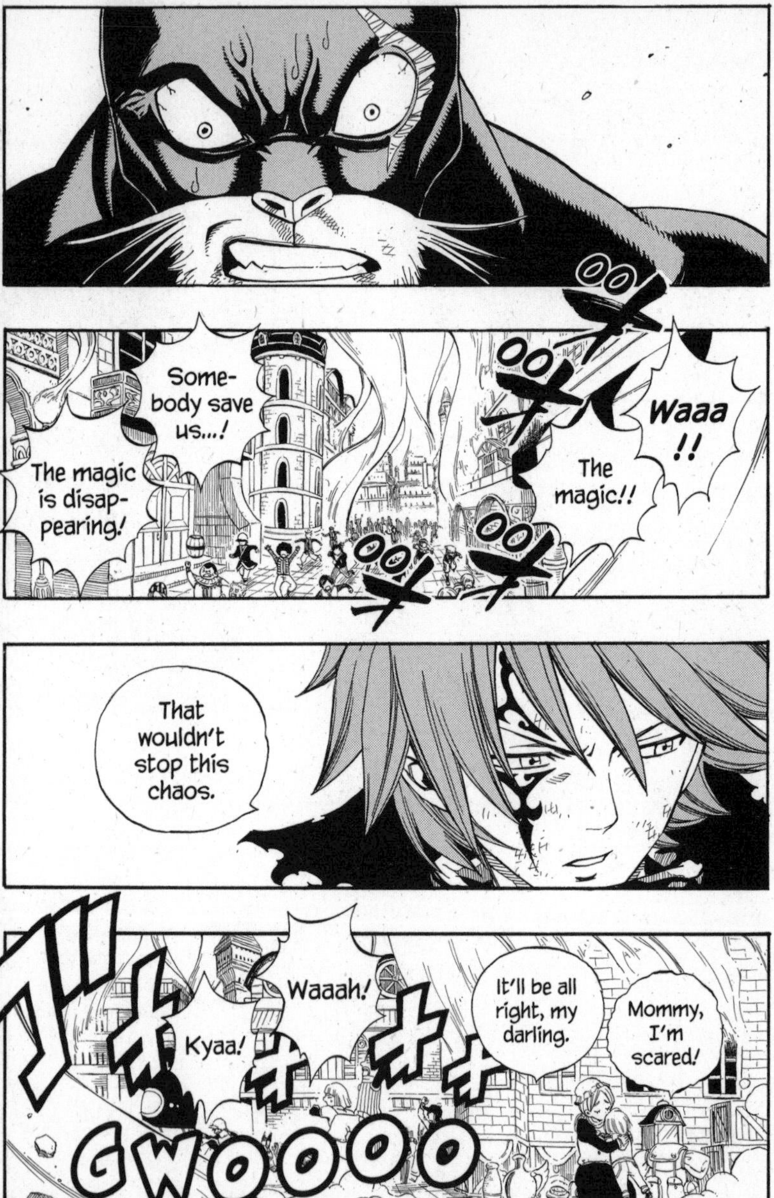
Waaa !!
The magic!!
Some-body save us...!
The magic is disap-pearing!
That wouldn't stop this chaos.
Mommy, I'm scared!
It'll be all right, my darling.
Waaah!
Kyaa!
GWOOOOO

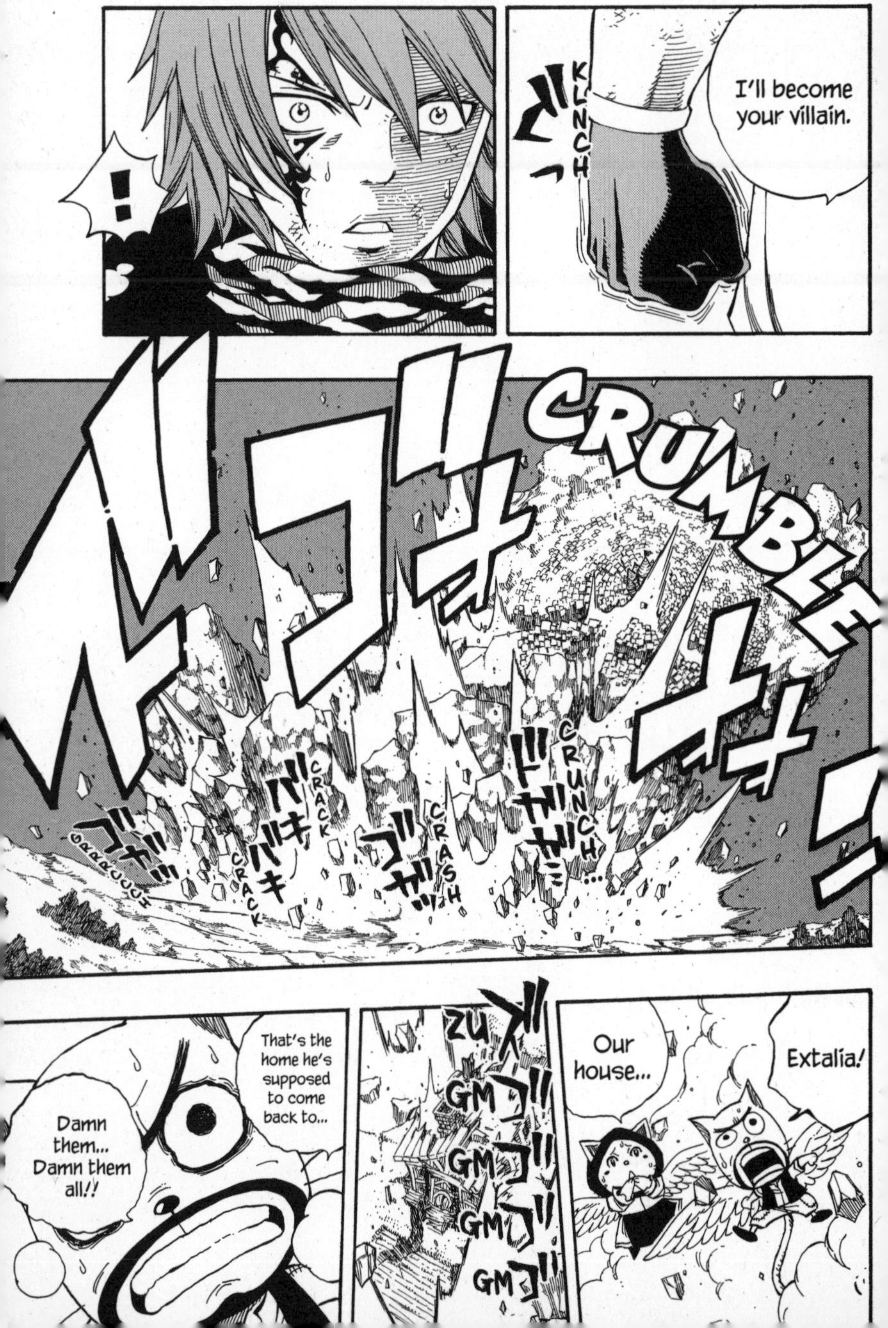
I'll become your villain.
KLUNCH
!
CRUMBLE
CRUNCH
CRASH
CRACK
CRACK
GRRRUUUH
Extalia!
Our house...
ZU
GM
GM
GM
GM
That's the home he's supposed to come back to...
Damn them... Damn them all!!

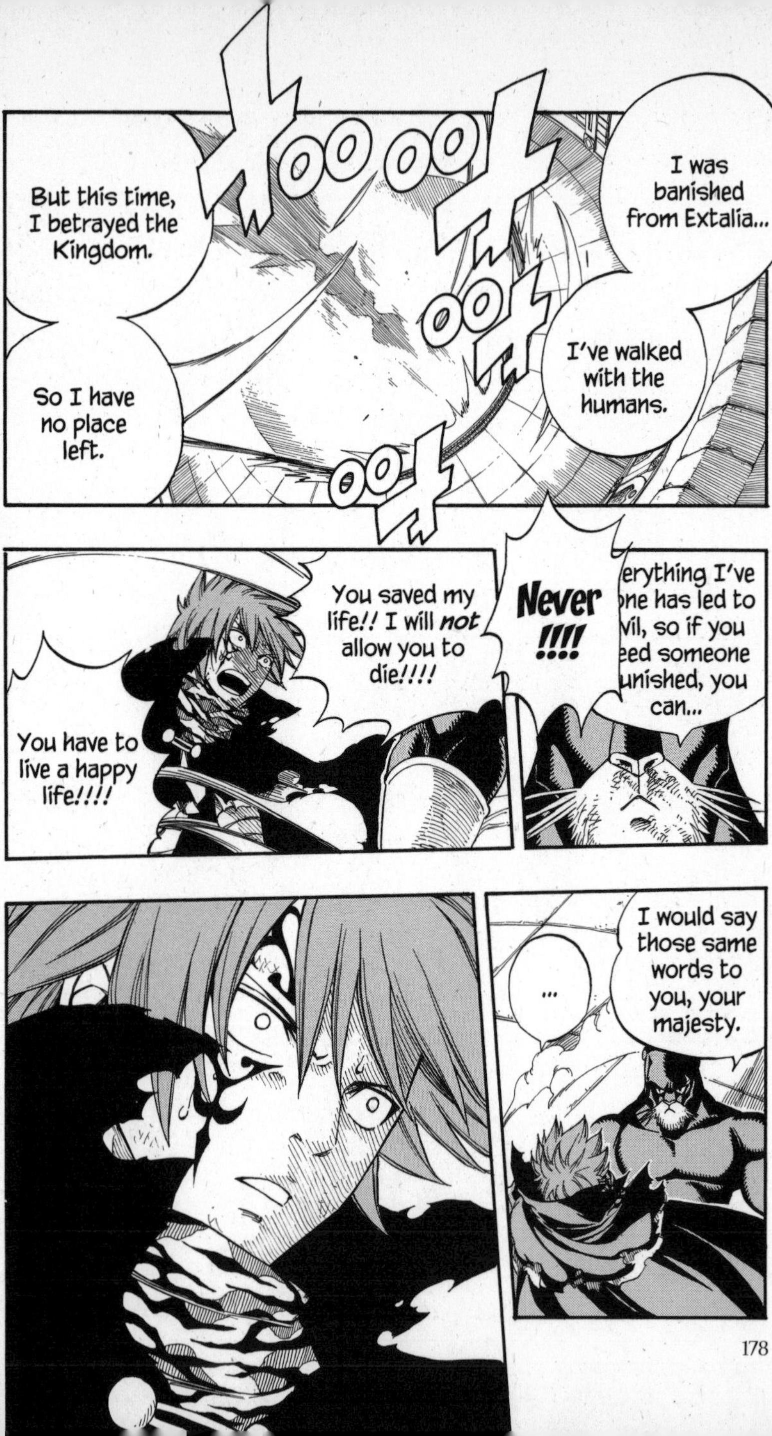
I was banished from Extalia...
I've walked with the humans.
OOOO
OO
OO
But this time, I betrayed the Kingdom.
So I have no place left.
erything I've one has led to vil, so if you eed someone unished, you can...
Never!!!!
You saved my life!! I will *not* allow you to die!!!!
You have to live a happy life!!!!
I would say those same words to you, your majesty.
...

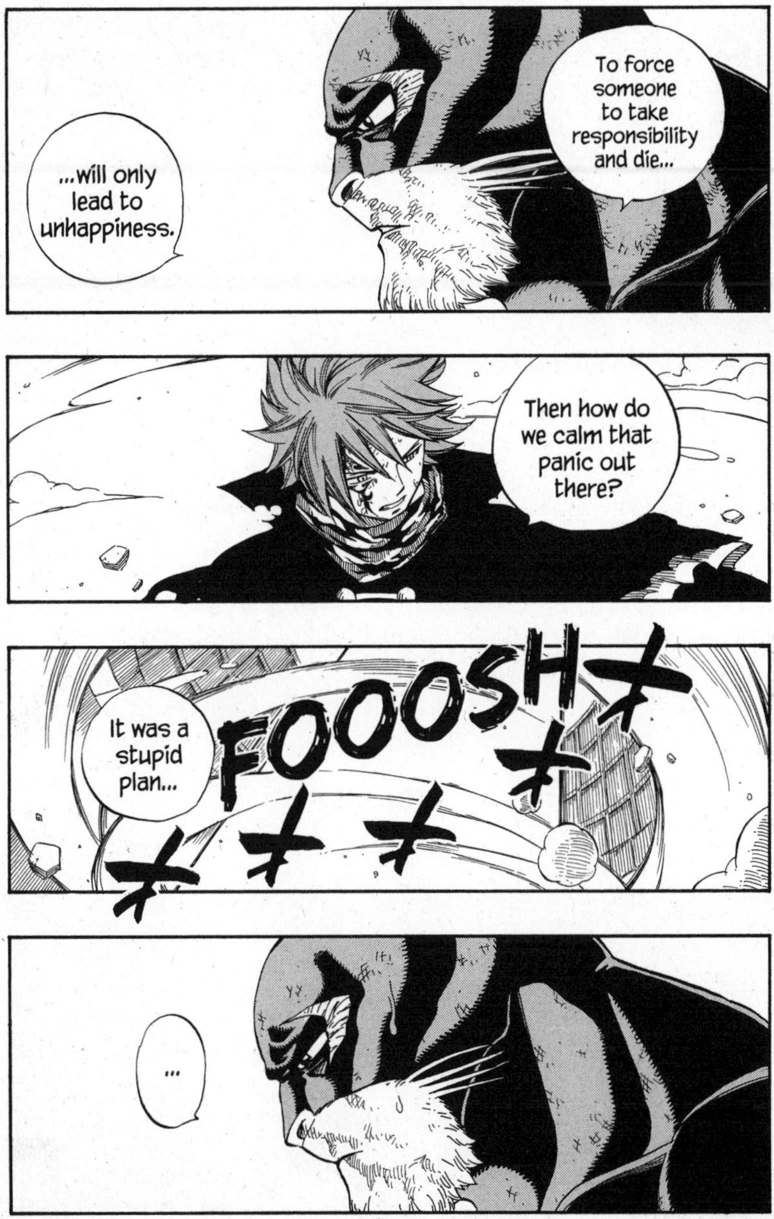
To force someone to take responsibility and die...
...will only lead to unhappiness.
Then how do we calm that panic out there?
FOOOSH
It was a stupid plan...
...

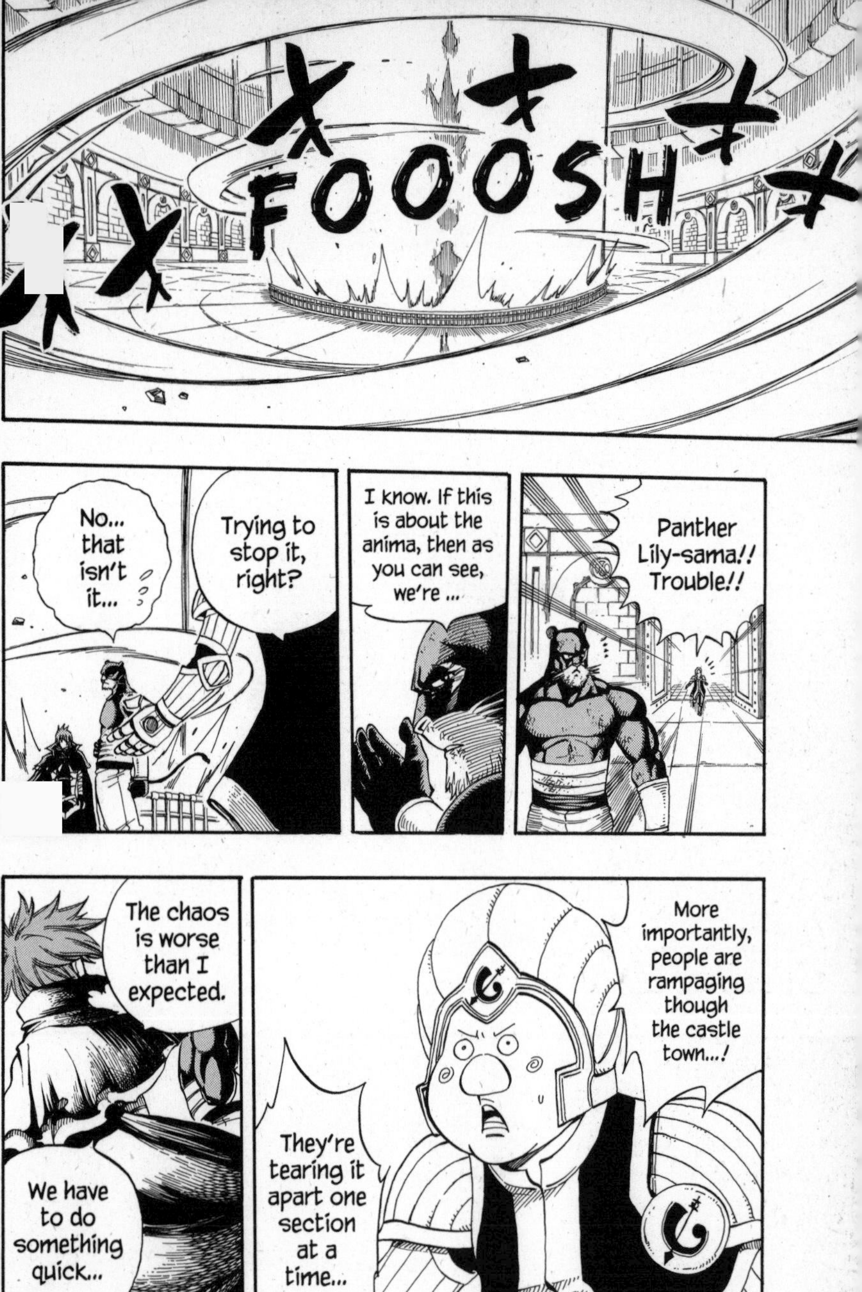
FOOOSH
Panther Lily-sama!! Trouble!!
I know. If this is about the anima, then as you can see, we're ...
Trying to stop it, right?
No... that isn't it...
More importantly, people are rampaging though the castle town...!
They're tearing it apart one section at a time...
The chaos is worse than I expected.
We have to do something quick...

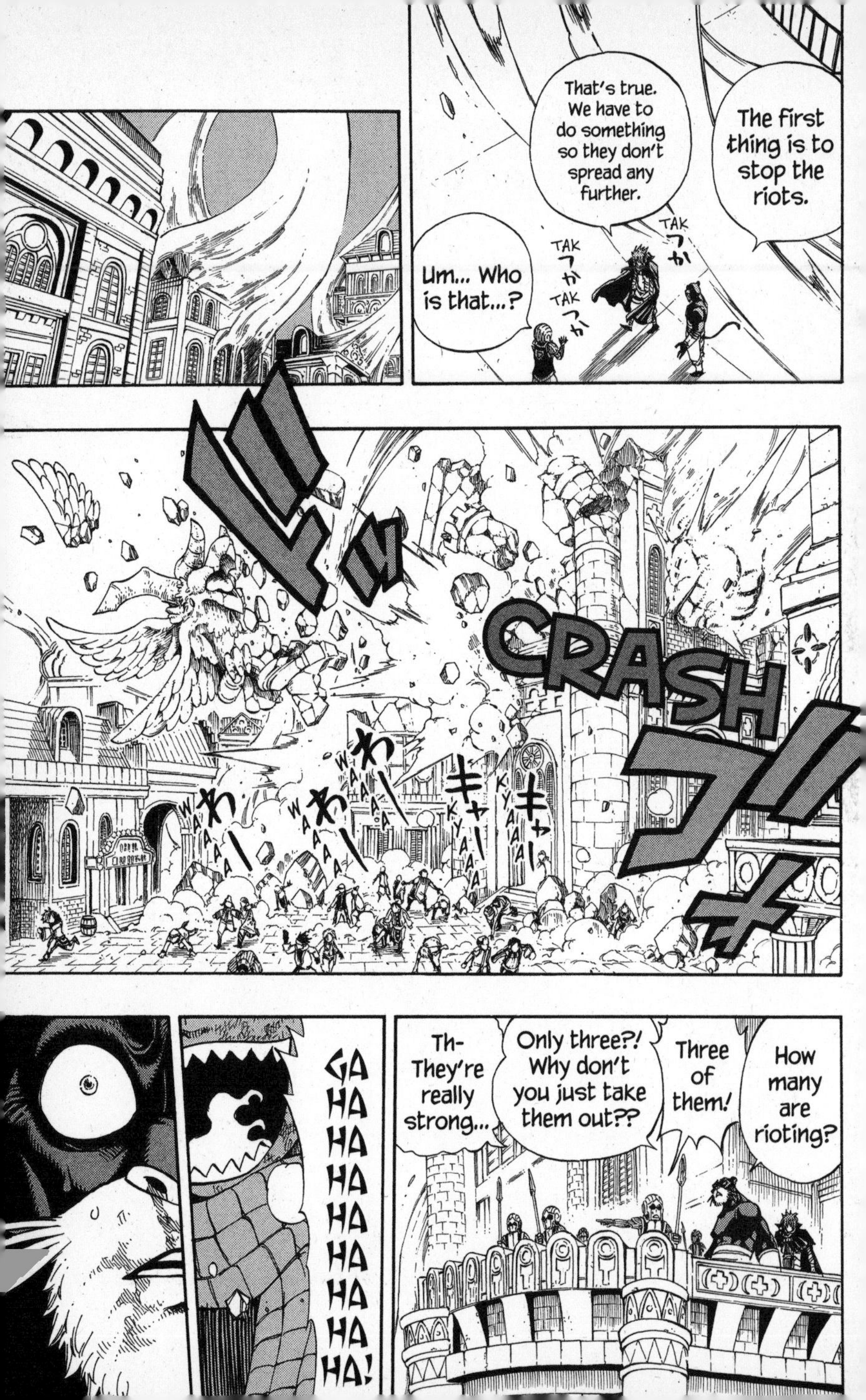

The first thing is to stop the riots.
That's true. We have to do something so they don't spread any further.
TAK つか
TAK つか
TAK つか
Um... Who is that...?
CRASH
WAAAAA わー
WAAAAA わー
WAAAAA わー
KYAAAA キャー
KYAAAA キャー
How many are rioting?
Three of them!
Only three?! Why don't you just take them out??
Th- They're really strong...
GA HA HA HA HA HA HA HA HA HA HA HA!

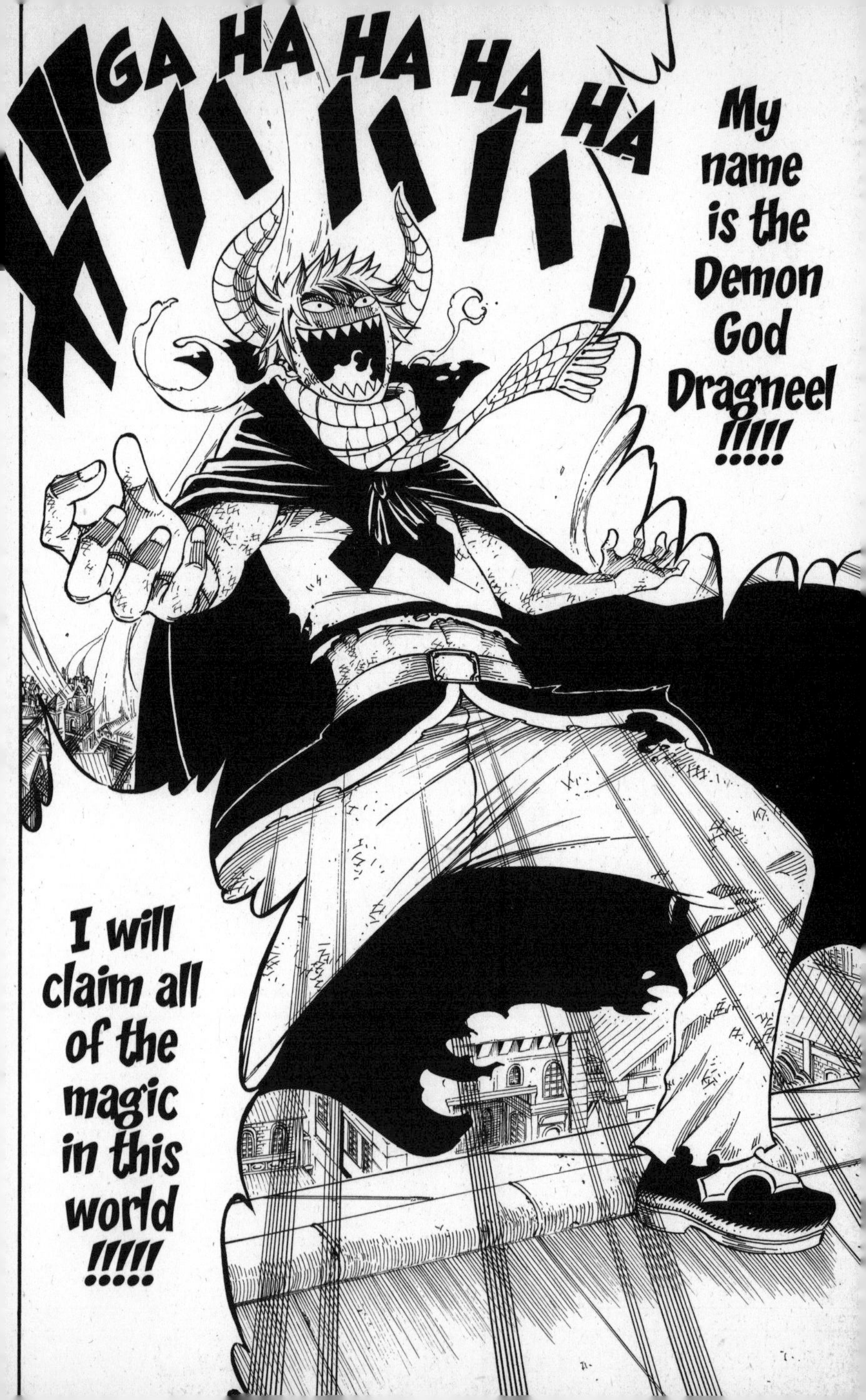
GA HA HA HA HA HA!!!
My name is the Demon God Dragneel!!!!!
I will claim all of the magic in this world!!!!!

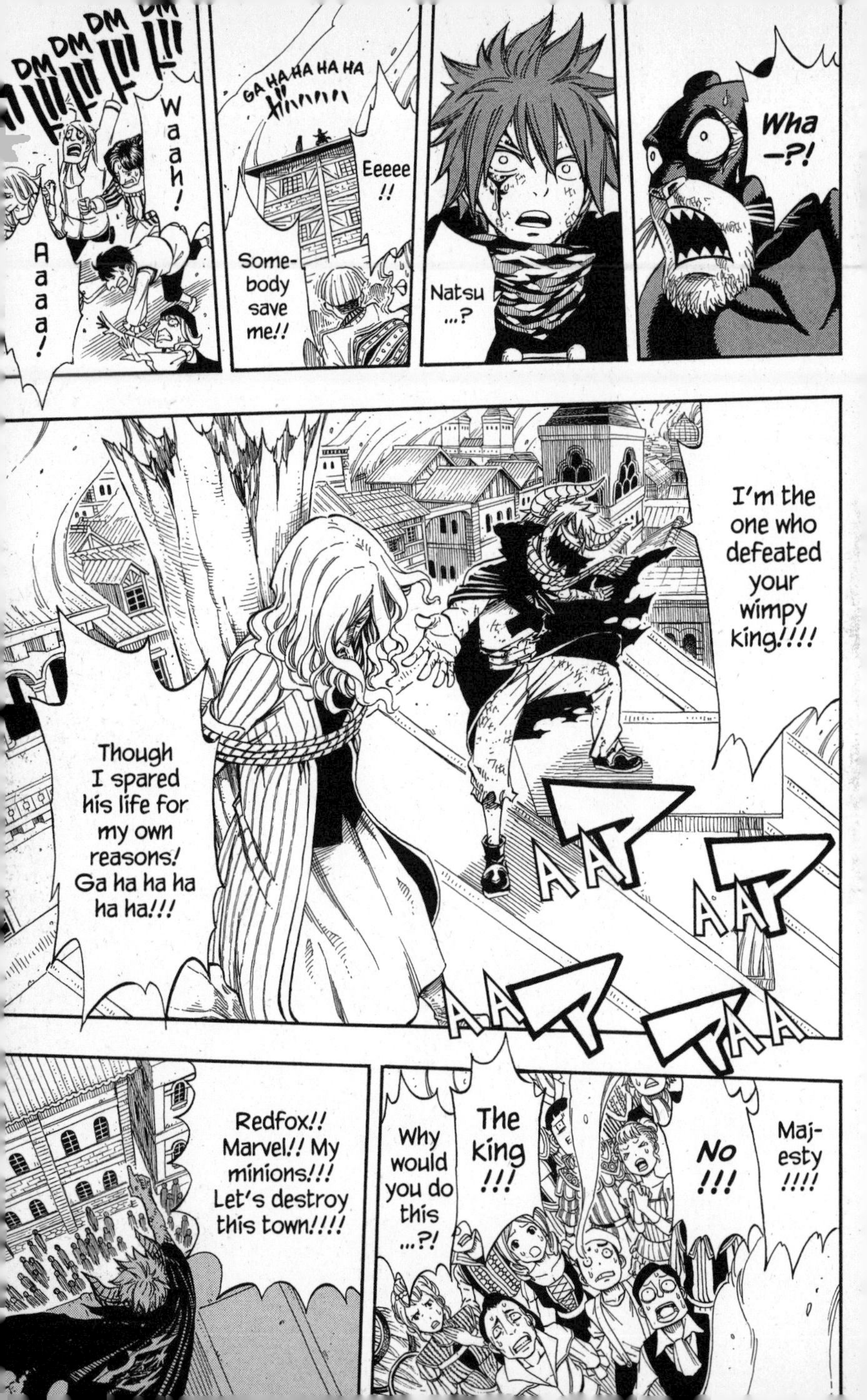
Wha—?!
Natsu ...?
GA HA HA HA HA
Eeeee!!
Some-body save me!!
DM DM DM DM
Waah!
Aaaa!
I'm the one who defeated your wimpy king!!!!
Though I spared his life for my own reasons! Ga ha ha ha ha ha!!!
AAAAAAAA
Maj-esty!!!!
No!!!
The king!!!
Why would you do this ...?!
Redfox!! Marvel!! My minions!!! Let's destroy this town!!!!

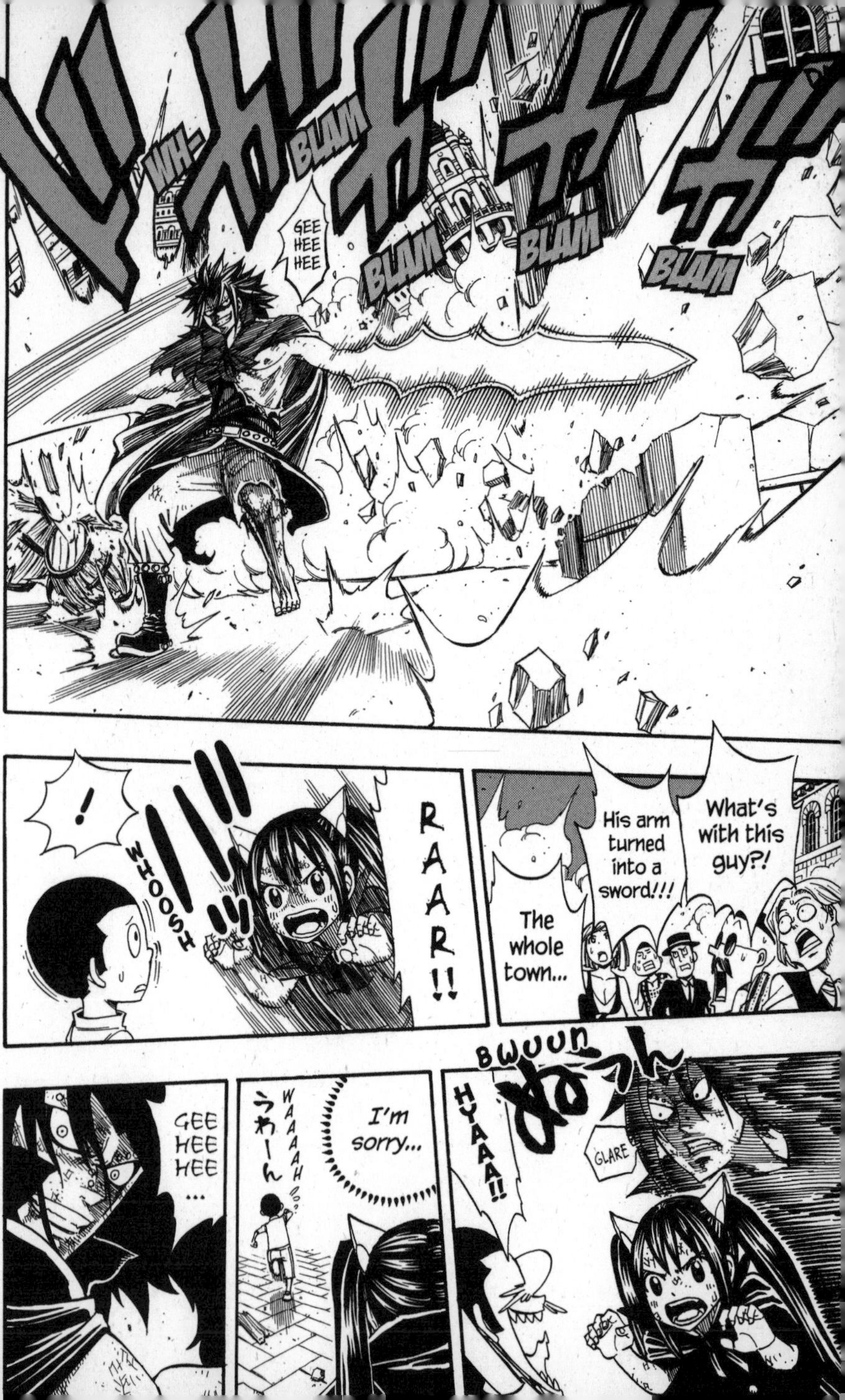
WH-
BLAM
BLAM
BLAM
BLAM
BLAM
GEE HEE HEE
What's with this guy?!
His arm turned into a sword!!!
The whole town...
RAAR!!
WHOOSH
!
BWUUN
GLARE
HYAAA!!
I'm sorry...
WAAAAH
うわーん
GEE HEE HEE ...

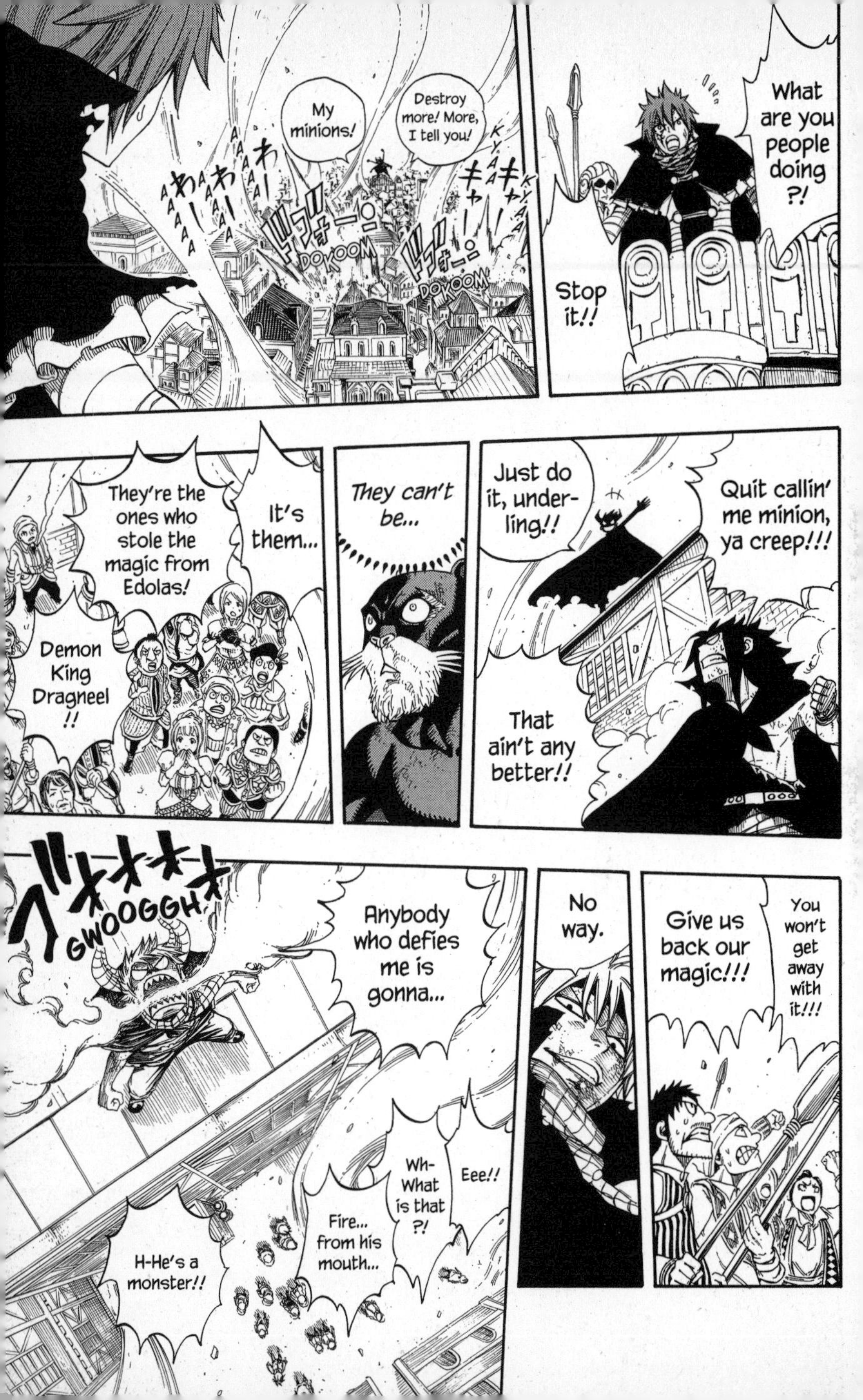
What are you people doing?!
Stop it!!
Destroy more! More, I tell you!
My minions!
KYAA
DOKOOM
DOKOOM
Quit callin' me minion, ya creep!!!
Just do it, under-ling!!
That ain't any better!!
They can't be...
It's them...
They're the ones who stole the magic from Edolas!
Demon King Dragneel!!
You won't get away with it!!!
Give us back our magic!!!
No way.
Anybody who defies me is gonna...
GWOOGGH
Eee!!
Wh-What is that?!
Fire... from his mouth...
H-He's a monster!!

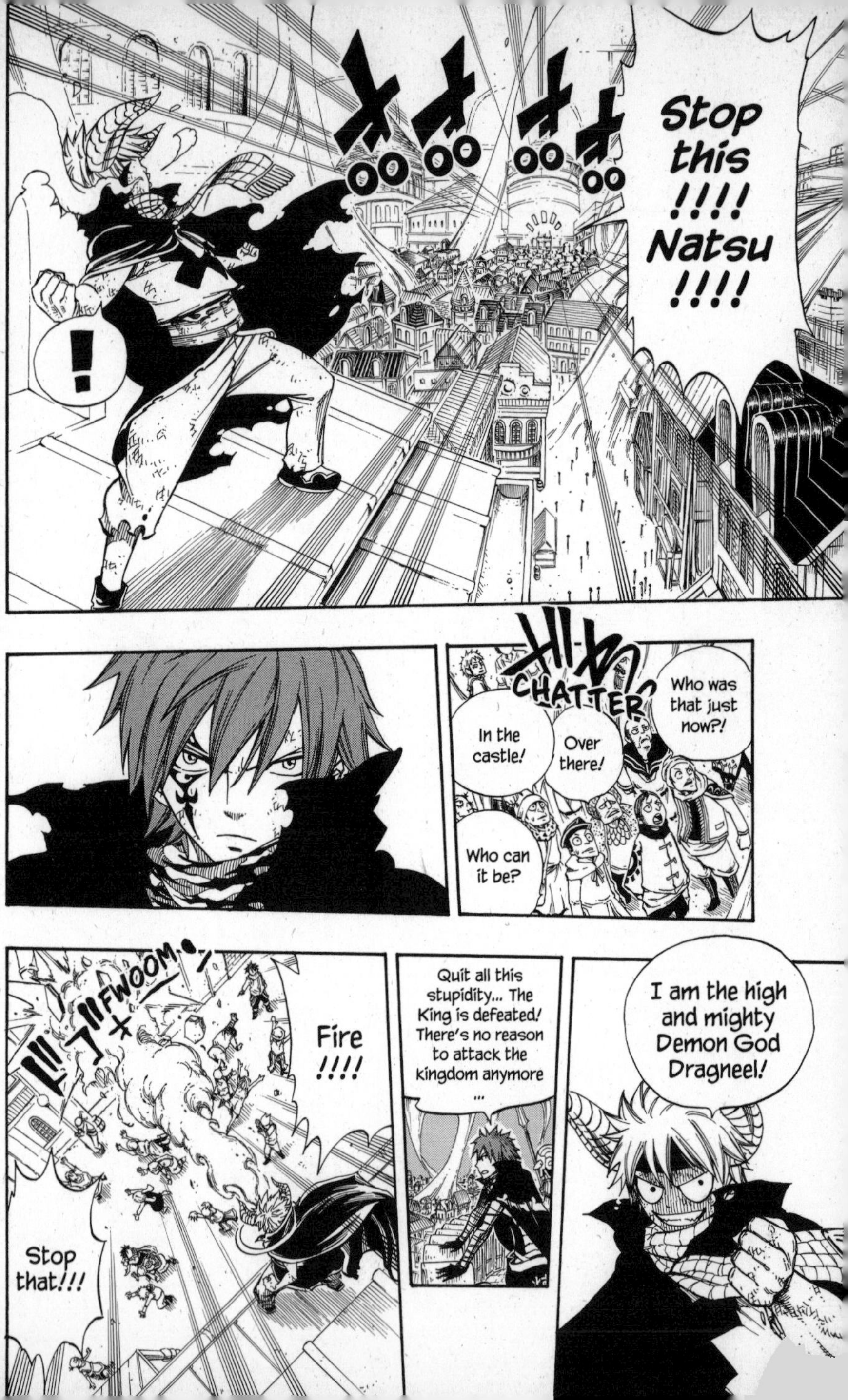
Stop this!!!! Natsu!!!!
oo oo oo oo
!
CHATTER
Who was that just now?!
Over there!
In the castle!
Who can it be?
I am the high and mighty Demon God Dragneel!
Quit all this stupidity... The King is defeated! There's no reason to attack the kingdom anymore ...
Fire!!!!
FWOOM
Stop that!!!

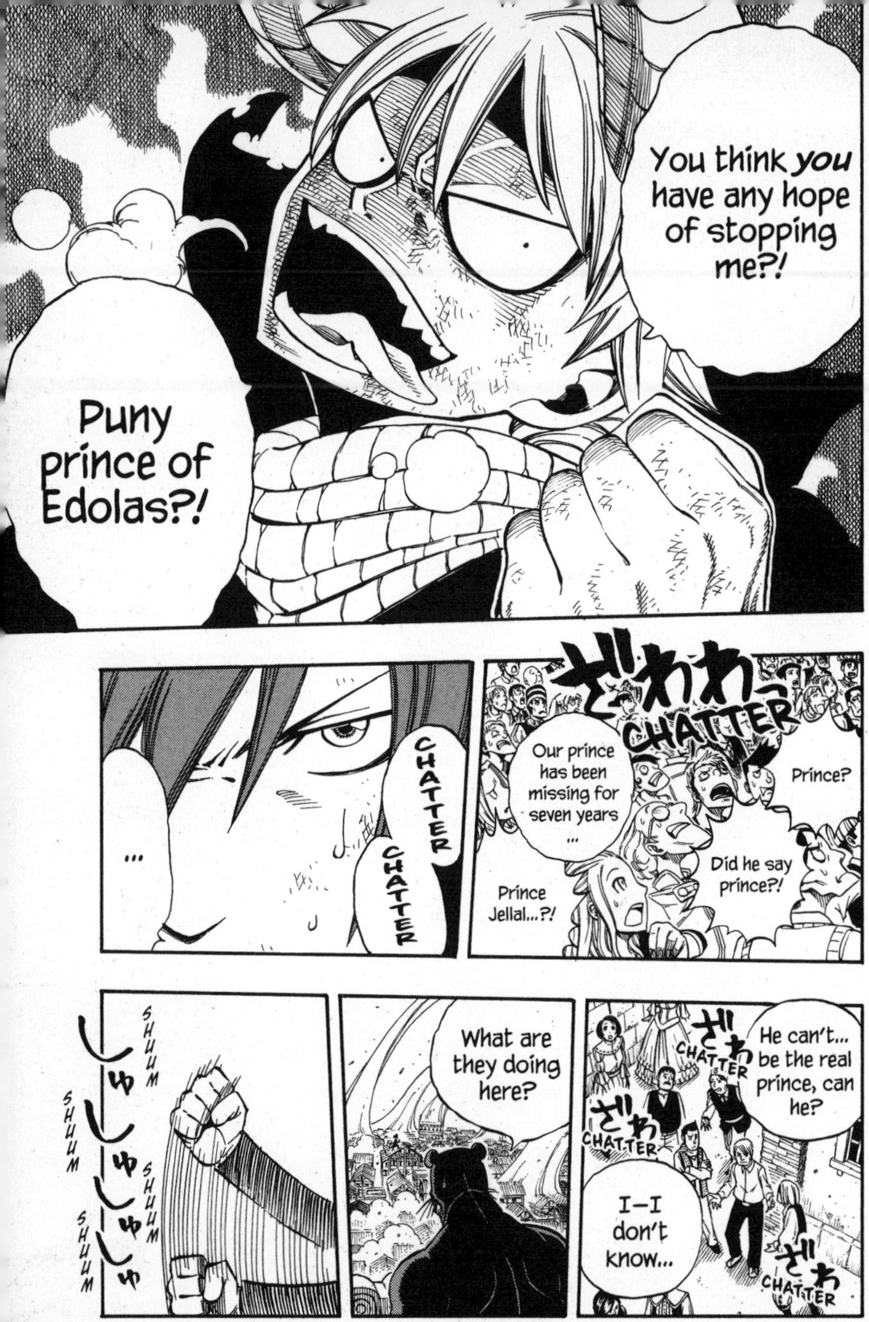
You think *you* have any hope of stopping me?!
Puny prince of Edolas?!
ざわわっ
CHATTER
Prince?
Our prince has been missing for seven years ...
Did he say prince?!
Prince Jellal...?!
CHATTER
CHATTER
...
ざわ
CHATTER
He can't... be the real prince, can he?
ざわ
CHATTER
I-I don't know...
ざわ
CHATTER
What are they doing here?
しゅ
SHUUM
しゅ
SHUUM
しゅ
SHUUM
しゅ
SHUUM

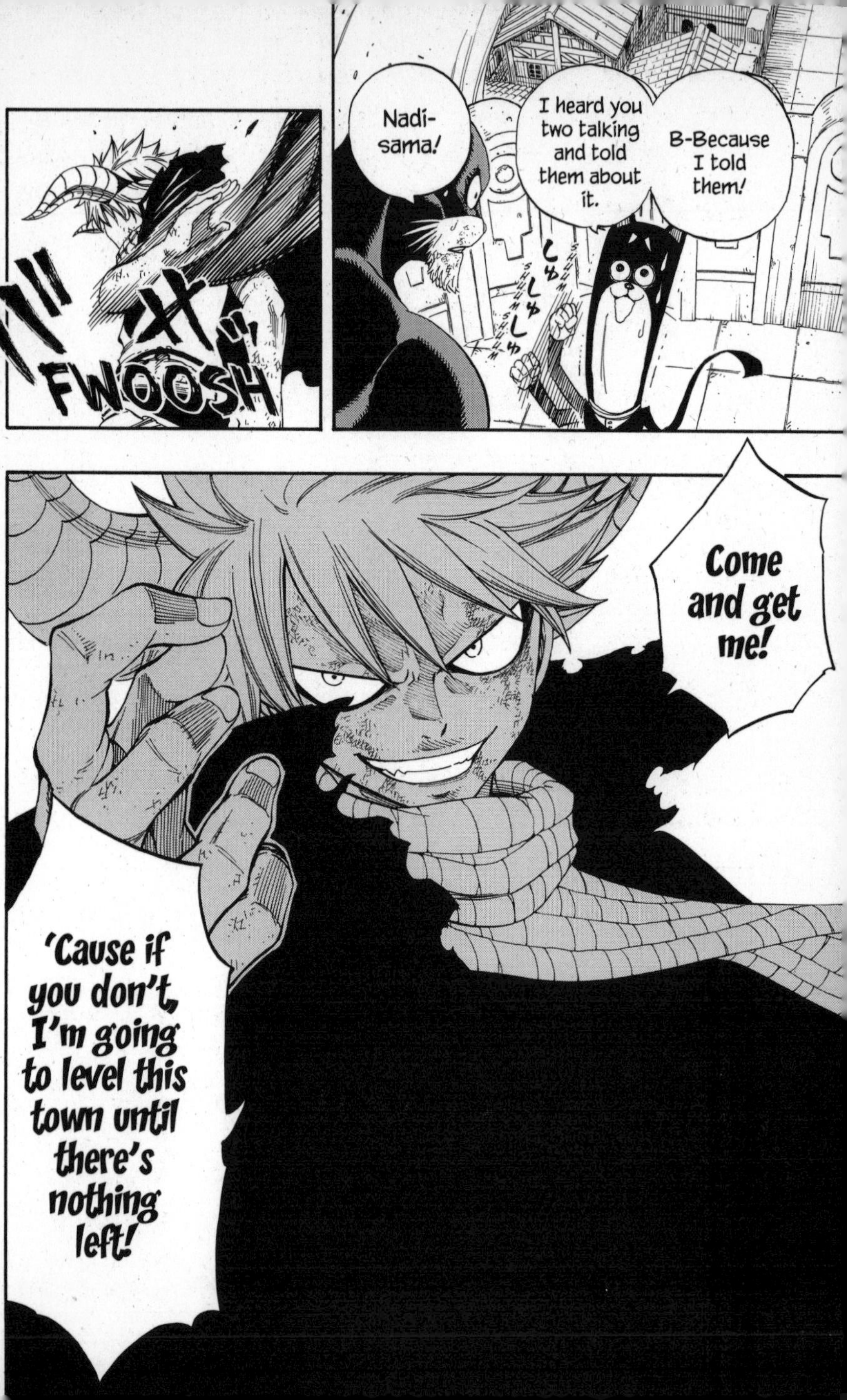
B-Because I told them!
I heard you two talking and told them about it.
Nadi-sama!
SHUM SHUM SHUM
FWOOSH
Come and get me!
'Cause if you don't, I'm going to level this town until there's nothing left!

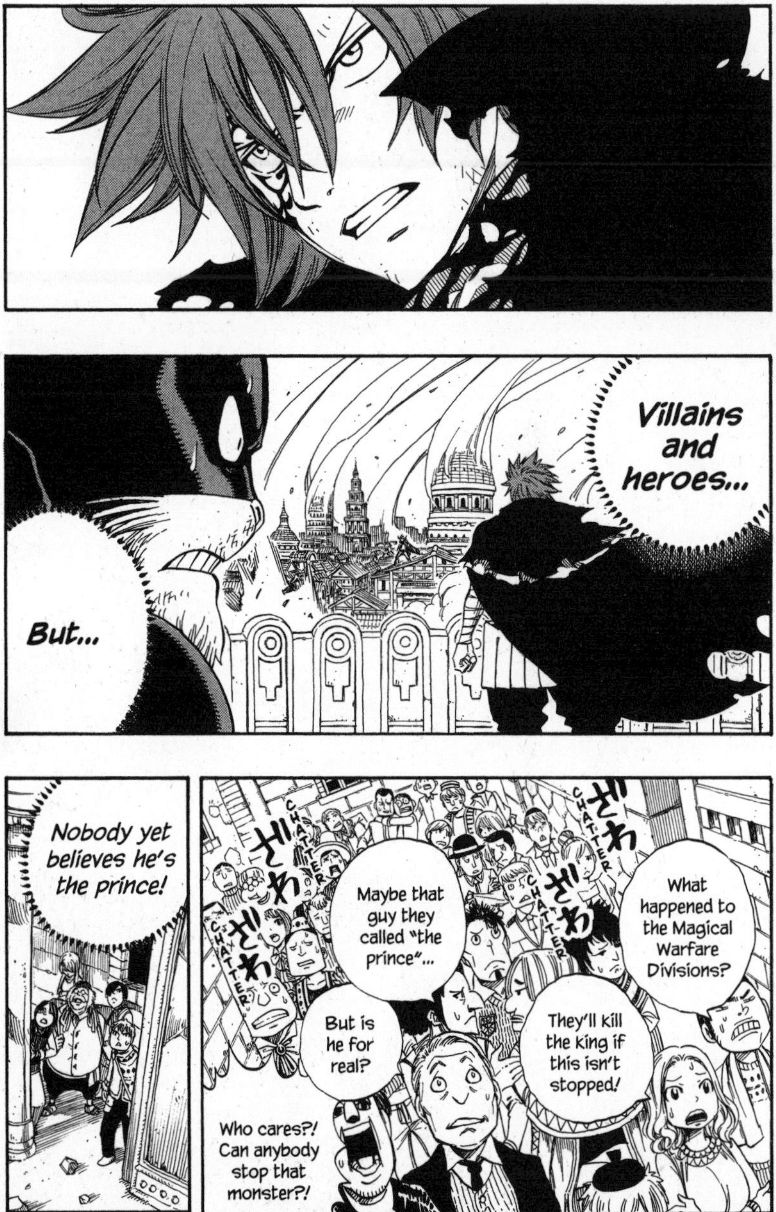
Villains and heroes...
But...
ざわ CHATTER
What happened to the Magical Warfare Divisions?
ざわ CHATTER
Maybe that guy they called "the prince"...
They'll kill the king if this isn't stopped!
ざわ CHATTER
ざわ CHATTER
But is he for real?
Who cares?! Can anybody stop that monster?!
Nobody yet believes he's the prince!

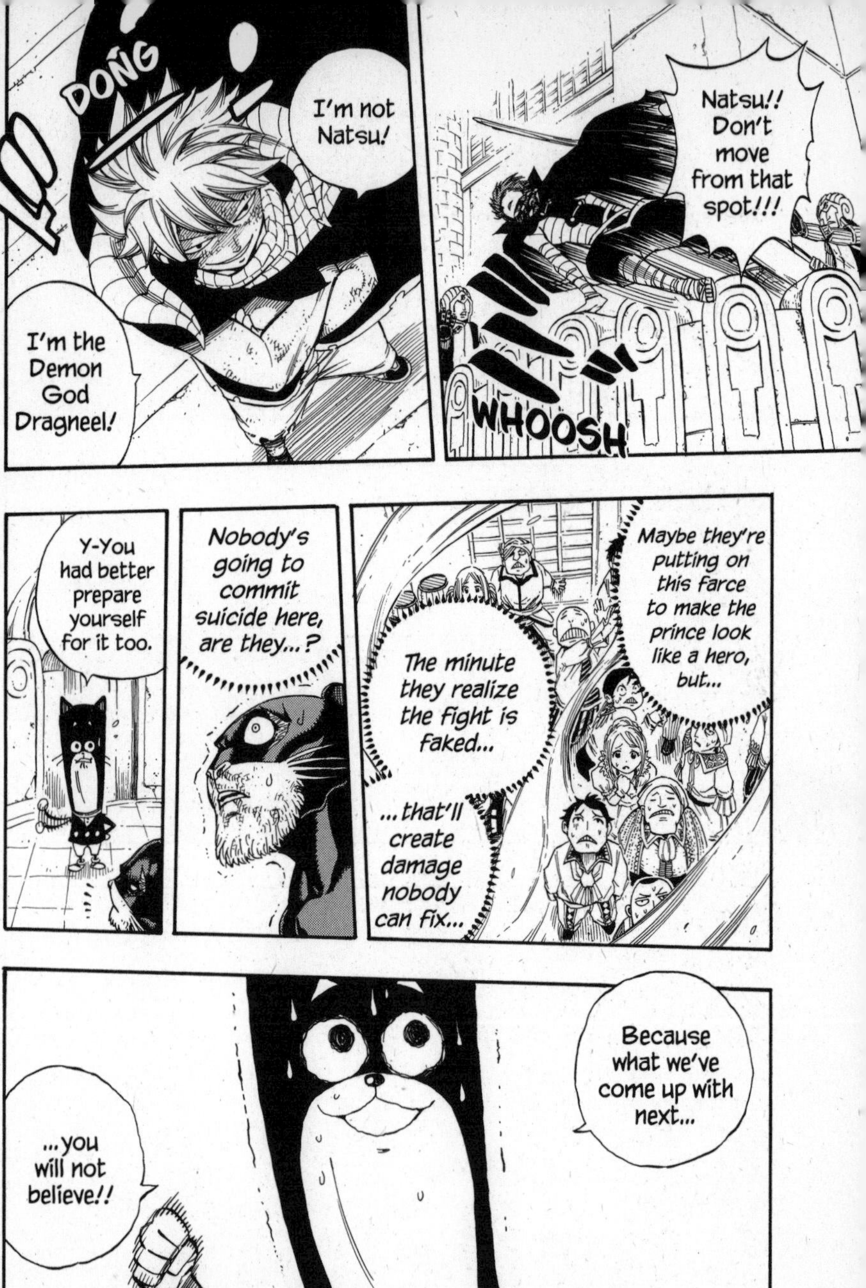
Natsu!! Don't move from that spot!!!
WHOOSH
DONG
I'm not Natsu!
I'm the Demon God Dragneel!
Maybe they're putting on this farce to make the prince look like a hero, but...
The minute they realize the fight is faked...
...that'll create damage nobody can fix...
Nobody's going to commit suicide here, are they...?
Y-You had better prepare yourself for it too.
Because what we've come up with next...
...you will not believe!!

TO BE CONTINUED

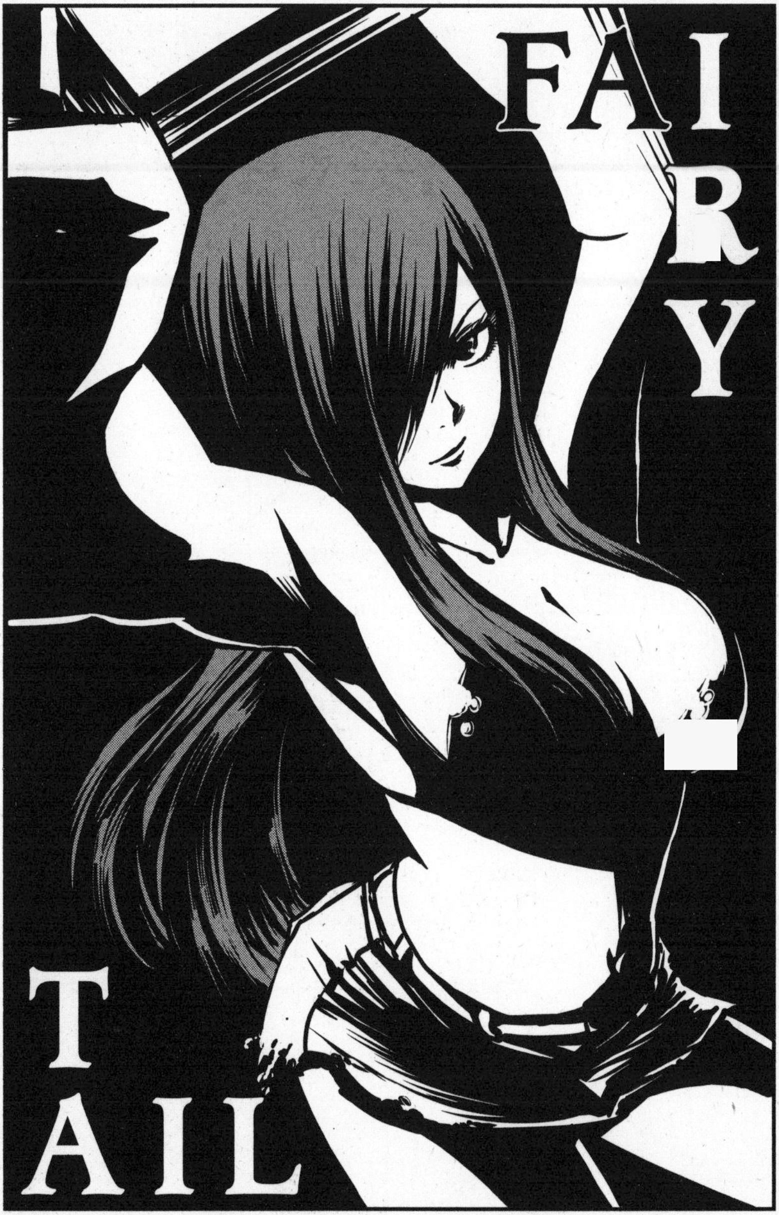
FAIRY
TAIL

EXTRA

Lucky

Happy's father, but that's a secret. His favorite things are fish and apples. He's fallen into the habit of saying, "Aye," and, "Kaaaah!"

Clap

A young male who loves to fly. His special ability is to be able to sleep while using Aera. He's only ever fallen to the ground once.

Marl

Happy's mother, but that's a secret. A wife who is always smiling and kind. Taught the "shape of a heart" to Carla.

Salvare

He's spent so much time in southern Edolas that he now has a thick southern accent. He's a skilled hunter.

Belletokia

A girl who loves pineapple. She wants to grow up to be a scholar. She considers her striped tail to be one of her most charming features.

Kurubushi

A young Exceed who wants to be a comedian. He often goes down to the ground to gather ideas for his comedy act. For some reason, he always seems to meet up with huge caterpillars.

Monmo

The leader of the children's detective squad. His hobby is collecting unique sticks. He's weak but fast.

Go-Go-Tiger

A slow-moving delivery cat. Kurubushi is always talking to him, but he never listens. He loves tomatoes and cucumbers.

Queen Chagot

The queen of Extalia, the country of the Exceed. She can see future events.

Mejeer

One of the Four Elders of Extalia. He's worried about his aging eyes, but it's his policy to never wear glasses.

Martam

One of the Four Elders of Extalia. He's taken care of Chagot ever since she was a baby.

Nichiya

Commander of the Imperial Guard of Extalia. A warrior who loves beautiful scents (perfumes). He leads the hundred-cat-plus Royal Guard.

Mysdroy

One of the Four Elders of Extalia. He was present when Chagot hatched from her egg, and one of her wings was gone.

Nadi

The Kingdom of Extalia's Minister of State. He's the one charged with helping to run the Kingdom. For some reason, he's always shaking his arm.

Muganto

One of the Four Elders of Extalia. He's the only one who knows that the queen's egg was extremely weak, so the queen gave one of her wings to the egg.

Panther Lily

Commander of the First Magical Warfare Division. Due to his breaking an old Exceed tradition, he was banished from his mother country. A very loyal warrior.

Continued from the left-hand page. ⬇

Lucy: And as you read in previous volumes, my father is now in the Akarifa Trade Guild.

Mira: Natsu, Gray, Erza, Gajeel and Wendy have no parents, right?

Lucy: Levy-chan and Juvia both said they don't have any parents.

Mira: So there are unexpectedly a lot of BEEEEP in the BEEEEP

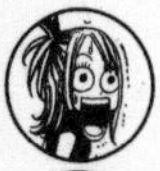
: Mira-san!! Somebody just bleeped out your words!

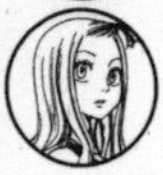
: Oh, dear.

Lucy: Not only that, but I hear that you don't even know about this backstory thing, Mira-san!

Mira: Is that so? Then I guess we'll just have to leave it at that.

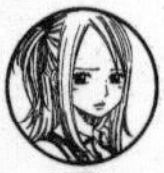
: But looking at it like this, there sure are a lot of people without parents, huh...?

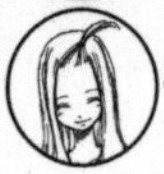
: But the guild is like our family, right?

Lucy: (I guess I should be happy that one of my parents is still alive.)

So where exactly do Natsu and Happy live?

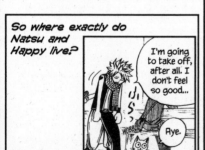

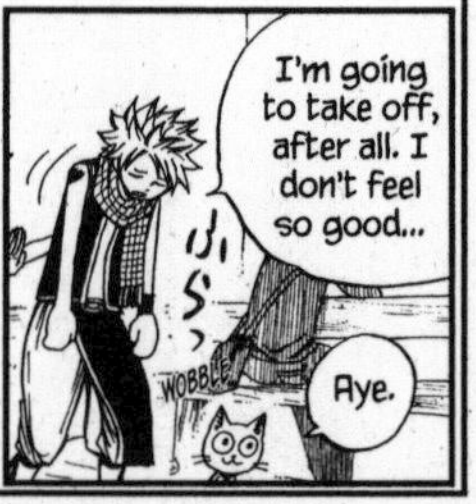
I'm going to take off, after all. I don't feel so good...
WOBBLE
Aye.

Lucy: I'm very curious about that too!!

Mira: They have a place of their own on the outskirts of Magnolia.

Lucy: What kind of place is it?

Mira: A very normal place. It will show up in Volume 24, so enjoy the anticipation! ♡

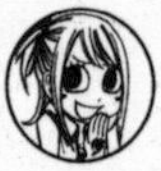
: Heh heh heh! Once I know where it is, I'm going to sneak in!!

Mira: Sneak in? Whatever for?

Lucy: To show them what it feels like when they do it to me!! I'm going to make him scream,
"This is my room!!"

Mira: A woman of puny ambitions.

Lucy: Huh? It's to surprise them!! Every time I go home, somebody is always there! That's gotta end!

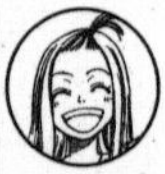
: Then I'll help you out!

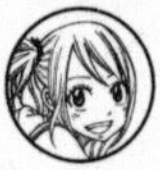
: Really? Mira-san!

Mira: Sure! It'll be really fun! ♡ Natsu and Happy will come back from a job, and Lucy will be there waiting saying, "Wel•come•home•honey! ♡"

Lucy: ...

Mira: Then Lucy will say, "Do you want dinner first, or a bath first, or maybe, ME first? ♡"

Lucy: Maybe we should just watch the sunset in silence, Mira-san.

Mira: Maybe you're right.

EMERGENCY REQUEST! EXPLAIN THE MYSTERIES OF FAIRY TAIL!

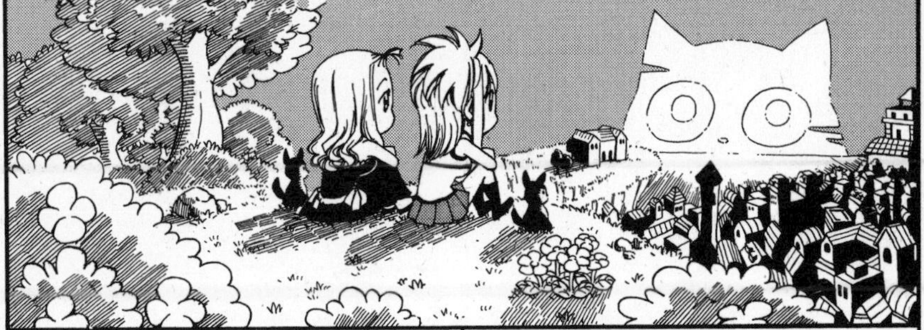

On Magnolia Hill...

Lucy: Mira-san, the setting sun is pretty, huh?

Mira: What's wrong? Why are you so sentimental all of a sudden?

Lucy: It's nothing, really. You know... We just got this question.

Why don't Lucy's Sex-Appeal Missions ever work?

BWAA
AAN

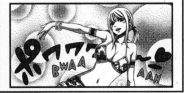

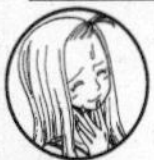

: Oh, dear.

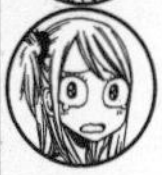

: You mean it's never worked even once...?

Mira: Hm...
Seduce Count Everlue→Fail
Get Into Weekly Sorcerer→Fail
Miss Fairy Tail Contest→Fail
Last Volume Against Hughes→Fail

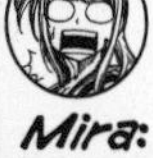

: You're right. Not once!!!

Mira: But remember that this reader asked why it failed. In other words, he's saying, "It would have worked on me," right?

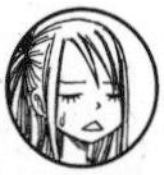

: Your sympathy is almost as bad as the question, so let's move on to the next one.

Doesn't anybody in the guild have parents?

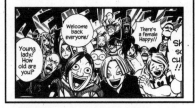

There's a female Happy!!
Welcome back everyone!
Young lady! How old are you?

Mira: What a good question!

Lucy: It doesn't really come up in the story a lot, huh?

Mira: This is foreshadowing to something in the backstory, so I really can't say much about it...

Lucy: Are you sure you're even supposed to say that much?

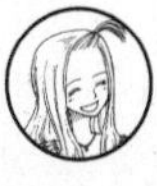

: Then I'll just say what I can... First Elfman and I lost our mother when we were little, and that was the impetus that made us enter the guild.

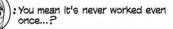

Continued on the right-hand page.

TAIL d'ART

The Fairy Tail Guild d'Art is looking for illustrations! Please send in your art on a postcard or at postcard size, and do it in black pen, okay? Those chosen to be published will get a signed mini poster! ♪ Make sure you write your real name and address on the back of your illustration!

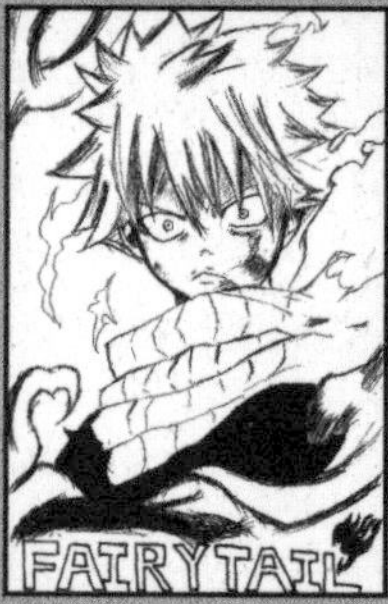
FAIRY TAIL

▼Angry Natsu. I think it's cool how he's becoming one with the flames.

Yamaguchi Prefecture, Asuka

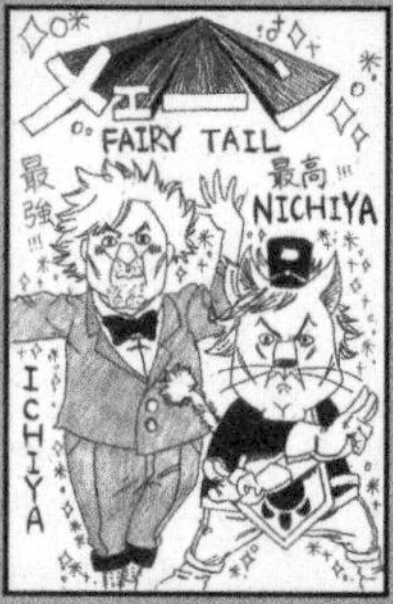
FAIRY TAIL
最強
最高
NICHIYA
ICHIYA

▼A dream (?) collaboration. They both have wonderful voices!

Nagasaki Prefecture, Haruhi

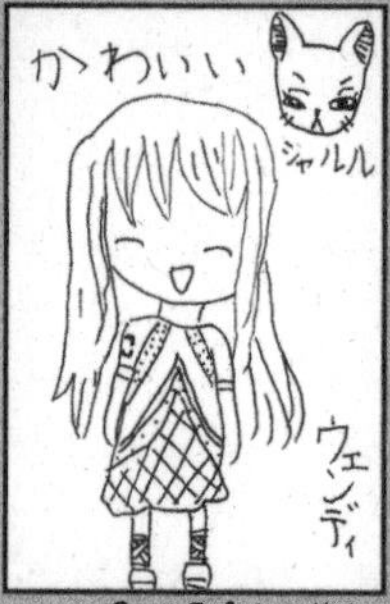
かわいい
シャルル
ウェンディ

▼Thanks! I'm going to be hard at work drawing Carla and Wendy too!

Gunma Prefecture, Y-tan

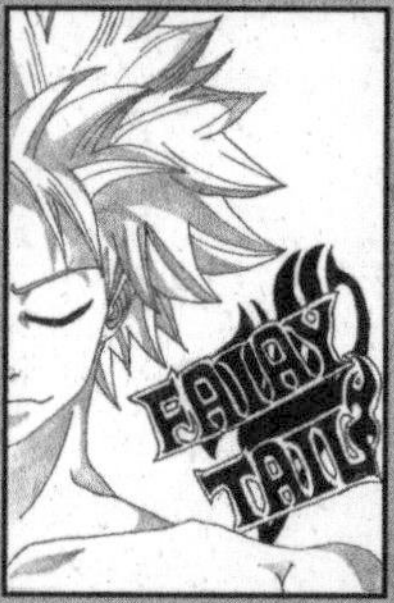
FAIRY TAIL

▼Natsu in a quiet place... A very rare picture.

Chiba Prefecture, Yūta Horii

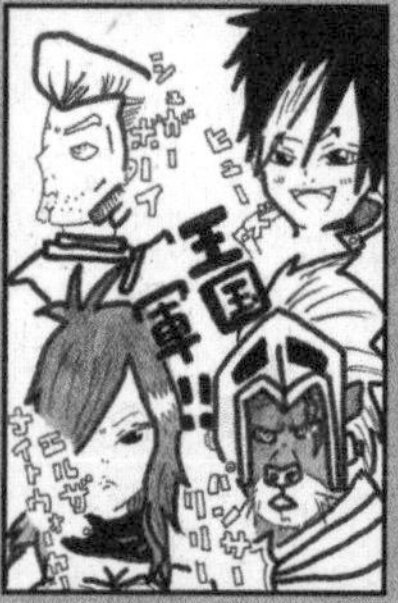
王国軍!!

▼Just a short while back, I met the first person who ever said, "I love Sugarboy!"

Osaka, Kaoru Koga

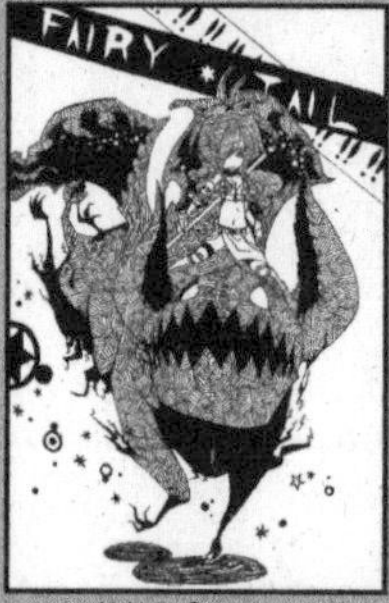
FAIRY TAIL

▼It's Nightwalker-san!! Hey, wait! This drawing's good!!

Aichi Prefecture, Yuzu-hime

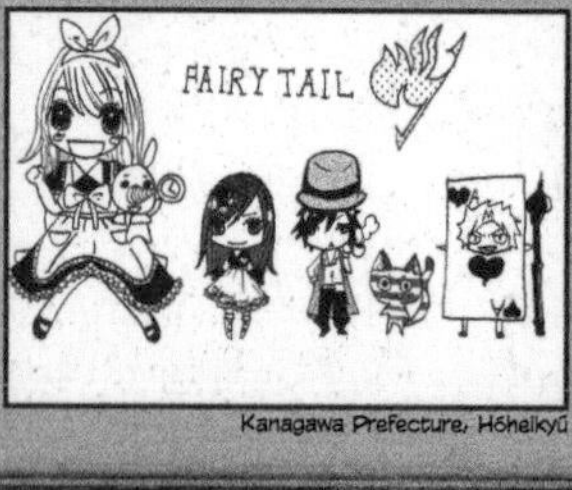
FAIRY TAIL

▼It's Alice!! Everybody's so cute! And it's very well drawn!!

Kanagawa Prefecture, Hōheikyū

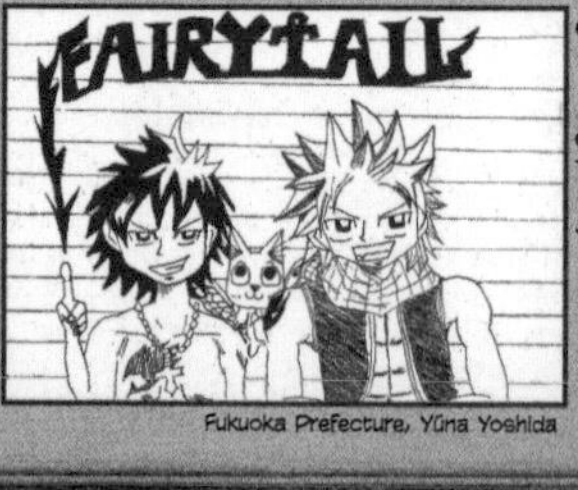
FAIRY TAIL

▼They can say whatever they like, but they really do get along pretty well.

Fukuoka Prefecture, Yūna Yoshida

Send to Hiro Mashima, Kodansha Comics
451 Park Ave. South, 7th Floor New York, NY 10016

FAIRY GUILD

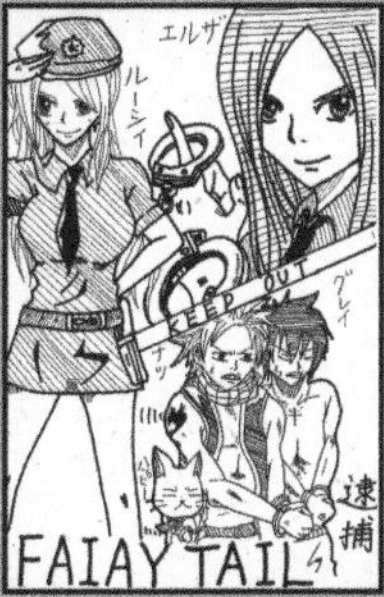

エルザ
ルーシィ
KEEP OUT
グレイ
ナツ
逮捕
FAIAY TAIL

Shizuoka Prefecture, Rocchi

▼Yeah, I guess they would get caught… in many different ways.

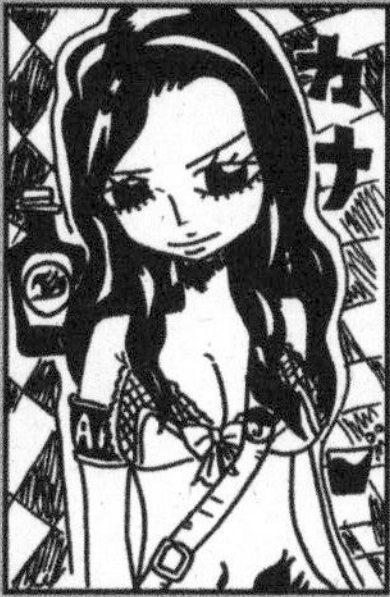

カナ

Tokyo, Kaminari

▼Cana's time is coming really soon! You have that to look forward to!

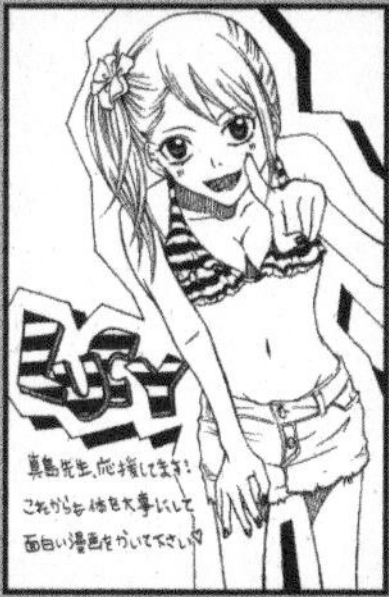

LUCY
真島先生、応援してます!
これからも体を大事にして
面白い漫画をかいて下さい♥

Hyogo Prefecture, Hikaru Matsunaga

▼Thanks for the note!! I'm doing my best!

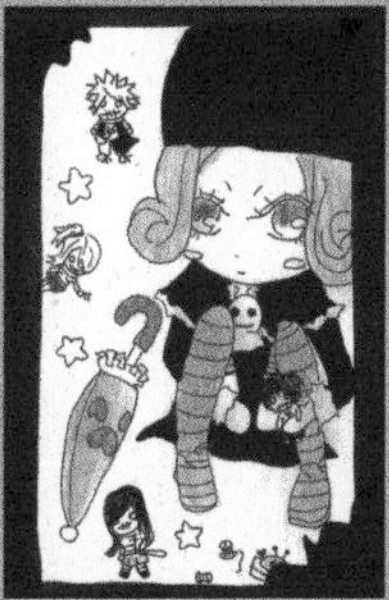

Hokkaido, Hikari Matsuda

▼So will there be a huge change in Juvia next volume or not…?

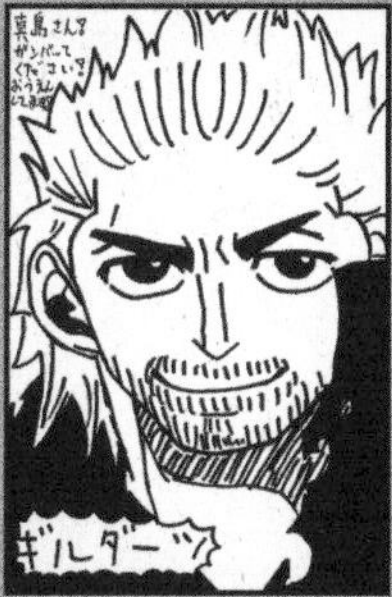

ギルダーツ

Tokyo, Ayaka Saito

▼I really like the strong old guy type! And I think he's going to be more active soon.

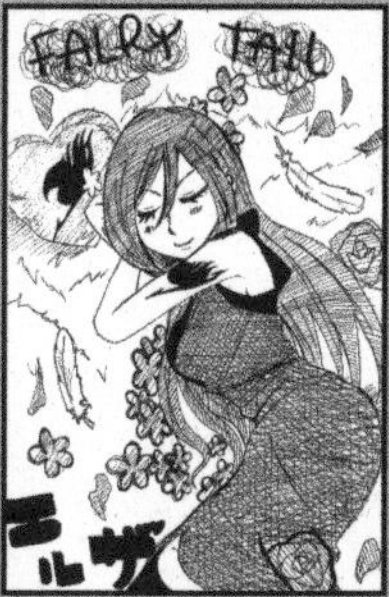

FAIRY TAIL
エルザ

Kagawa Prefecture, Saki Nakanishi

▼A really relaxed-looking Erza asleep…. What a great picture!

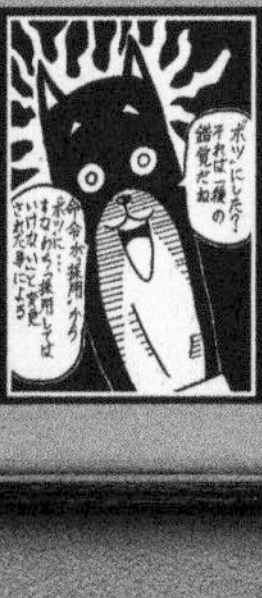

Chiba Prefecture, Yûya Miyata

▼The person came right out and said, "I don't really like Nad!" on the back of the postcard.

REJECTION CORNER

By sending in letters or postcards you give us permission to give your name, address, postal code and any other information you include to the author as is. Please keep that in mind.

Spot the Differences!

This image is just like the title page for Chapter 195 on page 151! But if you look very closely, you may spot differences... There are ten differences!! Can you find all of them?

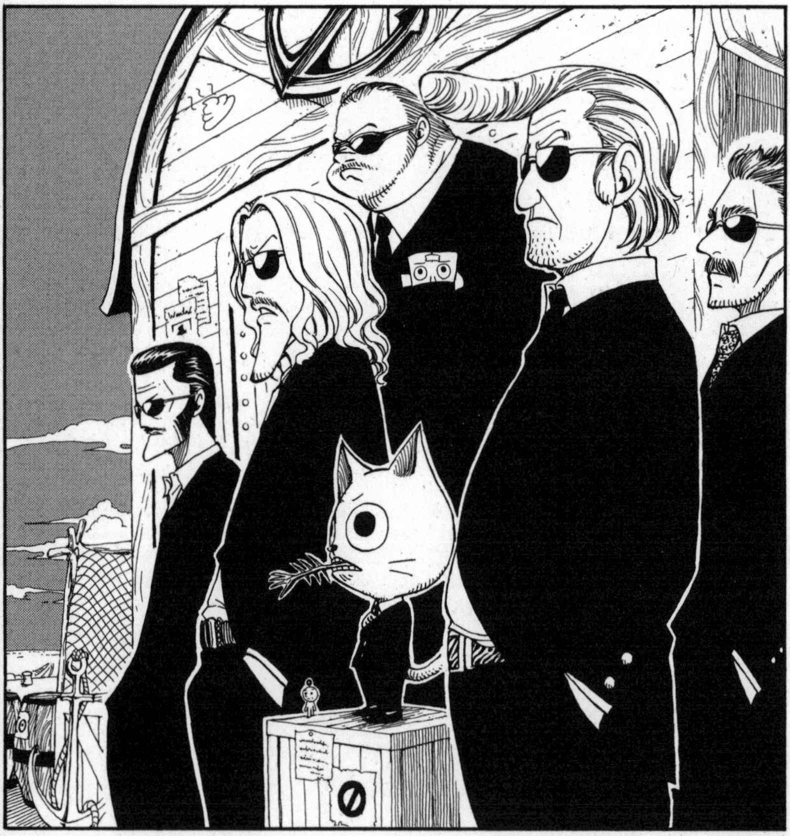

Afterword

あとがき

This time, I present the France Trip Diary!! I thought I'd be completely buried in work before the trip, but actually I found some free time here and there. Actually this was my second time going to France, but last time, due to tight scheduling, I wasn't able to go to the palace of Versailles. So this time I was determined!! That's where Marie Antoinette was and all that stuff, right? Well, it was just amazing! I was moved!! Also, French cooking is delicious! The cheese fondue they have there was especially dangerous!! I couldn't stop!! And as a result, I gained a few kilos on the trip.

Now, thanks to the wonderful people who showed up for the signing, and the fantastic efforts of the staff, it turned out to be a huge success. I drew and signed for some 600-700 people over the course of three days. This country of France is so far away from Japan, so I was very thankful that so many fans would come to see me! And I was incredibly happy to meet my French fans. I couldn't say much aside from the simplest conversation (greetings), but it was really fun! I especially want to thank the members of the staff who exhausted themselves in their efforts to make it a good signing!! I want to go back again someday soon.

Come to think of it, I wrote last time that I'd like a signing in Japan too... Well, like a drumbeat, events just kept moving along, and I had a signing the other day in Akiba. So I want to say to all of the people who came and to the staff here in Japan too, thank you so much!!! And I'll be doing another signing as soon as I get the chance!!

Erza Nightwalker Ver. 2

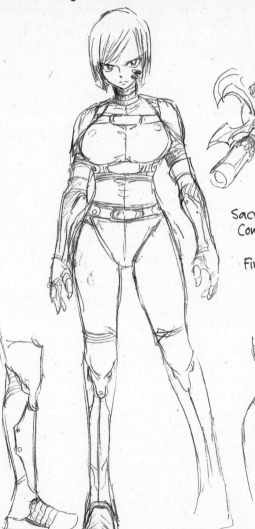

Sacred Spear Ten
Commandments

Final form:
Ravelt

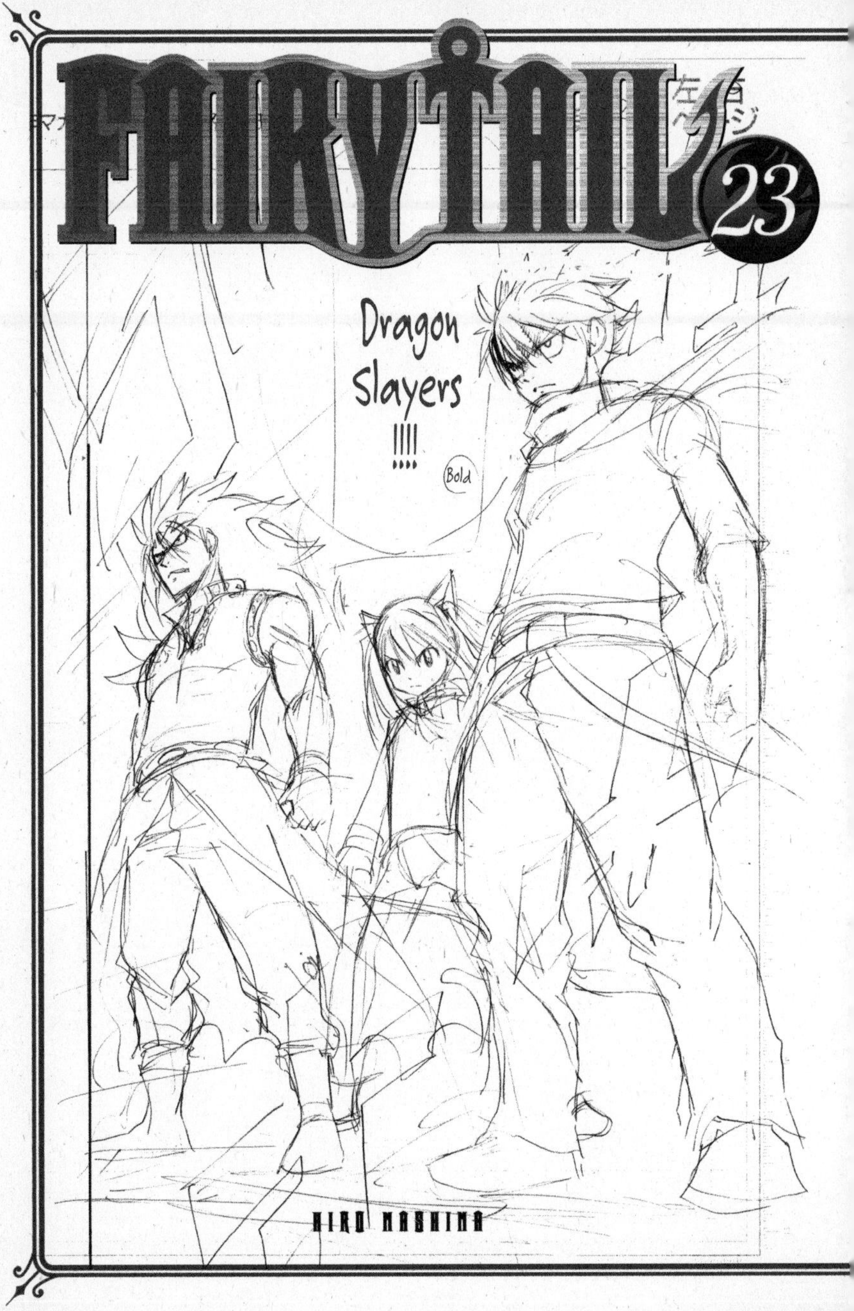
FAIRY TAIL
23
Dragon
Slayers
!!!!
Bold
HIRO MASHIMA

Preview of *Fairy Tail*, volume 24

We're pleased to present you with a preview from Fairy Tail Vol. 24, coming in March 2013 from Kodansha Comics. See our Web site (www.kodanshacomics.com) for more details!

FAIRY TAIL
24
Hiro Mashima
Creator of Rave Master

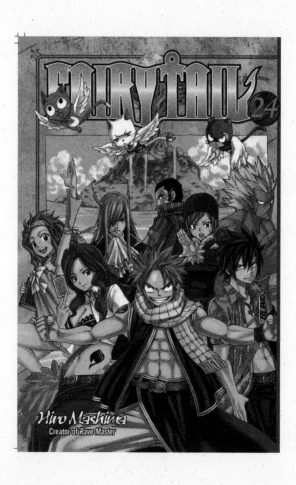

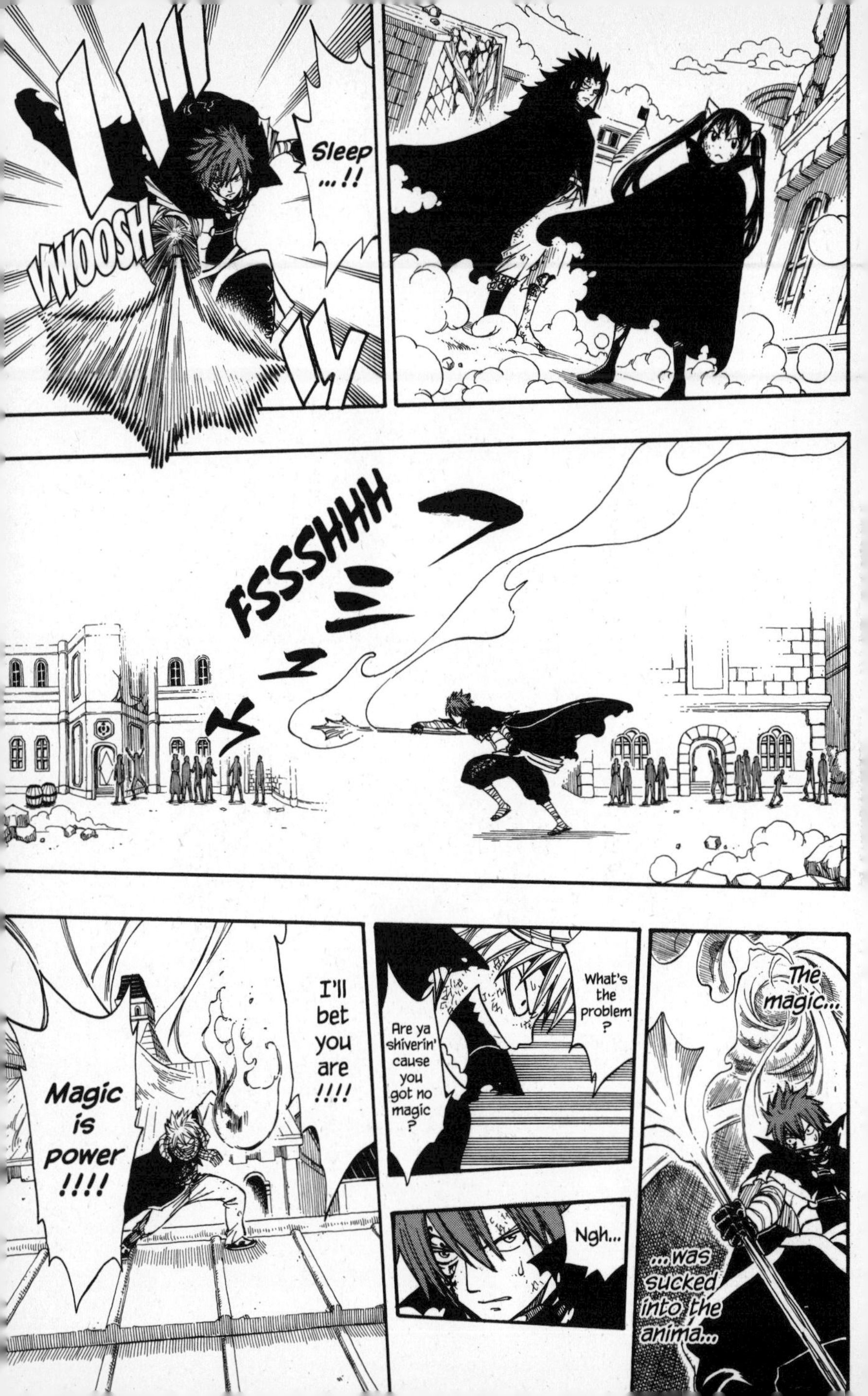
Sleep ...!!
VWOOSH
FSSSHHH
The magic...
...was sucked into the anima...
What's the problem?
Are ya shiverin' cause you got no magic?
Ngh...
I'll bet you are!!!!
Magic is power!!!!

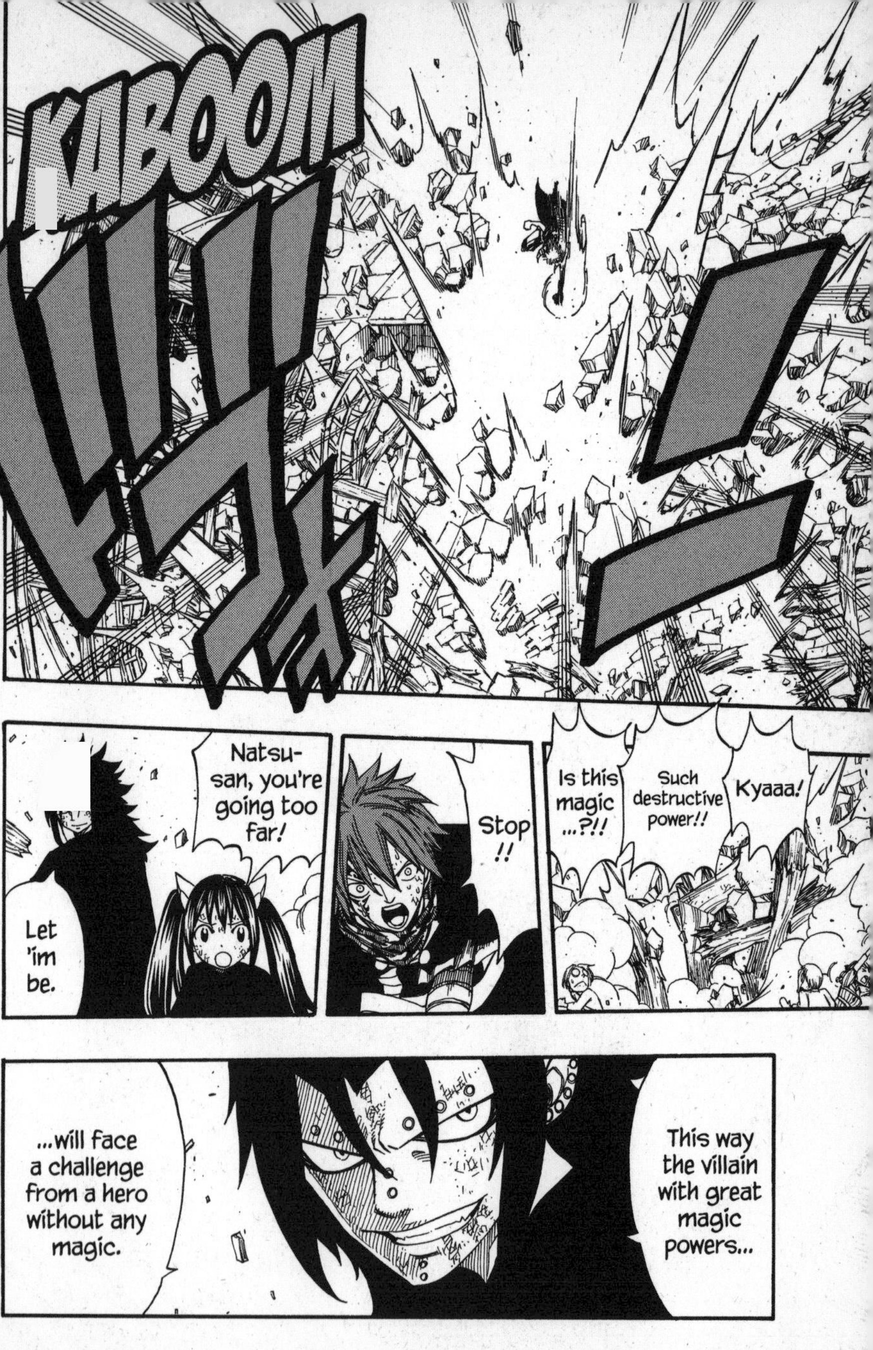
KABOOM
Kyaaa!
Such destructive power!!
Is this magic ...?!!
Stop !!
Natsu-san, you're going too far!
Let 'im be.
This way the villain with great magic powers...
...will face a challenge from a hero without any magic.

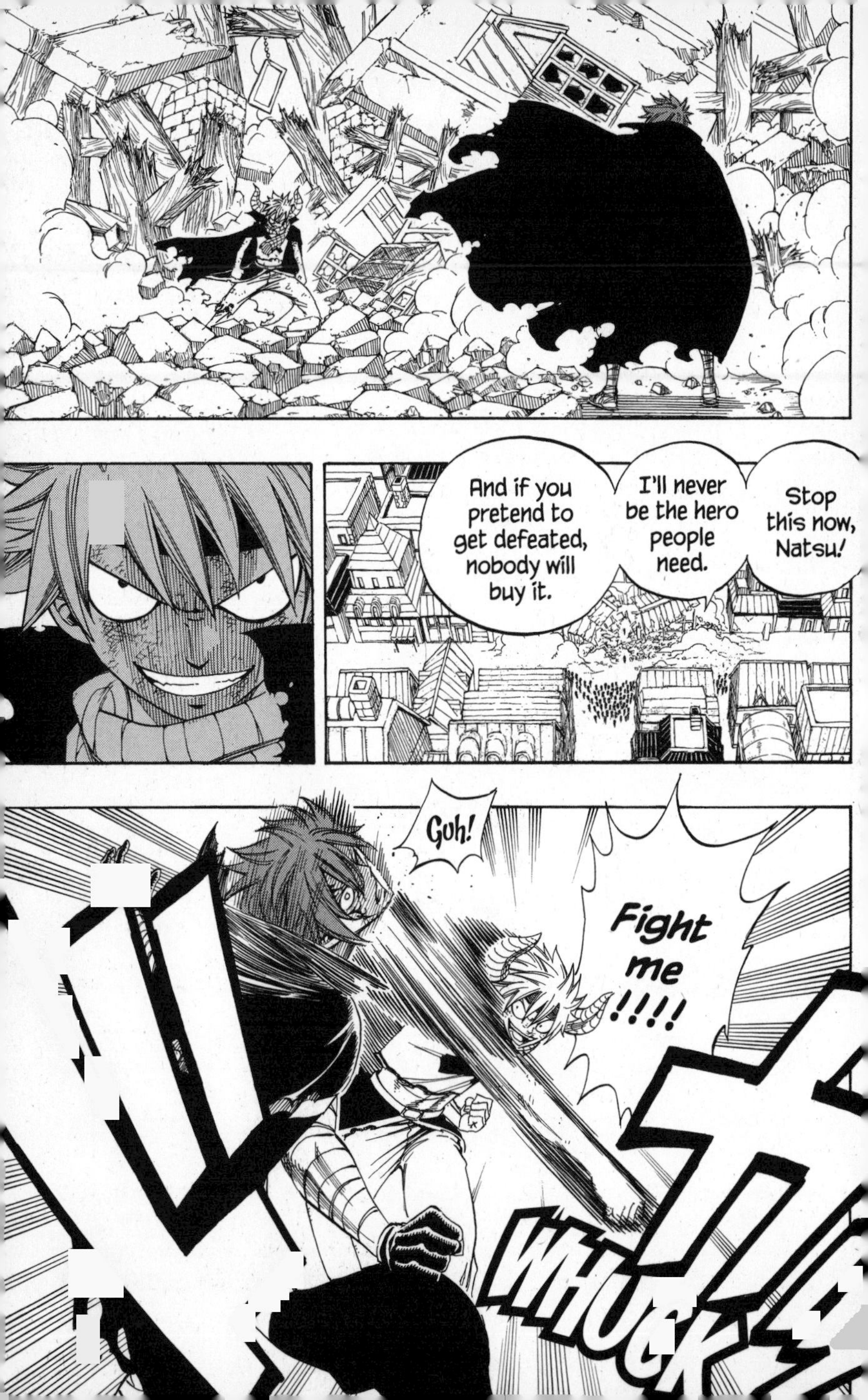
Stop this now, Natsu!
I'll never be the hero people need.
And if you pretend to get defeated, nobody will buy it.
Fight me!!!!
Guh!
WHUCK

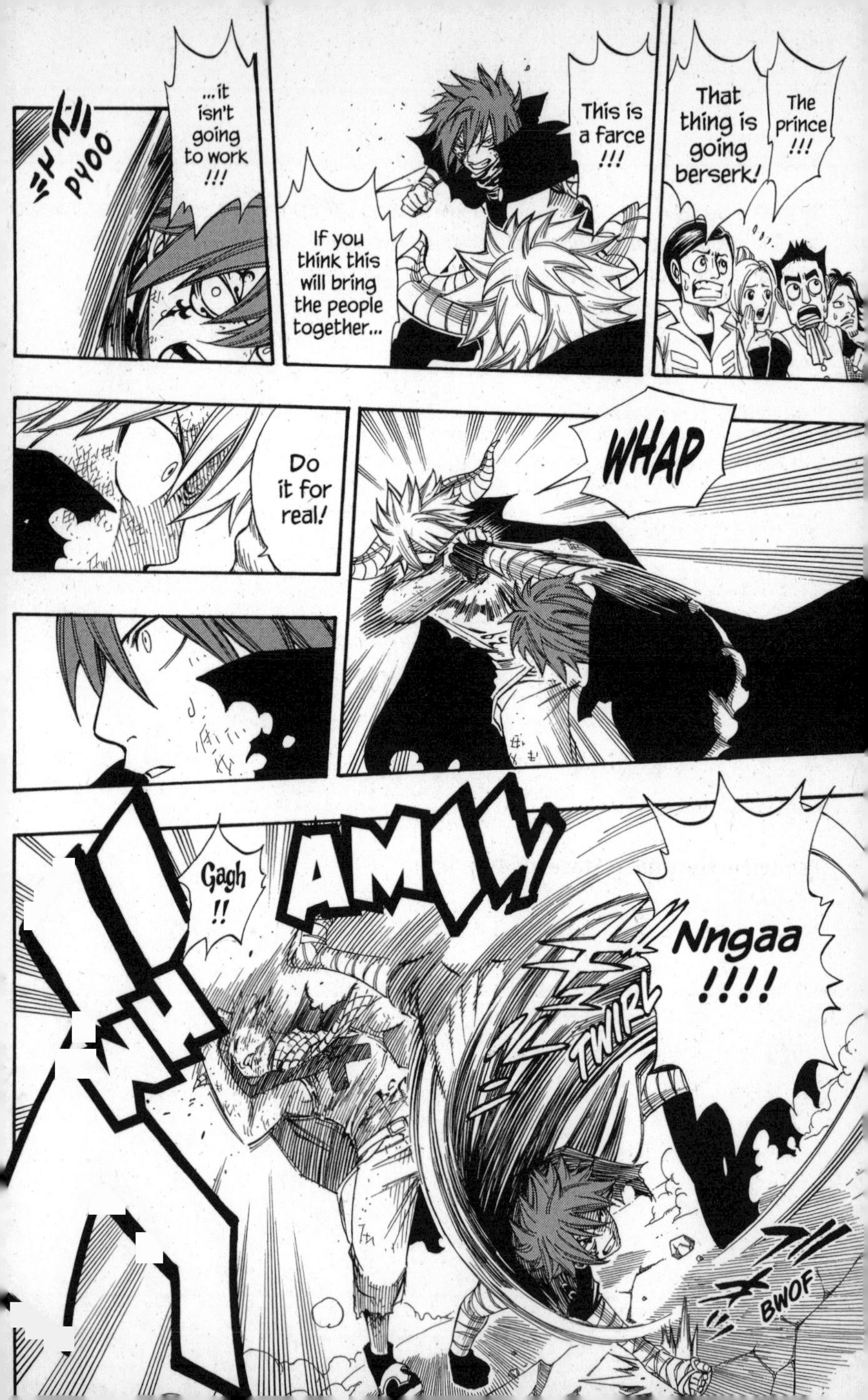
The prince!!!
That thing is going berserk!
This is a farce!!!
If you think this will bring the people together...
...it isn't going to work!!!
PYOO
WHAP
Do it for real!
Nngaa!!!!
TWIRL
BWOF
Gagh!!

Fairy Tail volume 23 is a work of fiction. Names, characters, places, and incidents are the products of the author's imagination or are used fictitiously. Any resemblance to actual events, locales, or persons, living or dead, is entirely coincidental.

A Kodansha Comics Trade Paperback Original.

Published in the United States by Kodansha Comics, an imprint of Kodansha USA Publishing, LLC, New York.

Publication rights for this English edition arranged through Kodansha Ltd., Tokyo.

First published in Japan in 2010 by Kodansha Ltd., Tokyo.
ISBN 978-1-61262-060-2

Printed in the United States of America.

www.kodanshacomics.com

9 8 7 6 5 4 3 2 1

Translator: William Flanagan
Lettering: Deron Bennett

TOMARE!

止まれ
[STOP!]

You're going the wrong way!

Manga is a completely different type of reading experience.

To start at the *beginning*, go to the *end*!

at's right! Authentic manga is read the traditional Japanese way—om right to left, exactly the *opposite* of how American books are ead. It's easy to follow: Just go to the other end of the book and read ch page—and each panel—from right side to left side, starting at e top right. Now you're experiencing manga as it was meant to be!